EUROPEAN VISION and the
SOUTH PACIFIC

European Vision and the South Pacific

Second Edition

Bernard Smith

Yale University Press
New Haven and London · 1985

Designed by Gillian Malpass
Filmset and printed in Hong Kong through Bookbuilders Ltd

Library of Congress Cataloging in Publication Data

Smith, Bernard William.
  European Vision and the South Pacific.

  Previous ed. published as: European vision and the South Pacific, 1768–1850.
  Bibliography: p.
  Includes index.
  1. Australia in Art. 2. Philosophy of Nature. 3. Art, Colonial—Australia. I. Title.
N7399.7.S6 1985   709′.4   84-21947
ISBN 0-300-02815-6

Contents

Preface to the Second Edition

WHEN the first edition of this book appeared, an ahistorical approach prevailed in the social sciences, and the history of art was largely confined to the study of works of approved aesthetic merit. Today an historical approach is no longer dismissed by social scientists with the degree of confidence so common a quarter of a century ago, and art historians have broadened the field of their interests considerably. Furthermore, the assured posture of the 'scientific' observer, secure in his own capacity to view the *other* with an wholly objective and neutral gaze, is much less common in academic circles today than it was then.

When it first appeared, this book played a part in that coming change, particularly in the fields of Pacific and Australian studies. By providing a wealth of historical evidence that the perception of Europeans (as manifest in their artefacts) was culture-bound when confronted by the (for them) new world of the Pacific, it gave support to a new generation of anthropologists, ethnohistorians and others, who had come to realise and take an interest in the inescapable relativity of their own perceptions.

The use of the term 'European vision' declared a belief in a cognitive theory of perception: that seeing is conditioned by knowing. But the book nowhere suggested that Europeans (or for that matter the members of any other ethnic or cultural grouping) are incapable as individuals of seeing what is actually before them, or that they are incapable of knowing that they are in the presence of the (for them) new, though they may well find, and usually do find, difficulty in assembling appropriate words, images, symbols and ideas to describe accurately their experience. It was assumed that it is possible, with the exercise of reasonable care, to distinguish accurate and faithful description from the distortions and errors so frequently attendant upon the interpretation of the novel. The book was not written as an apologia for an extreme cultural relativism.

Extreme culture relativism was, however, implicit in some readings of the text when the book first appeared. The most common such reading was that eighteenth-century Europeans saw Pacific peoples as 'noble savages'. Another was that the impact of Europe upon the island societies was fatal. Neither thesis is supported by the evidence advanced here. Even in the eighteenth century the 'noble savage' was but one of a number of competing and conflicting stereotypes by means of which Europeans sought to accommodate themselves to the existence of the newly-discovered Pacific societies, and it was certainly not the most influential. Nor was any 'fatal impact' of Europe on the Pacific a concern of the text; if anything it was precisely the opposite: the significance of the impact of the Pacific upon Europe.[1] And it is pleasing to note in this connection that since the appearance of the first edition research has been undertaken, of a parallel kind, into the European perception of other non-European parts of the world. A notable example was the Cleveland Museum's exhibition, *The European Vision of America*, organised in connection with the

vii

bicentenary of the USA, and the important publications that flowed from it.[2] The first edition, it may also be noted, raised sharply and from a new perspective the question of white Australian racialism, and thus stimulated, if it did not inaugurate, the modern discussion of this question.

Although the method and point of view adopted in the book have been influential, the two major themes around which it was written have never become the subject of serious discussion. This is to be regretted because they raise important issues.

The first, and perhaps the more important, advanced the view that in the century preceding the publication of *The Origin of Species* (1895) the Pacific region provided a challenging new field of experience for Europeans, one which placed unprecedented pressure upon the Biblical creation theory and provided, simultaneously, a wealth of new evidence out of which was fashioned eventually the first scientifically credible theory of evolution. That theory was not simply an ideology but an attempt to account accurately for what had been observed.

Two years after the publication of the first edition, Thomas Kuhn published his influential essay, *The Structure of Scientific Revolutions* (1962). Because Kuhn was primarily concerned with assembling a conceptual structure for the understanding of the real history of science he did not, within the short compass of an essay, take into consideration 'external social, economic and intellectual conditions'.[3] It was not that he entirely denied the significance of external factors for a full understanding of the history of science, but that he claimed for them no more than that 'explicit consideration of effects like these would not, I think, modify the main thesis developed in this essay, but it would add an analytic dimension of first-rate importance for the understanding of scientific advance'.[4] One would have expected a consideration of external factors acting upon scientific thought to do even more than that, to, in short, provide the kind of test that Kuhn's hypothesis stands in need of before it can be held to be valid. A history of science that excludes the influence of external conditions or appeals to them only to add 'an analytic dimension' sounds like a contradiction of terms.

That said, it must also be said, however, that Kuhn's thesis is not brought into question by the account of the emergence of evolutionary theory outlined in this book, and the account could be translated readily into the Kuhnian terminology. It would then run along these lines. The so-called 'non-descript' flora and fauna collected from the Pacific, the nature of its coral formations, and so forth, provided an unbearable number of anomalies for the Creation theory and the Linnean paradigm. The tension that thus developed between a wealth of anomaly and a poverty of theory is revealed in, among other things, the successive shifts at this time in taxonomic schemata. The situation was not resolved until the publication of a scientifically credible theory of evolution in terms of natural selection. The anomalies of the old paradigm then became substantive evidence for the new.

The present book in this way provides support for Kuhn's hypothesis by taking external factors into account, but it issues from a materialist account of historical change that poses by default the question: if the opening of the Pacific was not the prime external factor contributing to the emergence of a scientifically acceptable theory of evolution, what external factor, if any, did play that role? Or must we conclude that the idea of evolution itself is one that is to be explained entirely within the problematics of biological science and the inventive minds of biologists? It was surely in such islands of intellectual autarchy that evolution first found its most redoubtable opponents.

What is even more fascinating for the historian of ideas is that evolution as a scientific theory, which is undoubtedly a better way of understanding the history of life on the planet, could be transformed so readily into an ideology for the pursuit of power, and become a superior strategy for the control and subjugation of technologically weaker peoples. By contrast the Enlightenment notion of the noble savage was an ambiguous instrument. It tended to civilise the transactions of cultural contact, and it also tended to subvert European self-confidence, becoming an intellectual instrument in the hands of the revolutionary overturners of European society. 'Natural selection', however, became an effective instrument for the maintenance of European power. As soon as it was transformed from a biological to a social explanation of the history of life, and 'the survival of the fittest' became a popular slogan on the tongues and in the minds of European settlers in non-European regions, evolutionary theory became a powerful anodyne for the suppression of guilt when dealing with 'lesser breeds without the law': an instrument for control, subjugation, and all too often—as in the case of the Tasmanians and Terra del Fuegians—extermination. In the Pacific it was not only trade and commerce that followed the flag but also 'scientific' theory. In this regard it is worth noting that whereas in Europe evolutionary theory was strenuously opposed by organised religion, in the Pacific it combined with social Darwinism, in the business of destroying traditional Pacific societies.

The second main theme of the book is the contention that the predominant mode in nineteenth-century landscape painting arose from the need to discover and to evoke what was typical. Here, too, the lack of critical comment has been understandable but regrettable. Art-historical method during the 1950s consisted largely in assembling an aesthetically pre-determined sequence of art masterpieces and linking them by means of stylistic and iconographic analysis. Although the practice was fleshed out to some extent with a measure of 'social context', such was rarely crucial to the accounts. Visual records that did not pass the initial aesthetic selection were usually excluded. The practice of the time was admirably demonstrated in the comprehensive *Pelican History of Art* series that was initiated during the 1950s. In its forty-odd volumes no place was found for the arts of the Pacific region, that is to say, one-third of the earth's surface. They were, presumably, either too 'primitive' or too 'provincial' to find a significant place in the series: irritating anomalies within the prevailing paradigm of art history.

Within that practice this book was also something of an anomaly since its main concerns lay not with art masterpieces but with visual images produced primarily for the purposes of information, and devoted itself not so much to explicating the creative role of artists in their societies (the central myth of art history) but to the use of visual documents for a clearer understanding of the European penetration of the Pacific.

It was from such a perspective that the notion of 'typical' landscape as the predominant mode of nineteenth-century landscape painting emerged. The European control of the world required a landscape practice that could first survey and describe, then evoke in new settlers an emotional engagement with the land that they had alienated from its aboriginal occupants. The well-known accounts of the development of nineteenth-century landscape that are still to be found in the general histories, couched as they are entirely in terms of European cultural movements and categories (classicism, romanticism, naturalism, impressionism, etc.) are of little value in attempting to understand the underlying structure of the situation, in which Europeans are undertaking the physical and emotional mastery of the world. Such cultural categories obscure the conceptual underpinnings of landscape throughout the century by the dominating categories of the descriptive sciences (botany, zoology, geology, geography, meteorology, anthropology, etc.) by means of which landscapes and their inhabitants were effectively described and brought under control. Only then were the conventional cultural categories of European landscape used to endow the new in its typicality with a familiar European gloss. But to accept such categories at their face value is to obscure what is structurally novel about landscape practice during the nineteenth century.

In the new edition I have endeavoured to take into account a good deal of original work that has been published since the first edition, and to remove some errors and misleading emphases; otherwise the text of the book remains substantially as it was. But I have attempted to note and often comment upon recent research where it bears upon major themes and topics considered, and the bibliography has been updated. But it would be impossible to take account of all the relevant publication that has appeared since 1960, even if one knew of it, and that attempt has not been made. The new edition is more fully illustrated, and includes colour where it is often useful, as in the case of the work of William Hodges, for a better understanding of the artist's intentions.

Finally, I wish to thank the Yale University Press for its decision that the book should be republished in a second and expanded edition and particularly its editor, John Nicoll, and his staff at the London Office, for their help in seeing the edition through the press.

B. S.
University of Melbourne
January 1984

Preface to the First Edition

THIS book arose, in the first instance, from an inquiry into the origins of European art in Australia begun fifteen years ago and published in 1945.[1] That inquiry revealed the need to investigate the beginnings of European art in the south Pacific more fully; beginnings which may be traced from 1768 when professional artists first began to voyage in the South Seas. How did they see this new world of the Pacific? Did their entry into it stimulate thought and affect in any way traditional forms of expression? Such questions, it seemed, were worth asking.

It soon became clear that the study of European art in contact with the Pacific involved a more general problem: the relation between art and science during the late eighteenth and early nineteenth centuries. For this reason this book has become a study in yet another chapter in the long history of the relation between art and science. While it is believed that the association of art and science during the period under discussion is here treated with sufficient breadth to elucidate the association more fully than hitherto, the investigation is centred upon a study of European reactions to the Pacific. It remains to be seen whether other studies, centred upon art in Europe itself or in America at this time, yield similar conclusions or modify them. The conclusions may be stated briefly here at once.

The first artists to voyage among the lands and peoples of the Pacific, while doing all they could to cast its unfamiliar world into the pictorial conventions of the time, also assisted, some unwittingly and some with a growing appreciation of what they were doing, in creating a different form of landscape art, which is best described as typical. The origins of typical landscape may be traced in the topographical and the picturesque modes of landscape-painting; and the new form arises partly in response to the increasing impact of science upon art, and partly as a result of the discovery by Europeans of the beauty of the world beyond Europe.

The idea of the typical in landscape-painting parallels in point of time the emergence of the idea of organic evolution in science. It will be shown that in the Pacific these two matters were closely connected. In both is to be witnessed the abandonment of classical ideals of order, for an order based on a closer scrutiny of things in themselves. In its mature forms, the typical landscape provides an artistic counterpart to the biological explanation of life upon the planet provided by the theory of organic evolution. The main outline of this argument is developed in Chapters 1 to 5, 7 and 12. Chapters 6, 8, 9, and 10 are concerned with a cognate theme: the beginnings of European art in Australia. Although themselves distinct, each theme helps to illuminate the other; and certainly the second cannot be understood without recourse to the wider references of the first. For this reason they have been kept together—as they arose in the process of research.

It is a pleasant duty to mention that Dr. K. Badt's *John Constable's Clouds*,[2] Dr. O. Pächt's 'Early Italian Nature Studies',[3] and Professor Wind's 'The Revolution in History Painting'[4] have been most suggestive and are, in a sense, germinal to the central argument of the study. It will be obvious that it also owes much to Professor A. O. Lovejoy's studies in the history of ideas. An initial acknowledgement is due to the British Council for the award of a research grant which enabled me to begin working specifically on the subject in England in October 1948. My greatest debt is to the members of the staff of the Warburg Institute for their helpful interest in my work and their stimulating criticism—above all to the invaluable discussions and splendid advice of Mr. Charles Mitchell. A further grant from the Australian National University made it possible for me to continue work on the subject in the Department of Pacific History during 1954–5. For this later phase of my research my thanks are specially due to J. W. Davidson, Professor of Pacific History at the Australian National University, for his advice, his careful reading and comments upon the drafts, invariably of value, and for an approach to the study of history which found a subject concerned with the history of art and related ideas as much a part of general historical studies as those fields of history more familiar to Australian historians.

I am also grateful to Mr. Charles E. Buckley, Mr. Croft Murray, Professor W. G. Constable, Mr. Gerard Hayes, Sir Maurice Holmes, Dr. Averil M. Lysaght, the late Mr. Paul Oppé, and Mr. Michael Robinson, who have sent me information and been kind enough to answer my questions. I owe a special debt of gratitude to Mr. R. A. Skelton, for continued kindness in this regard. His extensive knowledge of the graphic records of Cook's voyages has been of inestimable value.

All future research workers in the graphic records of the Pacific and of early art in Australia and New Zealand will be deeply indebted to Mr. Rex Nan Kivell for assembling over many years his unique collection of pictures and books of Pacific interest now owned by the Commonwealth National Library, Canberra. It will be apparent how much I am indebted to this collection.

I am also indebted to librarians, archivists, and many other persons, both in Australia and abroad. To Miss Mander Jones, formerly Librarian of the Mitchell Library, Sydney, and to the library's efficient and courteous staff, especially Miss S. Mourot, my debt is beyond measure. During two years in Canberra, Mr. Hardd White, Librarian of the Commonwealth National Library, and his staff, especially Mrs. W. D. Fanning, provided never-failing assistance. Mr. A. L. G. MacDonald, Librarian of the National University, and his staff helped immeasurably by drawing upon the collective resources of libraries throughout the country. I also owe a good deal to the help of Miss W. Radford and the research staff of the Public Library of New South Wales; to Mrs. Henry J. Howell, jun., Librarian of the Frick Art Reference Library, New York, and her research staff; to Mr. James Packman, Librarian, Royal Empire Society, London; to the City Librarians of Hobart and Launceston, Tasmania; Mr. Robert Sharman and Mr. P. K. Eldershaw of the Tasmanian State Archives, Hobart; Mr. Anthony Wood, County Archivist, Warwick; Miss D. A. Leech, City Archivist, Coventry; Mr. R. M. Anderson, Chief Botanist and Curator, Botanic Gardens, Sydney; Dr. W. Bryden, Director, Tasmanian Museum and Art Gallery and his assistant, Mr. S. de Teliga; Mr. W. Currell, Director of the Queen Victoria Museum, Launceston; Mr. Ernest Simpson, City Library, Coventry; Professor O. H. K. Spate and Dr. D. Freeman of the Australian National University; the late Miss Margaret Kiddle, of the University of Melbourne; Miss E. Boyes, of Newton, Hobart; Mr. F. J. Patrick, City Librarian, Birmingham; Mlle M. G. Madier, Librarian, Museum National d'Histoire Naturelle, Paris; and Mr. M. D. McLean of the Dumfriesshire Libraries; Messrs. Spink & Sons, London; and the Neilson Park Trust, Vaucluse House, Sydney. Although the main draft of the manuscript was completed at Canberra prior to my joining the Department of Fine

Arts of the University of Melbourne, my colleagues Dr. Ursula Hoff and Mr. Franz Philipp have often provided helpful comments on a subject somewhat outside their usual fields, and I am especially grateful to Professor J. T. A. Burke for his most generous interest in every stage of the book, his unfailing co-operation, and his tireless and stimulating discussion of the issues involved in a field so closely connected with his own. I also received help of a most material kind from Professor J. C. Beaglehole, whose knowledge of Pacific exploration is unrivalled, from Mr. Charles Mitchell, already mentioned, from Mr. L. F. Fitzhardinge of the Australian National University, and from Dr. L. Bodi of the University of New South Wales. All four read the manuscript and provided comments which have been invaluable when preparing the book for the press. Mr. T. S. R. Boase was also kind enough to find time to read the half-finished manuscript during a busy visit to Australia in our winter of 1956. Nor can I refrain from thanking Professor J. A. La Nauze for drawing my attention to a passage in Macaulay which at least one Australian schoolboy did not know. None of my friends of course are responsible, except where I have said so, for anything in the book.

Finally my thanks are due to Mrs. L. Gale and Miss E. H. Richmond for their help in typing the text and index, and to Mr. G. F. James and my wife who assisted me in correcting the proofs.

B. S.
University of Melbourne
January 1959

1. Introductory: The European and the Pacific

IN the year 1768 the Royal Academy was established and the Royal Society promoted Cook's first voyage to the South Seas. The two events fittingly represent two influential attitudes to nature current in English eighteenth-century thought. The formation of the Academy constituted the official recognition in England of those neo-classical theories of Italian origin which had been transmitted to Britain through French theorists like de Chambray and de Piles. Nature, it was said, was to be rendered by the artist not with her imperfections clinging to her but in her perfect forms; what those perfect forms were the artist could only learn by a close study of the masterpieces of the ancients and their Renaissance disciples. The Royal Society, on the other hand, approached nature in a different way, appealing to travellers, virtuosi, and scientists to observe carefully, record accurately, and to experiment.

Now the opening of the Pacific provided a new world for the philosophers of nature. But it was the empirical approach of the Society and not the neo-classical approach of the Academy which flourished under the impact of the new knowledge won from the Pacific. For though the discovery of the Society Islands gave initial support to the belief that a kind of tropical Arcadia inhabited by men like Greek gods existed in the South Seas, increasing knowledge not only destroyed the illusion but also became a most enduring challenge to the supremacy of neo-classical values in art and thought. The effect of this challenge is to be observed in painting, in poetry, in the theatre, and even in ideas concerning the nature of the universe. The opening of the Pacific is therefore to be numbered among those factors contributing to the triumph of romanticism and science in the nineteenth-century world of values. Whilst it will be shown how the discovery of the Pacific contributed to the challenge to neo-classicism in several fields, more particular attention will be given to the impact of Pacific exploration upon the theory and practice of landscape painting and upon biological thought. For these two fields provide convenient and yet distinct grounds in which to observe how the world of the Pacific stimulated European thought concerning the world of nature as a whole; in the case of the former as the object of imitation and expression, in the case of the latter as the object of philosophical speculation.

The empirical observation of nature, exemplified in the keeping of ships' logs and seamen's journals, was an established part of British maritime practice a great many years before the foundation of the Royal Society in 1660. And from its inception the Society placed a high value upon the information to be gained from such logs and journals. The information they contained included not only verbal and numerical data but also graphic records in the form of maps and profiles of coasts. Now both Captain Cook and Joseph Banks inherited the traditions of empirical observation derived from maritime practice and the precepts of the Society. Banks, too, was subjected to the influence of the Society of Antiquaries which had received a charter in 1750 and sought to bring habits of close observation, description, and explication to the study of the past, especially as revealed by its material remains, in order to place

1. Henry Roberts, *The Resolution*, watercolour, 21¼ × 15 in. (*c.* 1774). Mitchell Library, Sydney. PXD11. f. 34. By permission of the Trustees of the State Library of New South Wales

1

the writing of history upon a firmer and more objective footing. On Cook's *Endeavour* an important step was taken to advance the techniques of objective observation and recording employed on far voyages by the use of trained scientific observers and professional artists. Also the voyage was, it must be remembered, the first large scientific maritime expedition in whose promotion the Society played a major role. Partly for this reason the Pacific, although the last great ocean to be explored by Europeans, was, curiously enough, the first large region beyond Europe that modern scientific method came fully to grips with. But there are two other closely associated reasons. Firstly, sea travel over great distances was considerably safer than land travel in the last decades of the eighteenth century. Secondly, the scientific examination of the Pacific, by its very nature, depended upon the level reached by the art of navigation. As soon as it was possible to control scurvy and to construct reliable chronometers, the archipelagos of the Pacific yielded information of value to the ocean-going scientist far more readily than did the continental masses of Asia, Africa, and America to their land-travelling colleagues. A vessel like Cook's *Resolution* (Plate 1), despite her deficiencies, combined the values of a fortress and a travelling laboratory. Land-travelling scientists had no hope of competing with the results of a Cook, a Flinders, or a Dumont d'Urville. In this regard the case of John Ledyard is illuminating. Ledyard, a marine on the *Resolution* during Cook's third voyage, attempted an overland expedition across Siberia in 1786 for Banks, after returning from the Pacific. He was arrested at Yakutsk, thrust across the Polish frontier to arrive penniless and ragged at Regensburg begging a few guineas in the name of Sir Joseph. In 1789 Ledyard died of fever in Cairo while about to set out in search of the source of the Niger.[1] The interiors of the great continents remained virtually unknown while the islands of the Pacific were visited by one scientific voyage after another.

Indeed so well known did the islands of the South Seas become following the publicity given to Cook's voyages that the natural productions and native peoples of the Pacific became better known to European scientists than the natural productions and peoples of many less distant regions. The plan of operations adopted by Banks and Cook on the *Endeavour* became standard practice for many later expeditions. It is not unlikely that Gilbert White had the achievements of his friend Banks in mind when he recommended to Thomas Pennant (a friend both of Banks and White) a programme for a naturalist's tour of Ireland. The programme suggested was virtually identical with that employed so successfully by Banks in the Pacific some six years before:

> Some future faunist, a man of fortune, will, I hope, extend his visits to the Kingdom of Ireland; a new field, and a country little known to the naturalist. He will not, it is to be wished, undertake that tour unaccompanied by a botanist, because the mountains have scarcely been sufficiently examined; and the southerly counties of so mild an island may possibly afford some plants little to be expected within the British Dominions.... The manners of the wild natives, their superstitions, their prejudices, their sordid way of life, will extort many useful reflections. He should also take with him an able draughtsman.[2]

Now the empirical approach to nature, despite its standing in philosophy and science, played little part in the theory and practice of landscape-painting in England at the time of the establishment of the Royal Academy. Claude was the model held up by Reynolds to those who sought to perfect the art of landscape. When the empirical approach to nature did begin to influence English landscape-painting during the later decades of the eighteenth century, it began to influence the art, naturally enough, through those scientific disciplines concerned with the description and analysis of the structure, vegetation, and atmosphere of the earth's surface. For the landscape-painter shared with the botanist, geologist, and meteorologist certain common fields of interest and, in a sense, similar materials of study, however different the purposes of scientist and artist.

During the second half of the eighteenth century the sciences of botany, geology, and meteorology, in company with a number of other sciences based on exacting empirical research, were beginning to perfect their techniques and modes of classification. An essential condition for the progress of these new sciences was the collection of evidence from all parts of the world. Consequently, the scientific voyages to the Pacific played an important part in their programmes and did much to stimulate an interest in them. Now such sciences as botany, zoology, and the nascent science of ethnology, made extensive use of draughtsmen to assist in the description of material observed or collected. It was the business of the botanical and zoological draughtsmen to depict with great care and accuracy the appearance and structure of type specimens upon which new species might be erected. A great deal of artistic talent was absorbed between 1750 and 1850 in thus serving the biological sciences as they sought to perfect the descriptive and systematic phases of their respective disciplines.

On scientific voyages, however, professional artists trained in art schools and academies worked side by side with nautical and scientific draughtsmen. Frequently they were called upon to do similar work. At all times they were exposed to the influence of scientists and naval officers trained in the empirical habits of observation championed by the Royal Society and the Navy. In consequence their mode of perception became increasingly less dominated by neo-classical theories of art and increasingly more influenced by empirical habits of vision.

The mode of perception and expression which artists thus tended to acquire as a result of the conditions imposed upon them on scientific voyages is not to be equated with a naïve and unselective naturalism. Neo-classical theory had stressed the supreme importance of the unity of mood and expression in the highest forms of landscape art. Analytical and empirical observation, however, tended toward the disruption of such unity, forcing the artist to look at the world as a world of disparate things. But these 'things', the rocks, plants, animals, people, and atmospheric conditions perceived by the painter acquired a new significance under the pressure of scientific inquiry. As scientists came to question the teleological position implicit in the view of nature as a great chain of being, they tended to seek an explanation for the origin and nature of life in the material evidence provided by the earth's surface. The intense study of rocks, plants, animals, people, and the laws governing climatic conditions acquired a new significance even for the landscape-painter. For such things held the clue to the meaning of nature and the origin of life. It was most desirable, therefore, that the artist should depict them accurately, for it was only by the closest scrutiny and the most careful description that they could be made to yield their meaning. Furthermore, it became increasingly clear that certain essential relationships existed in the world of nature between certain types of rocks, plants, animals, and climates. These ecological relationships were quite different from the relationships imposed by the neo-classical landscape-painter in the search for a unity of mood or expression. They were only to be revealed by a careful empirical study of nature and were the object of scientific inquiry. Under the influence of science, however, ecological principles began to determine increasingly the forms of unity which the landscape-painter imposed upon his material.

An early example of the type of relationship which art began to take over from

3

science at this time is to be found in botanical and zoological illustration. One of the important features of the description of a new species was the description of its habitat. Consequently, illustrators of animals usually placed them in their appropriate environmental setting. During the period under discussion this became a more frequent practice in the illustration of plants also. The relationship which existed between a species and its habitat could, however, be extended to all the species peculiar to a particular habitat. The placing of plants, animals, and primitive peoples in their appropriate environmental situation became a matter of increasing importance for the landscape-painter. In this tendency lay the implicit recognition of the intimate connexion between the objects in a landscape and the environmental and climatic situation of which the landscape as a whole was both a representation and a symbol. Thus landscapes came to be painted in which the rocks, plants, animals, peoples, and atmospheric conditions depicted were selected and organized to characterize the *type* of landscape painted. In this practice is to be observed a further expression of that interest in types which had gained such impetus in the scientific world from the work of Carl von Linné.[3] His work in the classification of plants and animals was extended to the classification of clouds by meteorologists and the classification of climates by geographers. In this situation there arose the desire to represent in works of art what may best be called typical landscape, a form of landscape the component parts of which were carefully selected in order to express the essential qualities of a particular kind of geographical environment. Landscape-painters became fully conscious of the fact that the world contained distinct types of scenery with their own forms of visual unity. Such unity was only to be achieved by an appreciation of the essential character and beauty of each scenic type.

In this study the emergence of the idea of typical landscape is traced from the appearance of scientific illustrations used by geologists and natural historians, and the interests of a circle of virtuosi centred upon Sir Joseph Banks. The idea was given more complete expression in the practice and writings of William Hodges in whose work it begins to impinge upon the world of taste and neo-classical values. Through Alexander von Humboldt the typical landscape was given a theoretical justification and championed as an artistic programme for painters. Humboldt's writings were very widely read and influenced the thoughts of such men as Karl Gustav Carus and John Ruskin. Through the work of such men the idea of typical landscape was elaborated and became the common property of nineteenth-century artistic thought. Now although the factors which united to produce this new approach to landscape were by no means confined to European experience in the Pacific, it will be shown that Pacific exploration played a significant part both in its emergence as an art and in its theoretical formulation.

Typical landscape is one aspect of the growing influence of the biological sciences which Pacific exploration did so much to stimulate. The stimulus operated with great effect at the empirical level, for the Pacific, naturally enough, provided scientists with a vast amount of new data. Concerning Matthew Flinders's voyage, for instance, Joseph Dalton Hooker wrote, 'the botanical results ... have been ... incomparably greater, not merely than those of any previous voyage, but than those of all similar voyages put together'.[4] The stimulus, however, was also felt at the level of theory. Despite their empirical methods most eighteenth-century biologists sought to relate their findings to a cosmology Aristotelian in its origins. 'If we consider the generation of Animals', wrote von Linné, 'we find that each produces an off-spring after its own kind ... and that from each proceeds a germ of the same nature with its parent; so that all living things, plants, animals, and even mankind themselves, form one "chain of universal Being", from the beginning to the end of the world.'[5] Scientists working in the Pacific, however, found it increasingly difficult to classify their material according to the presuppositions of this cosmology. Sir James Edward Smith, the first President of the Linnean Society, put the difficulty in this way:

> When a botanist first enters on the investigation of so remote a country as New Holland, he finds himself as it were in a new world. He can scarcely meet with any fixed points from whence to draw his analogies; and even those that appear most promising, are frequently in danger of misleading, instead of informing him. The whole tribes of plants, which at first sight seem familiar to his acquaintance, as occupying links in Nature's chain, on which he is accustomed to depend, prove, on a nearer examination, total strangers, with other configurations, other economy, and other qualities; not only the species themselves are new, but most of the genera, and even natural orders.[6]

Confronted with such problems natural philosophers not infrequently suggest novel solutions. Indeed, interest in the formation of coral islands, and in the plants, animals, and native peoples of the Pacific may be said, in general, to have promoted thought along evolutionary lines. Pacific voyages stimulated the reflections of Erasmus Darwin, Lord Monboddo, and a number of minor writers. And during the first half of the nineteenth century, three scientists, Charles Darwin, Joseph Dalton Hooker, and Thomas Henry Huxley, whose joint efforts did so much to establish organic evolution as an acceptable scientific explanation of the history of life on earth, spent the crucial formative years of their lives as naturalists on scientific voyages to the Pacific region.

European experience of the Pacific by thus helping to promote thought along evolutionary lines challenged the supremacy of neo-classical values in cosmological theory as it had helped to challenge those values in the theory and practice of landscape-painting. For these reasons alone European experience of the Pacific is not without significance for the history of European art and ideas. Even so, it is to be stressed that the impact of Pacific experience upon European art and thought is only to be observed operating within an intricate interplay of ideas in which, for the most part, European observers sought to come to grips with the realities of the Pacific by interpreting them in familiar terms. Both classical antiquity and the traditions of Christian thought provided a stock of attitudes and preconceptions which Europeans continually brought to bear upon their experience of the Pacific.

European attitudes to Pacific peoples provide an illuminating example. The first European visitors to Polynesia tended to view the natives as noble savages, an attitude with its roots deep in the thought of classical antiquity. It is possible to distinguish two forms of this primitivistic approach[7] to Pacific peoples: a soft primitivism, applied mainly to the inhabitants of the Society Islands, and a hard primitivism, applied to such peoples as the Fuegians, the Maoris, and the Australian aborigines. The primitivistic interpretation of Pacific peoples was, however, severely challenged by evangelical thought during the last decade of the eighteenth century. Soft primitivism, more closely associated with deistic thought and neo-classical values, was singled out for the most severe attacks by evangelical critics; the notions of austerity and fortitude associated with hard primitivism being somewhat more congenial both to Calvinistic Christianity and to the romantic interest in the historical origins of the northern nations of Europe. Nevertheless, Christian thought, with the decline of deism, found any kind of belief in the natural virtue of pagan savages repugnant and did much to spread the belief that the native peoples of the Pacific in their natural state were depraved and ignoble.

Such preconceptions both as to the nobility and to the ignobility of Pacific peoples

5

exhibited considerable vigour in popular thought despite the objective investigations of scientists, educated missionaries, and travellers. Nevertheless, Europeans gradually became aware of the physical and social factors which differentiated one people from another. In the end scientific method triumphed in the description both of nature and man.

Historians of Pacific exploration have tended to neglect the importance of investigations undertaken by the scientific and artistic components of voyages of discovery. As a result of Banks's decision to sail with Cook there was added to research in the physical sciences, of direct interest to the Admiralty and the Royal Society, the interests of a virtuoso specializing in the biological sciences together with the interests of his attendant artists. Banks proved beyond doubt the value of those recommendations for equipping exploratory voyages with naturalists and artists which had been urged from time to time throughout the eighteenth century both in England and in France. In 1748 Richard Walter, in his popular edition of Anson's *Voyage*, argued strongly for the inclusion of skilled draughtsmen on such expeditions. He drew attention to the fact that in 1712 Amédée François Frézier (1682–1773) had been sent by Louis XIV, surreptitiously, on a merchantman to draw draughts and plans of coastlines and fortified positions along the South American coast, for potential use in smuggling and naval assault. But Walter saw the value of skilled draughtsmanship in a much wider context, and his arguments deserve to be quoted in full for they must have exercised a strong influence upon Banks, in preparing for the *Endeavour* voyage. We know, incidentally, that he took copies both of Frézier[8] and Anson with him, for he quotes from both in his *Journal*. Walter's views were crucial for the development of Banks's plan for combining verbal and visual records:

> ... I cannot ... but lament, how very imperfect many of our accounts of distant countries are rendered by the relators being unskilled in drawing, and in the general principles of surveying; even where other abilities have not been wanting. Had more of our travellers been initiated in these acquirements, and there had been added thereto some little skill in the common astronomical observations, (all of which a person of ordinary talents might attain, with a very moderate share of application) we should by this time have seen the geography of the globe much correcter, than we now find it; the dangers of navigation would have been considerably lessened, and the manners, arts and produce of foreign countries would have been much better known to us, than they are. Indeed, when I consider, the strong incitements that all travellers have to acquire some part at least of these qualifications, especially drawing; when I consider how much it would facilitate their observations, assist and strengthen their memories, and of how tedious, and often unintelligible, a load of description it would rid them, I cannot but wonder that any person, that intends to visit distant countries, with a view of informing either himself or others, should be unfurnished with so useful a piece of skill. And to inforce this argument still further, I must add, that besides the uses of drawing, which are already mentioned, there is one, which, though not so obvious, is yet perhaps of more consequence than all that has been hitherto urged; and that is, that those who are accustomed to draw objects, observe them with more distinctness, than others who are not habituated to this practice. For we may easily find, by a little experience, that in viewing any object however simple, our attention or memory is scarcely at any time so strong, as to enable us, when we have turned our eyes away from it, to recollect exactly every part it consisted of, and to recall all the circumstances of its appearance; since, on examination, it will be discovered, that in

6

some we were mistaken, and others we had totally overlooked: But he that is employed in drawing what he sees, is at the same time employed in rectifying this inattention; for by confronting his idea copied on the paper, with the object he intends to represent, he finds in what manner he has been deceived in its appearance, and hence in time acquires the habit of observing much more at one view, and retains what he sees with more correctness than he could ever have done, without his practice and proficiency in drawing.[9]

In France, some eight years later, Charles De Brosses (1709–77) published his highly influential *Histoire des Navigations aux Terres Australes* (1756). It stressed the importance of taking both naturalists and natural history draughtsmen on voyages of exploration, and it too was included in Banks's *Endeavour* library. It is strange however that Bougainville, who was so much influenced by De Brosses in the conception and planning of his voyage to the Pacific (1766–9), did not take a competent natural history draughtsman with him. His naturalist Philibert Commerson, though well-trained and enthusiastic, possessed neither the patience nor the skills of a good scientific draughtsman. It was left therefore to Banks to establish the value in practice of taking skilled artists on scientific voyages and of collating verbal and visual observations.

Banks's success set the organizational pattern for the later exploratory work in the Pacific by England, France, Russia, and America; research in the biological sciences being undertaken along with research in the physical sciences. And to these inquiries there came to be added the objective and comparative study of native peoples, a study greatly promoted by the work of the Forsters, father and son, during Cook's second voyage, and officially written into La Pérouse's instructions. Furthermore, it must be stressed that the scientists of these great voyages inherited the rational enthusiasm of the Enlightenment and went to the South Seas ambitious to discover man and the world. As John Reinhold Forster put it: 'My object was nature in its greatest extent; the Earth, the Sea, the Air, the Organic and Animated Creation, and more particularly that class of Beings to which we ourselves belong.'[10] Their enthusiasm was not altogether misplaced; for in the hundred years after 1768 the Pacific Ocean became one of the finest schools for scientists in the world and stimulated European thought concerning man and nature both in art and in science.

2. Cook's First Voyage

'It is a strange thing', wrote Bacon in his essay *Of Travel*, 'that in sea-voyages, where there is nothing to be seen but sky and sea, men should make diaries, but in land-travel wherein so much is to be observed, for the most part they omit it.' [1] Such an observation, from the pen of an early champion of empiricism, serves well to illustrate the connexion already existing in Elizabethan times between sea voyaging and empirical observation. By 1588 British explorers were already being advised in their official instructions to keep daily diaries. In that year Thomas Randolfe, Elizabeth's ambassador to the Russian Emperor, provided three Englishmen, James Bassendine, James Woodcocke, and Richard Browne with a commission for discovery in the north-eastern seas. 'Take with you paper and ynke', his instructions advised them, 'and keepe a continuall journall or remembrance day by day, of all things as shall fall out worth the knowledge, not forgetting or omitting to write it, and note it, that it may be shewed and read at your returne.' [2]

From its foundation in 1660 the Royal Society appreciated the value of journals kept by seamen and travellers who embarked upon far voyages. In order that such journals should be accurate and comprehensive the Society included in the first volume of its *Philosophical Transactions* a set of 'Directions for Seamen, bound for far voyages'. It prefaced them with the following explanation:

> It being the Design of the *Royal Society*, for the better attaining the End of their Institution, to study *Nature* rather than *Books*, and from the Observations, made of the *Phenomena* and Effects she presents, to compose such a History of Her, as may hereafter serve to build a Solid and Useful Philosophy upon; They have from time to time given order to several of their Members to draw up both *Inquiries* of things Observable in forreign Countries, and *Directions* for the Particulars, they desire chiefly to be informed about. And considering with themselves, how much they may increase their *Philosophical* stock by the advantage, which *England* enjoyes of making Voyages into all parts of the World, they formerly appointed that Eminent Mathematician and Philosopher Master Rook, one of their Fellowes, and Geometry Professor of Gresham College, to think upon and set down some Directions for *Sea-men* going into the *East* and *West-Indies*, the better to capacitate them for making such Observations abroad, as may be pertinent and suitable for their purpose; of which the said Sea-men should be desired to keep an exact *Diary*, delivering at their return a fair Copy thereof to the *Lord High Admiral of England*, His Royal Highness the Duke of York, and another to *Trinity-House* to be perused by the Royal Society. [3]

The Society's 'Directions' were mainly concerned with the assembling of verbal and numerical data. But one direction involved the graphic arts. The fourth in the list enjoined seamen to 'make Plotts and Draughts of prospects of Coasts, Promontories,

2. Coastal profiles from *Abel Janszoon Tasman's Journal*, ed. J. E. Heeres (1898)

Islands and Ports, marking the Bearings and Distances, as neer as they can'.[4] Not only maps but also profiles of new or little-known coasts were considered an essential part of a seaman's journal. The Dutch navigator Abel Tasman, for instance, made considerable use of coastal profiles to illustrate his *Journal* of the voyage of the *Heemskirk* and *Zeehaan* (1642–3) when he discovered Tasmania and New Zealand (Plate 2). Recognition of the usefulness of skill in drawing among seamen was one of the reasons which led to the establishment, on the advice of Sir Christopher Wren, Samuel Pepys, and others, of a Drawing School at Christ's Hospital in 1693. The Drawing School was attached to the Mathematical School which trained boys for the Navy, and the drawing of sea-views and coastal profiles were among the chief items taught by the Drawing Master.[5] The Drawing School at Christ's Hospital helped to raise the standard of draughtsmanship in the Navy during the eighteenth century. It thus, indirectly, helped to further the aims of the Royal Society.

In the same year that the Drawing School was established at Christ's Hospital, the philosopher John Locke published his *Thoughts Concerning Education*, in which he stressed the importance of drawing as an accomplishment in the general education of a young gentleman:

> When he can write well and quick, I think it may be convenient not only to continue the exercise of his hand in writing, but also to improve further the use of it in drawing, a thing very useful to gentlemen on several occasions, but especially if he travel, as that which helps a man often to express in a few lines well put together what a whole sheet of paper in writing would not be able to represent and make intelligible. How many buildings may a man see, how many machines and habits meet with, the ideas whereof would be easily retained and communicated by a little skill in drawing, which being committed to words are in danger of being lost, or at best ill retained in the most exact descriptions? I do not mean that I would have your son a perfect painter; to be that to any tolerable degree will require more time than a young gentleman can spare from his other improvements of greater moment; but so much insight into perspective and skill in drawing as will enable him to repeat tolerably on paper anything he sees, may, I think be got in a little time.[6]

With the support of men like Pepys and Locke, the practical value of drawing for recording information became widely accepted during the first half of the eighteenth century. Drawing was introduced as part of the curriculum at the Portsmouth Naval Academy in 1733, and in consequence of the views expressed in Anson's *Voyage*, quoted in the previous chapter, a directive was issued by the Admiralty to commanders afloat 'that officers qualified in draughtsmanship should be employed wherever and whenever possible to provide plans and sketches of ports, watering places, anchorages, coasts and wherever troops could land "taking particular care,

when in *Foreign Parts*, not to do anything to give Umbrage or offence to the Governors, or Inhabitants, of Places in Friendship with the King'' '.[7]

Another way in which the graphic arts were called into the service of empirical observation is to be observed in the use of engravings to illustrate letters and papers published in the *Philosophical Transactions*. These engravings, which were used from the early issues onwards, were almost invariably intended to be nothing more than useful illustrations to supplement the written account. But during the second half of the eighteenth century an increasing number of professional artists were employed to make scientific illustrations. Consequently some of the engravings which appeared in the *Transactions* during that period possessed an arresting visual appeal quite apart from what they were intended to illustrate. Among such illustrations are to be numbered the hand-coloured engravings which were used to illustrate William Hamilton's descriptions of the eruptions of Mount Vesuvius which he observed in 1767, 1776, 1777, and 1791.[8] Hamilton made drawings of the changing aspect of the volcano during eruptions to assist his own observations. He also trained a young Neapolitan artist, Pietro Fabris, to make numerous sketches of all stages of the eruptions observed. Concerning the 1767 eruption Hamilton wrote: 'From my villa situated between Herculaneum and Pompeii, I had watched the growing of this little mountain,[9] and by taking drawings of it from time to time, I could perceive its increase most minutely; I make no doubt that the whole of Mount Vesuvius was formed in this manner.'[10] Thus Hamilton's drawings were used to assist his observation and his published engravings are, equally, an integral part of his descriptions of the eruptions he observed (Plate 3). In donating a collection of volcanic earths to the Society in 1769 he also presented a pictorial device which, in some respects, anticipated both the Vesuvius paintings of Joseph Wright of Derby and the *Eidophusikon* of Philip de Loutherbourg. After describing his gift of volcanic earths Hamilton added: 'I have also accompanied that collection with a current of lava from Mount Vesuvius; it is painted with transparent colours, and, when lighted up with lamps behind it, gives a much better idea of Vesuvius, than is possible to be given by any other sort of painting.'[11] Hamilton later published his observations more fully in *Campi Phlegraei* (1776) with illustrations by Fabris, 'completed under my eye, and by my direction, with utmost fidelity, and . . . as much taste as exactness' and 'in which each stratum is represented in its proper colours'.[12]

In 1767, the year that Hamilton was making use of drawings executed on the spot to assist his geological observations of Vesuvius, Joseph Banks (later one of Hamilton's close friends) was becoming increasingly interested in the uses of drawing and engraving for the promotion of botanical studies. Banks, like Hamilton, was a virtuoso.[13] Both his great-grandfather and his grandfather had been antiquaries. It was an antiquary who successfully nominated him for membership of the Royal Society at the age of twenty-three. The programme of the Society of Antiquaries, as it was reconstituted in the mid-eighteenth century, suggested, *inter alia*, that 'fit persons' might be sent 'to travel over England and abroad' to inspect books and manuscripts, to draw ancient fortifications, Castles, Churches, Houses, Tombs, Inscriptions, Epitaphs, &c.[14] In practice professional topographical artists had been employed by the gentlemen antiquaries during the previous century; the most notable example being the employment of Hollar by Thomas Howard, Earl of Arundel, the 'father of Vertu in England'. Hollar made topographical drawings for the Earl upon his travels, published illustrations of exotic plants and animals, and plates illustrating the costumes of the old and new worlds. He also made a personal visit to Tangier to draw records of the town and garrison life there.[15] Years later Banks's artists were to range over a similar repertoire of subjects. As a young man archaeology claimed Banks's attention. He examined barrows, commenting on their meaning and origin.[16] In 1766 he collected plants when he went with his friend Lieutenant Phipps to Newfoundland. Upon his return he employed the most renowned botanical illustrator of the day, Georg Dionysius Ehret (1708–70),[17] to illustrate some of the plants he had collected.[18] It was at this time that the use of art in the service of science emerged as one of the central interests of his life. In later years he was to employ many botanical artists, including several Germans and Austrians attracted to England by his patronage of scientific draughtsmanship.

Banks's enthusiasm for the scientific illustration of exotic plants extended, among his circle of friends, to the scientific illustration of exotic animals. Their enthusiasm may be estimated from the reception given to the news of the arrival of a penguin from Patagonia. Thomas Pennant wrote to Banks excitedly:

> Let me hope that the Patagonian Penguin had set for its picture, that Mr Brook's Percnopteru will not depart this life without having its image preserved to be transmitted to posterity by Mr Paillou's pencil; that the image of these and many others may for the benefit of the curious and making of proselytes to our divine science be multiplied by engraving and that we may with unabated zeal pursue the path we have begun by our four plates.[19]

And in another letter to Banks a fortnight later Pennant wrote: 'Is your Penguin drawn? I dream, I rave of it'.[20]

The penguin was drawn, not by Peter Paillou however, but by Sydney Parkinson, the son of a quaker brewer of Edinburgh, who began to paint flowers for Banks in 1767.[21] The drawing was engraved and used to illustrate Pennant's article on the Penguin in the *Philosophical Transactions* (Plate 4).[22] An endeavour has been made to portray the bird in its natural environment: it stands facing the sea, upon a promontory, with an arched rock behind it. Pennant, interested in the habitat of each animal which he studied, found the accurate portrayal of environmental setting a question of considerable interest. In his autobiography he recounts how Peter Paillou painted pictures for him of climatic regions, each with its appropriate animals: 'He painted for my hall, at Downing, several pictures of birds and animals, attended with suitable landscapes. Four were intended to represent the climates. The frigid zone and

4. *The Patagonian Penguin*,
engraving after Sydney
Parkinson, *Phil. Trans.* lviii
(1768), pl. 5

an *European* scene of a farm yard, are particularly well done....'[23] Throughout his lifetime Pennant, like Banks, continued to employ artists in pursuing his study of natural history. One artist, Moses Griffith (1749–*c*. 1809), worked with him for many years.

In Pennant's paintings at Downing, showing exotic animals in their natural climatic settings, there lay an incipient programme for the landscape-painter radically different from the neo-classicism predominant in British landscape-painting during the 1760's. An early formulation of this programme was provided by Thomas Falconer,[24] a friend both of Banks and Pennant, in a letter to Banks. In 1768 Banks had projected, probably with Linnaeus's tour in mind, a voyage to Lapland. In a letter of advice to Banks concerning the proposed tour Falconer insisted upon the value of coloured drawings of all natural phenomena observed:

> We shall expect ... a particular account of some of those wonderful scenes which are mentioned in the Oration of Linnaeus. You take a designer with you, and it would be easy to sketch out some of the views. Travellers in general confine themselves to the works of Art; and by giving us only Towns or Churches, exhibit nothing but a tedious uniformity. The appearance of Nature is varied in every Climate: an Alpine scene is different from a Derbyshire landscape; and if your designer would stain his drawing, it would point out the colour of the Soil and verdure, with the nature of the Rocks, and would enable us here to have a full idea of the Country, which no description possibly can.[25]

While insisting that Banks should take a landscape-painter with him, Falconer also appears to be making an implicit criticism of travellers who employed artists upon grand tours. For the travellers mentioned who confine themselves to works of art are almost certainly the grand tourists, whose depictions yielded, for Falconer, a 'tedious uniformity'. So he outlined a programme for the landscape-painter which, for 1768, was rather unusual. Certainly all would agree that nature differed in different regions, but it was not, according to neo-classical theory, the concern of the artist to busy himself with these differences. The landscape-painter seeking to produce works of art of lasting value should seek rather to reveal the uniformity underlying the apparent differences to be observed in nature. While it was readily admitted that accurate representations of plants, animals, and buildings could serve many useful purposes, art of this kind occupied a low position in the hierarchy of neo-classical values. Falconer's statement, however, contains an implicit criticism of the low status awarded such art by the connoisseurs. According to him the landscape-painter should seek out the permanent geological and climatic features of the landscape he is painting in order to present 'a full idea' of the region concerned. Landscape-painting instead of revealing the uniformity of nature is to reveal her geographical variety.

Falconer had written his letter to Banks in February 1768. By April it was settled that Banks should voyage with Cook to the South Pacific in the *Endeavour*. Consequently Falconer's letter contained a programme which Banks was to put into operation not in Lapland but in the South Seas.

In consequence of the prestige attained by Banks, after his return from the Pacific, the ideas concerning art and nature discussed between Pennant, Falconer, and himself upon the eve of his departure, began to make some impact upon the world of taste. For throughout his life Banks's interests continued to be divided between the world of science and the world of taste. Although he did not consider himself a connoisseur of the visual arts, he had many friends both among artists and connoisseurs.[26] And through the patronage which he was able to extend both directly and indirectly—by virtue of his long Presidency of the Royal Society (1778–1820)— his own views on art came to exercise an influence upon late eighteenth-century taste.

At an early age Banks had become a member of the Society of Arts, a society which, significantly enough, sought to establish a closer relationship between science, technology, and art.[27] In 1774 he was elected a member of the Society of Dilettanti and continued to be for many years one of its most distinguished and honoured members, acting as its secretary for a period of eighteen years (1778–97).[28] Since its foundation in 1732 this dining society of wealthy and travelled amateurs had played a key role in the promotion of neo-classical taste in the visual arts both at home and abroad. In it Banks became acquainted not only with artists like Sir Joshua Reynolds (elected 1766) and patrons like Sir George Beaumont (elected 1784), but also with distinguished classical antiquaries like Sir William Hamilton, Charles Townley, Richard Payne Knight, and James ('Athenian') Stuart—the man responsible for nominating him for membership. For many years Banks kept the Society's marbles in his own house at Soho Square; and his fellow-neighbour Richard Payne Knight became one of his closest friends. Reynolds painted him as a thoughtful man among convivial friends in the second of his two group portraits of members of the Dilettanti (Plate 5).

Yet despite his close association with some of the most learned classical antiquaries and men of taste of the day, Banks himself had little sympathy with classical idealism in the visual arts. Joseph Farington summed up Banks's taste in art briefly but adequately when he wrote: 'Accuracy of drawing seems to be a principal recommend-ation to Sir Joseph'.[29] The artists with whom Banks associated and to whom he extended his patronage were men whose works are notable for their precision of draughtsmanship and the rendering of visual statements without resort to adornments of style. One of his associates was Paul Sandby whose work is notable for its clarity of draughtsmanship and its simpicity of vision.[30] Sandby travelled with Banks on a tour of Wales,[31] and the virtuoso also acquired many of the artist's finest drawings. Banks was also the friend of Johan Zoffany, whose 'neat, polished, highly finished German style' with its 'tendency to the lively and minute imitation of natural objects' must have appealed to him.[32] While making a tour of Holland in 1773 Banks visited the cabinet of the Princess of Orange at The Hague and examined several paintings. 'One of Oxen and a Shepherd painted by Potter pleased me much', he wrote in his Journal, 'immencely high finishd but absolute nature.'[33] The work of Pieter van Loo[34] and Thomas Bewick[35] also appealed to him, and he appears to have been particularly interested in the work of Joseph Wright.[36] George Stubbs, that eighteenth-century master of visual empiricism, painted a dingo and a kangaroo (Colour Plate 1) for him.[37] In 1774 Banks was a prominent member of a club which included artists and scientists among its members and met at Young Slaughter's Coffee House.[38] Indeed already by 1773 he had established a reputation among his friends for the way in which he was making use of artists in the service of scientific accuracy. In that year Falconer, by way of complimenting Banks upon the results of his tour of Iceland and the Hebrides, criticized Martin's *Description of the Western Isles of Scotland* (1703) for being insufficiently objective. Banks's use of artists was, according to Falconer, one of the factors which helped to make his account of the Hebrides more impersonal and more accurate:

> ... the remarks of an English traveller would be more consonant to an English ear; for we all judge by comparison and a Scotch traveller would not consider a place as barren, which we should regard as worth nothing. For this reason Martin and others have given us a false idea of the western islands; and your remarks will set the world right in many particulars wherein they were ill-instructed before. Your precision of measures, and the advantage of able artists, are a great point, for when we judge by description we form an opinion through the medium of another man's understanding, who generally compares it with something else he has seen.... The French use the terms magnifique and superbe to the close and dirty lanes of Paris.... What an assistance is it then to truth to have the objects delineated by one common measure which speaks universally to all mankind.[39]

But the production of accurate graphic records in the Pacific was not such a simple matter as Falconer supposed. For Banks's artists, coming from Europe, were themselves subject to the same preconceptions as the European public. Furthermore, the position and requirements of Banks himself were ambivalent. Though a distinguished and scrupulous amateur scientist he was also a gentleman embarking upon a most unusual grand tour, and in his journals he sought to cater both for the men of taste and the natural historians. His position is admirably summed up in his own reply to those who thought he should perform the grand tour of Europe: 'Every blockhead does that, my Grand Tour shall be one round the whole globe.'[40] To the programme and results of that tour we must now turn.

The *Endeavour*, under the command of Lieutenant James Cook, sailed from Plymouth on 26 August 1768. Cook was to observe the 1769 transit of Venus across the face of the sun and to seek the much-discussed southern continent. His *Secret Instructions* also laid upon him other duties very much in the spirit of the Royal Society's 'Directions for Seamen, bound for far voyages'. Among other things he was instructed:

5. Sir Joshua Reynolds. *The Society of Dilettanti II*, canvas, 78 × 59 in. (1777–9). London, Society of Dilettanti. From left: Lord Mulgrave (1744–92); Lord Dundas (1741–1820); Lord Seaforth (1744–81); Hon. Charles Greville (1749–1809); John Charles Crowle (died 1811); Duke of Leeds (1751–99); Sir Joseph Banks (1743–1820)

... carefully to observe the Nature of the Soil, and the Products thereof; the Beasts and Fowls that inhabit or frequent it, the fishes that are to be found in the Rivers or upon the Coast and in what Plenty; and in case you find any Mines, Minerals or valuable stones, you are to bring home Specimens of each, as also such Specimens of the Seeds of Trees, Fruits and Grains as you may be able to collect, and Transmit them to our Secretary, that We may cause proper Examination and Experiments to be made of them.

You are likewise to observe the Genius, Temper, Disposition and Number of the Natives. . . .

You are to send by all proper Conveyances to the Secretary of the Royal Society Copys of the Observations you shall have made of the Tranist of Venus; and you are at the same time to send to our Secretary, for our information, accounts of your Proceedings and Copys of the Surveys and drawings you shall have made.[41]

The Royal Society had promoted the voyage by appealing to George III who promised £4,000 and a ship of the Navy. The *Secret Instructions* reveal the joint responsibility of the Royal Society and the Admiralty for the voyage, and emphasize its scientific nature. In the tradition of the Society they made faithful reporting a daily duty.

Cook was admirably fitted for his task. He was described in the *Transactions* by Dr. Bevis as 'a good mathematician, and very expert at his business'.[42] As an hydrographer his achievements were unequalled in his time.[43] The official objectives of the voyage were therefore in the most capable hands. But to these official objectives were added the interests of Joseph Banks and his party. The party included the Swedish naturalist, Daniel Carl Solander (1736–82), and an assistant naturalist, Herman Diedrich Spöring, together with two artists, Alexander Buchan and Sydney Parkinson. Banks employed Buchan as his topographical artist, but very little is known about him. An epileptic, he was seized with a fit during an excursion in Tierra del Fuego, when two of the company perished with cold, and died four days after the *Endeavour* reached Tahiti. 'His loss to me is irretrievable', wrote Banks in his *Journal*, 'my airy dreams of entertaining my friends in England with the scenes I am to see here

6. *Eucalyptus Terminalis*, photograph of a specimen collected in 1770 on Cook's first voyage. British Museum (Natural History)

7. Sydney Parkinson,
Eucalyptus Terminalis, pencil,
$18\frac{1}{4} \times 10\frac{3}{4}$ in. 'Plants of
Australia', iii, f. 139 (1770).
Botanical Library, British
Museum (Natural History)

8. Frederick Polydore
Nodder, *Eucalyptus
Terminalis*, watercolour,
$21\frac{3}{8} \times 13\frac{7}{8}$ in. 'Plants of
Australia', iii (1778), f. 139.
Botanical Library, British
Museum (Natural History)

9. *Eucalyptus Terminalis*,
engraving (*c.* 1780)

have vanished. No account of the figures and dresses of the natives can be satisfactory unless illustrated by figures; had Providence spared him a month longer, what an advantage it would have been to my undertaking, but I must submit.'[44]

Banks's original intention had been that the drawings executed on the voyage should fall into two groups: faithful copies of singular plants and animals, from Parkinson; drawings of savages and scenery that would entertain his friends at home, from Buchan. But, with the death of Buchan, Banks called upon Spöring and occasionally Parkinson to make drawings of people and places encountered. Parkinson when not working on natural-history drawings for Banks kept a personal diary, compiled vocabulary lists of Pacific languages, and drew figures and scenes for his own personal interest and pleasure. He was thus torn, as we shall see, between the needs of the scientist and the tastes of the grand tourist.

A great deal of Parkinson's work upon the voyage consisted of drawing specimens of plants collected by the naturalists. Solander described all new plants collected and attempted to classify them, but the vast amount of new and strange material created major problems in classification. His notebooks abound with erasures and cancellations of specific and generic names first allotted to the specimens collected.[45] Described and classified by Solander, a new plant was then sketched by Parkinson sufficiently to record the shape, size, coloration, and principal parts of the foliage and flower. It was then preserved. After returning to England, Solander wrote up a full description and Banks employed artists to make finished drawings from Parkinson's sketches. These drawings were later engraved under Banks's personal supervision. Parkinson made 955 drawings of plants (675 sketches, 280 finished drawings) during the voyage.[46] An idea of the method of recording new plants followed by Banks and his party may best be gained by considering a single case.

During their voyage along the Australian coast Solander and Banks collected some leaves of a tree which Solander described and named *Metrosideros salicifolia* and later *Metrosideros obliqua*.[47] Parkinson made a pencil drawing of the leaves and flowers of the plant (Plate 7). Eight years later Frederick Nodder[48] made the finished drawing for Banks (Plate 8). Nodder based the disposition of the leaves and flower upon Parkinson's rough sketch, the notes on the back of which gave hints for colouring, viz. 'the stamina white, receptacles pale green the stalks the same the leaves a pale blue green with a yellowish nerve in the middle'. Banks then had an engraving (in reverse) made from Nodder's drawing (Plate 9). These drawings and the engravings may be compared with an original dried type specimen brought home by Banks and preserved in the British Museum (Natural History) (Plate 6). Although the disposition of the foliage is, naturally enough, somewhat different, the essential botanical facts have been recorded faithfully from specimen to published engraving. Yet the quality of Parkinson's finished work is unquestionable. (Colour Plate 2).[49]

Parkinson, although trained as a botanical draughtsman, also made many drawings of coastal profiles during the voyage, as did Buchan and the naturalist Spöring. Although the drawing of profiles was traditional among mariners, the standard of draughtsmanship in the British navy in this field in the 1760's was not particularly high. The profiles drawn by Captain Samuel Wallis (Plate 10)[50] who preceded Cook to Tahiti were little more than practical off-shore guides to the identification of new coasts. But Banks's topographic and natural-history draughtsmen readily took to the naval practice and succeeded in producing (perhaps at Cook's suggestion) coastal profiles of an order of accuracy beyond naval standards. On 7 October 1769, for instance, the coast of New Zealand first came into view. On the following day Cook entered in his Journal: 'The land on the Sea-Coast is high, with white steep cliffs and

1. George Stubbs, *Kangaroo* (detail), $23\frac{3}{4} \times 27\frac{1}{2}$ in. (1772–3). Parham Park, Sussex. By kind permission of the Trustees of the Parham Estate

Convolvulus grandiflorus.

"Otahité"

Sydney Parkinson pinx 1769.

2. Sydney Parkinson, *Convolvulus grandiflora*. Stictocardia tiliaefolia (Desrousseaux). Hallier f. Signed Sydney Parkinson, 'Otahite'. $18\frac{1}{2} \times 11$ in. (1769). Botanical Drawings by Sydney Parkinson, Botanical Library, British Museum (Natural History)

3. William Hodges, *Isle of Mayo distant 2 miles and the Hill B West*, wash, sheet 13 × 19 in. (1772). Mitchell Library, Sydney. By permission of the State Library of New South Wales

5 (following pages). George Forster, *Ice Islands* (detail), gouache, 10½ × 15 in. (c. 1772). Original sketches . . . collected by Admiral Isaac Smith. Mitchell Library, Sydney. PXD11. 30. By permission of the Trustees of the State Library of New South Wales

4. William Hodges, *The Cape of Good Hope*, canvas, 38 × 49¼ in. (1772). National Maritime Museum, London. On loan from the Department of Defence—Navy

7. William Hodges, *View of Part of the Island of Ulietea* (Raiatea), canvas, 13 × 19¼ in. (1773). National Maritime Museum, London. On loan from the Department of Defence—Navy

6 (preceeding pages). William Hodges, *Province of Oparee* (Pare) (detail), panel, 30 × 48½ in. (c. 1775/6). National Maritime Museum, London. On loan from the Department of Defence—Navy

8. William Hodges, *View of the Islands of Otaha and Bola Bola*, (Tahaa and Pora Pora), canvas, 13 × 19¼ in. (1773). National Maritime Museum, London. On loan from the Department of Defence—Navy

back inland are very high mountains, the face of the Country is of a hilly surface and appeares to be cloathed with wood and Verdure.'[51] Parkinson made a profile of the landfall which was published later in his *Journal of a Voyage to the South Seas* (Plate 11). It is just as impersonal in its topographical fidelity as Cook's description. By such means a natural-history draughtsman learned how to document a new coastline in a manner similar to the documentation of a new plant. Publication by means of engraving made the appearance of the coast available to navigators just as the publication of engravings of new plants made them available to botanists.

Cook, the Admiralty, the Royal Society, and even Banks, in his capacity as botanist, required of draughtsmen accurate visual documents, nothing more and nothing less. But Banks, as already observed, was on his grand tour. He realized correctly that not only his friends but the whole British public would be seeking something more visually exciting than topographical and botanical documents. So he set Spöring the task and encouraged Parkinson to make views of the scenes Buchan was to have painted in the South Seas.[52] Parkinson, for the most part, brought the same topographical fidelity to the work as he did to his coastal profiles. But whereas they were drawn purely for the purpose of documentation irrespective of their subject interest, the landscape views and ethnographical illustrations which Parkinson made

10. Samuel Wallis, *Osnaburg* (Meetia) *Island*, pen drawing, $9\frac{3}{4} \times 16\frac{1}{4}$ in. (1767). Nan Kivell Collection 31, National Library of Australia, Canberra

11. *View of the North side of the Entrance into Poverty Bay and Morai Island in New Zealand*, engraving after Sydney Parkinson, from his *Journal* (1773), pl. xiv

were chosen because they were curious enough to be interesting to a virtuoso: picturesque views of waterfalls (Plate 12), grottoes, river and bay scenes such as any artist travelling with a grand tourist to Italy might have painted for his patron. And to this normal repertoire of picturesque subject-matter, the Pacific added many exotic and curious scenes—native houses and canoes (Plate 13), Tahitian dancing girls, the Polynesian *marae*, and so on.[53] Consequently, in Parkinson's work the appeal of picturesque scenery is mingled with the appeal of the exotic. In this regard also Parkinson's work foreshadows that of many artists who voyaged to the Pacific in later years.

Some idea how the conflicting ideals of art and science both engaged Banks's interest may be obtained by a study of his description of a natural arch discovered in Tolaga Bay, New Zealand:

> We saw . . . an extraordinary natural curiosity. In pursuing a valley bounded on each side by steep hills, we suddenly saw a most noble arch or cavern through the face of a rock leading directly to the sea, so that through it we had not only a view of the bay and hills on the other side, but an opportunity of imagining a ship or any other grand object opposite to it. It was certainly the most magnificent surprise I have ever met with; so much is pure nature superior to art in these cases. I have seen such places made by art, where from an inland view you were led through an arch 6 ft wide, and 7 ft high, to a prospect of the sea, but here was an arch 25 yards in length, 9 in breadth, and at least 15 in height.[54]

In this description Banks might satisfy the exacting requirements that a friend like Falconer might demand and also demonstrate as Falconer wished that nature was

12. Sydney Parkinson, *View up the River among rocks* (Society Islands), pencil and wash, $9\frac{1}{2} \times 11\frac{1}{2}$ in. (1769). British Museum Add: MS. 23921.7b

28

superior to art, but the language is nevertheless that of a young gentleman of taste vindicating his decision to go south with Cook. For Banks's description is carefully composed like a painting: in the foreground the arch, the sea behind, the hills on either side, and to give a centre to the view, an imaginary ship.

Here was a scene that would entertain Banks's friends. Spöring made a pencil drawing of it, full of detail but in the spirit of Banks's picturesque description (Plate 14). It was later engraved with appropriate embellishments for Hawkesworth's *Voyages*. Later in the voyage, however, Parkinson copied Spöring's original drawing in outline into his sketch book and then developed for his own personal pleasure a picturesque vignette, in which Hogarth's serpentine curves of beauty are substituted for Spöring's topographic detail (Plate 15).[55]

About a fortnight later, they came upon a similar curiosity. At Mercury Bay a Maori *pa* had been built upon an arched rock surrounded by the sea at high water. Here was a curiosity which combined the appeal of the picturesque with the appeal of the exotic. '... what made it most truly romantic', wrote Banks in his journal, 'was that much the greater part of it was hollowed out into an arch, which penetrated quite through it.'[56] Spöring made a sketch of the village upon the rock (Plate 16) which was engraved for Hawkesworth's *Voyages* (Plate 17). The engraver, however, has altered the drawing, increasing the scale of the sketch by reducing the size of the man standing on the rock to the left. Furthermore, by decreasing the size of the native craft, by adding the long boat and the native canoe in the foreground and the birds, clouds, and distant mountains, the engraver invested the scene with a grandeur Spöring's careful drawing did not possess.

It was thus possible to adopt two attitudes to new landscapes: they could be documented faithfully after the manner of coastal profiles, or they could be composed picturesquely in the manner of geological curiosities.[57] These two attitudes, revealing two types of interest in Pacific phenomena, persist in the published engravings.

13. Sydney Parkinson, *New Zealand War Canoe*, pen and wash, 11¾ × 19 in. (1769). British Museum, Add. MS. 23920.46

29

14. H. D. Spöring, *The Arched Rock, Tolaga Bay*, pencil, $10\frac{3}{4} \times 16$ in. (1769). British Museum Add. MS. 23920. f. 39

15. Sydney Parkinson, *A Perforated Rock in New Zealand* (Tolaga Bay), pen and wash, $11\frac{3}{4} \times 14\frac{3}{4}$ in. (1769). British Museum, Add. MS. 23920.40b

16. H. D. Spöring, *A Perforated Rock fortified on the Top*, pencil, 11 × 16 in. (1769). British Museum Add. MS. 23920.42a

17. *A Fortified Town or Village called a Hippah built on a perforated rock at Tolaga in New Zealand*, engraving after Spöring, in Hawkesworth, *Voyages* (1773), pl. xviii

Whilst Banks's interest in the arched rocks of New Zealand does, doubtless, derive from his interest in grottoes as a feature of the gardens he had visited,[58] his enthusiastic descriptions, and the engravings of them after Parkinson and Spöring, did play a part in promoting the *natural* grotto, as a popular item of romantic taste. Banks stressed, as we have seen, the superiority of natural grottoes to artificial grottoes. His accounts and the illustrations, through the works of Hawkesworth and Parkinson, became widely known to the European public, and were absorbed into the general context of European ideas. It is not unlikely, for instance, that they inspired the description of the enormous natural arch discovered by the shipwrecked company of Frenchmen in the fictitious *Découvertes dans la mer du Sud. Nouvelles de M. de la Peyrouse.*[59] It was described by one of the company as follows:

> J'avoue que je ne pus me défendre d'un premier mouvement d'admiration à la vue de cet étonnant ouvrage de la nature. Qu'on se figure un pont d'une seule arche de plus de 800 toises de large, d'environ 600 pieds de haut dans sa moindre élévation, et de 200 brasses au moins de longueur. La mer entroit par ce chemin jusqu'au fond de la baye, qui s'élargissant ensuite prodigieusement à droite de à gauche, formoit un magnifique bassin presque rond, d'environ quatre lieues et demie de large en tous sens.[60]

This description, in turn, is possibly the basis for the 'stupendous rocks, with an arched bridge' which August von Kotzebue two years later took as the setting for the final scene of his play on the tragic voyage of La Pérouse.[61] The play was performed, in English, at Convent Garden in 1799.[62]

The 'grottoes' of New Zealand appealed directly to current rococo taste. This made their detached observation difficult. But they stimulated also Banks's interest in geological curiosities. In his use of the botanical draughtsman, Parkinson, to depict curious New Zealand rocks is foreshadowed his later use of another botanical draughtsman, John Frederick Miller, to depict the basaltic formations of Fingal's Cave on the Isle of Staffa. In both situations, but more particularly in the latter, the technical precision of botanical illustration was adapted to the depiction of landscape structure as a whole.

In 1772, after cancelling the projected voyage with Cook in the *Resolution*, Banks decided upon a visit to Iceland with the intention of examining the antiquities and topography of the island. It was on this trip that Banks visited the Isle of Staffa and wrote the first extensive scientific description of the formation known as Fingal's Cave. It created the widest interest. In it, once again, Banks mingled the delight of a virtuoso in the oddities of nature with the objective accuracy required of a member of the Royal Society. Once again he pointed to the supremacy of the works of nature over the works of man, finding in Fingal's Cave a measure of the limitations of classical art:

> Compared to this what are the cathedrals or palaces built by men! mere models or playthings, imitations as diminutive as his works will always be when compared with those of nature. What is now the boast of the architect! regularity the only part in which he fancied himself to exceed his mistress, Nature is here found in her possession, and here it has been for ages undescribed. Is not this the school where the art was originally studied, and what has been added to this by the whole *Grecian* school? a capital to ornament the column of nature, of which they could execute only a model; and for that very capital they were obliged to a bush of *Acanthus*. How amply does nature repay those who study her wonderful works![63]

18. *Bending Pillars in Staffa*,
engraving after John
Frederick Miller by P.
Mazell, in Pennant, *Tour in
Scotland* (1774 edn.), pl. xxx

19. *View of Booshala from the
cliff above it*, engraving after
John Frederick Miller by P.
Mazell, in Pennant, *Tour in
Scotland* (1774 edn.), pl. xxix

20. *Fingal's Cave in Staffa*,
engraving after John
Frederick Miller, by P.
Mazell, in Pennant, *Tour in
Scotland* (1774 edn.), pl.
xxviii

But to this rhapsody upon the beauties of nature was appended a long detailed description of the basaltic formations upon the island, together with measurements. Banks's account of Staffa was published in his friend Pennant's *Tour of Scotland* (1774 edition) together with engravings after Miller, who accompanied Banks to Iceland. These engravings, like Banks's verbal description, seek to combine documentary precision with an artist's general impression of the natural beauties of Staffa. It is to be noted in *Bending Pillars in Staffa* (Plate 18) how Miller, the draughtsman, and Mazell, a specialist in engraving subjects of natural history, have rendered the shape and articulation of the basaltic pillars with the same care and precision that they were accustomed to expend upon the illustration of a new species of plant or animal. The landscape is, in one sense, a scientific diagram, but in another sense it provides evidence of a new and more analytical approach to the beauty of nature as revealed in landscape art. For the Staffa engravings (Plates 18–20) are not merely diagrams; clearly they seek to portray graphically that delighted enthusiasm in the unusual results of nature's handiwork which runs through so many of Banks's descriptions. Such engravings mark a distinct advance upon previous illustrations of geological curiosities, such as those provided by T. H. Tischbein to illustrate an article[64] on basaltic formations in Hessen published in the *Philosophical Transactions* for 1771 (Plate 21). For Tischbein's rocks are drawn as though laid upon the soil. They are not seen as a basic element in the structure and contour of the terrain. By comparison Miller's engraved drawings are already hinting at a more analytical, more penetrating approach to the depiction of land forms in landscape-painting.

In Banks's description of Staffa there was also a challenge for the architect. Was not architecture first studied in the school of nature? The question had, of course, been asked long before—and answered—by Vitruvius. But the time was propitious that it should be asked again. Many years later that visionary architect J. M. Gandy took up Banks's challenge when he exhibited his drawing *Architecture: Its Natural Model* at the Royal Academy in 1838 (Plate 22). The long description expanded the sentiments Banks had expressed sixty-four years before, and the drawing itself contained many 'natural bridges' drawn from travel books, and gave Fingal's Cave pride of place in the right-hand corner. As visions should be, it was prophetic. During the next century architecture was to relinquish gradually an aesthetic of regularity for an aesthetic of 'natural' forms—to replace the classic by the organic. In this regard Gandy foreshadowed Ruskin as Ruskin foreshadowed F. L. Wright.

Making faithful records of the native peoples of the Pacific proved to be more difficult than making accurate records of plants, animals, or landscapes.[65] There was, for instance, the question of size. In 1642 Tasman had written concerning the Tasmanian aborigines: 'There can be no doubt there must be men here of extraordinary stature.'[66] And at the other extremity of the Pacific, there had accumulated by 1768 a formidable body of evidence that the natives of Patagonia were giants.[67] The Captains Harrington and Carmen had come back in 1704 with stories of the giants. Byron, in 1764, only four years before Cook sailed in the *Endeavour*, corroborated their story. He described a Patagonian chief of 'gigantic stature' who 'seemed to realize the tales of monsters in a human shape'.[68] Byron's meeting with this chief was illustrated in Hawkesworth's *Voyages*, the chief being made, in accordance with Byron's description, to tower above the Englishman (Plate 23). But Byron had no professional artist with him. The illustration therefore was not an independent report based on direct observation, nor was it visual reportage in which observations were heightened by artistic devices. It was simply an illustration

21. *A Basalt-Rock near Gudensburg in Hassia* (Hessen), engraving after T. H. Tischbein, *Phil. Trans.* lxi (1771), pl. 18, p. 583

22. J. M. Gandy, *Architecture: Its Natural Model*, watercolour, $27\frac{1}{4} \times 14\frac{1}{2}$ in. (1838). Soane Museum, London

23. *John Byron's Landing in Patagonia,* engraving, in Hawkesworth, *Voyages* (1773), pl. xxiii

24. *A Sailor giving a Patagonian Woman some Biscuits for her Child*, engraving, in *A Voyage round the World in His Majesty's Ship the Dolphin*, (1767), frontispiece.

25. Alexander Buchan, *A Man of the Island of Terra del Fuego*, watercolour, $14\frac{1}{2} \times 10\frac{1}{2}$ in. (1769). British Museum. Add. Ms 23920. f.16

26. *Two Californian Women, the one in a bird's skin the other in that of a deer*, engraving by John Pine, in Shelvocke, *Voyage Round the World*, London (1726), pl. f.p. 404

based on a written statement. Indeed an anonymous account of Byron's voyage published in 1767 depicted an English sailor whose height reached only to the Patagonian hips (Plate 24). Banks, as already indicated, had taken his artists to the Pacific to avoid such expressions of 'opinion through the medium of another man's understanding'.

Banks was anxious to correct misconceptions about the size of Patagonians. It was, indeed, his first real test as an observer. So he described them carefully in his *Journal*: 'the men are largely built, but very clumsy, their height being from five feet eight inches to five feet ten inches, and all very much the same size. The women are much smaller, seldom exceeding five feet.'[69] Both Buchan and Parkinson made drawings of the Fuegians and both showed them to be normal in height. Buchan's drawings are models of documentary realism. The native is not shown in a landscape setting. The figure is isolated to reveal proportion, posture, expression, modes of dress and equipment (Plate 25). Yet we know from his field sketches that Buchan was not a highly skilled figure draughtsman, and in developing finished drawings from his sketches he probably had recourse to John Pine's engraving of *Two Californian Women* (Plate 26) in Shelvocke's *Voyage*, a copy of which was in Banks's little *Endeavour* library.[70] And when Parkinson drew Fuegians he disposed them according to the dictates of picturesque compositions and settings (Plate 27). On the voyage as in the case of landscape, the rival claims of art and science influenced the depiction of natives.

It was no easy matter to bring an objective account of the Fuegians before the notice of the British public. Hawkesworth summarized the evidence for and against the existence of giants in Patagonia in the introduction to his *Voyages*, and concluded:

Upon the whole, it may reasonably be presumed, that the concurrent testimony of late navigators, particularly Commodore Byron, Captain Wallis, and Captain Carteret, Gentlemen of unquestionable veracity, who are still living, and who not only saw and conversed with these people, but measured them, will put an end to all doubts that have been hitherto entertained of their existence.[71]

The statement provided natural philosophers, like Lord Monboddo, who preferred to believe in the existence of Patagonian giants, with useful support. The 'negative'

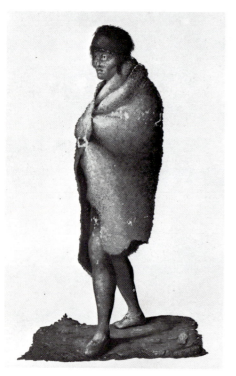

27. Sydney Parkinson, *Natives of Terra del Fuego with their Hut*, pen and wash, 11 × 19 in. (1769). British Museum, Add. MS. 23920.13

evidence of Cook and Banks was accepted as in no wise superior to that of earlier navigators. In 1774 Monboddo claimed that Hawkesworth's summary of the evidence weighed heavily in favour of the existence of the giants:

> ... many will not believe that there is in our species the common variation of great and small, from the size of ten or eleven feet, to that of two or three. As to the first, Mr Hawkesworth, in the introduction to the late Collection of voyages round the world, has fairly stated the evidence on both sides; by which I think it is proved, as much as a fact of that kind can well be, unless we shall set mere negative evidence against positive, that men of such a size are to be found in the southern parts of the south continent of America.[72]

Popular collections of voyages and travels continued to include illustrations of Patagonian giants years after the publication of Hawkesworth's *Voyages*, as for instance an English collection of *Voyages* (1773–4),[73] which illustrates a giantess (Plate 28) and a French collection (1788), which illustrates a giant (Plate 29), receiving Commodore Byron.

Hawkesworth's account of the 'giants' of Patagonia was not the only way in which his *Voyages* vitiated the accounts of the voyage written by Cook and Banks. There was a more subtle way in which accounts of native peoples could be falsified.[74] Alexander Buchan's original drawing of a native hut in *Tierra del Fuego* (Plate 30) certainly corroborated Cook's statement that the Fuegians were 'perhaps as miserable a set of People as are this day upon Earth'.[75] But the original drawing was so altered by Giovanni Cipriani (1728–85), who redesigned it for the engraver, Francesco Bartolozzi (1730–1813), that its graphic effect was to contravert Cook's considered opinion (Plate 31).

Neither Buchan's original drawing nor Cook's opinion of the Fuegians became available to the eighteenth-century public in its original form. In the hands of Hawkesworth the picture of the Fuegians was altered subtly but extensively. Hawkesworth saw them as hard primitives, modern exemplars of the austere virtuous lives led in classical time by such peoples as the Spartans and the Scythians.[76] And he spoke as though the eyewitnesses, Cook and Banks, saw them in a similar fashion:

> What bodily pain they might suffer from the severities of their winter we could not know; but it is certain, that they suffered nothing from the want of innumerable articles which we consider, not as the luxuries and conveniences only, but the necessaries of life: as their desires are few, they probably enjoy them all; and how much they may be gainers by an exemption from the care, labour and solicitude, which arise from a perpetual and unsuccessful effort to gratify that infinite variety of desires which the refinements of artificial life have produced among us, is not very easy to determine: possibly this may counter-balance all the real disadvantages of their situation in comparison with ours, and make the scales by which good and evil are distributed to man, hang even between us.[77]

Although Cook and Banks refrained from thus philosophizing upon the Patagonians, they did write a similar comment upon the Australian aborigines into their journals.[78] Hawkesworth simply switched the comment from one people to the other; and indeed, the Patagonians and Australians served many later writers as interchangeable examples of hard primitives. Such comments by Banks and Cook were as much based, we may assume, upon the prevalent cult of the noble savage as upon their own personal observations. The cult was manifest not only in philosophical writings but in the widely read romances of the day, such as François de Salignac de la Mothe-Fénelon's *Télémaque* (1699), a highly popular book for the young throughout the eighteenth century. Hawkesworth himself made an English translation of *Télémaque*[79] four years before he published his *Voyages*, and it is a book Banks is likely to have been acquainted with in his youth.[80] Such romances did much to fashion the mental climate of the time. In this regard it is to be noted that Hawkesworth's view that the Fuegians did not suffer from the lack of things we should consider necessities and enjoyed all their desires because they had so few, is paralleled in Fénelon's description of the people of his ideal kingdom of *Bétique*:

28. *A Patagonian Woman Receiving Commodore Byron*, engraving in *An Historical Account of Voyages round the World* (1773–4), ii, pl. f.p. 11

29 (far right). *Entrevue de Biron avec les Patagons*, engraving in Bérenger, *Voyages* (1788–9), v, frontispiece

30. Alexander Buchan,
*Inhabitants of the Island of
Terra del in their Hut*, water-
colour, $10 \times 14\frac{1}{2}$ in. (1769).
British Museum, Add. MS.
23920.14a

31. *A View of the Indians of
Terra del Fuego in their Hut*,
engraving after Cipriani by
Bartolozzi, in Hawkesworth,
Voyages (1773), pl. 1

32. *Natives of Terra del
Fuego*, engraving by J. F.
Read, in Cook's *Voyages*
(pub. W. Wright, 1843), i.
pl. f.p. 8

Il y a plusiers mines d'or et d'argent dans ce beau paiis. Mais les habitans, simples et hereux dans leur simplicité, ne daignent pas seulement compter l'or et l'argent parmi leurs richesses; ils n'estiment que ce qui sert véritablement aux besoins de l'homme.[81]

Again, the life of the Fuegians caused Hawkesworth to ask his readers whether, living exempt from 'care, labour, and solicitude', the natives may not be better off than Europeans. That was the same kind of question the inhabitants of Bétique asked Adoam:

Peut-on nommer bien, un superflu qui ne sert qu'à rendre les hommes mauvais? Les hommes de ces pays sont-ils plus sains et plus robustes que nous? Vivent-ils plus longtems? Sont-ils plus unis entre eux? Mènent-ils une vie plus libre, plus tranquille, plus gaie? Au contraire, ils doivent être jaloux les uns des autres, rongés par une lâche et noire envie, toujours agitéz par l'ambition, par la crainte, par l'avarice, incapables des plaisirs purs et simples, puisqu'ils sont esclaves de tant de fausses nécéssitez dont ils font dépendre tout leur bonheur.[82]

If Hawkesworth's and Banks's accounts were coloured by their classical learning and neo-classical romances like *Télémaque*, then, equally, Buchan's original drawing was falsified by the conventions of neo-classical artists. Buchan's drawing answers closely to a description of a Fuegian village written by Banks.[83] Both men, doubtless, visited the village at the same time.

Cipriani made extensive alterations in redrawing Buchan's sketch evidently to bring it into line with Hawkesworth's interpretation of the Fuegians. He has made the six squalid figures in the sketch more comely and graceful, and has added four more at the entrance of the hut;[84] the two figures introduced at the right suggest a Tobias and Angel prototype. These additional figures transformed the state of miserable wretchedness depicted by Buchan into the state of primitive elegance imagined by Hawkesworth. The transformation is helped greatly by the introduction of a land-scape setting—a Claudean tree in the foreground, Salvator Rosa's rocks and knotty branches, the mountainous background, together represent the state of untamed nature as Rousseau and Fénelon conceived it. Cipriani's drawing was then engraved faithfully by Bartolozzi for Hawkesworth's *Voyages* (Plate 31). Falsified as the engraving was it provided none the less a model for later illustrators of Pacific voyages. A degraded form of Cipriani's design appears, for instance, in an 1843 account of Cook's voyages (Plate 32). The two little naked amorini have been discreetly removed as befitted an account written with an eye upon evangelical opinion. And the landscape setting has been transformed from Rosa's picturesque sublimity to the coconut palms of a tropical Elysium, despite the fact that the latitude corresponded to Britain's, that it was a land of beech (*Fagus betuloides*) and birch (*Fagus antarctica*), and the weather so severe when Cook was first there that snow fell in January and two of Banks's coloured servants perished from exposure to the cold. But despite these changes the two adult figures, which Cipriani had first conjured from his extensive repertoire of noble types to embellish Buchan's drawing, still served, more than half a century after his death, to illustrate the shivering inhabitants of Patagonia.

Landscape settings became an important element in the ennobling of savages. Portraits of natives devoid of such settings tend, on the whole, to be more truthful. Parkinson's portrait of a *New Zealand Man*, for example, despite European echoes in the man's features, was intended to provide a faithful portrait of a Maori chieftain and his manner of adornment (Plate 33). In this case the engraver did not depart materially from the original drawing (Plate 34). Significantly, this is the only engrav-

ing in Hawkesworth in which a native figures prominently that was not subjected to some kind of idealizing by engravers, and it is the only illustration in which a native is not shown in a landscape. On the other hand, it is to be noted that the *Gentleman's Magazine*, in reviewing Parkinson's account of the voyage, praised the fidelity with which the engravings therein depicted the distinctive features of natives of the Pacific together with their typical dresses and ornaments. By implication the reviewer criticized Hawkesworth as one of those editors who 'intent on gaining the characters of fine writers and elegant artists, have departed from the simplicity of Nature to give a scope to the decorations of Art'.[85] It was ironical that Hawkesworth's modifications of his source-material was brought about by his desire to present striking examples of the 'simplicity of Nature' as revealed by the Pacific. Parkinson's book was praised because both in its descriptions and illustrations it did more than Hawkesworth's *Voyages* to distinguish one type of native people from another. It is significant that, for the most part, Parkinson's book does not portray natives in landscape settings. Parkinson's approach was more ethnographic, less primitivistic, than Hawkesworth's. But his book was not readily available until 1784,[86] so that Hawkesworth's book, the creation of a writer and of artists with strong neo-classical interests, became the main source of information on Cook's first voyage.

Neither Banks nor Cook saw the Fuegians as noble savages, though Hawkesworth did.[87] The Tahitians were a different proposition. Banks was more disposed than Cook to take a kindly view of them.[88] Their customs suggested parallels with classical antiquity. They sang in praise of their visitors like ancient Greeks. 'These gentlemen', wrote Banks, 'like Homer of old, must be poets as well as musicians.'[89] The chieftains became sentimentalized Greek heroes for the voyagers, four of them obtaining classical pseudonyms until their native names were mastered. 'Hercules' was named for his strength; 'Ajax', for his grim countenance; 'Epicurus', for his appetite;

33. Sydney Parkinson, *Portrait of a New Zealand Man*, pen and wash, $15\frac{1}{2} \times 11\frac{3}{4}$ in. (*c.* 1769). British Museum Add. MS. 23920.54a.

34. *The Head of a New Zealander*, engraving after Parkinson, in Hawkesworth, *Voyages* (1773), pl. 13

41

'Lycurgus', for his justice in returning a snuff-box stolen from Banks.[90] Though such comparisons were playful, it is to be remembered that the eighteenth century viewed the ancient Greeks as gifted children who had lived at the dawn of civilization, themselves noble savages. The Doric order, for example, was venerated not so much for its beauty of proportion as for the sublimity of its primitive grandeur and simplicity.

The parallel between Tahitians and Greeks was not, however, initiated by the *Endeavour*'s company. Wallis's reports had already suggested such parallels in England, and the French navigator, Louis de Bougainville, who visited Tahiti in April 1768, a year before Cook, compared the Tahitians to Greek gods. 'I never saw men better made, and whose limbs were more proportionate: in order to paint Hercules or a Mars, one could nowhere find such beautiful models.'[91] A naked young Tahitian girl on the deck of his ship appeared 'as Venus . . . herself to the Phrygian shepherd, having . . . the celestial form of that goddess'.[92]

The noble savage, as already noted, is always closely related to his natural setting, for he was, in a sense, a personification of the eighteenth-century belief in the nobility and simplicity of Nature, that very Nature which when rightly understood would, according to the deists, reveal God to man. Consequently, the noble Tahitians were identified closely with the tropical luxury of their island. Just as the Patagonians became identified in Hawkesworth's mind with Fénelon's hard primitives, so the Tahitians became identified in the mind of Bougainville and Banks with the soft primitives of classical mythology, such as the inhabitants of Elysium. 'One would think himself', wrote Bougainville, 'in the Elysian fields.'[93] And he proceeded to write a description which stamped itself permanently upon the imagination of Europe. The country was so rich, the air so salubrious that people attained to old age without its inconveniences. Indeed, the island was a healer. Men rotten with scurvy regained strength after spending one night there. 'Everyone gathers fruits from the first tree he meets with, or takes some in any house he enters.'[94] Bougainville was fond of walking about the island and what he saw transported him with delight. 'I thought I was transported into the garden of Eden; we crossed a turf, covered with fine fruit trees, and intersected by little rivulets, which kept up a pleasant coolness in the air, without any of those inconveniences which humidity occasions. . . . We found companies of men and women sitting under the shade of their fruit trees . . . everywhere we found hospitality, ease, innocent joy, and every appearance of happiness amongst them.'[95] The land, in short, was like Paradise before the Fall of Man, and the people lived in a natural state of innocence enjoying its bounty. Their state of innocence was symbolized for Bougainville by an incident he recounts: 'We were stopped by an islander, of a fine figure, who lying under a tree, invited us to sit down by him on the grass. We accepted his offer: he then leaned towards us, and with a tender air he slowly sung a song, without doubt of the Anacreontic kind, to the tune of a flute, which an Indian blew with his nose: this was a charming scene, and worthy of the pencil of a Boucher.'[96] Similar stories told by Captain Wallis of trees that grew bread and palms that supplied milk, created a sensation in England.

Banks was just as enthusiastic; to him as to Bougainville, Tahiti was the Golden Age come again. The sexual freedoms of the people filled him with admiration and delight, but in his English way, he was more circumspect about it than the Frenchman. His private opinions are nowhere better expressed than in the short paper which he wrote for Count Bentinck (while visiting Holland in 1773) in order to amuse the Princess of Orange. He called it Thoughts on the manners of Otaheite. Banks claimed that Tahitian women were the most elegant in the world. European ladies outvied them in complexion, but in all else the Tahitians were superior. Their clothes were natural and beautiful, such as were found in Europe only upon statues and antique gems, or in the paintings of the great Italians who knew how to clothe their angels and goddesses in loose natural folds just 'as the Tahitians now wear them'. Such clothing followed Nature, and so grateful Nature had endowed the Tahitians with beautiful bodies. 'Such the Grecians were from whose model the Venus of Medicis (*sic*) was copied.' Their bodies were so beautiful that they 'might even defy the imitation of the chizzel of a Phidias or the Pencil of an Apelles'.[97] And to Banks the country was just as beautiful as the people: '... the scene that we saw', he wrote in his journal, 'was the truest picture of an Arcadia of which we were going to be kings that the imagination can form.'[98]

Tahitian society by suggesting parallels with Greek society also suggested a novel approach to the study of Greek civilization. Perhaps a study of the islanders of the Pacific might throw new light upon the manners and customs of the ancient world? Bougainville and Banks had compared the Tahitians to ancient Greeks. Years later Richard Payne Knight, the classical scholar, and close friend and neighbour of Banks, found it illuminating to compare the Greeks in their Golden Age with contemporary Tahitians. There need be little doubt that Knight had the Tahitians in mind when he wrote in his *Analytical Enquiry into the Principles of Taste* (1801):

> It has been observed by travellers that the attitudes and gestures of savages, particularly those of high rank among them, are extremely dignified and graceful; which arises from their being unperverted and unrestrained, and therefore expressing naturally and emphatically the sentiments of the mind; which, in men who have obtained their rank, as men always do in the early stages of civil society, by their talents and courage, will of course be bold and elevated, if not polished and refined.
>
> In the fine age of the arts in Greece, civilisation had just arrived to that state, in which the manners of men are polished, but yet natural; and consequently their attitudes and gestures expressive and emphatical, without ever being coarse or violent.[99]

The comparison of contemporary primitive societies with ancient cultures had, of course, begun before the opening of the Pacific.[100] But the wealth of primitive cultures suddenly revealed to the world by Cook helped to promote the comparative study of society, and to bring a more empirical approach to classical studies.

An empirical approach is also present from the beginning in the European observation of Polynesians. For we must not be misled by the colourful parallels developed by Bougainville, Banks and others, into thinking that all Polynesians evoked classical visions of the Golden Age in the eyes and minds of their first eighteenth-century European observers. Solander, for example, kept a list of Polynesian words, in which a name list is prominent, doubtless for the very practical purpose of daily communication with the islanders and the identification of individuals. His list reveals a fascinating diversity of response. While *Tuboura Tomaidi* is certainly described as 'our chief friend Lycurgus' and *Oteatea* is described as a 'fine Grecian girl' others, doubtless less powerful and influential and not perceived as members of the Tahitian 'nobility' are described in much more homely terms. *Noahao* was described as a 'french girl', and *Omay* as 'Mrs Yellow face'. *O Bualha* was called 'Square Kate' and *Tehea* as 'Mrs fine eyes'. *Toimata* was described as a 'fine wild woman' and *Tuahao* as 'sniggle mouthed Jack'.[101] Yet it was the classical vision which first permeated the European imagination. The ignoble day of 'sniggle mouthed Jack' lay in the not so distant future.

Tahitian life also stimulated moral speculation among Europeans. It prompted

Cook, not given to abstruse speculation, to write, 'in the article of food these people may almost be said to be exempt from the curse of our forefathers; scarcely can it be said that they earn their bread with the sweat of their brow, benevolent nature hath not only supply'd them with necessarys but with abundance of superfluities.'[102] Hawkesworth echoed the sentiments without Cook's qualification: 'They seem', he wrote, 'to be exempted from the first general curse "that man should eat his bread in the sweat of his brow".'[103] Tahiti became a deist's argument against the necessity of Revelation. Tahitian morality, Hawkesworth argued, like Tahitian clothing, was natural. 'These people have a knowledge of right and wrong from the mere dictates of natural conscience.'[104] Was not morality, after all, a matter of social custom? 'We must indeed estimate the virtue of these people, by the only standard of morality the conformity of their conduct to what in their opinion is right.'[105] Perhaps, suggested Hawkesworth, they are happier than we are. Why then should we stand in judgement upon them! Reflection upon Tahitian society was helping to promote unconventional thought upon the nature of morality.

There were certain features of Tahitian society, however, that not even Hawkesworth could reconcile with a deistic paradise of innocence and natural virtue. The licentious dances, the prostitution and infanticide practised by the *arioi*, the strange funerary customs, and those symbols of paganism, the *marae* and *tupapa'u*,[106] shocked a good deal British public opinion. The virtuoso in Banks found such things engaging to his curiosity, the deist in Hawkesworth found them rich topics for reflection, but to most God-fearing Englishmen, from Dr. Johnson to the itinerant Methodist preachers, it was only too apparent that these so-called innocents of nature were depraved and benighted savages. No matter how much men enthused about Tahiti, it was recognized from the beginning—the evidence was in Hawkesworth for everyone to read—that there were two sides to Tahiti, a light side and a dark side. So that when men came to reflect upon the island and its people the two sides invariably rose in their minds. Tahiti proved that there was once a Golden Age; Tahiti also proved it had long passed away. The island entered into the more serious and reflective levels of European art and thought not as a symbol of the normality of human happiness but as a symbol of its transience. The theme appeared early in the work of artists and poets.

The emergence of the theme in its Tahitian context is to be noted first in the

35. Sydney Parkinson, *View in the Island of Huaheine with an Ewharra and a small altar with an offering on it*, wash, $9\frac{1}{4} \times 14\frac{1}{4}$ in. (1770). British Museum Add. MS. 23921.

engraving entitled '*Ewharra*' *in Huaheine* (Huahine) by William Woollett, after Parkinson, published in Hawkesworth. In Tahiti, Banks had observed a funerary object and described it carefully. 'It consisted of a chest whose lid was nicely sewed on, and very neatly thatched over with palm-nut leaves; the whole was fixed on two poles by little arches of very neatly carved wood. These poles seemed to be used in carrying it from place to place.'[107] Parkinson made a wash drawing which answered to Banks's description which he called *View in the Island of Huaheine with an Ewharra and a small altar with an offering on it* (Plate 35). Apart from the mourning figure at the left the drawing is straightforwardly topographical. Now *Ewharra* meant house. Banks asked a native boy what the house was. The boy replied, 'Ewharra no Eatua', which Banks translated as 'the house of God'. Hawkesworth, in recounting the incident remarked upon the 'general resemblance between this repository and the Ark of the Lord among the Jews'.[108] Seeking to emphasize the significance of the resemblance, Hawkesworth listed Woollett's engraving after Parkinson as *A View in the Island of Huaheine; with the Ewharra no Eatua, or House of God* (Plate 36). For the most part, Hawkesworth's account of the voyage was roundly criticized for not being Christian enough, but in this case a funerary practice suggested a biblical rather than a classical comparison. Woollett, who was noted for his ability to invest his plates with dramatic intensity, has endowed Parkinson's sketch with a melancholy grandeur. In order to do so he made considerable alterations. A tree, from another sketch by Parkinson, has been introduced on the left. Part of the middle distance has been thrown into shadow so that the two figures that stand out as black shapes in the foreground of the sketch are picked out strongly with a shaft of light, which, passing them, lights up the *Ewharra*, with its offering to the dead before it, so uniting the solemn theme. The discordant elements in Parkinson's sketch, the store-house and the figures near the boat, have been discarded while the light and graceful coconut palms, more suggestive of tropical luxury than the theme warrants, have been relegated to a corner. On the other hand, the mournful leaves of the casuarina have been enlarged considerably, while the distant mountains have been introduced to give a touch of grandeur. When we notice the figure gazing thoughtfully at the *Ewharra*, the abandoned boat, and the leaves of the lily introduced into the lower left corner without the sanction of the sketch, we realize that Woollett sought to provide his engraving with a meaningful intensity quite lacking in Parkinson's sketch. Parkinson's documentation has been transformed, in the words of Falconer, 'through another man's understanding', into a contemplative and melancholy setting. It has become an essay on the theme of human transience in a new setting, the sub-tropical abundance of a southern Arcadia.

36. *A View in the Island of Huaheine; with the Ewharra no Eatua, or House of God*, engraving after Parkinson by W. Woollett, in Hawkesworth, *Voyages* (1773), ii, pl. 6

Hawkesworth's *Voyages* quickly aroused widespread interest in the Pacific throughout Europe. Although the book was expensive and obviously aimed to satisfy the taste of the *cognoscenti*, its contents soon reached a wide section of the British public.[109] But for all its popularity the book aroused violent criticism. Hawkesworth, it was said, had handled his sources, the journals of Cook and Banks, too freely; he had introduced 'dark and difficult' speculations into the narrative; and he had been indiscreet in his description of some of the more erotic Tahitian customs. Such descriptions, as contemporary versifiers were quick to point out, were not calculated to improve the morals of the British nation:

> One page of *Hawkesworth*, in the cool retreat,
> Fires the bright maid with more than mortal heat;
> She sinks at once into the lover's arms,
> Nor deems it vice to prostitute her charms;
> 'I'll do', cries she, 'What Queens have done before';
> And sinks, *from principle*, a common whore.[110]

Unwittingly, Hawkesworth had provided a rich fund of material for the satirists. Banks figured prominently in Hawkesworth's account of the voyage, and Banks, like Hawkesworth himself, was fair game for the satirist. There were many people in Britain who regarded him as a wealthy and ambitious young eccentric who had risen rapidly to public and court favour as the result of an unusual jaunt to the South Seas.[111] They thought of him as something of a charlatan, professing an interest in botany but actually possessing little genuine scientific knowledge. Many, indeed, concluded, after reading Hawkesworth, that he was more interested in exotic women than exotic plants. Most of the satirical poems evoked by Hawkesworth's *Voyages* take this point of view. The author of *Transmigration* (1778), for instance, wrote:

37. *Amusemens des Otahitiens et des Anglais*, engraving, in Bérenger, *Voyages* (1788–9), viii, frontispiece

ATTEND, ye swarms of MODERN TOURISTS,
Yclept, or Botanists or Florists:
Ye who ascend the cloud-capt Hills,
Or creep along their tinkling Rills;
Who scientifically tell
The Wonders of each COCKLE-SHELL;
And load the Press with Publications,
With *useless, learned* DISSERTATIONS.
Ye who o'er Southern Oceans wander
With simpling B—ks or sly S—r;
Who so familiarly describe
The Frolicks of the wanton Tribe,
And think that simple Fornication
Requires no sort of Palliation.
Let Wanton Dames and Demireps,
To *Otaheite* guide their Steps;
Their Love's delicious Feasts are found;
There Joys *so innocent* abound!
Behold, a Queen her Gul o'er-reaches;
First steals, and then she wears his Breeches.
Such luscious Feats, when told with Ease,
Must Widows, Matrons, Maidens please;
Nor can they blush at having read
What ye so modestly have said:
Yet though ye strive to dress your Story,
And make (what is your Shame) your Glory,
With us this makes no Variation;
Still is it simple FORNICATION,
Whether in DRURY'S ROUNDS ye sport,
Or frisk in OBEREA'S COURT.

38. *Representation of the Heiva at Otaheite*, engraving after Daniel Dodd by Royce, in [John Rickman], *Journal of Captain Cook's last Voyage to the Pacific Ocean* (1781). Pl. f.p. 156

39. *A View of the inside of a house in the Island of Ulietea, with the representation of a dance to the music of the country*, engraving after Cipriani by Bartolozzi, in Hawkesworth, *Voyages* (1773), ii, pl. 7

Bougainville had called Tahiti *la Nouvelle Cythère*, and the island became notorious throughout Europe in the popular mind as a land of free-love. The erotic attractions of Tahiti were dealt with in great detail in chap-book verse and graphically illustrated in such engravings as *Amusemens des Otahitiens et des Anglais* in Bérenger's *Voyages* (Plate 37), and Daniel Dodd's convivial reduction (Plate 38) of Cipriani's stately interpretation of a dance in Raiatea based upon Parkinson's original field drawings (Plate 39).

Now although the lampooning of Banks and Hawkesworth, together with the detailed exploitation of the more 'salacious' passages in Hawkesworth's *Voyages*, were the immediate concern of the satirists, the poems which the *Voyages* evoked were written against a background of general ideas to be related to, or modified by, Pacific exploration. Four of these ideas need to be discussed here briefly in connexion with the poems, namely, the belief in an ideal southern kingdom, the deep conviction in the transience of earthly happiness, the idea of the universe as a chain of universal being, and the long-standing belief that things in the southern hemisphere were somehow inverted or at least governed by laws which differed from those governing the northern parts of the world.

All the poets presented Tahiti as an ideal kingdom, even if only ironically. For the island appeared to be the substantial embodiment of those ideal Austral kingdoms which political satirists had found so useful during the preceding century or more to measure the shortcomings of European society. In Tahiti, it seemed (as Banks said), the Golden Age still lingered. The belief was best expressed in the poem, *Otaheite*, published in 1774:

> Here, ceaseless, the returning Seasons wear
> Spring's verdant Robe, and smile throughout the Year
> Refreshing Zephyrs cool the noon-tide Ray,
> And Plantane Groves impervious Shades display.
> The gen'rous Soil exacts no Tillers' Aid
> To turn the Glebe and watch the infant Blade;
> Nature their vegetable Bread supplies,
> And high in Air luxuriant Harvests rise.
> No annual Toil the foodful Plants demand,
> But unrenew'd to rising Ages stand;
> From Sire to Son the long Succession trace,
> And lavish forth their Gifts from Race to Race.
> Beneath their Shade the gentle Tribes repose;
> Each bending Branch their frugal Feast bestows:
> For them the Cocoa yields its milky Flood,
> To slake their Thirst, and feed their temp'rate Blood;
> No ruddy Nectar their pure Bev'rage stains,
> Foams in their Bowl and swells their kindling Veins.

Despite such passages as this, nowhere do the poets succumb entirely to the simple-minded belief that Tahiti and its people represented a Golden Age or Garden of Eden. The Society Islands might indeed be as beautiful as the Garden of Eden but man there, like all living men, not being innocent, lived only upon transitory pleasures. That was the essence of the general opinion. For all their bawdy couplets the poets clung to a Christian rather than a classical interpretation of life in Tahiti. And whether they treat their themes with mock-heroic melancholy, or more seriously, their reflections upon life on the island quickly turns into reflections upon the vanity of earthly pleasures. Immediately after he had drawn his picture of Tahiti as an island paradise, the author of *Otaheite* proceeds to ask the crucial question:

> Can cruel Passions these calm Seats infest,
> And stifle Pity in a Parent's Breast?
> Does here Medea draw the vengeful Blade,
> And stain with filial Gore the blushing Shade;
> Here, where Arcadia should its Scenes unfold,
> And past'ral Love revive an Age of Gold!

Hawkesworth himself had given the answer in the affirmative. Not the knowledge of death merely, but ritual murder, sullied the innocence of the southern paradise. Tahiti was seen from the beginning, by poets and artists, as a tainted paradise—its pleasures fitful, physical, and transient.

In the above connexion it may be noted that two of the earliest poems evoked by Hawkesworth, *An Epistle from Oberea . . . to Joseph Banks*, and *A Second Letter from Oberea . . . to Joseph Banks*, both by John Scott,[112] are built upon the theme of the waywardness of human affections. The poems, which tell how Queen Oberea yearns for her lover Banks, are modelled upon Ovid's *Oenone Paridii*. Like Oenone, Oberea pines for the day when her lover will return:

> But vain the wish, and vain th'impassioned sigh,
> Corporeal pleasures are but born to die.
> What tho' with thee, beneath the bread-tree's shade,
> In every form of wanton love I've laid;
>
> . . . . . .
>
> The transport's fled, and nought is left behind,
> Save the cold comforts of a restless mind.

Even in such a highly erotic poem as John Courtenay's *Epistle (Moral and Philosophical) from an Officer at Otaheite* (1774) it is not long before reflection upon the transience of earthly pleasures makes an appearance. With delicate irony Courtenay pictures Tahiti as an island wherein the people still live as in the Age of Innocence:

> Naked and smiling, every nymph we see,
> Like Eve unapron'd, 'ere she *robb'd the tree*
> Immodest words are spoke without offence,
> And want of decency shews innocence.

But innocent happiness, Courtenay proceeds to point out, cannot last for long. The amorous enjoyments lead directly to disease and death. For the French—it was, according to the English poets, most certainly the French—had introduced venereal disease into the island paradise. And Courtenay wrote in mock-heroic vein:

> Alas, what human bliss is long compleat
> For ever changing man's precarious state!

It is by no means surprising that English satirists should point to the shortcomings of this new Pacific island paradise and greet it with shouts of ribald laughter. The temper of English thought in the third quarter of the century was not of a kind likely to take to tales about an earthly paradise without question. As presented by Hawkesworth and Bougainville, the Tahitians were essentially soft primitives, and the attractions of soft primitivism held no great appeal for English thought in the later eighteenth century. Soft primitivism led to a life of luxury, sloth, and degeneration. A decade before Hawkesworth's *Voyages* appeared, Dr. Johnson had written the classical rebuttal of soft primitivism as an ideal of human happiness in his *Rasselas* (1759). Soon after the appearance of the *Voyages*, George Forster was to argue, from his personal observation on Cook's second voyage, that the typical vices of soft primitivism had begun to develop in Tahitian society even before the arrival of Europeans. Again, evangelical opinion in England, increasing at the time in power and influence, was scandalized by Hawkesworth's descriptions of Tahitian morality. More than one poetaster setting out to lampoon Banks and make the most of Hawkesworth's suggestive passages ended upon a tone both patriotic and pious. Tahiti, they said, might indeed be Paradise, or something like it, if Britain would only accept the challenge of history and take a knowledge of Christ to the Tahitian peoples:[113]

> On Minds which thus untaught thus darkling stray,
> To pour the radiant Beams of heav'nly Day;
> To point where Nature the great Outline draws,
> Where Truth reveal'd gives Sanction to her Laws;
> To bid th' intemperate Reign of Sense expire,
> And quench th' unholy Flame of loose Desire;
> Teach them their Being's Date, its Use and End,
> And to Immortal Life their Hopes extend,
> How great the Triumph!—But to whom assign'd?
> What Nations rise the Teachers of Mankind?

Such an appeal was calculated to impress a British public growing increasingly conscious of a sense of religious obligation to pagan savages and also growing increasingly patriotic following a series of remarkable military victories. For by the 1770's 'English people had become passionately proud of their contemporary history'.[114] The enormous success of West's *Death of Wolfe* and William Woollett's engraving after it, bear witness to the new patriotic feeling. Similarly the patriotic note is frequently sounded in the poems based on Hawkesworth's *Voyages*. *Otaheite* begins on a patriotic note, Courtenay's *Poetical Epistle* (1775) ends on one. William Falconer's *Shipwreck* published in 1762 ran through many editions and did much to introduce the British seaman as a popular and patriotic figure to poets. *Otaheite* follows this convention, praising those British sailors who under Cook braved all the extremities of heat and cold, the diseases of the tropics, the terrors of cannibalism, not to enslave savages for gold like the Spaniards or give venereal diseases to the Tahitians like the French, but all for the cause of British science. Through the patient work of the British sailor the Great Design of the universe, the universal chain of being, is at last to be slowly revealed to man in all its astounding magnificence:

> Thus toils the Sage whose penetrating View
> Dares Nature to her inmost Depths pursue.
> He marks how animated Life descends
> Progressive, and in Vegetation ends;
> Inspects each Series through the great Design,
> Each vital Point that fills th' unbounded Line;
> Through endless Systems darts his piercing Eye,
> And undismay'd attempts Infinity.

How much more worthy of praise, says the poet, are such scientific voyages as these than those arm-chair naturalists—the 'minutely learned' who 'with petty care, impale a beetle or a moth insnare'. The scientific voyagers will reveal at the end of their labours how every species of plant and animal has its appointed place in nature's chain, and how every region upon the face of the earth is capable of producing just those forms of happiness peculiarly suited to the human inhabitants of the region. The latter notion, mentioned by Hawkesworth (as already quoted) in discussing the Patagonians, was a special application of the philosophical optimism propounded by Soame Jenyns and William King.[115] It was the purpose of the laws of nature, these writers claimed, to keep each species in its own special sphere for the sake of the personal well-being of the individual members of the species, and for the system as a whole. 'Earth worms', wrote Gilbert White in 1777, 'though in appearance a small

50

and despicable link in the chain of Nature, yet, if lost, would make a lamentable chasm.'[116] And Thomas Falconer in his long letter to Banks of 15 February 1768, already quoted in part, advised him: 'If you travel near the sea coast it would be part of your scheme to collect *Testacea*. I suppose they would have little beauty in the eyes of mere curiosity; but they are a part of the great chain of nature, and may be compared with our own. One use of such a comparison would be to see the gradual influence of different climates.'

It was indeed widely held both by naturalists and writers that Cook's scientists, aided by his seamen, would gradually complete the picture of the universe as a vast ordered chain of being which had been partially known to man from earliest times. But this ancient preconception came into conflict gradually with another preconception possessing antecedents quite as venerable as the chain of being. The ancients had claimed that things in the Antipodes were different from things in the northern hemisphere; monsters dwelt there; the normal laws of nature did not hold, in fact, they were reversed.[117] It was into such a world that Britain's intrepid scientists and seamen had pressed:

> Climes, where the Sun, with unremitting Blaze,
> Pours the full ardour of his fiercest Rays;
> Regions of Ice, on whose deserted Plains,
> Inverting Nature's Law, stern Winter reigns;
> Where never Spring with genial Influence rose,
> Unbound the Glebe and thaw'd the eternal Snows,
> Patient they trod....

The idea of an antipodal inversion of natural laws was not an easy one to reconcile with the idea of a carefully ordered hierarchy both physical and moral which was securely held together by the laws of nature. In the example quoted above the idea of antipodal inversion occurs in a simple geographical context but it could be extended, as we shall see, to the field of biology. There was already a hint of the idea applied, half-mockingly, in the field of morals, in *An Epistle from Mr. Banks* wherein Banks is made to exclaim concerning the Tahitians: 'What's vice in us, in you is virtue clear.' These minor hints in the satirical poetry of the time may be taken to indicate the presence of the idea of antipodal inversion in the background of British reflection upon Pacific phenomena. It was, as will be shown, to play its part in the nineteenth-century challenge to the chain of being as an adequate explanation of the nature of the universe. The author of *Otaheite* seems to have sensed the significance of the opening of the Pacific for European thought when he chose as his motto for the poem these lines from Seneca:

> Venient annis
> Secula seris, quibus Oceanus
> Vincula rerum laxet, et ingens
> Pateat Tellus, Tiphysque novos
> Detegat orbes.

For the motto was aptly chosen. In the succeeding century the exploration of the Pacific was to play a significant role in loosening the bonds of classical thought both in art and in science.

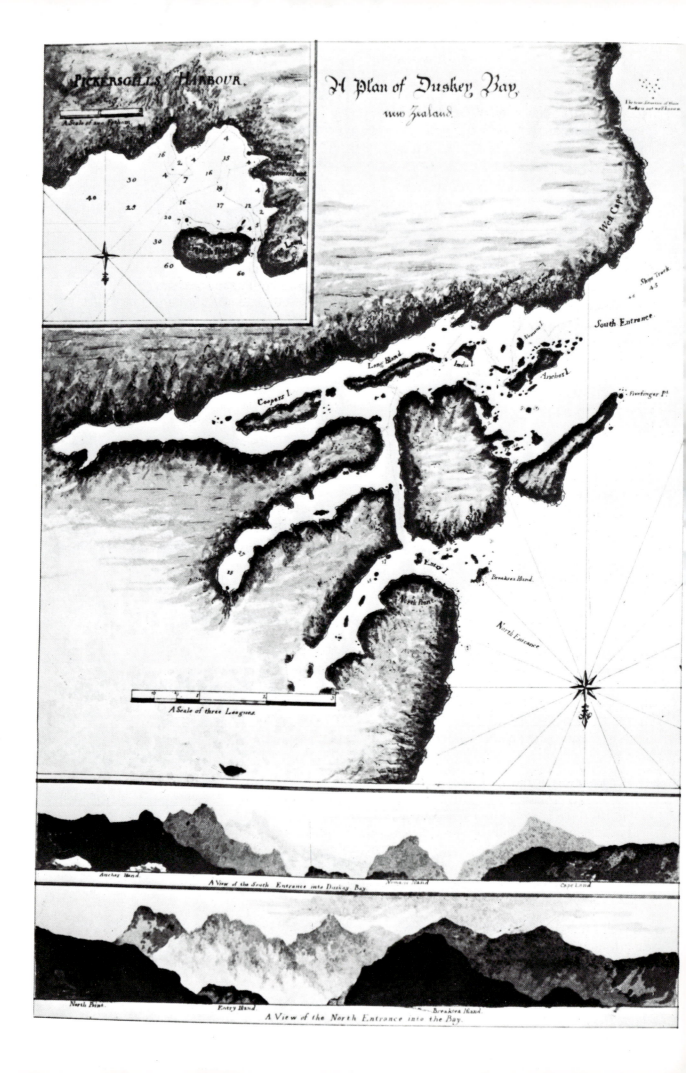

PICKERSGILLS HARBOUR.

A Scale of ... Fathom.

A Plan of Duskey Bay,
new Zealand.

West Cape

Ship Track
45

South Entrance

Fivefinger Pt.

Long Island
Coopers I.
Anchor I.
India I.
Nomans I.

North Point
Entry I.
Breaksea Island.

North Entrance

A Scale of three Leagues.

Anchor Island.   A View of the South Entrance into Duskey Bay.   Nomans Island.   Cape Land.

North Point.   Entry Island.   Breaksea Island.   A View of the North Entrance into the Bay.

3. Cook's Second Voyage

DURING the voyage of the *Endeavour* Cook's official tasks and Banks's interest in natural history were successfully pursued without friction and both men benefited from the association. Banks was well aware how much his own advancement owed to the voyage. 'I was about twenty-three when I began my peregrinations', he wrote to William Hooker years later, '... if I had listened to a multitude of voices that were raised to dissuade me, I should now have been a quiet country gentleman, ignorant of a number of things I am now acquainted with.'[1] Science, too, benefited from the union of astronomy, navigation, and natural history.[2] Yet the voyage did not satisfy those who, like Alexander Dalrymple, still maintained that a large continent existed in the Southern Ocean. Cook agreed that another voyage was required to settle the question, and Banks was keen to sail again with his artists and naturalists: 'O how glorious to set my heel upon the Pole! and turn myself round three hundred and sixty degrees in a second', he wrote, in high spirits, to Count Lauragais, in December 1771.[3] Banks's party was to have included Daniel Carl Solander, his companion and professional botanist on the *Endeavour*; Johan Zoffany (1734–1810), the well-known portrait- and genre-painter; John Frederick Miller and James Miller, natural-history draughtsmen and John Cleveley, marine painter. In addition, Banks was anxious to recommend Joseph Priestley (1733–1804), philosopher and chemist, but drew back from recommending him because some clergymen on the Board of Longitude objected to his religious principles. James Lind (1736–1812), physician and astronomer, was invited to embark in Priestley's place.

But Banks fell foul of the Navy Board when he claimed that the cabins of Cook's ship for the voyage, the *Resolution*, were too small for the needs of his party. Having failed to gain his way in having certain structural alterations made to the vessel, Banks and his party retired from the expedition.[4] A letter which Banks wrote explaining the reason for his retirement addressed to the Earl of Sandwich, First Lord of the Admiralty, provides further evidence of the high value Banks placed upon the use of professional artists in the making of accurate records and the winning of new knowledge:

> When it was first proposed to me by your Lordship to go to the South Seas again ... I joyfully embrac'd a proposal of all others the best suited to my Disposition and Pursuits. I pledg'd myself then to your Lordship and have since by the whole tenor of my Conversation and Correspondence pledg'd myself to all Europe not only to go the Voyage but to take with me as many able Artists as the Income of my Fortune would allow me to pay; by whose means the learned World in general might reap as much benefit as possible from those Discoveries which my good Fortune or Industry might enable me to make.[5]

Banks's retirement from the *Resolution* may indeed have put 'a check to the rising expectations of the literati', as one publisher suggested,[6] but it is clear that the

40. Joseph Gilbert, *A Plan of Dusky Bay and Views of the North and South Entrances into Dusky Bay* (views $4\frac{1}{2} \times 13\frac{1}{4}$ in.) (1773). British Library, Add. MS. 15500 f.3

Admiralty's appointment of William Hodges (1744–97), as painter, and the Forsters, as naturalists, arose from Bank's outstanding work on the Endeavour. The appointment of naturalists and artists became thenceforward a normal feature of the organization of scientific voyages.

Sydney Parkinson served under Banks; William Hodges served under Cook. The distinction is significant. For Hodges's work came to be associated much more closely than Parkinson's with the interests of seamen and of physical science while voyaging upon the *Resolution*. Partly on account of the nature of the voyage which took place over vast unknown tracts of ocean and partly on account of the interests of his companions, Hodges's art came to be influenced considerably by his observation of the atmosphere and the weather.

The accurate observation of unusual atmospheric disturbances was an established feature of naval practice. The Royal Society's *Directions for Seamen, Bound for Far Voyages*, quoted above, enjoined mariners 'to observe and record all extraordinary *Meteors*, Lightnings, Thunders, *Ignes fatui*, Comets, etc., marking still the places and times of their appearing, continuance, etc.'[7] Soon after Banks knew that he was to sail on the *Endeavour*, his friend Falconer had sent him a letter full of advice on these matters:

> To relieve the mind, it may be worthwhile to note the variations of the air, and, as you will change the seasons of the year, to mark the gradual transmission of summer and winter from what it is in our northern hemisphere. We shall expect too some observations on those electrical lights so often seen about vessels in those seas, which are often mentioned simply as facts, but the state of the air at that particular time, with the consequential effects have been never distinctly noted.[8]

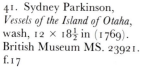
41. Sydney Parkinson,
Vessels of the Island of Otaha,
wash, 12 × 18½ in (1769).
British Museum MS. 23921.
f.17

The study of meteorological phenomena, however, was not one of Banks's central interests, and Parkinson's drawings reveal only a passing interest in effects of light and atmosphere—as when, for instance, in a drawing made in Tahaa he depicts sunrays

breaking through clouds in the background (Plate 41). Indeed, his training as a botanical draughtsman, his limited abilities as a landscape-painter, and the still primitive condition of water-colour as an art medium in the 1760's, made the rendering of atmospheric effects an extremely difficult matter for him. Even so, what his hands could not render his eye most certainly saw. This is revealed by a lengthy note he entered in one of his sketch-books:

> mem. that the water within the Reefs . . . seagreen . . . brownish towards the edge of the Reef . . . the breakers white . . . in many bays have taken notice that the sea . . . green colour with the tops of the waves white, this stript and streakt with a dark colour of a purple cast occasioned by the intervention of the clouds between sun and water. In a calm where there is a swell the water appears undulated with large and pale shades and at other times it is quite smooth streakt here and there with dark colour occasioned by what sailors call cats paws on the water when there is a wind coming or rain it appears very black upon the water and when nigh it is full of p(ur)pling waves which spread themselves in streaks on the smooth water, the sky in general is very uniform often times blue mottled with white clouds. in a storm the sea is dark bluish black here and there a pale blue, the tops of the billows white with a number of white streaks all near the surface of the water.[9]

Clearly Parkinson possessed the ability to apply the precise and analytical observation with which he was accustomed to describe and paint a flower to the description of the transient colour effects of sea, cloud, and sky. But his stained monochrome washes provided him with little opportunity to record his observations graphically.[10]

On the *Resolution* all the scientific company became intensely interested in the study of light and atmospheric effects. One reason is to be found in the great length of the voyage, so much of which was passed out of sight of land in high southern latitudes abounding with unusual visual phenomena. A more immediate reason, however, is to be found in the publication early in 1772 of Joseph Priestley's *History of the Present State and Discoveries relating to Vision, Light and Colours*.[11] In this book Priestley discusses a great variety of visual phenomena such as *ignes fatui* and marine phosphorescence. Had he travelled with Cook, as originally intended, such things would have received his closest attention.

As it turned out it was John Reinhold Forster (1729–98) and his son George (1754–94)[12] who helped to cover the field left vacant by the withdrawal, first of Priestley and then Lind. The elder Forster had had a varied career. A pastor of Nassenhuben (near Danzig) and a distinguished scholar and naturalist, he had been commissioned by Catherine to inspect the Russian colonies in Saratov. But his irascible temper led him to quarrel with the Russian government. Arriving in England his own career began to parallel, in some ways, that of Joseph Priestley. He became, like Priestley, a member of the Royal Society, and he accepted an appointment as professor of natural history at the nonconformist academy at Warrington, where Priestley had been classical tutor from 1760 to 1767. Like Priestley, Forster combined a passion for empirical observation with a delight in general philosophical speculation. He subscribed to Priestley's book on light and doubtless took his copy with him on the *Resolution*. His own *Observations made During a Voyage round the World on Physical Geography, Natural History, and Ethnic Philosophy* (1778) contains a great number of observations upon light and atmospheric phenomena. In these fields it is a kind of supplement to Priestley's book. John Reinhold Forster's son George was at the beginning of a career even more distinguished than that of his father.[13] His *Voyage round the World*—the most readable of all accounts of Cook's voyages—also abounds with descriptions of unusual visual phenomena. On the voyage his particular duty was to draw specimens of natural history collected by his father, an art in which he had already acquired considerable skill.

William Wales (1734–98), one of Banks's nominees, was appointed astronomer and meteorologist on the *Resolution*. Although he quarrelled with the Forsters, he possessed, like them, the keenest interest in all forms of atmospheric phenomena. Indeed, he could well claim that in this field his knowledge was more professional. He had already been employed by the Admiralty to observe the transit of Venus at Fort Churchill in Hudson's Bay (1769) while Cook was at Tahiti. The published results of these observations and his accounts of the voyage to Fort Churchill; the *Original Astronomical Observations, made in the course of a Voyage towards the South Pole* (1777),[14] which he compiled jointly with William Bayly, the astronomer of the *Adventure* (Cook's other vessel); and his manuscript Journal on the *Resolution*, 1772–4, all reveal his preoccupation with meteorological phenomena.[15]

It must also be remembered that a close study of effects of light upon the colour of the sea was of great practical importance to seamen. Only by correctly interpreting such effects was it possible to forecast weather changes and navigate unknown seas safely. The practical importance of the observations was emphasized by the senior Forster:

> Wherever there is an extensive bank or shoal, there the colour of the seawater is changed; but even this is subject to many exceptions; sometimes we find places which are amazingly clear, and the ground, at the depth of several fathoms, may be seen plainly . . . sometimes the sea assumes a grey hue, and seems turbid, as if it had lost its limpidity. But often you are deceived by the situation of the sky and clouds. Dark, cloudy weather involves likewise the whole ocean in a grey hue. A serene and clear sky tinges the waves with the finest berylline or blueish-green colour. If a cloud appears, it gives to a spot of the sea a hue quite different from the rest; and, if not well attended to, often alarms the navigator with the fear of soundings or even shoals. A judicious eye, conducted by long experience, can alone distinguish properly in these cases.[16]

The artist, William Hodges, was thus thrust among a circle of professional scientists and seamen all keenly interested in visual phenomena, a circle even less disposed than Banks's party on the *Endeavour* was to allow the claims of taste to vitiate the truth of observation.

There were a number of seamen on the *Resolution* skilled in charting, and three of them, Henry Roberts, Joseph Gilbert, and Isaac Smith, included coastal profiles and harbour views in their logs. Many of Hodges's own drawings[17] and paintings are elaborate off-shore views of coasts and harbours; and it is clear that he was influenced by the naval regard for strict accuracy in drawing the outlines of hills and coasts. In his work, therefore, we may observe naval practice exerting an influence upon an artist trained in neo-classical traditions of landscape-painting (Plate 42, Colour Plate 3). On the other hand, Hodges exerted an influence upon the work of his naval companions. Joseph Gilbert, for instance, in his profiles and harbour views used brushwork freely instead of a pen, adopted a three-toned scheme of wash drawing in indian ink to give depth to his profiles, and sought to catch some effects of light in his work. Indeed, Gilbert's coastal views of Dusky Bay (Plate 40),[18] reveal that interest in atmospheric effects which captured the interest of the voyaging scientists.

It is possible, of course, that Hodges, even before he embarked on the *Resolution*, was aware of the difference between the type of landscape preferred by connoisseurs who had made the grand tour, and that preferred by influential virtuosi like Banks and

ISLE of MAYO diftant 7 Miles and the Hill B West

ISLE MAYO when the Hill C bears NWBN diftant 1 League

Pennant. Hodges had begun life as an errand boy to William Shipley (1714–1803), the artist who had founded the Society of Arts, and had himself won premiums for river views from the Society in 1762, 1763, and 1764.[19] It is not unlikely that either at Shipley's school, in the rooms of the Society of Arts, or in such places as Rawthmell's Coffee Inn, where artists and scientists forgathered, he had listened to discussions upon the relative merits of classical idealism and faithful topography in landscape art. While painting scenes for the theatre at Derby, Hodges probably met Joseph Wright.[20] It is likely that his work even at this time was not unaffected by the intense interest in science that was then stirring in the Midlands.[21]

But Hodges was also the pupil of Richard Wilson and through Wilson absorbed the principles of classical idealism in landscape-painting so well that he has been described as 'probably the most accomplished painter of fake Wilsons'.[22] Nevertheless, an early work exhibited in the Society of Artists Exhibition (1766), already revealed features that were to mark his Pacific paintings, the paint being 'more loosely handled, and more liquid in quality'[23] than Wilson's. This suggests that Hodges may have become interested in the special problems involved in rendering effects of light in landscape-painting before he joined the *Resolution*. But the decisive factor which impelled his art towards naturalism may be assumed to have been his association with scientific companions on the voyage.

Cook sailed from Plymouth on 13 July 1772 and stopped at Madeira and Porto Praya, in the island of St. Jago, for supplies. At both places Hodges made drawings of harbour views from the *Resolution*.[24]

The expedition arrived at Cape Town on 29 October and remained there until 22 November. In describing his stay at the Cape, Cook wrote: 'Mr. Hodges employed himself here in drawing a view of the Cape, town, and parts adjacent, in oil colours; which was properly packed up, with some others, and left with Mr. Brandt, in order to be forwarded to the Admiralty by the first ship that should sail for England.'[25] In another letter Cook mentions that the painting is a large one.[26] It was, almost certainly, the painting by Hodges, *The Cape of Good Hope* (Colour Plate 4), now at the National Maritime Museum, Greenwich. From its aspect it is clear that Hodges certainly drew, and quite probably painted, the picture from the *Resolution*, working in the security of the great cabin, the large windows of which gave him a view aft which was both wide and commanding.' This may partly account for its fresh *plein air* qualities.[27] But a more decisive reason may be found. The painting is still essentially a coastal profile, with a profile's insistence upon topographical accuracy, but it is a profile into which a keen interest in atmospheric phenomena has entered.

57

One of the prime reasons for Hodges's interest in atmospheric phenomena was, doubtless, the friendship which sprang up between himself and Wales. Hodges was twenty-eight, Wales ten years his senior. In the small circle of scientists, which comprised in addition to themselves, the two Forsters and the elder Forster's assistant, Anders Sparrman, they seem to have been drawn close together, a companionship assisted, perhaps, by a common dislike of the Forsters.[28] They explored islands together[29] and Wales later defended Hodges against criticism levelled at his drawings by George Forster.[30] On one occasion Wales wrote in his journal concerning a matter he had been unable to see himself: 'this is the substance of what I had from Mr. Hodges whose intelligence I have made use of before and I dare say it is pretty just.'[31] As a result of this friendship Hodges, on the voyage at least, appears to have developed a more empirical and more experimental attitude to his painting.

That a thoughtful and experimental attitude prevailed among the scientific company in general is revealed by both Anders Sparrman and George Forster. Sparrman observed how the seamen treated the scientistis as a special group: '. . . all the passengers who did not belong to the ship's company proper were called "experimental gentlemen", or gentlemen of adventure; and although the human race . . . tends to retain old customs, everyone and everything on this voyage tended to novelty and experiment.'[32] That this attitude frequently led to a study of atmospheric conditions is suggested by George Forster's remark: 'In the uniform life which we led between the tropics, where we found weather, wind, and sea, almost constantly favourable and agreeable, the mind catched at every little circumstance that could give the hint to a reflection.'[33]

It is against this background that we must seek to interpret Hodges's intentions when painting the *Cape of Good Hope*.[34] The weather conditions prevailing at the Cape at the time were extremely squally. A detailed meteorological record was kept by Wales during the period, which requires to be quoted in detail for the light it throws on Hodges's painting:

> *Thurs. Oct. 29th 1772.* About 19H came to an Anchor in Table Bay, and moor'd with Cable each way. Green Point bearing NWbN about a mile distant, and the Church SWbW; and soon after the Adventure came to an Anchor between us and the Town.
> *Fri. Oct 30th.* Brisk wind and Cloudy Weather, with rain at times.
> *Sat. Oct 31st.* Brisk wind and Cloudy with squalls and Rain at times.
> *Sun. Nov 1st.* Brisk wind at NW with Flying clouds and rain at times.
> *Tues. Nov 3rd.* Moderate breeze from the NE and Cloudy for the most part.
> *Nov. 4th to 14th.* Employ'd making Various Observations on the Shore (my observation book). The wind and weather during this time very irregular; being sometimes dead calm and in an hour or two blowing in such Violent Gusts that it was with utmost difficulty that we prevented the two Observatories from being blown away. At the same time the state of the Air was every wit as uncertain being very seldom either clear or cloudy for more than two or three hours at a time. This Uncertainty of the weather I conceive is entirely owing to the town being situated at the foot of the Table Mountain, which by its height attracts to itself vast quantities of Moist vapour; and these are dispersed again every two or three hours by the strong Gales which blow from thence in every direction. It is not uncommon to see the Top of this mountain, alternately, clear and covered with thick Clouds five or six times a day.

Now in the painting, a large oil which must have taken Hodges many days to paint, he has sought to render, not a visual transcript of certain conditions of light and

58

air as seen in a moment of time (in the impressionist manner), but a faithful and naturalistic account of the typical weather conditions prevailing during the expedition's stay at the Cape. It will be noted that his point of view corresponds with the position of the *Resolution* as recorded by Wales on 29 October, Green Point being out of the picture to the right. Hodges has chosen to render a moment when the afternoon sun breaking through the clouds behind the Lion's Head suddenly illuminates the stormy sky and strikes with dramatic sharpness upon the slopes of Table Mountain, the Devil's Peak, the town and fort, and the *Adventure* riding at anchor. But the moment has been chosen not only because it was pictorially dramatic but also because, on the evidence of Wales's weather record, it was typical. Hodges must have seen the light breaking through cloud thus not once but many times during his stay at the Cape. The masterly handling of the light upon the *Adventure*, the fort, and the town are almost impressionistic in their immediacy. Only in their ordered disposition does Hodges reveal the painting's tenuous affiliation with the neo-classical landscapes of Richard Wilson. When completed the picture became a graphic illustration of those very weather conditions which Wales described so carefully on 14 November 1772—a day on which the painting itself must have been nearing completion. For four days later it was packed up, as Cook informs us, ready for consignment by the first ship returning to England.[35]

That Hodges's painting should be so closely related to the scientific work of the voyage is not surprising. By this time Cook and the Admiralty had begun to realize the significance of the high value which Banks placed upon professional artists as scientific recorders. 'The Admiralty shewed no less attention to science in general', wrote Cook, 'by engaging Mr. William Hodges, a Landscape Painter, to embark in this voyage, in order to make drawings and paintings of such places in the countries we should touch at, as might be proper to give a more perfect idea thereof, than could be formed from written description only.'[36]

Still more unusual visual effects awaited Hodges in the Antarctic. For many months the *Resolution* worked its way among ice in high southern latitudes where the normal pictorial components of classical landscape were simply not to be found. Instead of foreground copses framing prospects of pastoral happiness and plenty, and backed by blue hills and golden skies, Hodges found only ice, water, mist, and light from which to compose his drawings.

In the Antarctic, Hodges confined his work to wash and water colour drawings. These reveal his continued interest in painting light and atmospheric effect.[37] In order to capture these effects he adopted a technique involving the use of three (or occasionally four) tones laid in broad washes. By suppressing detail and heightening tonal contrast he was able to suggest varied effects of luminosity—especially the effect of light upon ice. An examination of the skies in these drawings suggests that he attempted to reproduce actual cloud effects studied. Occasionally he made drawings which are magnificent studies of sea and sky (Plate 43).

The *Resolution and Adventure Taking in Ice for Water* (Plate 44) may be taken as an example of Hodges's wash-drawing technique. The artist's first interest here is to render the effects of light from a sun, low in the sky, illuminating the sails of the vessels sharply against grey clouds and an ice grotto with its complicated reflections. The grotto answers closely to a description of one written by George Forster:

> The shapes of these large frozen masses, were frequently singularly ruinous, and so far picturesque enough; among them we passed one of great size, with a hallow in the middle, resembling a grotto or cavern, which was pierced through, and admitted light from the other side.[38]

The grotto, a conventional item of taste, has here become almost entirely an essay upon the effects of light in high latitudes.[39] Inspired no doubt by Hodges's efforts, and with little to draw in the way of plants and animals in those icy regions, George Forster himself, on one occasion at least, essayed with considerable success a study in gouache of Antarctic light. In his *Ice Islands* (Colour Plate 5), this interest in light on ice overrides all other considerations, blurring and modifying the contours, uniting ice, water, and sky in one shimmering texture, and reducing the grotto to a minor pictorial component. The light suffused above the horizon is, doubtless, a representation of the ice-blink mentioned by Wales and Forster upon several occasions.[40] The ice in the background is flushed with a roseate hue while the sky emits a yellow glow which is reflected by the foreground ice. Anders Sparrman wrote a description which answers closely to the scene recorded in the drawing:

> On the 26th [December 1772], ... one of the icebergs ... was transformed into the loveliest scene imaginable. The glow of the setting sun fell upon this iceberg, which was as clear as crystal, so that its many thousand crevices and chasms shone like gold, in a clear scintillating yellow, while the rest of the mass reflected a rich purple colour.[41]

It was in seeking to carry out his commission and record such scenes graphically that Hodges was drawn to the problems involved in depicting light naturalistically. In the *Island of South Georgia* (Plate 45) the simple economy of Hodges's tonal technique has transformed what might have been a conventional coastal profile into a dramatic statement in which topographical accuracy is united with a striking atmospheric effect.

61

In the Pacific Hodges was confronted with quite different visual problems but his solutions again reveal an original mind. In his wash drawing of canoes (Plate 46) he essays with surprising success the problem of painting objects upon water seen directly against the sun. Using the same breadth and economy of statement present in his Antarctic drawings he here succeeds by sufficiently sharpening tonal contrasts in the foreground to create the illusion of sunlit waves. Hodges handled his washes with swift brevity to gain effects purely visual, as in his rendering of the man in the prow of the foreground canoe, the cutting of the rear canoe by the edge of the drawing, and his method of suggesting by oblique shadows the position of the source of light.

Hodges's *plein air* approach is revealed in the oil paintings which he completed in the Pacific. In the *Province of Oparee* (Pare), he takes up again the problem of painting into 'the eye of the light' (Colour Plate 6). But in this painting the light is suffused through mists rising over the islands. Hodges here breaks quite free from neo-classical formulas; the roseate hue diffused over sea and sky is something quite different from the golden sunset glow of Claude and Richard Wilson. Again Hodges uses a canoe truncated by the base-line of the painting as a foreground motif—a most unclassical device. The imperceptible gradation of tone to suggest spatial recession towards a far-distant horizon, the wide distribution of highlights over the painting rendered with a swift liquid impasto, and the radiation of suffused light over everything are unusual features to find in an English eighteenth-century landscape-painting. His *View of Part of the Island of Ulietea* (Colour Plate 7) and *View of Otaha and Bola Bola* (Colour Plate 8) in their 'direct and vivid observation of the thing seen' anticipate Turner's sketch for *Walton Bridges* by more than a quarter of a century. Hodges, in short, presented himself with a problem more common to artists in the nineteenth century—the painting of landscapes filled with strong sunlight.

Hodges, however, was not the only one to notice the effect of sunshine in determining the character of the Tahitian landscape. He may well have been a member of the party which climbed to the head of one of the valleys of Pare, whence it enjoyed a view described in words that could fittingly be used to describe Hodges's painting:

> The prospect from hence was delightful; the reef which surrounded O-Taheitee, the bay with the ships, and numerous canoes, and the whole plain of Matavai with its beautiful objects, lay as it were under our feet, while the meridian sun threw a steady and calm light on the whole landscape.[42]

When the *Resolution* returned to England Hodges was employed by the Admiralty at £250 per annum to complete the paintings and drawings he had brought home with him in preparation for the publication of the voyage. The scientific nature of the voyage, as we have seen, had drawn Hodges to the study of light and atmosphere but upon his return to England he felt the need to direct the appeal of his paintings to a more varied audience than the Resolution's scientific company. Nevertheless, their approval of his representation of matters of fact remained an important consideration. But Hodges was also an aspirant to membership of the Royal Academy.[43] Consequently, in making his finished paintings for the Admiralty he began to pay more attention to the neo-classical taste of the time as enunciated by Reynolds. Several of the paintings he made for the Admiralty (or replicas of them) were exhibited at the Academy in 1776 and 1777.

In painting landscapes for the Academy, Hodges had the current veneration of Claude to guide him. Tahiti provided an ideal subject in which to combine classical idealism and scientific accuracy because in that island, as it was generally agreed, nature herself approached the classical ideal. Claude's paintings evoked dreams of the

46. William Hodges, *Canoes*, *Tahiti*, wash, 10½ × 15 in. (1773). Mitchell Library, Sydney, PXD11. 15a. By permission of the Trustees of the State Library of New South Wales

47. William Hodges, *Oaitepeha Bay*, (Tautira Bay) *Tahiti*, or 'Tahiti Revisited', canvas, 36½ × 54½ in. (1776). National Maritime Museum, London. On loan from the Ministry of Defence-Navy, L36–19

Golden Age; so did nature in Tahiti. In 1776 Hodges exhibited *A View Taken in the Bay of Otaheite Peha* (Tautira Bay) at the Academy. This painting is probably identical with his *Oaitepeha Bay, Tahiti* (Plate 47, Colour Plate 10), in the National Maritime Museum. An examination of this latter will, in any case, reveal how Hodges sought to resolve the interests of the men of taste and the men of science.

He began with a classical framework. The group bathing, the winding river, and the deep-toned central distances screening the mountainous background, proceed from Claudean principles of composition as modified by Wilson. Conventional classical motives, however, have been replaced by others typical of Tahiti: plantations of bread-fruit and coconut-palm replace olive-tree and cypress, a group of Tahitian girls bathing replace Arcadian shepherdesses, the precipitous peaks of the interior of the island replace the hills of the Campagna. Even so the mood evoked recalls the paintings of Claude in its poetic evocation of Arcadian happiness. But the colours of the Italianate landscape have here been heightened into an effect more tropical, and the clouds upon the mountain tops owe as much to Hodges's talks with Wales as to his training under Wilson. Indeed, here, as in so many of his paintings, Hodges's search for a faithful rendering of the atmosphere has had the effect of broadening his brushwork, a point of technique particularly noticeable in the foreground.[44] It is in fact his rendering of tropical atmosphere charged with luminous vapour which imposes a visual unity upon the composition. The pictorial expression of the atmosphere has become the main subject of the painting symbolizing the island's fertility and providing at the same time a rational explanation for the island's Arcadian beauty. For Hodges also had to satisfy the scientists. Consequently the girls must be painted not as ideal beauties but with their typical tattoo markings; the houses under the bread-fruit groves on the slopes of the hills rendered accurately if unobtrusively; and the exotic vegetation depicted so as not to offend the prying eye of the botanist.

By these means Hodges sought to satisfy both the men of taste and the men of science. And into the picture Hodges has also interwoven two well-established aspects of the island-paradise theme. On the one hand, the life free of moral restraints is suggested by the exotic beauty of the nude bathing girls, while on the others, the vanity of earthly pleasures and the mystery and melancholy of death is suggested by the ancestral image (*tii*) which towers above the bathers and the *Toupapa'u* with its shrouded corpse in the distance on the extreme right.[45]

When we compare this painting with engravings published in Hawkesworth's and Cook's *Voyages*, it becomes clear that Hodges is asserting the existence of the Tahitian paradise not by pointing to classical parallels of dress, physique, and customs with their idealistic associations but by seeking for an explanation and a unifying factor in the salubrity of the climate. The luxury of Tahiti was for Hawkesworth and the verse satirists of the day a problem in morals and theology, a problem which Hodges sought to answer rationally by reference to climate. That this is so becomes clearer if we regard the South Sea compositions, which Hodges completed after his return, as considered reflections upon the documentary work he made on the spot. Such paintings may be compared with advantage to the reflections of other members of the *Resolution*'s company written after their return. By such comparisons we are enabled to gain a clearer idea of the picture, which formed in the minds of those in the best position to know, concerning the essential nature of the Tahitian Arcadia. In these reflections is to be found the search for a scientific explanation of the island's beauty in the nature of its climate. John Reinhold Forster's graphic description of Tahiti provides us with the best possible insight into the intrinsic meaning of *Oaitepeha Bay*:

64

O-Taheitee and all the high islands, are in general more happy and fertile, than the low islands, and those of a moderate height. The high hills in the middle of the first, attract by their situation, all the vapours and clouds that pass near them; there are but few days, on which their summits are not involved in fogs and clouds; and though it does not constantly rain there, yet such a regular supply of moisture is derived from these hills, that their very tops are crowned with lofty trees, and their sides fringed with shrubs and agreeable plants during the whole year; and all the surrounding valleys collect in their bosom the salutary humidity, which is not absorbed by these plants, and which is generously screened by them against the sun's power; so that in every one a gentle stream is collected from the smaller rills, which unite into one bed. This rivulet the natives stem here and there by wears, made of large stones, in order to water the plantations of eddoes; the frequent trees that are growing along the banks of the sweet purling stream, extend their shady branches, give a coolness to the virgin-water, and thus bring refreshment, and the principles of bread-fruit, apple and cloth trees, and bannana's (sic), and spreads happiness and plenty. These rivers become the fountains and chief causes of the great variety of fruit, which grows everywhere; they enliven the picturesque scenery, and afford a cooling liquor for the inhabitants.[46]

In this rational and yet poetic explanation of the island's beauty we have a close parallel to the documentary and ideal elements in Hodges's painting. For it is at heart quite unclassical. The painter is seeking to gain the authority and prestige of classical landscape for another kind of landscape altogether: a form of landscape the compositional elements of which were determined not by reference to states of mind but by reference to the interrelation of the facts and scientific laws determining the nature of a given environment. Topography, of course, had always been given a humble place at the bottom of the academic table, but here was an attempt to elevate exotic topography to the high places reserved for the ideal landscapes of Claude, the heroic landscapes of Poussin, and the picturesque landscapes of Salvator Rosa.[47] It is not surprising that such an attempt to broach the elevated frontiers of the ideal should have been made by means of pictorial representations of an island which had constantly reminded travellers of classical antiquity. It would have been a more difficult business to find a respectable correlative for the ice islands of Antarctica. One, however, was available for the representation of the New Zealand landscape, based upon the authority of Salvator Rosa.

The Royal Society, as already observed, required travellers to record most carefully all atmospheric disturbances observed. Such an occurrence the *Resolution*'s company observed off Cape Stephens, in the South Island of New Zealand on 17 May 1773, when four waterspouts formed and dispersed quite close to the vessel. Detailed accounts of the phenomenon were recorded by all the scientists aboard and Hodges made sketches of the incident from which an engraving was made and published in Wales and Bayly's *Astronomical Observations* (1777), to supplement their written account (Plate 48).

But Hodges also decided to use the incident in order to combine a scientifically observed natural wonder with a study of nature in the sublime. In his *View of Cape Stephens* (Plate 49) the *Resolution* is shown beating against the variable winds which accompanied the appearance of the waterspouts, the heavy sea breaking against the high cliffs of Cape Stephens, from which depend stunted trees tossed in the gale. It is all in the manner of Salvator Rosa, and Hodges must have been frequently reminded of Rosa's paintings while the *Resolution* was on the New Zealand coast, as George Forster was when he wrote:

48. *Waterspouts in Cook's Straits, New Zealand*, engraving after William Hodges, in Wales and Bayle, *Astronomical Observations* (1777), pl. 4

49. William Hodges, *A View of Cape Stephens (New Zealand) with Waterspout*, canvas, 54 × 76 in. (1776). National Maritime Museum, London. On loan from the Department of Defence-Navy, L36–9.

... the view of rude sceneries in the style of *Rosa*, of antediluvian forests which cloathed the rock, and of numerous rills of water ... altogether conspired to complete our joy; and so apt is mankind, after a long absence from land, to be prejudiced in favour of the wildest shore, that we looked upon the country at that time, as one of the most beautiful which nature unassisted by art could produce.[48]

New Zealand landscape, then, could be portrayed in the manner of Rosa whose work had the *imprimatur* of Reynolds and the connoisseurs. To Reynolds the manner of Rosa though inferior to the grand style, nevertheless, possessed great merit because it revealed a lively imagination. And, more significantly, such landscapes as Rosa painted could be contrived from diverse elements providing they were united and harmonized by the controlling imagination.[49] Hodges's problem was, in short, to give to his own documentary art with its own particular discipline, 'that sort of dignity which belongs to savage and uncultivated nature'. Now a careful examination of George Forster's description of the phenomenon and Hodges's painting of it, reveals that the painter followed the meteorological report closely:

> In the afternoon, about four o'clock, we were nearly opposite Cape Stephens, and had little or no wind. . . . On a sudden a whitish spot appeared on the sea in that quarter, and a column arose out of it, looking like a glass tube; another seemed to come down from the clouds to meet this, and they made a coalition, forming what is commonly called a waterspout. A little while after we took notice of three other columns, which were formed in the same manner as the first. . . . Their base, where the water of the sea was violently agitated, and rose in a spiral form in vapours, was a broad spot, which looked bright and yellowish when illuminated by the sun. The column was of a cylindrical form, rather encreasing in width towards the upper extremity. These columns moved forward on the surface of the sea, and the clouds not following them with equal rapidity, they assumed a bent or incurvated shape. . . . In proportion as the clouds came nearer to us, the sea appeared more and more covered with short broken waves, and the wind continually veered all round the compass, without fixing in any point. We soon saw a spot on the sea, within two

50. Richard Wilson, *Ceyx and Alcyone*, canvas, 40 × 50 in. (*c.* 1767–8). National Museum of Wales, Cardiff

hundred fathoms of us, in a violent agitation. The water, in a space of fifty or sixty fathoms, moved towards the centre, and there rising into vapour, by the force of the whirling motion, ascended in a spiral form towards the clouds. Some hailstones fell on board about this time, and the clouds looked exceedingly black and louring above us. Directly over the whirlpool, if I may so call the agitated spot on the sea, a cloud gradually tapered into a long slender tube, which seemed to descend to meet the rising spiral, and soon united with it into a strait column of a cylindrical form. We could distinctly observe the water hurled upwards with the greatest violence in a spiral, and it appeared that it left a hollow space in the centre. . . . After some time the last water-spout was incurvated and broke like the others, with this difference, that its disjunction was attended with a flash of lightning, but no explosion was heard. Our situation during all this time was very dangerous and alarming; a phenomenon which carried so much terrific majesty in it, and connected as it were the sea with the clouds, made our oldest mariners uneasy and at a loss how to behave. . . . We prepared indeed for the worst, by cluing up our topsails; but it was the general opinion that our masts and yards must have gone to wreck if we had been drawn into the vortex.[50]

Hodges kept quite close to this description, but has added other features. The *pa* at the extremity of the Cape was in fact built upon an isolated rock in Queen Charlotte Sound, and the flashes coming from it were not observed simultaneously with the waterspouts but on the following morning. Forster writes: 'About five o'clock the next morning we opened Queen Charlotte's Sound, and about seven we saw three flashes rising from the south end of the Motu-Aro, where a *hippah*, or strong hold of the natives, was situated.'[51] Cook and Banks visited this *pa* on the first voyage, and Hodges depicts the fissure which Hawkesworth describes as separating the fortified village from the mainland.[52] Hodges has also added seals such as were found at Dusky Bay; and a recollection of the Maori family, which he drew when the *Resolution* put in there, is doubtless the source of the noble savage family which he has painted upon the rocks in the foreground. The painting as a whole is intended, therefore, to create a dramatic and dignified representation of a terrifying but true phenomenon of nature as it was witnessed near the savage landscape of New Zealand. To endow the landscape with its typical features is the function of the *pa*, the seals, and the native family.

The painting is, however, more than an assemblage of observations. The model for the composition appears to have been Wilson's *Ceyx and Alcyone* (Plate 50). The compositions of *Cape Stephens* and Wilson's *Ceyx* are strikingly similar, the tree motif in the top right foreground of the Wilson is repeated with little alteration in the Hodges. The *Ceyx* appears to have been particularly well known to Hodges for Farington says that drawings of the painting by Hodges were sold as Wilson's at Sandby's sale in 1811.[53] Both paintings, however, look back to Wilson's *Niobe* and it is, perhaps, not too fanciful to see in Hodges's painting an attempt to solve the problem of relating an action of supernatural grandeur to a naturalistic landscape which Wilson attempted, according to Reynolds, so unsuccessfully in the *Niobe*.[54] In both paintings a composition of strong diagonals is adapted to the expression of nature in a dark and terrifying mood, and in both the dramatic effect is mainly produced by vivid effects of light. But there the comparison ceases: whereas Wilson looked back to a Nature controlled by the gods of classical mythology, Hodges looks toward exotic *mirabilia* to create an effect 'akin to the supernatural'; whereas Wilson peoples his landscape with Apollo and the children of Niobe, Hodges peoples his with the noble savages and

animals of a romantic country discovered by the enterprise of British seamen. Some twenty years later Coleridge was to present himself with quite a similar problem in literature, and to solve it by comparable means. And it seems likely that William Wales's scientific enthusiasm for the study of the atmosphere became a source of inspiration to both painter and poet.[55]

    Hodges's *Oaitepeha Bay* forms a striking contrast with his *Cape Stephens*. One reveals how Tahiti became identified with classical landscape, the other how New Zealand became identified in the minds of Hodges, Wales,[56] and the Forsters with romantic landscape. The one thing the two paintings have in common is Hodges's sustained interest in atmospheric effects. Neverthelss, both paintings represent a compromise with academic taste. But this is not true of all the paintings of the South Seas executed after his return to England. His *Matavai Bay* (Plate 51) carried the direct vision of his South Sea wash drawings on to the walls of the Academy of 1776. In this painting the precepts of classical composition are reduced to a minimum; only the relatively darker foreground tones and the masts of the canoes on either hand remain to indicate the traditional affiliations of the composition. Apart from this, the painting has become a study in Tahitian light. The canoes cut by the framing vertical edges of the picture are devices which suggest more lateral space than the picture contains. With this feeling for amplitude is united a feeling for depth attained by tonal degradation ranging from the sharp contrasts of the foreground to the barely perceptible transitions of the horizon. *Oaitepeha Bay*, as we have seen, seeks to evoke echoes of the classical world—*le mirage océanien*—as a foil to its atmospheric and topographic motifs. But in *Matavai Bay* the motifs do not arouse traditional associations. The study of light here becomes an

51. William Hodges, *A View of Matavai Bay in the Island of Otaheite*, canvas, 54 × 76 in. (1776). National Maritime Museum, London. On loan from the Ministry of Defence-Navy, L 36–17

end in itself and the unifying factor in the composition: hard flat light from native cloth, or light soft and broken from surf foaming over a reef, iridescent from a headdress, dappling the tops of trees on a wooded headland, caught by the crests of waves, a sail-rope, or a sail filled with wind, or light diffused into haze, reveal Hodges's sustained interest in purely visual effects.

The way in which Hodges's artistic interests varied between the current intellectual interests of his time and his interest in the study of light may be estimated by comparing Woollett's engraving, *The Monuments of Easter Island* (Plate 52), after one of Hodges's drawings, with an original oil painting which Hodges made of the monument from sketches completed on the island (Colour Plate 11).

William Woollett, as we have already seen, had invested Parkinson's '*Ewharra*' in *Huaheine* with a conventional melancholy, frequently associated with Arcadian scenery at the time. George Keate, for instance, whose *Account of the Pelew Islands*, is discussed below, wrote a two-act play, *The Monument in Arcadia*, in 1773. In it the consciousness of death gradually destroys the innocent happiness investing an Arcadian situation. In 1755 Richard Wilson painted *Et in Arcadia Ego* (Plate 53), a painting which Hodges probably knew well. The substance of the melancholy theme was introduced by a simple transition into an engraving illustrating the statues discovered upon Easter Island.

Cook reached Easter Island in March 1774. The statues he found there, he suggested, were not idols, as Jacob Roggeveen had suggested when he discovered the island in 1722,[57] but 'monuments of antiquity' marking the burial places of certain tribes or families.[58] They had not been erected by the contemporary inhabitants, who could not even provide a satisfactory account of them. The scientists believed that the monuments were used to commemorate the dead of the present inhabitants but also saw them as an indication of the passing of a more civilized people. George Forster wrote: 'We marched to an elevated spot, and stopped a little while to take some refreshments, and to give Mr. Hodges time to draw some of the monuments, near one of which we found an entire skeleton of a man.'[59] The subject must have appealed to Hodges. In 1768 he had exhibited a painting at the Society of Artists called *A View of a Druid's altar in Pembrokeshire*. Here were ruins even more mysterious in the South Seas. The mystery asked for some kind of explanation. George Forster pointed out that since the monuments were 'so disproportionate to the present strength of the nation, it is most reasonable to look upon them as the remains of better times.'[60] This led to the suggestion that the people of the island, whom Cook's company found living in a very poor condition, once enjoyed a more flourishing state. The monuments came to be seen as the records of a decayed civilization. Consequently, the solitary native outlined against the ocean, in Woollett's engraving after Hodges, rests on his staff, like the shepherd in Wilson's *Et in Arcadia Ego*, and contemplates, like him, the symbols of mortality. The basket of fruit held by the native, the giant leaves of the banana tree, the profusion of plants that embroider the rocks, are emblems of a South Sea island paradise. Yet even here, the engraving clearly suggests, the savage must remember human transience and contemplate the brevity of happiness. The idea held a strong appeal for both classical and Christian attitudes of mind and the engraving frequently reappeared, usually in debased and popular forms, in later accounts of Cook's voyages (Plate 54).

Hodges's oil painting *The Monuments of Easter Island* (Colour Plate 11) offers a striking contrast to the engraving of the subject. The emphasis in the engraving is literary and reflective; the emphasis in the oil is essentially visual. In the latter Hodges has treated the subject with a characteristic breadth of handling as an essay in the depiction of light and weather. In the engraving there is only a vestige of the dramatic

52 (facing page top). *The Monuments of Easter Island*, engraving after William Hodges by William Woollett, in Cook, *Voyage Towards the South Pole* (1777), pl. xlix

53 (facing page bottom). Richard Wilson, *Et in Arcadia Ego*, canvas, 43 × 53½ in. (1755). Lady Elizabeth Byng, Wrotham Park, Barnet, Herts. Reproduced by courtesy of the owner

54. *Monuments on Easter Island*, woodcut, in Cook, *Voyages* (ed. J. Barrow, 1874), f.p. 238

71

55. *The Landing at Middleburgh* (Eua), *One of the Friendly Islands*, engraving after Hodges by J.K. Sherwin, in Cook, *Voyage towards the South Pole* (1777), pl. liv

56. *The Landing at Erramanga*, engraved after a painting by Hodges by J. K. Sherwin, in Cook, *Voyage Towards the South Pole* (1777), pl. lxii

stormclouds emerging from the sea which determine the mood of the painting; and the enormous skeleton which dominates the central foreground of the engraving as a *memento mori* finds its parallel only in a small skull of quite secondary importance to the emotional tone of the painting. The composition is rudimentary and naturalistic, put down without much regard for neo-classical precepts. The statues are blocked in broadly with an eye mainly to the visual patterns they help to establish against the sky. It is the sharp contrasts which their mellow sandstone and red tufa set up against the deep green of the storm-cloud rather than their melancholy associations which made the monuments of pictorial interest for Hodges. The broad handling and interest in atmosphere suggests that the painting may have been executed on the voyage, though not on Easter Island, where their stay was much too short for such an ambitious work.

The above comparison between the engraving and the painting of *The Monuments of Easter Island* serves to indicate that the neo-classical and literary element is con-

57. *Telemachus and Mentor in the Island of Calypso* (detail), engraving after Angelica Kauffmann by Bartolozzi (1786)

siderably stronger in the engravings after Hodges, published in Cook's *Voyages*, than in Hodges's original paintings. In this connexion a class of engravings published in Cook's *Voyage towards the South Pole* which illustrates his landings on certain Pacific islands deserves special mention. The *Landing at Middleburgh* (Eua) (Plate 55), the *Landing at Mallicolo* (Malekula), and the *Landing at Erramanga* (Eromanga) (Plate 56) are stated to have been engraved from paintings by Hodges. Some of the figures are unlike Hodges's paintings of natives: those of the *Landing at Middleburgh* are sentimentalized neo-classical versions of the noble savage drawn in the manner of Angelica Kauffmann and may be compared with Bartolozzi's engraving after her *Telemachus and Mentor in the Island of Calypso* (Plate 57). Proof that Hodges did not draw the figures for one of these 'landing' engravings is to be found on the original drawing for the figures in the *Landing at Erramanga* (Plate 58) in which the signature of Cipriani, though cut at the base, is clearly discernible. Hodges made a practice of using other artists to draw his full-length figures for him.[61] The neo-classical style in which these

58. G. B. Cipriani, drawing for *The Landing at Erramanga*, pen and wash, $12 \times 15\frac{1}{4}$ in. (*c.* 1776). Public Archives of Canada, Ottawa, Hodges-Webber drawings, 1–7

59. William Hodges, *Tu*, red chalk, $21\frac{1}{4} \times 14\frac{1}{2}$ in. (1773). National Library of Australia, Canberra, R. 755

60. *Otoo King of O-Taheite Drawn from nature by W. Hodges*, engraved by J. Hall, in Cook, *Voyage towards the South Pole* (1777), pl. 38

'landing' engravings are executed suggested that those in charge of the publication of the official version of Cook's second voyage felt that the landings in question—with their implications of British sovereignty—were of sufficient historical moment to be illustrated in the elevated style of history-painting. Cipriani was a natural choice for such figure work, being one of the best-known history-painters in England at the time, and well versed in the precepts of neo-classical composition. It is to be noted that the engraved portraits of natives published with the 'landing' engravings are executed in a more realistic style. Though most are faithful in visual fact to the original drawings the differences are at times striking. The engraver Hall, for example, quite lost the subtle psychology of Hodges's drawing of Tu (Plate 59), reducing him to a sullen, pop-eyed savage (Plate 60). Tu later became Pomare I, the first King of the Pomare dynasty. Thus in Cook's *Voyage towards the South Pole* is to be found, once again, an endeavour to cater for the men of taste and the men of science. But upon this occasion also, as when Hawkesworth's *Voyages* appeared, the appearance of noble savages in a supposedly scientific work was singled out for attack. It came on this occasion from an informed member of the expedition. George Forster, in his own account of the voyage, paid several tributes to Hodges's artistic abilities but he could not refrain from drawing attention to the gross absurdity of the *Landing at Middleburgh*:

> Mr. Hodges designed this memorable interview in an elegant picture, which has been engraved for captain Cook's account of this voyage. The same candour with which I have made it a rule to commend the performances of this ingenious artist, whenever they are characteristic of the objects, which he meant to represent, obliges me to mention, that this piece, in which the execution of Mr Sherwin cannot be too much admired, does not convey any adequate idea of the natives of Ea-

oowhe or of Tonga Tabbo. The plates which ornamented the history of captain Cook's former voyage, have been justly criticised, because they exhibited to our eyes the pleasing forms of antique figures and draperies, instead of those Indians of which we wished to form some idea. But it is also greatly to be feared, that Mr. Hodges has lost the sketches and drawings which he made from NATURE in the course of the voyage, and supplied the deficiency in this case, from his own elegant ideas. The connoisseur will find Greek contours and features in this picture, which have never existed in the South Sea. He will admire an elegant flowing robe which involves the whole head and body, in an island where the women very rarely cover the shoulders and breast; and he will be struck with awe and delight by the figure of a divine old man, with a long white beard, though all the people of Ea-oowhe shave themselves with muscle-shells.[62]

Since the designs here criticized so trenchantly were probably not the artist's own but Cipriani's, or one of his associates, Hodges, with his name on the published engraving, was placed in a difficult position. His friend Wales, however, came to his defence.[63] The form which the defence took is itself an illustration of the method used by a neo-classical history-painter, and it is likely that Wales used Hodges's own arguments to justify the engraving—arguments, indeed, which Cipriani might have helped to frame. The history-painter before commencing a design was bound to study his sources and to seek in them descriptions of the manners and characters of his actors and the historic scenes in which they participated. But these descriptions should be adaptable to an ideal presentation of the facts. Accordingly, Wales, in defending Hodges, points to the fact that George Forster himself when describing the natives of the Friendly Islands used such phrases as 'elegant', 'features full of sweetness', 'exquisitely proportioned', and so on. These are the phrases seized upon by the neo-classical designer to justify the florid elegance of the scene. But such treatment of a people so little known to Europeans, and so little available to them, constituted a breach of faith in honest reporting.[64] The criticism, as we shall see, was not lost upon Hodges.

Hodges's oil-paintings, however, tended to evoke criticism for quite a different reason from those advanced by Forster against the *Landing at Middleburgh*. Hodges's interest in the rendering of atmosphere and light had an effect upon his technique: it led to a breadth of handling, directness of brushwork, the use of strong tonal contrasts, and a wide distribution of highlights in impasto. The reception which this technique received from contemporary critics may be judged from the review of his *War Boats of the Island of Otaheite* (Plate 61), a very large painting which he exhibited in the Academy of 1777:

> Mr. Hodges, who in last year's exhibition had several views of bays etc. about the Island of Otaheite, has this year a large piece exhibiting the war boats of that Island, and a view of part of the Island of Ohamaneno, etc. The public are indebted to this artist for giving them some idea of scenes which before they knew little of. It is surprising, however, that a man of Mr. Hodges's genius should adopt such a ragged mode of colouring; his pictures all appear as if they were unfinished, and as if the colours were laid on the canvas with a skewer.[65]

Comments of this nature gained currency. Edward Edwards stated that as Hodges had trained 'under a master not over careful in finishing his pictures, he copied of Wilson's defects than of his perfections, in consequence of which, his works in general have too much appearance of neglect, which has been considered as the effects of slovenliness allied with the affectations of mastery. In all his productions he discovered too little attention to the true similitude of the objects he represented.'[66] And Edward Dayes wrote: 'the colouring is too monotonous, and sometimes heavy, with an abruptness in the light and shade approaching to hardness'.[67] Clearly, these critics did not appreciate that Hodges's technical eccentricities had developed because he had for many years addressed himself to the problem of painting tropical light in the Pacific, and later in India.

Hodges visited India in 1778 and, gaining the patronage of Warren Hastings, remained there six years. His *Travels in India* (1793) reveals his continued interest in effects of light and atmosphere. Extensive travel had made him aware how greatly light and colour can vary in different climatic regions. In this connexion it is important to note that he was not only the first professional English landscape-painter to visit the South Seas but also the first to visit India.[68] One of the first observations he was to make concerning his Indian travels concerned itself with the different emotional effects induced by different conditions of light and air. Concerning the Indian climate he wrote:

> The clear, blue, cloudless sky, the polished white buildings, the bright sandy beach, and the dark green sea, present a combination totally new to the eye of an Englishman, just arrived from London, who, accustomed to the sight of rolling masses of clouds floating in a damp atmosphere, cannot but contemplate the difference with delight: and the eye thus gratified, the mind assumes a gay and tranquil habit, analogous to the pleasing objects with which it is surrounded.[69]

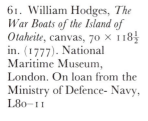

61. William Hodges, *The War Boats of the Island of Otaheite*, canvas, 70 × 118½ in. (1777). National Maritime Museum, London. On loan from the Ministry of Defence- Navy, L80–11

On another occasion he described the onset and dispersal of a storm which reveals the keeness of his weather observations, a faculty sharpened, doubtless, by his years on the *Resolution*:

62. *Portia's Garden, Merchant of Venice, Act v sc. 1*, engraving after William Hodges by J. Byrne (1790)

At this season of the year it is not uncommon, towards the evening, to see a small black cloud rising in the eastern part of the horizon, and afterwards spreading itself north-west. The phenomenon is always attended with a violent storm of wind, and flashes of the strongest and most vivid lightning and heavy thunder, which is followed by rain. These storms sometimes last for half an hour or more; and when they disperse they leave the air greatly freshened, and the sky of a deep, clear, and transparent blue. When they occur near the full moon, the whole atmosphere is illuminated by a soft but brilliant silver light, attended with gentle airs, as Shakespeare has expressed—

> 'When the sweet wind did gently kiss the trees
> And they did make no noise.'[70]

The beauty of the moonlit nights he experienced in India left a lasting impression upon Hodges. The subject which he chose to illustrate for Boydell's 'Shakespeare Gallery' was, fittingly enough, *Portia's Garden* (Plate 62)—a stage set which must have recalled for him the still, moonlit nights of India.[71]

In his enjoyment of moonlit landscape—one of the notable indications of the deepening sensitivity to natural beauty so characteristic of the art and poetry of the last quarter of the eighteenth century—Hodges may be compared with Joseph Wright of Derby. Wright had begun to apply his special interest in the sources of light to landscape-painting after his return from his Italian tour of 1773–5.[72] In Hodges's case the interest in painting moonlight effects is most probably an aspect of that general interest in atmospheric effects stimulated by his Pacific voyage. The scientists aboard the *Resolution* observed halos and coronae around the moon with great interest and described them in detail. 'Our people had the felicity of enjoying the sight of the moon', wrote Cook on one occasion, after weeks of stormy weather.[73]

On another occasion, at Tahiti, George Forster wrote: 'All night the moon shone in a cloudless sky, and silvered over the polished surface of the sea, while the landscape lay before us like the gay production of a fertile and elegant fancy.'[74] Such experiences prepared Hodges for the enjoyment of those moonlight scenes which he describes with such evident enjoyment in his *Travels in India* and which enter so frequently into his Indian paintings.

When Hodges returned from India in 1784, he was the most widely travelled English landscape-painter of his day. But, like Banks, he had not made the usual tour of Italy. Hodges realized that the landscape-painter who travelled outside Europe found himself confronted with special problems. George Forster's criticism of the *Landing at Middleburgh* had already underlined the dangers of applying the precepts of classical idealism to exotic scenes. And in his *Travels in India* Hodges took pains to state what he considered to be the requirements of the artist-traveller.

> A painter for such pursuits ought necessarily to be endowed with three great qualities; a perfect knowledge of his art, and with powers to execute readily and correctly; judgment to choose his subjects; and fancy to combine and dispose them to advantage. The first I must suppose him possessed of; in the second is included the choice of subject, with the knowledge of all the parts necessary for such a subject; and in the third is included the combination of all the different parts, so as to produce a general effect: but the imagination must be under the strict guidance of a cool judgment, or we shall have fanciful representations instead of the truth, which, above all, must be the object of such researches. Everything has a particular character, and certainly it is the finding out the real and natural character which is required; for should a painter be possessed of the talents of a Raphael, and were he to represent a Chinese with the beauty of a Grecian character and form, however excellent his work might be, it would still have no pretentions to reputation as characteristical of that nation.[75]

The passage has a familiar ring. Reynolds, in his Second Discourse, indicated three stages in an artist's development. These are paralleled by the three qualities Hodges finds necessary to the travelling artist. Furthermore, there are verbal echoes in Hodges's statement which suggests that he might have been attempting to write his own gloss on Reynolds's pronouncements. The requirements set forth by both artists have much in common. It is only Hodges's third quality of the travelling artist which differs fundamentally from Reynolds's third stage of artistic growth. Yet even these, at first glance, have something in common. There does not seem, at bottom, much difference between the ability 'to discriminate perfections that are incompatible with each other',[76] as Reynolds puts it, and Hodges's desire that the artist-traveller should find out the 'real and natural character' of his scenes. But Reynolds is not suggesting that artists should discriminate between differences of race and climate in their paintings. he is referring to the theory of modes: the beautiful subject should be treated evenly and smoothly; the picturesque subject, with a more vigorous touch, and so on. Each mode has its own type of perfection which a mature artist should recognize. Hodges himself had worked according to the theory of modes when he painted *Oaitepeha Bay* and *Cape Stephens*. For he treated the former with the smoothness and harmony befitting the classical character of the subject, and the latter with the breadth and vigour befitting the romantic character of the subject. But in his discussion of the qualities desired in the travelling artist he has given the theory a geographical twist. The 'particular character' which travelling artists should seek out is not the particular kind of handling demanded by the aesthetic qualities of the

78

subject, as whether, for instance, it partakes of the beautiful, the sublime, or the picturesque; it is the particular character determined by race, climate, and vegetation.

Hodges, it is to be stressed, is not merely extolling the virtues of topographic art, he is suggesting a means whereby topography may reach out and embrace the whole character and history of a region, and thereby occupy a higher place in the hierarchy of painting. Hodges's travels about the world had suggested to him a way in which landscape-painting, a neglected art, might be made to rival history-painting itself, still situated as it was in his day, at the theoretical apex of pictorial art. He makes this clear in the last paragraph of his book which he was to elaborate still further in later years:

> Many other tours in that interesting country (i.e. India) might be undertaken by the enterprizing artist. We know that the whole coast of Malabar possesses pictures-que beauty equal to any country on earth; and how valuable would be the representation of that scenery, whether as a natural object, or as connected with the history of the country, and the manners of the people? Pictures are collected from their value as specimens of human excellence and genius exercised in a fine art; and justly are they so: but I cannot help thinking, that they would rise still higher in estimation, were they connected with the history of various countries, and did they faithfully represent the manners of mankind.[77]

Another way in which landscape-painting could be endowed with the full dignity of history-painting occurred to Hodges towards the end of his painting career, after a return from a visit to the Continent which had taken him during 1790 as far as St. Petersburg. Late in 1794 he completed two large paintings, known as the *Effects of Peace* and the *Effects of War* and, renting some rooms, exhibited them in Old Bond Street together with twenty-three other paintings. He also issued a catalogue in which he inserted some new reflections on landscape painting:

> Upon maturely reflecting upon the nature of my profession, I have been led to lament a defect, and humbly to endeavour a remedy. I found that in the ancient and many of the modern masters of landscape, the greatest combinations of nature, and the most exact similitude, the happiest composition, and pencilling governed by the hand of Truth. But I confess there seemed very rarely to me any moral purpose in the mind of the artist. . . .
>
> It could not escape me that other branches of the art had achieved a nobler effect—History exhibited the actions of our heroes and our patriots, and the glory of past ages—and even Portrait, though more confined in its influence, strengthened the ties of social existence. To give dignity to landscape is my object. Whatever may be the value of my exertions, the design to amend the heart while the eye is gratified will yield me the purest pleasure by its success. I may flatter myself with an influence that will never be acknowledged; and the impression of these slight productions may be felt in juster habits of thought and conduct consequently improved. . . . Perhaps the enthusiasm of the artist carries me too far; but I hope and trust that my progress in this design may be serviceable to my country and to humanity.[78]

But Hodges's attempt to inject moral values into landscape-painting met with no immediate success. His paintings aroused the severe displeasure of Frederick Augustus, the Duke of York and second son of George III. The Duke visited the exhibition in January 1795, a few weeks after he had returned to London from

Flanders, where as Commander of the British expeditionary force he had been defeated disastrously by the French Revolutionary army under Carnot and had been lucky to escape being taken prisoner. He ordered that the exhibition be closed because of the political nature of the subjects. According to Edward Edwards the Duke asserted that 'no artist should employ himself on works which might tend to impress the mind of the inferior classes of society with sentiments not suited to the public tranquillity'. It was effectively the end to Hodges's career as a painter. With England at war with France and with the fear engendered by the French Terror at its height, people suspected of democratic sympathies feared for their lives. By March Hodges had decided to leave London, and sent no paintings to the Royal Academy exhibition of May 1795. In June he auctioned his collection of paintings at Christie's at the worst possible time, and received little for them. Retiring with his family to Devon he invested in a bank, but the firm could not withstand the severe banking crisis of March 1797. He died in great financial distress on 5 March 1797 from what was reported as 'gout in the stomach'.[79] But Farington asserted that he poisoned himself with laudanum.[80]

Hodges occupies a place in the development of English landscape-painting not dissimilar from that occupied by West in the development of English history-painting. That Hodges failed to gain fame where West succeeded is no cause for surprise. Like his master Wilson, Hodges found landscape-painting a precarious livelihood. But Hodges, like West, sought to commemorate contemporary and topical events of historic significance. Like West, he painted scenes in lands unknown to Greeks and Romans. As West sought to appeal to the 'law of the historian', so Hodges sought, in the end, to appeal to the laws of the historian and the natural historian. Like West, he sought to capitalize upon the popular and patriotic appeal of exotic wonders. And, lastly, in such paintings as *Oaitepeha Bay* and *Cape Stephens* he evolved a style of 'mitigated realism' in landscape which sought to combine the documentary art of the scientific voyages with the classical art of the academies.

Despite his failure as a painter it is arguable that Hodges's innovations went farther than West's and were fraught with more significance for the history of painting though the direct influence of his art was apparently small. In seeking to endow landscape-painting with moral values he foreshadowed Turner and Ruskin. On the other hand, his wash drawings of Antarctica, his *Cape of Good Hope*, *Matavai Bay*, and *Monuments of Easter Island* are fearless attempts to break with neo-classical formulas and to paint with a natural vision. He might well have been speaking of his own art when he wrote of Indian portrait-painting: 'A constant study of simple nature, it is well known, will produce a resemblance which is sometimes astonishing, and which the painter of ideal objects can never arrive at.'[81]

The arrival of Captain Furneaux in July 1774 with Omai, a native of Huahine, created a sensation in England.[82] Received with honour as a guest of Banks and the Earl of Sandwich, he mingled in fashionable circles with a natural grace and became a lion of London society (Plate 64). Reynolds painted a full-length portrait of him which reveals both how fashionable society adopted him as one of its members while viewing him at the same time as an exemplar of the noble savage (Plate 63), and Hodges painted for the famous surgeon, John Hunter, one which was much less idealized, more frankly realistic (Colour Plate 12). In the Reynolds portrait, an idealized exotic landscape elevates Omai's character, while the bare feet, the flowing robe, and the classic gesture (not unlike Reynolds's adaptation of the Belvedere Apollo in his earlier portrait of Keppel), all suggest its affinities with antiquity. Yet the painting is not so much a portrait of a noble savage as that of a self-confident

63. Sir Joshua Reynolds, *Omai*, canvas 236 × 146 in. (1775). Castle Howard, Yorkshire. Reproduced by courtesy of Mr. George Howard

80

civilized patrician.[83] In sharp contrast, Hodges's portrait of Omai, in keeping with the artist's quest for truth, has provided us with a much more faithful document of Omai's appearance. It accords well enough with Solander's verbal description of Omai, given in a letter written on 19 August 1774.

> He is very brown, allmost a[s] brown as a Mulatto. Not at all hansome, but well made. His nose is a little broadish, and I believe that we have to thank his wide Nostrills for the Visit he has paid us—for he says, that the people of his own country laughed at him upon the account of his flatish Nose and dark hue, but he hopes when he returns and has many fine things to talk of, that he shall be much respected.[84]

Hodges could not have painted Omai prior to his arrival in England in July 1774. He painted no known portraits of native peoples in oils during the voyage, indeed his stocks of oils were limited and were exhausted well before the *Resolution* returned to Cape Town. In any case Omai travelled back to London on the *Adventure* with Furneaux. As a low-born Raiatean he was not the kind of person who would normally have been depicted by Hodges, even in crayon, during the voyage. The engraving by Caldwall in the official account of the voyage (1777) was probably executed from a lost drawing by Hodges.

For the verse satirists, however, Omai, as noble savage, became a stock-figure of great use in the attack upon the morals and manners of contemporary society. The first of these was John Scott's *Second Letter from Oberea, Queen of Otaheite, to Joseph Banks, Esq., ... Brought over by his Excellency Otaipairoo, Envoy Extraordinary and Plenipotentiary from the Queen of Otaheite, To the Court of Great Britain. Lately arrived in his Majesty's Ship, the Adventure, Capt. Furneaux.* The satire, which was published in 1774, before any accounts of the second voyage in book form had appeared, returned to the already much-exploited passages in Hawkesworth, attacked the morals of the court, and transformed the theme of Arcadian melancholy (treated with dignity by Woollett) into mock heroics:

> But vain the wish, and vain th' impassion'd sigh,
> Corporeal pleasures are but born to die;
> What tho', with thee, beneath the bread-tree's shade,
> In ev'ry form of wanton love I've laid;
> What tho', at court, amidst my frolic ring,
> My self the vainest, and the fondest thing,
> What tho', entranc'd upon the rolling wave,
> Mutual we talk'd of joys, and mutual gave;
> The transport's fled, and nought is left behind
> Save the cold comforts of a restless mind.

Yet, despite its satire, the poem has some tenderness of feeling which reveals that Scott was not unaware that the figure of Omai, while still useful as a satirical device, was also a symbol of the life of nature around which much emotion and sentiment had gathered. He was half-serious and conscious of the romantic susceptibility of his readers when he wrote in a footnote to the poem:

> The language of Otaheite is so inexpressibly beautiful and melodious, that Oberea's letter may, with great propriety, be decreed a love song—The Author has only to wish he had been able, in this translation, to have done justice to the peculiar tenderness of its sentiments, and the unusual harmony of its periods.[85]

Despite such concessions to romantic sensibility a satirical temper continued to

OMIAH, the Indian from OTAHEITE, presented to their MAJESTIES at Kew, by Mr Banks & Dr Solander July 17, 1774.

64. *Omai, the Indian from Otaheite presented to their Majesties at Kew, by Mr Banks and Dr Solander, July 17, 1774*, unsigned engraving. Nan Kivell Collection, National Library of Australia, Canberra

dominate the poetry evoked by the South Pacific written during the 1770's. In 1775 the most virulent of all the poems of the Cook 'cycle' was published. It was called *An Historic Epistle, from Omiah to the Queen of Otaheite; being his Remarks on the English Nation*. An exhaustive denunciation of fashionable society is here put into the mouth of Omai who, as representative of the natural life, proceeded to condemn the evils and luxuries of Europe:

> Can *Europe* boast, with all her pilfer'd wealth,
> A larger store of happiness, or health?
> What then avail her thousand arts to gain
> The store of every land and every main:
> Whilst we, whom love's more grateful joys enthrall,
> Profess one art—to live without them all.

Omai then assails the condition of religion in England. First he criticizes the Established Church:

> Here bloated bishops loll in purple coach,
> On turtle dine and luxuries reproach
>
> .   .   .   .   .
>
> Whilst hackney curates starving on the town,
> *Retail* divinity for half a crown;

and, second, the Evangelists:

> Heav'n has no room, but merely to contain
> A cassockt, canting, methodistic train.

Both the warlike propensities and the imperial ambitions of European states are singled out for attack, for they,

> ... in cool blood premeditately go
> To murder wretches whom they cannot know.

83

Urg'd by no inj'ry, prompted by no ill,
In forms they butcher, and by systems kill;
Cross o'er the seas, to ravage distant realms,
And ruin thousands worthier than themselves.

Then in savage but clever burlesque the poet proceeds to castigate the evils of the day: the exploitation of honour, the pseudo-science of the virtuosi, and the chicanery of the law. It is all due, he concludes, to the senseless complexity of European civilization:

Not rul'd like us on nature's simple plan,
Here laws on laws perplex the dubious man.

Written in a similar satirical vein to *An Historic Epistle*, is *Seventeen Hundred and Seventy Seven; or, a Picture of the Manners and Character of the Age. In a Poetical Epistle from a Lady of Quality*. Omai had been taken back to Huahine when Cook left on his third voyage in July 1776. But the lady of the poem urges him to return because England has need, she points out, of many such natural men. Tourist connexions between England and Tahiti should be fully established for the people of the two islands have much to learn from one another. Tahitians will find many pleasures according to their enjoyment in England and in return they should be able to give 'the last polish to the sons of taste'. It is high time that an English *arioi* was established; time, too, that Tahitian fashions displaced the invidious domination of Italy. How much more would the sons of the nobility learn if they would only go to the South Seas instead of the Mediterranean for their grand tours! Thus in the same year that Hodges was introducing Tahitian motifs into the Italianate landscape, poets were using Tahitian customs to lampoon the servile veneration of anything Italian which they saw prevailing in fashionable society:

Nature and Art our souls in vain adorn,
The sober fear us, Macaronies[86] scorn;
That hateful race, disgraceful to our age,
Nor beauty warms, nor kindness can engage.

    .   .   .   .   .

Are these the men, these fading forms of air,
To bound the wishes of a British fair!
Hence, shadows, hence! unreal mockries rove,
Disgrace of manhood, and despair of love!
That maid's reproaches and the matron's gibe
To caves and wilds shall hunt the baneful tribe;
Still may derision wait the females' pain
Who looks for joy from such a flimzy train.

Come then, ye sons of Nature, and restore
The race of love, or pleasure is no more.
Our silken youths for you shall cross the line,
To dress your females and your boards refine;
Each travell'd peer shall bless you in his tour
With arts of play, and secrets of amour.
Yours, be our feathers, tinsels, paints, and lies,
Our playful frolicks, and our deep disguise:
Ours, be that want of feeling, or that pride,
Which bravely boasts what common mortals hide.
In pleasure's sources, what a gainful trade!

Of mutual science, what exchanges made!
Then shall perfection crown each noble heart,
When southern passions mix with northern art;
Like oil and acid blent with social strife,
The poignant sauce to season modish life.

It was a short step from the use of Tahitian life to criticize the shortcomings of English society, to the claim that European civilization would corrupt life in the Pacific islands. These evil effects are not stressed in satirical verse before 1779. At most they constitute a minor theme subsumed and softened by the more general theme of Arcadian transience, or else associated with the patriotic reminder that it was the French and not the English who introduced venereal disease into Tahiti.

In France, however, corruption by Europeans provided Diderot with the central subject of his *Supplément au voyage de Bougainville*, which he wrote in 1772. Diderot used a literary device common since the sixteenth century. An old Tahitian who had been silent during Bougainville's stay in the island rises and makes an impassioned speech as the French leave, deploring and denouncing this European intrusion into their island paradise:

> Nous sommes innocens, nous sommes heureux, et tu ne peux que nuire à notre bonheur. Nous suivons le pur instinct de la Nature, et tu as tenté d'effacer de nos âmes son caractère … tu as infecté notre sang.… Nos champs seront trempés du sang impur qui a passé de tes veines dans les nôtres, où nos enfans condamnés à mourir et à perpétuer le mal que tu as donné, aux pères et aux mères et qu'ils transmettront à jamais à leurs descendans.[87]

Diderot's *Supplément* was not printed, however, until 1796; and Hawkesworth, though entertaining sentiments similar to Diderot's, was sufficiently discreet not to condemn the voyages he had been paid to write. Not so George Forster. He admired the social equality of an island where a king could paddle his own canoe without loss of dignity. But he saw that already the simplicity and social equality of the Society Islands was giving way to luxury and inequality—as a result, he claimed, of the indolence of the chiefs. This trend, he argued, would be hastened by European intrusion. He therefore condemned European contact with the peoples of the Pacific:

> It were indeed sincerely to be wished, that intercourse which has lately subsisted between Europeans and the natives of the South Sea islands may be broken off in time, before the corruption of manners which unhappily characterizes civilized regions, may reach that innocent race of men, who live here fortunate in their ignorance and simplicity.[88]

And on another occasion he wrote:

> If the knowledge of a few individuals can only be acquired at such a price as the happiness of nations, it were better for the discoverers and the discovered, that the South Sea had still remained unknown to Europe and its restless inhabitants.[89]

George Forster's reflections provided the basis of the *Injured Islanders: or, the influence of art upon the Happiness of Nature*, a poem by Gerald Fitzgerald.[90] Again, the *Heroides* provided a form suited to the melancholy theme. But on this occasion it is Captain Wallis, the discoverer of Tahiti, and not Banks, whose absence is mourned by the forsaken Tahitian queen, Oberea. And whereas Scott was mainly concerned to lampoon Banks, Fitzgerald turns Oberea's unhappiness into a paradigm of the misfortune that has befallen all her people. The poem is thus of interest in that, while

85

preserving the pattern adopted by Scott's earlier satires, it witnesses to quite a different kind of emotional response to the native peoples of the Pacific. Sentiment replaces satire. Oberea's love for Wallis has destroyed her love for her country—no longer can she enjoy its natural pleasures. The poet, closely following suggestions from Forster, shows how European trade is quickly corrupting and degrading island life. An aura of sentimentality still surrounds everything Tahitian, but the sentimentalized heroes of the simple life are becoming sentimentalized victims of European corruption.

The idea of the noble savage was grounded in the belief that primitive man lived in harmony with natural laws that were universal, coherent, harmonious, and complete, and were, moreover, understood instantaneously by man through the agency of his reason. These laws are accessible to all men if only they would live as rational beings. They constituted for Voltaire the whole duty of man:[91]

> La morale uniforme en tout temps, en tout lieu ...
> C'est la loi, de Platon, de Socrate, et la vôtre.
> De ce culte éternal la Nature est l'apôtre.
> Cette loi souveraine en Europe, au Japon,
> Inspira Zoroastre, illumina Solon.

By about 1777, however, a sufficient number of accounts of travel in the Pacific existed to reveal the great disparity which existed between the universal laws of nature of the philosophers and the physical forces of nature studied by travellers in the Pacific. Instead of the *lex naturae*, revealed to man by virtue of his rationality, nature came increasingly to be considered as a climatic force operating upon the vegetable, animal, and human worlds alike. In the writings of the Forsters, M. Taitbout,[92] and Hodges, nature is conceived as a concrete geographical force acting upon men from without through the agency of climate. The guiding principles, if not the direct influence, now appear to proceed from the work of the Abbé du Bos,[93] Montesquieu[94] and Winckelmann.[95] George Forster, in his account of the voyage, discusses the effects of climate upon the physical, moral, and social condition of the primitive peoples he observed in the Pacific. J. R. Forster published such discussions in a more systematic form in his *Observations*, which appeared a year after his son's book. The *Observations*, in more ways than one, is a remarkable book.[96] The elder Forster was a learned man in several fields of contemporary science. The study of comparative philology, botany, and physical anthropology were special interests. In this last field he was acquainted with the work of Blumenbach, the pioneer craniologist, and the anatomical researches of John Hunter. Scornful of those philosophers who only studied mankind in their cabinets[97] or who only observed highly civilized nations, J. R. Forster came to believe, with some justification, that he was something of a pioneer in scientific method. He took as his object nothing less than 'the history of man in general, considered as one large body'. His method included the careful observation, recording and assembling of all facts bearing upon the life of primitive man. By an extensive use of the comparative method—he constantly contrasts the people of one island group with another—and the use of evidence gained from such distinct disciplines as meteorology, physiology, botany, geology, anatomy, and philology, he sought to study man as a whole. 'My object was nature in its greatest extent; the Earth, the Sea, the Air, the Organic and Animated Creation, and more particularly that class of Beings to which we ourselves belong'.[98] By equipping himself as a trained observer and then studying primitive man in the field, he became a pioneer of social anthropology. Likewise, through his own work and the great influence which his son was to exert later upon forming the interests of Alexander von Humboldt, he may be counted as one of the fathers of modern geographical science.[99] It may be noted that J. R. Forster's desire to study man as a whole also animated the thinking of Herder in writing his *Ideen zur Philosophie der Geschichte der Menschheit* (1784–91). 'As everything in the world has its philosophy and science', he wrote, 'there must also be a philosophy and science of what concerns us most nearly, of the history of mankind at large.'[100] And it was in the *Ideen* that J. R. Forster received what was perhaps his finest tribute. Herder learned much from the *Observations*,[101] and wrote:

> The Ulysses of these regions (i.e. the South Pacific), Reinhold Forster, has given us such a learned and intelligent account of the species and varieties of the human race in them, that we cannot but wish we had similar materials for a *philosophico-physical geography* of other parts of the world, as foundations for a history of man.[102]

J. R. Forster, asserting that climate acted upon the physiology of man to affect his mental, moral, and social life, claimed that the native peoples of the most favourable climatic regions of the earth, such as the inhabitants of the tropical islands of the Pacific, retain something of the 'original happiness' of man. The primitive peoples of less-favoured regions, such as the Fuegians and Tasmanians, have fallen from a state of original happiness to a degraded preternatural state. Climate, however, can be modified by the effects of education, whereby man can raise himself from his primitive condition by his own resources. J. R. Forster was thus no thorough-going climatic determinist. His theory combined the notion of climatic control with both the idea of chronological degeneration—a falling away from original happiness—and the idea of progress, achieved through education. This theory, as he applied it to the peoples of the Pacific, helped to modify considerably the simpler primitivistic conceptions of Pacific islanders given currency by the writings of Bougainville and Hawkesworth.

In the year following the publication of J. R. Forster's *Observations* a pamphlet was published in Paris entitled *Essai sur l'isle d'Otahite située dans la mer du Sud et l'esprit et les mœurs de ses habitans*. Written by M. Taitbout its purpose was to assist in some way 'operer la revolution générale et tant desirée, et à qui l'esprit humain devra un jour l'association libre, entière et parfaite de tous les hommes'.

Like John Reinhold Forster, Taitbout emphasizes the great need for compiling a stock of exact information concerning native peoples, and claims, again like Forster, that natural man is very much what the climate makes him. His ideas on climatic control, however, were drawn directly from Montesquieu; and his discussion of the life of the savage owes much, if indirectly, to Rousseau's *Discours sur l'inégalité*. It is perhaps unlikely that Taibout read Forster's *Observations* but he did read George Forster's *Voyage* and other accounts of Cook's first two voyages. His essay, indeed, is largely a scissor-and-paste series of interpolations from them. When he discusses, for instance, the growth of inequality among the Tahitians, the ill effects of labour and prostitution upon the lower classes of the island, and the equally bad effects of idleness and luxury upon the higher classes, he is not expressing his own ideas[103] but borrowing directly from George Forster. Taitbout's pamphlet is of interest, not for the originality of its ideas, but because it reveals how notions of geographical control deriving from Montesquieu and applied by the Forsters to the islanders of the Pacific, could provide a rational explanation for the soft primitivism with which Bougainville, Hawkesworth, Banks, Diderot, and others, had endowed the peoples of the Society Islands, and add point and fire to a revolutionary pamphlet.

The ideas of the Forsters concerning the effect of climate upon primitive people are also traceable in contemporary English poetry. They occur, for instance, in the first book of Cowper's *Task*, which the poet began to write in July 1783, in a passage clearly inspired by his reading of Pacific voyages. For Cowper, as for the Forsters, the civilized life is more calculated to make man virtuous than the life of nature. Natural man is a fierce creature who only acquires civilized habits slowly:

> Blest he, though undistinguish'd from the crowd
> By wealth or dignity, who dwells secure,
> Where man, by nature fierce, has laid aside
> His fierceness, having learnt, though slow to learn,
> The manners and the arts of civil life. (ll. 592–6.)

Cowper had heard of those virtues which were said to ennoble the harsh and austere lives of primitive peoples dwelling in hard environments, but he was most doubtful about the existence of such virtues. In a passage immediately preceding the one quoted above he describes a crowd of gypsies as rather brutalized human beings, who at most, possess a certain animal vigour and resistance to disease. But the virtues of hard primitivism are for Cowper as harsh and unattractive as the people who possess them. It is only in civilized countries that,

> ... virtue thrives as in her proper soil;
> Not rude and surly, and beset with thorns,
> And terrible to sight, as when she springs
> (If e'er she spring spontaneous) in remote
> And barb'rous climes, where violence prevails,
> And strength is lord of all; but gentle, kind,
> By culture tam'd, by liberty refresh'd.

And, so proceeds Cowper's thought, if virtue is to be found in primitive man, it is certainly not to be found among those who live in extremely cold climates. The primitive inhabitant of such regions rises little above the level of the brute:

> His hard condition with severe constraint
> Binds all his faculties, forbids all growth
> Of wisdom, proves a school in which he learns
> Sly circumvention, unrelenting hate,
> Mean self-attachment, and scarce aught beside.
> Thus fare the shiv'ring natives of the north,
> And thus the rangers of the western world,
> Where it advances far into the deep,
> Towards th'antarctic.

The people of the tropical islands of the Pacific are a little better off than such Laplanders and Fuegians, but not much better, for their easy life allows them to sink so easily into luxury and vice:

> Ev'n the favour'd isles,
> So lately found, although the constant sun
> Cheer all their seasons with a grateful smile,
> Can boast but little virtue; and, inert
> Through plenty, lose in morals what they gain
> In manners—victims of luxurious ease.
> These therefore I can pity, plac'd remote
> From all that science traces, art invents
> Or inspiration teaches; and enclosed
> In boundless oceans, never to be pass'd
> By navigators uninformed as they, ...

In these passages, even in the matter of allowing the Tahitians (quite obviously he is thinking of them) a little natural virtue while decrying the degeneration that a bountiful climate brings with it, Cowper is thinking along lines similar to the Forsters.

Henry James Pye (1745–1813), who became Laureate in 1790, in his long poem *The Progress of Refinement*, published in the year that Cowper began the *Task*, expressed similar views concerning the virtues of savages. The poem is concerned with showing how taste and the arts have been transmitted from the earliest times from one civilized society to the next. For Pye, as for John Reinhold Forster and Cowper, refinement is an educational process. Primitive societies, on the other hand, are dominated by the climate and the soil:

> What else exists beneath the cope of heaven
> Is to the savage tribe of wanderers given,
> Who unrestrain'd by precept or by law,
> From climate, and from soil, their difference draw. (ll. 731–4.)

Primitive man is neither naturally good nor naturally bad; he is what the climate makes him:

> Amid the wild expanse of southern seas
> Where the blest isles inhale the genial breeze,
> The happier native in the fragrant grove

65. William Hodges, *The Taj Mahal*, oil on canvas, 39 × 49½ in. (*c.* 1785–95). National Gallery of Modern Art, New Delhi (Acc. no. 2316)

Woos the soft powers of Indolence and Love:
But where more keen the ray, more rude the gale,
Manners less mild and harsher laws prevail;
Till in the sad extremes of polar frost,
The sacred beam of human reason lost,
Man scarcely rises from the shaggy brood
That prowl insatiate o'er the icy flood. (ll. 741–50.)

It is possible that Pye gained his ideas concerning the moral state of savages directly from reading the works of the Forsters, for he enjoyed reading travel books. It was Pye, Hodges tells us, whose influence and persuasion induced him to publish his *Travels in India*.[104] Its importance was acknowledged by Reynolds in his Thirteenth Discourse (1786): 'The Barbaric splendour of those Asiatic Buildings, which are now publishing by a member of this Academy, may possibly . . . furnish an architect, not with models to copy, but with hints of composition, and general effect, which would not otherwise have occurred.'[105]

Travels in India was the first book to introduce the British public (and through it Europe) to the beauties of Islamic architecture. Confronted by the beauty of the Taj Mahal (plate 65), which he painted more than once, Hodges wrote:

The effect is such as, I confess, I never experienced from any work of art. The fine materials, the beautiful forms, and the symmetry of the whole, with the judicious choice of situation, far surpasses anything I ever beheld.[106]

It was doubtless the shock of realising that the beauties and perfection of Islamic architecture were little known and less appreciated by Europeans that led Hodges to give serious thought to the history and origins of architecture. In *Travels in India* he republished an essay on architecture which he had first published[107] separately to accompany plates of Indian views issued after his return from India in 1784. This essay which thus first appeared so shortly after the poems of Cowper and Pye, also depends largely upon the idea of climatic control to explain the behaviour of primitive peoples. A product of Hodges's extensive travelling the essay sought to explain the emergence of architectural styles in terms of climate and building materials. His ideas, doubtless, owe something to Vitruvius, but the real stimulus to his thought, as he himself tells us, came from his travels:

Thus far I can venture to state, not only from what I have read, but likewise by a stronger conviction, from what I have seen in the various climates and parts of the world in which I beheld mankind, in almost every stage of negative or positive civilisation.[108]

66. *A Column taken from the Temple of Vis Visha at Benares Engraved by T. Medland, from a drawing taken on the spot by W. Hodges R. A., in Hodges, Travels in India* (1793)

Hodges's essay was directed against the classical as the sole standard of architectural excellence. Admitting the great beauty of Greek architecture, he asserts that there is no reason at all why it should be admired exclusively. Egyptian, Hindu, Moorish, and Gothic architecture also possess majesty, boldness, and magnificence. Yet people affect to despise them simply because their forms are more varied and cannot be reduced to the precise rules of Greek art (Plate 66). But, says Hodges, the excellence of architecture does not depend upon simplicity, strength, and elegance, and upon columnar beauty; it depends rather upon the great masses and forms of the buildings themselves, upon their strength and symmetry, and their convenience for the people who use them. 'That Greek architecture comprises all that is excellent in art, I cannot help considering as a doctrine which is in itself as erroneous and servile, as in its

90

9. Sydney Parkinson, *Three Maori Canoe paddles from Cook's first voyage*, wash and watercolour, $11\frac{5}{8} \times 9$ in. (*c*. 1769). British Library, Add. MS 23920, f. 71a

10 (following pages). William Hodges, *Oaitepeha* (Tautira) *Bay, Tahiti* (detail). Also called 'Tahiti Revisited'. Canvas, $36\frac{1}{2} \times 54\frac{1}{2}$ in. (1776). National Maritime Museum, London. On loan from the Ministry of Defence—Navy

12. William Hodges, *Omai*, panel, 24 × 20 in. (*c.* 1775–7). Royal College of Surgeons, London

11 (preceeding pages). William Hodges, *The Monuments of Easter Island* (detail), canvas, 30½ × 48 in. (*c.* 1775/6). National Maritime Museum, London. On loan from the Ministry of Defence—Navy

13. John Webber, *Poedooa (Poetua), Daughter of Oree, Chief of Ulietea (Raiatea), one of the Society Islands*, canvas, 57 × 37 in. (*c.* 1780). National Library of Australia, Canberra

No 1

Toha

14. P.G. de Loutherbourg, *Toha*, watercolour, 7½ × 12 in. (1785). National Library of Australia, Canberra. (*Towha*, here seen in martial dress, was the supreme god of Tahiti in the *Omai* pantomime.)

consequence it is destructive of every hope of improvement.'[109] Perhaps our veneration for Greek art, Hodges suggests, is the result of our education. Examining his own mind on the matter, he finds himself agreeing 'from habit and education' that no buildings are more beautiful than Greek temples. And yet he also finds himself 'entertaining a similar partiality for countries, where different models have been brought to an equal perfection.'[110] Travel had given Hodges a comprehensive and eclectic taste in architecture more common in the succeeding century. Architecture, he wrote, begins from simple prototypes. Men are born neither with tools to build with nor with any innate ideas concerning the forms of the buildings in which they should dwell. They are born with a native awareness of their needs and with abilities to improve their situation—'as the country affords, and as the climate will suggest'.[111] In past ages even the kings of Ithaca and Britain sought shelter in the hollow trees and thick foliage of the forest. Today primitive people still imitate such shelters as those, but make them more permanent:

> They appear evidently imitated in the wigwams of the torpid, wretched, unsettled Pecherais on the frozen coast of Terra del Fuego; of the equally independent, but not more fortunate New Hollanders, in a milder climate; and of the more civilized and sagacious hunting savages of North America.[111]

Wigwams such as these, Hodges continued, are similar in form from country to country, they differ only in the nature of the materials. When, however, the 'wandering families of hunters and fishermen' become stationary and grow into large numbers, they proceed to give their dwellings 'as much amiability and conveniency' as their climates, materials, and manner of life will admit of. Even so they are not likely to deviate from the original form of the wigwam to any great extent, rather, the original form will be improved and embellished,

> ... into the various thatches and huts which I have seen in the South Sea Islands, and which the Negroes on the Coast of Guinea, and the Hottentots, inhabit; high and low, circular or square, open at all sides, inclosed with palisades, matting, or wicker work, hurdles, lattice, or mud walls. They will raise them on piles above the ground, and, as it were, suspend them in the air, in countries where the dampness of the soil, or sudden inundations, would endanger their lives and property; as on the banks of the Marannon, or Oroonoko, in Guiana, and in the inland parts of Surinam: they will keep them low, and, as it were, sink them under ground, in cold climates, where heavy blasts of wind and snow teach them such methods of self-defence. Wandering nations of herdsmen, fishermen and warriors, such as the Arabs, Calmucks, Mongols, Tonquesees, Tartars, Esquimaux, Greenlanders, Laplanders, Samojedes, and Osticks, find in the skins of their cattle, of their flocks, and of their fishes, materials; and in their camels, horses, bullocks, and fishing boats, conveyances of portable huts, and imitations of their original wigwams, huts and tents, which in shape will differ more or less according to the different materials they are made of.[112]

All such buildings, Hodges believed, would retain their original forms to the extent that the builders themselves remained unmixed and unassimilated with other racial groups, and each nation 'will regard their primitive habitations with the same eye of partiality as they are prejudiced in favour of their particular countries.' However, when a people grows opulent, ambitious, and powerful, the original dwellings are enlarged and embellished. When members of a tribe or nation migrate to other lands, they take the style of their dwellings with them. The genius of the people will at last stretch and improve the style 'to the last degree of perfection of which it is capable.'[113] This, Hodges claims, is what happened to Greek and Roman architecture. It also happened to Chinese architecture which was based on a bamboo-tent prototype. In Chinese architectural construction the slender and tapering form of the bamboo admitted both of higher proportions and of wider intercolumniation than the marble blocks of the Greeks. It follows therefore that the Chinese ideal of architectural beauty differs fundamentally from the Greek ideal being based upon different constructional principles. It follows equally that it is misleading to apply Greek canons of beauty to the principles and methods of Chinese buildings. Hodges, it will be seen, in his attack upon the authority of Greek architecture foreshadows, in some ways, the modern architectural theory of functionalism:

> Architecture undoubtedly should, and must be adapted, to all climates and countries which mankind inhabit, and is variously, more than any other art, influenced by the nature of the climate and materials, as well as by the habits and pursuits of the inhabitants.[114]

Architecture in short, Hodges concluded, is to be understood as the 'spontaneous produce of genius in different countries; the necessary effects of similar necessity and materials'.[115] It followed that each style possessed its own peculiar form of beauty.

Clearly these reflections upon architecture parallel in more ways than one Hodges's reflections upon landscape-painting; and both arose from a deep awareness of the variety of climates and cultures upon the face of the globe. But the functional element in his reflections upon architecture appears to owe something to the writings of Carlo Lodoli, to whom he is doubtless referring when he writes: 'I have not read Father Ladola's famous dissertation on the absurdity of the misplaced and unprincipled imitation of Greek architecture.'[114] Even though he had not read the dissertation, he appears to have come under the influence, albeit indirectly, of Lodoli's ideas.

It has been suggested that the belief in the natural virtue of primitive man would have passed out of common currency much earlier than it did, had it not been for the discovery of the Society Islands.[116] There is, however, evidence which suggests that the opposite view, namely, that man had risen stage by stage from a lower to a higher form of existence, was promoted by information won from the Pacific as a whole.[117] Some of it has already been discussed. There is reason to believe that, although at the outset of Pacific exploration the accounts of Bougainville and Hawkesworth stimulated the notion that the Society Islands preserved something of the Golden Age, the steady accumulation of information concerning natural history and man in the Pacific contributed materially to the eventual triumph of the idea of evolution over primitivistic theories during the second half of the nineteenth century. While it may be said that the Pacific contributed much to one of the last chapters of the long history of primitivism, it also began to contribute to theories of evolution from the moment they became influential in eighteenth-century thought.

Lord Monboddo (1714–99) was one of the early champions of the theory of evolution. During the last quarter of the eighteenth century he became widely known throughout Europe as the advocate of a theory of progress which asserted that man and the higher apes belong to the same species. Man in his original state, he claimed, following Rousseau, lived an isolated and brutish existence. In his *Origin and Progress of Language* (1773–6), Monboddo made extensive use of material which he found in accounts of Pacific voyages. It is true that he followed the view then widely held that 'the golden age may be said yet to exist in some of the countries that have been discovered in the South Sea, where the inhabitants live, without toil or labour, upon the bounty of nature in those fine climates.'[118] But Monboddo was careful to warn his readers that the idea of the Golden Age, transmitted to Europeans by the ancients, had been 'embellished and exaggerated after the manner of poets'. The legend, he claimed, only serves to reveal that man in his natural state was a frugivorous animal living very simply upon herbs and fruits produced spontaneously from the earth. That man was not originally an animal of prey 'seems to be proved by what M. Bougainville relates' concerning his landing upon the Falkland Islands: 'all the animals came about him and his men; the fowls perching upon their heads and shoulders, and the four-footed animals running among their feet.' They would not have acted so, said Monboddo, were it true that man was by nature a beast of prey. Even so, most natives, at some time or other, became cannibals, any doubt of this being entirely removed by the testimony of Banks and Solander in their voyage to the South Seas, 'where they found, in the country called New Zealand, a people who fed on human flesh; but were, in other respects, far from being a barbarous or inhuman people.'[119] Man, Monboddo pointed out, when he becomes a beast of prey, unlike other carnivores, shows no distaste for the flesh of his own species.

In support of his argument that man in his original condition lived in a brutish state, Monboddo cited several ancient authors, particularly Diodorus Siculus, supporting their evidence by the accounts of modern travellers. He mentions the case of the fish-eaters of south-west Arabia, from Diodorus, who 'went naked, and lived entirely by fishing, which they practised without any art, other than that of making dikes or mounds of stones, to prevent the fish that had come with the full tide into the hollows and gullies upon that coast, from going out again with the ebbing tide, and then catching them in these ponds as in a net.'[120] Now this, Monboddo points out, is precisely the fishing method used by the New Hollanders today, as described to us by Dampier. 'This Dampier', he wrote, 'appears to me to be one of the most accurate and judicious of our modern travellers; so that, when we find him agreeing in his account of the customs of barbarous nations, with an ancient historian, whom I am persuaded he never read, nor perhaps ever heard of, we can hardly doubt of the truth of the fact.'

The second case cited by Monboddo, again taken from Diodorus, is that of the *Insensibles*. These people lived promiscuously with other animals, particulary with seals, but the most extraordinary thing about them was that they never used water or any other kind of liquid. 'This, I think', wrote Monboddo, 'is less incredible than what more than one modern traveller has told us of people in the South Sea, that when they had occasion to be long at sea, supplied the want of liquids by drinking sea-water.'[121] Monboddo made considerable use of Charles de Brosses's *Histoire des navigations aux terres Australes* (1756). From de Brosses he cited Jacques L'Hermite, a traveller who found the Fuegians living like brutes: 'without religion, or policy, or any the least regard to decency'.[122] De Brosses also provided Monboddo with Roggeveen's report of having found an island in the Pacific where, so far as he could ascertain, the people had no form of government. And it was in de Brosses that Monboddo read of certain islands 'in the South Sea, to the north of the line', visited by Drake, 'where he found inhabitants who had the nails of their fingers about an inch long, which he understood served them for offensive arms.'[123] Therein also he read of a people encountered by Jacob Le Maire in New Guinea, 'who used their teeth as an offensive weapon, and bit like dogs.' Among such people, Monboddo observed, 'if there was any government . . . it must have been very imperfect, and of late institution.'

Monboddo draws all his examples, it will be observed (with the significant exception of the New Zealand cannibals), from voyages published prior to those of Bougainville and Hawkesworth. It was these last, of course, which had given fresh life to the belief that man in his natural state was happy and virtuous. It appears clear that Monboddo did not think of the life in the Society Islands as constituting the original condition of man at all. For him such a state was better exemplified by the accounts of Fuegians and New Hollanders, who lived a life closer, as he said, to animals. That Monboddo was greatly interested in Pacific exploration as a new field for the study of man is clearly revealed by a remark made after discussing the cases of natural men from the Pacific already quoted above. 'This is all', he wrote, 'so far as I have observed, that has hitherto been discovered in the South Sea concerning the natural state of men there. But we have reason to expect from those countries, in a short time, much greater and more certain discoveries, such as I hope will improve and enlarge the knowledge of our own species as much as the natural history of other animals, and of plants and minerals.'[124]

Monboddo, then, gained many of his ideas concerning the nature of man from his reading of South Sea voyages, and his ideas, in their turn, influenced at least one author of an imaginary voyage to the Pacific in describing a people encountered there. This was the author of *The Travels of Hildebrand Bowman, Esquire, into Carnovirria, Taupiniera, Olfactaria, and Auditante, in New Zealand; in the Island of Bonhommica, and in the powerful Kingdom of Luxo-Volupto, on the Great Southern Continent. Written by Himself; who went on shore in the Adventure's large Cutter, at Queen Charlotte's Sound New Zealand, the fatal 17th December 1773; and escaped being cut off, and devoured with the rest of the Boat's crew, by happening to be a-shooting in the woods; where he was unfortunately left behind by the Adventure* (1778). As the title suggests, Bowman's *Travels*, though introduced by circumstances attending Cook's second voyage, really belongs to the fictitious voyage literature so frequently used as a vehicle for satire during the seventeenth and eighteenth centuries. The motto on the title-page of the book at once reveals the author's interest in the notions of Monboddo: 'An Ape, and Savage (cavil all you can), Differ not more, than Man compared with Man.' His descriptions of the Taupinierans reveals the author following rather closely Monboddo's notions of a people in a pure state of nature. Bowman's Taupinierans lived in caves by the sea, where they huddled together during the day snorting and snoring 'in the midst of putrid fish and their own nastiness',[125] coming forth at night to hunt for shell-fish which, eaten raw, was their sole diet. Bowman recounts how he succeeded in dragging a male member of the species out of a cave and examined it in the light of day when he found that apart from its bushy beard it was quite naked and that, although it possessed human form, the face resembled that of a hog and had eyes like a mole (Plate 67). These people were too stupid and sluggish to aspire to any form of personal adornment, neither tattooing nor ear and nose ornaments being found upon them. After overcoming an initial revulsion at the sight of such loathsome creatures, Bowman succeeded in making friends with one of the Taupinieran boys. 'All animals', the author points out, 'when young, are prettier, and more playful, than those come to maturity.'[126] The acquaintanceship enabled him to make a further discovery. 'One evening when we were at romps, I discovered to my great surprise, that he had a short tail, like that of a young pig; being scarcely able to believe my own feeling, I examined it over and over, and found it an undoubted truth.... both sexes were furnished with these small appendages.'[127] Monboddo had described primitive fish-eaters, cave-dwellers, and people furnished with tails. On the question of tails the author indirectly admitted his indebtedness to Monboddo's book in the process of making a satirical thrust at the Scottish philosopher's credulity:

> I am apprehensive that my veracity may be here liable to suspicion; which has set me on reading books of travels, and examining the opinions of authors on that

67. Engraved illustration in
*The Travels of Hildebrand
Bowman* (1778)

subject, since my return home. Great was my joy, to find that several travellers had seen men with such rear appendixes; which a learned judge in the northern part of this island has made a collection of, and, after a thorough examination, gives entire credit to. It is also very satisfactory to me, that this my account of the Taupinierans, will give a singular pleasure to this learned gentleman; who has been sneered at by some smatterers in knowledge, on this very account.[127]

One other quality of Bowman's Taupinierans deserves mention. They were nocturnal animals:

Their blindness in the day, and clear-sightedness in the dark, became from repeated observations a fact not to be doubted by me; however contrary it may be to the common course of nature all over the world, both in men and most kinds of animals. I shall not pretend to account for this phenomenon, unless the resemblance of their eyes to those of moles, may be thought sufficient for that purpose. But it may be asked, Did nature form those people's eyes, on purpose for their peculiar way of living in the side of that mountain?[128]

The nocturnal nature of the people finds no parallel in Monboddo and may be taken as another extension to the field of biology of those ideas of antipodal inversion so often present in the descriptions of the political institutions of southern utopias.

103

Another factor which helped to stimulate the idea of progress at this time was the wide interest being taken in zoophytes. The copious collections of corals brought back from the Pacific helped greatly to augment this interest. These plant-animals as they were called were said to occupy a crucial link in nature's chain since they constituted the link between the plant and the animal kingdoms. 'As the *zoöphyte* is in the middle betwixt the vegetable and animal', wrote Lord Monboddo, 'so *man* appears to occupy the space betwixt the several classes of animals.'[129] The crucial task of identifying the zoophyte (actinozoa) as an animal and not a plant had fallen to John Ellis in his *Essay towards the Natural History of the Corallines* (1755). Ellis's scientific interests possessed a strong aesthetic cast. In 1751 he received a collection of 'sea plants' from Anglesey and Dublin and in order to preserve the rarer specimens remarkable for their colour:

> ... expanded them on paper in fresh water, laying out their ramifications with some exactness.... These when properly dried, I dispersed on thin boards covered with clean white paper, in such a manner as to form a kind of landscape .... designing a Variety of Hills, Dales and Rocks which made a paper ground work and keeping for the little trees which the expanded plants and corallines not inaptly expressed. [Plate 68]

With these miniature marine landscapes, the ancestors of today's indoor aquaria, Ellis amused the Princess Dowager of Wales and the young princesses.[130] Solander, who brought back many rare corals from the Pacific, co-operated closely with Ellis in his work and together they produced the second important work on the subject, the *Natural History of many Curious and Uncommon Zoophytes* (1786). The subject became one of considerable interest not only to virtuosi but also to the public. The Duchess of Portland assembled an enormous collection of corals. Indeed, when her collection came to the auction rooms the engraved frontispiece of the sale catalogue gave pride of place to the Portland vase from the neck of which protruded a great length of coral (Plate 69), a fitting reminder to prospective buyers that the Duchess's vast collection contained wonders both of nature and of art. And Sir Ashton Lever[131] devoted a room to zoophytes in his Museum which made a feature of Pacific curiosities. In 1786 the Austrian scientist, Ignatius Born,[132] in the course of praising Thomas Martyn[133] on the quality of his illustrations of natural history, exclaimed, in a letter to him: 'What gratitude would not the world owe you, Sir, if you would not undertake a work, such as this, on the Zoophytes!'[134] Born's desire for fine illustrations of the smaller marine animals was to be satisfied by those natural-history draughtsmen employed on scientific voyages during the first half of the nineteenth century.

Quite apart from the physical construction of corals the formation of coral islands suggested a solution to the problem of yet another vital link in the great chain of nature, namely that between the organic and inorganic worlds. Banks, Cook, and the Forsters had brought back descriptions of the coral islands of the Pacific. In 1778 John Whitehurst published his *Inquiry into the Origin and Formation of the Earth*. The formation of coral islands formed a crucial aspect of Whitehurst's inquiry.

Whitehurst was a clock-maker of Derby, a member of the Lunar Society, and a close friend of Erasmus Darwin and Josiah Wedgwood. He was also very well acquainted with William Hodges who married Whitehurst's niece upon returning from India.[135] Banks, Erasmus Darwin, and Hodges all subscribed to Whitehurst's book. In it he claimed that the Golden Age once had a real existence at the beginning of the world. The first land to arise from the all-embracing ocean of the earth consisted, he claimed, of small islands composed of the shells and corals of animals.

68. *Groupes of different Corallines growing on Shells, supposed to make this Appearance on the Retreat of the Sea at a very Low Ebbtide*, engraving after Charles Brooking by A. Walker, in John Ellis, *An Essay towards the Natural History of the Corallines* (1755), frontispiece

69. Frontispiece to the *Catalogue of the Portland Museum*, 1786.

Indeed all the lands of the world had such an organic origin. The primeval islands raised as they were only a few feet above the level of the sea received their moisture only through nocturnal dews, for in those days there was no rain, the sea-water was fresh, there were no mountains or storms, and the moon had not been formed. Whitehurst thus combined a belief in the idea of a Golden Age with a theory of cosmic progress. What is considerably more important, however, is that Erasmus Darwin incorporated Whitehurst's theory into his *Economy of Vegetation*, published in 1791;[136] a poem in which he foreshadows the theory of evolution to be stated more fully in his *Zoonomia* three years later. The poet is addressing the gnomes who attended the fiery birth of the planet when it was thrown from a volcano upon the sun:

> You trod with printless steps earth's tender globe,
> While ocean wrapp'd it in his azure robe;
> Beneath his waves her hardening strata spread,
> Raised her primeval islands from his bed,
> Stretch'd her wide lawns, and sunk her winding dells,
> And deck'd her shores with corals, pearls and shells.
>
> O'er those blest isles no ice-crown'd mountains tower'd
> No lightnings darted, and no tempests lower'd.
> Soft fell the vesper-drops, condensed below,
> Or bent in air the rain-refracted bow,
> Sweet breathed the zephyrs, just perceived and lost;
> And brineless billows only kissed the coast;
> Round the bright zodiac danced the vernal hours,
> And Peace, the cherub, dwelt in mortal bowers! (Canto 2, ll. 33–46)

In such passages Erasmus Darwin is seeking, as Hodges had sought in his painting *Oaitepeha Bay*, to contain new geographical knowledge within the framework of traditional classical forms. Neither attempt was entirely successful; but out of the painter's failure came an anticipation of naturalistic landscape, and out of the poet's, the first fully formulated theory of organic evolution.

4. *Cook's Third Voyage*

COOK sailed on his third voyage on 12 July 1776 with the *Resolution* and *Discovery*, the principal object being the discovery of a northern sea passage from the Pacific to the Atlantic. In the secret instructions issued to him he was required, among other things, 'to survey, make charts, and take views of such bays, harbours, and different parts of the coast, and to make such notations thereon, as may be useful either to navigation or commerce'. He was also required to observe the nature of the soil, animals, fowls and fish found on new coasts, and 'in case there are any peculiar to such places, to describe them as minutely, and to make as accurate drawings of them, as you can'.[1]

For the preparation of these graphic records Cook, apart from his own outstanding work, relied upon his officers and made a point of seeing that he had trained people to help him with the work. 'I had several young men', he wrote, 'who, under my direction, could be usefully employed in constructing charts, in taking views of the coasts and headlands near which we should pass, and in drawing plans of bays and harbours in which we should anchor.'[2]

On this voyage the number of supernumeraries borne on the books of the two vessels was reduced to a minimum. From the Admiralty's point of view they had proved difficult. Banks had quarrelled with the Navy Board, and Cook's relations with the Forsters were anything but pleasant. On this occasion, therefore, a naturalist was chosen from within the service. William Anderson (?1748–78), surgeon's mate on the *Resolution*, became in fact, if not in name, the expedition's naturalist, and William Ellis, surgeon's second mate on the *Discovery*, acted as a natural-history draughtsman. A professional draughtsman was, however, considered essential—the man chosen being John Webber (1752–98).

Webber was born in London, his father being a sculptor of Bern, where John received his first art training. His teacher was John Louis Aberli (1723–86), a German painter and engraver who specialized in the production of picturesque coloured views of Switzerland that were popular and widely imitated. From Bern the municipal authorities sent Webber to Paris to continue his studies where he worked under J. G. Wille.[3] In 1775 he proceeded to London and attended classes at the Royal Academy. A portrait of his brother Henry, a sculptor, which he exhibited at the Academy in 1776, attracted the attention of Dr. Solander and this led to his appointment as artist to the expedition.

Although Webber, like Parkinson and Hodges before him, assisted in the drawing of coastal and harbour views, and also of plants and animals, the preparation of such drawings was not his main responsibility. The type of picture he was expected to provide derived partly from those ideas concerning the supplementation of written records which Banks had sponsored and partly from the success of published accounts of the first two voyages. In other words his paintings had to be both faithful and entertaining. Or, as Cook himself put it:

... that we might go out with every help that could serve to make the result of our voyage entertaining to the generality of readers, as well as instructive to the sailor and scholar, Mr. Webber was pitched upon, and engaged to embark with me, for the express purpose of supplying the unavoidable imperfections of written accounts, by enabling us to preserve, and to bring home, such drawings of the most memorable scenes of our transactions, as could be executed by a professed and skilful artist.[4]

Consequently, Webber's work is essentially illustrative. He sought to depict as faithfully as he could not only memorable incidents but also the dresses, houses, and customs of the people visited on the long voyage. He drew vegetation both in its individual plant forms and in mass with great care and attention, as though he was seeking to satisfy the critical eye of professional botanists. Indeed, it is likely that the care which he took in thus depicting plant forms was influenced by the sustained interest in botany which characterized the three voyages. This must be stressed. For the minute precision of his rendering of plant forms is a feature only of his finished work. That he could draw with great fluency, considerable breadth, and with a feeling for amplitude and mass is revealed in the rough sketch, probably made on the spot (Plate 70) and in the wash drawing (Plate 71) of the *Resolution*'s company shooting sea-horses. The oil-painting of the subject which he exhibited at the Academy in 1784, as might be expected, was more closely finished (Plate 72). But it was his insistence upon botanical detail that frequently destroyed the pictorial unity of his finished work. Few water-colour painters of Webber's day sought out the minutiae of vegetation with the same zeal. The topographic painters, for instance, though they rendered buildings with accuracy, usually treated foregrounds and distances with considerable freedom, to add variety and interest to the composition.[5] Much eighteenth-century topographical painting uses foliage as a setting to some item of architectural interest. But Webber frequently makes an exotic plant: a coconut, a bread-fruit, or a plantain (Plate 73) the central interest of his painting, and renders botanical detail with care and accuracy up to the limits of his frame.[6]

Webber, however, lacked Hodges's experimental attitude to his art. He sought to represent tropical light and colour by tinted colour, which, at most, produced a paleness of tone. Certainly, the problem of depicting the brilliance of tropical light and colour was not to be solved by the tinted manner of early English water-colour.[7]

Webber was, a prolific worker and no voyage undertaken in the days before photography ever returned so well documented with pictorial illustrations. Nor had so great an area of the earth's surface come under one artist's observation. From the cold south in Kerguelen's Land to the cold north in Nootka Sound, Webber drew plants, animals, peoples, and landscapes in all their geographical variety—shamen, fetishes, human sacrifices, native masks, Chinese sampans, winter huts in Siberia, temples in Macao, New Zealand cannibals, South African Hottentots, Cook Islanders, Society Islanders (Colour Plate 13), Hawaiians. The people and the landscapes of all the five oceans of the globe came, as the eighteenth century put it, under his pencil.

By means of engravings Webber's illustrations were destined to find a very large public. When the official account of the voyage was published in 1784, its title-page stated that the three volumes contained 'a great Variety of Portraits of Persons, Views of Places, and Historical Representations of Remarkable Incidents, drawn by Mr. Webber during the Voyage, and engraved by the most eminent artists'. The time taken for the completion of the engravings was one of the reasons for the delayed

70. John Webber, *Sea Horses*, charcoal and wash, $5\frac{3}{8} \times 10\frac{1}{8}$ in. (1778). Public Archives of Canada, Ottawa, Hodges-Webber drawings, 1-10

71. John Webber, *Sea Horses*, pencil and wash, $6\frac{3}{8} \times 11\frac{3}{4}$ in. (1778). Public Archives of Canada, Ottawa, Hodges-Webber drawings, 1-11

72. John Webber, *A Party of the Resolution and Discovery shooting Sea Horses*, canvas, $49 \times 61\frac{1}{2}$ in. (*c.* 1784). The Admiralty, White-hall. By permission of the Government Art Collection (Admiralty Collection)

publication of the voyage. The fact that so many of London's best-known engravers in the two or three years before 1784 were spending a good deal of time on engraving exotic landscapes that were of special interest to virtuosi and naturalists like Banks, could not have passed unnoticed even in Academy circles. In this connexion it is perhaps not without significance that Reynolds in his 11th Discourse (1782) criticized just the kind of landscape which Webber had brought home from his extensive voyage round the world:

73. John Webber, *The Plantain Tree in the Island of Cracatoa*, coloured aquatint, in *Views in the South Seas*, London (1808), pl. iv

74. John Webber, *The Fan Palm, in the Island of Cracatoa*, coloured aquatint, in *Views in the South Seas*, (1808), pl. xvi

> A landscape painter certainly ought to study anatomically (if I may use the expression) all the objects which he paints; but when he is to turn his studies to use, his skill, as a man of genius, will be displayed in showing the general effect . . . for he applies himself to the imagination, not to the curiosity, and works not for the virtuoso or the naturalist, but for the common observer of life and nature.[8]

It was all very well for Reynolds to lay down the law, but in practice, in the professional practice of painting in England in the 1780's, things were never as clear cut as that. Landscape-painters found it necessary from time to time, if not actually to work for botanists and virtuosi, then to have some regard for their taste in drawing. And at the time, 'the common observer of life and nature' was frequently to be found upon his knees examining her smaller productions with all the enthusiasm, if not the knowledge, of virtuosi and professional botanists. Five years after Reynolds made his pronouncement the first issue of the *Botanical Magazine* sold 3,000 copies. In 1789 Gilbert White published his *Natural History and Antiquities of Selborne*, a book in which a passionate enthusiasm for the minutiae of landscape is manifest throughout. On Cook's third voyage Webber had drawn a *Fan Palm in the Island of Cracatoa* (Krakatoa), in which the palm itself was featured as the central interest and a native girl at right as

75. *Nymphaea Nelumbo* or
Sacred Egyptian Bean,
aquatint by Burke and
Lewis after Henderson
(1804). Robert Thornton,
The Temple of Flora
(1799–1807), pl. 30

merely a pictorial embellishment (Plate 74). Here was one way in which the precision of botanical illustration could influence the practice of landscape-painting. Twenty years after Webber drew his *Fan Palm*, Robert Thornton was publishing his great folio *The Temple of Flora* to which many distinguished artists contributed and in which flowers were shown in their natural settings (Plate 75). The art of botanical illustration and the art of picturesque landscape were beginning to meet on common ground—and each art was beginning to influence the other.[9]

Editions of Cook's *Voyages* were, of course, widely read in all the main languages of Europe. There were sixty-one engraved plates after Webber's drawings published with the official account of the third voyage. The greatest care was taken in their printing and publication and their fame soon spread throughout Europe. Herder, writing shortly after their publication, saw in them new opportunities for the comparative study of man: 'Cook's last voyage', he wrote, 'if we may trust what Fame says of its engravings, commences a new and higher period, the continuation of which in other parts of the world I ardently desire ...'.[10] These plates, frequently supplemented by earlier plates after Buchan, Parkinson, and Hodges, passed from edition to edition, and from engraver to engraver, for a period of some fifty years. During this period Europeans gained their knowledge of the Pacific to a considerable extent from Cook's *Voyages*, and the visual impression formed must have been due in large measure to the engravings (often distorted and degraded in the process of transmission from one translation to another). Until the 1830's these engravings held the field virtually unchallenged for the illustration of editions of Cook, and they had become the chief source for illustrations concerning the Pacific in all kinds of publications—travel books, geography texts, missionary tracts, and articles on the Pacific in journals, newspapers, encyclopaedias of costume and exotic wall-papers. Translated into the medium of woodcut, lithograph, and steel engraving they continued to do service throughout the second half of the century. Hodges had found it difficult to sell his landscapes of the Pacific and India, but towards the end of the century, stimulated by the romance of Cook's *Voyages*, the interest in the exotic landscape steadily grew. Between 1788 and 1792 Webber was able to publish a series of sixteen plates of Pacific views, which were etched and coloured by himself.[11]

The engravings published in Cook's *Voyages* provided new visual information about many previously quite unknown peoples, and greatly enlarged Europe's knowledge of the family of man. Dr. Jöppien has shown how important encyclopaedias of costume and 'gallery of nation' books were in this process of popular dissemination. But as artists copied the engravings so they altered them still further in the direction of European pre-conceptions, the anthropological and ethnographic intentions of the originals being diverted increasingly to fulfil the demands of taste and the intrinsic needs of decoration. A fascinating example is the hand-coloured etching published by St.-Sauveur, the finest of the costume encyclopaedists of the late eighteenth century. Depicting the people discovered as a result of the voyage of Cook and La Perouse, it was based on figures included in his *Encyclopédie des voyages* (1795–6) (Colour Plate 17). St. Sauveur's work in turn inspired the fine series of wall-papers produced by Josef Dufour at Macon in 1804, entitled *Sauvages de la mer Pacifique*. Arranged as a series of colourful panoramas they were sold as a set accompanied by a prospectus which advised that without leaving his own home 'the reader of the histories of travel can imagine himself among those nations ... and will become familiar with their costumes and the diversity of nature'.[12] These colourful elaborations however did more to satisfy the delight in the exotic which is such a prominent feature of the Empire style than it did to convey accurate information, which was now distanced four or some-times five times from the original field drawings upon which the designs were ultimately based.

Even for artists working in the field the depiction of the people of Oceania remained a problem. Although Webber drew exotic landscapes with great accuracy, his figure

76. John Webber, *Cook meeting Inhabitants of Van Diemen's Land*, pencil, pen and wash, 26 × 38⅜ in. (1777). Naval Historical Branch, Ministry of Defence, London

drawing retained the facility and attenuated proportions of much late eighteenth-century draughtsmanship, particularly in Switzerland (Plate 76).[13] When engravers like Bartolozzi and Sherwin came to engrave the plates for Cook's third voyage such stylistic features became even more pronounced and natives were still seen, for the most part, as noble savages, despite contemporary criticism of the engravings in Hawkesworth (Plates 77, 78). Herder, as we have seen, had high hopes concerning Webber's plates and expressed the wish that 'the accurate and natural-historic manner of delineating the human species ... be extended uninterruptedly to all regions of the globe.' But a note in the 1803 English edition of Herder's *Ideen*, by a friend of the translator who signed himself F (George Forster?), claimed that by comparison with Hodges's work

> ... still greater deviations may be suspected, to have been committed by the artist, who attended Cook's last voyage. Either he, or the engraver, to whose favourite tool the department of antarctic forms was entrusted, seems to have sacrificed the realities before his eyes to a faint reminiscence, and stale repetition of Cipriani-Beauties.[14]

Curiously enough the first Academician to protest against such a sacrifice of reality was, as we have seen, Hodges himself in his *Travels in India* (1793).

The publication of Cook's last voyage and the publication of copious extracts from it in journals and newspapers created widespread public interest in England during the 1780's. English landscape-painters like Alexander Cozens[15] and William Gilpin[16] read accounts of strange landscapes in Cook's *Voyages* with fascination. 'The latest Discoveries appear to engross conversation from the politest circles and throughout every class of the Kingdom', wrote Thomas Banks in the preface to his *Universal Geography* in 1784.[17] The Theatre Royal, Covent Garden, with an eye to something topical decided to stage *Omai: or a Trip Round the World* by John O'Keefe (1747–1833)

77. *A Young Woman of Otaheite, bringing a Present*, engraving after John Webber by Bartolozzi, in Cook and King, *Voyage to the Pacific Ocean*, London (1784), pl. 27

78. *A Young Woman of Otaheite, dancing*. Engraving after John Webber by J. K. Sherwin, in Cook and King, *Voyage to the Pacific Ocean*, London (1784), pl. 29

79. *Omai's Public Entry on his first landing at Otaheite*, engraving after Daniel Dodd by Royce, in [J. Rickman], *Journal of Captain Cook's last Voyage to the Pacific Ocean*, London (1781), f.p. 136

as its Christmas pantomime for 1785. First performed on 20 December 1785 it became a great success being repeated fifty times during the season, once by Royal Command. In the autumn of 1786 it was revived for another eight performances, and in the spring of 1788 for yet another eight.

It was ten years since Omai had visited England but the recently published account of his return to the Society Islands in Cook's *Voyage to the Pacific Ocean* brought him back into the public eye again. For example, John Rickman, the second lieutenant on the *Discovery*, published an anonymous account of Cook's third voyage in 1781. In it he provided a most graphic account of Omai's return to Tahiti. Among the many gifts showered upon him when he left London to return home with Cook was a sword from Banks and a suit of mail from Lord Sandwich, that had been specially fashioned for him by the armourers of the Tower of London. A couple of days after the *Resolution* arrived at Vaitepiha Bay, Tahiti, Omai was to be seen, according to Rickman's account, 'dressed cap-a-pie in a suit of armour ... mounted and caparisoned, with his sword and pike, like St George going to kill the dragon'. Daniel Dodd drew an appropriate illustration for Rickman's *Journal*, adding Cook himself as Omai's accompanying officer (Plate 79).

Needless to say, with such astounding material to work with, O'Keefe's pan-

tomime, like Dodd's illustration, did not keep close to historical fact. In the play Omai—actually the son of a dispossessed native of Huahine—is heir to the Tahitian throne. The opening scene reveals a *marae* in Tahiti by moonlight. Otoo, father of Omai and descendant of the legal kings of the island, is revealed invoking the ancestral genii to help his son to the throne. Towha, the guardian genius of Omai, appearing in the garb of a chief mourner, informs Otoo that Omai must visit England and win the hand of Londina. With his servant Harlequin (who with Columbine provides comic relief in escapades with Don Struttolando and a clown), Omai visits London, eventually gains Londina, and returns in triumph with her to Tahiti, stopping at many places visited by Cook on the way home. After outwitting the enchantress Oberea, Omai is enthroned with his queen in the final scene which takes place on the 'great bay of Otaheite at sunset'. The pantomime concludes as a mad prophet addresses the native ambassadors who have come from all over the Pacific to witness Omai's coronation. He enjoins them to swear fealty to their new sovereign who, because of his exalted position in being 'the owner of fifty red feathers, four hundred fat hogs, and the commander of a thousand fighting men and twenty strong-handed women to thump him to sleep', is acclaimed as a monarch well worthy of their reverence. Furthermore, the mad prophet concludes, because Omai has married Londina, King George will see to it that he never wants. A patriotic finale completes the pantomime when an English captain and sailors pay a choral tribute to Cook as an enormous painting of his potheosis is slowly lowered to the floor of the stage.

The pantomime, despite its preposterous plot, occupies an important place in the history of realism in theatrical costume and scenery. Philip de Loutherbourg was in charge of the costume and *décor*.[18] It was the last, the most realistic, and the most successful of his many commissions.[19] He built his production around arresting light effects and nautical *mirabilia*. The model for one of his scenes has fortunately been preserved (Plate 80). A review of the first night's performance[20] speaks of moonlit scenes, showers of hail, the moon red—and in eclipse—sunrise effects, a storm at sea, the snowy rocks of Kamchatka, and a 'dreary ice island'. Loutherbourg's source for both his dress designs (Plate 81, Colour Plate 15) and his stage scenery was the published engravings after Webber and Hodges. O'Keefe also made considerable use of Cook's account of the third voyage. Apart from the moonlit *marae* of the opening scene and the 'bay of Otaheite' of the final scene, Loutherbourg also introduced views in Kamchatka, Tongatabu, Hawaii. At the end of the pantomime the procession of the 'nations' included representatives from the Cook, Sandwich, and Society Islands,

81. P. J. de Loutherbourg,
Obereyaee, Enchantress, dress
design for the pantomime
*Omai: or a Trip Round the
World*, watercolour, $7\frac{1}{2} \times 12$
in. (1785). National Library
of Australia, Canberra

from Easter Island, and from Kamchatka, Oonalashka (Unalaska), Nootka, and
Prince William's Sound. For these costumes and settings realism of scenery and
costume were combined on a scale never before attempted on the stage—the whole
spectacle being put on at tremendous expense. The views of places visited by Cook
were 'all of them finished in a style so superior', wrote the *London Chronicle*'s reviewer,
quoted above, 'that they appear the product of a new effort in the art of painting,
untried before'. The splendour of the production lingered in the memory of playgoers
for many years. 'The success of this elegant entertainment seems to have stampt a
character upon the theatre itself, which has since constantly adhered to it', wrote J.
Boaden forty years later.[21] Here, then, in the theatre as in painting the representation
of exotic landscapes and peoples was a harbinger of naturalism. In this connexion it is
not without interest to note that Reynolds, like many other distinguished artists, was

117

present at the first night, and 'expressed the utmost satisfaction at all the landscape scenes'.[22]

The success of the pantomime did not pass unnoticed in Paris. In October 1788 *le Théatre de l' Ambigu-Comique* announced a pantomime in four acts *La Mort du Capitaine Cook* by M. Arnould. It followed the pattern of the *Omai* pantomime and was every bit as popular with the public. An English version of *La Mort du Capitaine Cook* was billed at Covent Garden in the following year. The announcement read: *The Death of Captain Cook: a grand Serious-Pantomimic-Ballet, In Three Parts. As now exhibiting in Paris with uncommon Applause with the original French Music, New Scenery, Machinery, and other Decorations*. While playing in London, separate productions were presented at Dublin, Hull, Limerick, and perhaps other provincial centres. The programme summary published in Limerick for the performance at the New Theatre Royal there, advertised the play 'as now exhibiting in London, Dublin and Paris, with universal applause'.

La Mort du Capitaine Cook is set in the island of O-Why-e (Hawaii). The curtain rises on a pleasant landscape with native huts dotted here and there, and a volcano in the distance. Émaï, a native girl with royal connexions, chooses Oki as her lover. During the marriage ceremony the rejected lover Étoé challenges his rival and is beaten in the struggle that follows. A storm rises and distress shots are heard from a ship at sea. In the second act Cook is received by the native king who gives him fruits in exchange for many gifts. A dance follows, Cook sitting beside the king. Later the king and his ladies go on board Cook's ship for refreshment, which makes the native warriors anxious for the king. But Cook and the king return to the shore. During a love scene between Émaï and Oki, Étoé attacks the latter who is saved by the timely intervention of Cook. A fight then ensues between the followers of Cook and the king, and the forces of Étoé, who is taken prisoner with a follower, and is about to be tortured when Cook fires a cannon in disapproval. The natives, frightened, give up the plan. But Étoé, still revengeful, stabs Cook in the back while he is pardoning him. In dying Cook shoots Étoé. In the last act a *marae* is seen in the centre of the stage, and the volcano erupts spectacularly and continuously as the pantomime draws to a conclusion. Sailors bring in Cook's body. The lovers Émaï and Oki 'plongés dans la plus profonde tristesse, et les yeux baignés de larmes, s'approchent lentement et en silence du marai, qu'ils contemplent quelques instants avec une doleur concentrée'. With this solemn echo of the death in Arcadia theme and a native funeral dance in honour of the hero Cook, the play concludes.

As with *Omai: or a Trip Round the World*, the success of the French play depended to a great extent upon the uses of realistic costume and the use of a spectacular naturalism in the presentation of the settings. The producers of the original French play felt that a special effort should be made to present it as realistically as possible. This is made clear in a printed account of the pantomime.

> On s'est proposé d'amener sur la scène un spectacle vraiment neuf et singulier, et qui offrît en même-tems quelqu' intérêt. La Mort tragique du Capitaine Cook, assassiné par des Insulaires qu'il combloit de bienfaits, a paru réunir tous ces avantages. On a tâché que ce célèbre Marin se montrât d'une manière digne de lui, autant que le permettoient les bornes qu'on a dû nécessairement se prescrire; et l'on sent bien que les convenances Théâtrales ne nous ont pas toujours permis de suivre la vérité à la rigeur. Nous l'avons rendue le mieux qu'il nous a été possible, dans le costume, les mœurs, les danses des Sauvages de la mer du Sud.[23]

In other words, the conventions of the theatre required that the death of Cook should not be presented with strict adherence to fact but that he should be presented ideally as a tragic hero.[24] On the other hand, the costumes and settings were to be presented as faithfully as possible. Idealized action and realistic staging was combined in the exotic pantomime.

When Banks retired from Cook's second voyage with his party of artists and naturalists Johan Zoffany, who was to have shipped aboard the *Resolution* with Banks, went instead to Italy.[25] In Italy he probably absorbed a good deal of the theory of neo-classical history-painting then so fashionable in Rome. Zoffany, however, maintained contacts with Banks and others who had travelled in the South Seas. In 1783, four years after his return from Italy, he visited India at the invitation—it is said—of his friend Hodges. It is possible that Hodges discussed with Zoffany (after the painter's arrival in Calcutta and before Hodges's departure for England in December 1783) some of the problems which beset the artist travelling in countries beyond Europe. It has already been shown how such problems were occupying Hodges's mind and how he was groping towards a theory of landscape-painting which would endow it with the dignified qualities of history-painting. How far was it possible in history-painting to combine the ideal style championed by Winckelmann and Mengs with the insistence upon faithful reporting required of honest ravellers? Fortunately, Zoffany had the highly successful precedent established by West's *Death of Wolfe* to rely upon in the field of history-painting, whereas Hodges had to work out the landscape problem for himself. After West's resounding success with his painting, and Woollett's engraving after it, the presentation of contemporary history in the manner of Hodges's and Cipriani's 'landing' engravings courted both public disapproval and trenchant criticism from well-informed—if not academic—sources.

82. Johann Zoffany, *The Death of Cook*, canvas, 54 × 73 in. (*c.* 1795). National Maritime Museum, London

83. *A Man of the Sandwich Islands with his Helmet*, engraving after Webber by J. K. Sherwin, in Cook and King, *Voyage to the Pacific Ocean* (1784), pl. 64

84. Battle relief from the Heroon at Gjölbashi-Trysa (*c.* 420–410 BC). Kunsthistorisches Museum, Vienna

Zoffany returned from India in 1789. A lover of the theatre and a man who had been closely associated with Garrick before the advent of de Loutherbourg, it is most probable that he saw *The Death of Cook* which was running at Covent Garden and in the provinces at the time of his return. Zoffany knew many of the friends of Cook and had probably met him. In the circumstances the play might well have suggested to the painter the subject for his history-painting, the *Death of Cook* (Plate 82), which he painted between 1789 and 1797.[26] Already several other painters including John Webber, D. P. Dodd, John Cleveley, and George Carter, had painted versions of the death of Cook.[27] These were all based more or less faithfully upon the account of Cook's death published in his *Voyage to the Pacific Ocean*—the painters seeking to produce nothing more than a popular pictorial account of the tragedy. Zoffany, however, sought to produce a monumental historical composition in the grand manner. The pantomime itself could have possibly suggested not only the subject but also, to some extent, the treatment of the subject. For the pantomime did, in fact, present Cook as an ideal tragic hero; but the costumes and sets were treated realistically. It is rather doubtful, however, whether the presentation of the pantomime could have taught Zoffany much that he had not known already. For his experiences in Rome and the precedent already established by West were all he needed to guide him. Zoffany used the pose of the *Discobolus* in Charles Townley's collection, for Cook's murderer, and posed Cook himself in the manner of the Dying Gaul. Thus the highly idealized figure of a noble savage was made to confront a figure even more noble, a tragic hero of empire, in a timeless and historical situation. What helped to make the classical echoes so plausible was the fact that the headgear of the Hawaiian chieftains (Plate 83) was similar to the helmet worn by the ancient Greeks (Plate 84). The Polynesian helmet helped to bridge the gulf between the neo-classical rendering of the protagonists and the realistic rendering of the costumes and settings. Zoffany's *Death of Cook* thus provides further evidence of the intrusion of naturalistic elements into the highest levels of academic painting. This empirical naturalism may owe something to the wide popular appeal which the subject held for all Englishmen at this time, but it undoubtedly owes most to those standards of faithful recording explicitly enunciated by Hodges, and championed by Banks and his influential circle of virtuosi and naturalists—a circle with which Zoffany was intimately associated.

The death and achievements of Cook were also commemorated by several poets. One of the first, and the most widely read, was Anna Seward's *Elegy on Captain Cook*, published in 1780, only a few months after news of Cook's death reached England. By the following year it had reached its third edition and a fourth (encouraged doubtless by the appearance of the official account of Cook's death in *A Voyage to the Pacific Ocean*) appeared in 1784. Anna Seward was a close friend and neighbour of Erasmus Darwin and the influence of his poetry is apparent in her poem. Like him she sought to incorporate scientific and geographical *mirabilia* within a poetic framework of heroic couplets, personification, and classical allusion. In seeking to portray Cook as a highly idealized and tragic hero while attempting at the same time to convey vivid impressions of the countries and regions through which he passed, she set herself a problem much like Zoffany's. But the result was considerably less successful; for the conjunction of classical mythology and exotic naturalism was more incongruous in poetry than in painting. This may be observed, for example, in her endeavour to adapt classical form and allusions to the romantic imagery of the polar seas:

> Light on the icy rock, with outstretch'd hands,
> The Goddess of the new Columbus stands.
> Round her bright head the plumy Peterels soar,
> Blue as her robe, that sweeps the frozen shore;
> Glows her soft cheek, as vernal mornings fair,
> And warm as summer sun her golden hair;
> O'er the hoar waste her radiant glances stream,
> And courage kindles in her magic beam,
> She points the ship its mazy path, to thread,
> The floating fragments of the frozen bed
>
> . . . . .
>
> While o'er the deep, in many a dreadful form,
> The giant Danger howls along the storm
> Furling the iron sails with numbed hands
> Firm on the deck the great Adventurer stands;
>
> . . . . .
>
> Round glitt'ring mountains hears the billows rave,
> And the vast ruin thunder on the wave—
> Appall'd he hears! but checks the rising sigh,
> And turns on his firm band a glistening eye.—
> Nor for himself the sighs unbidden break,
> Amid the terrors of the icy wreck;
> Not for himself starts the impassioned tear,
> Congealing as it falls;—nor pain, nor fear.

Reynolds in commenting upon West's *Death of Wolfe* and the *Omai* pantomime had given his sanction to naturalism in the presentation of contemporary events of historic significance—both real and imagined—when these events occurred in distant lands. It is of interest therefore to note that Dr. Johnson, the official guardian of classical values in literature as Reynolds was in painting, made a somewhat similar concession to the claims of exotic naturalism when he said to Anna Seward in reference to *The Colombiade*, by Madame du Boccage: 'Madam, there is not in it anything equal to your description of the sea around the North Pole, in your Ode on the death of Captain Cook.'[28]

W. Fitzgerald's *Ode to the Memory of the late Captain James Cook*, also published in 1780, is no better, as poetry, than Anna Seward's *Elegy*. It does, however, provide evidence of the effect which the news of Cook's death had upon current attitudes to the peoples of the South Seas. For Anna Seward the islanders are still people endowed with natural sensibility and a freedom of emotional expression which they have derived from the simplicity of the 'natural' life. For her the death of Cook resulted from the treachery of individual natives. But this is not the attitude taken by Fitzgerald for whom the death of Cook reveals the true nature of the savage:

> From old time had brooded here
> Incurious languor, sordid strife,
> Want rapacious, toil severe,
> (Ills that flow from savage life)
> Sullenness, with low'ring eye,
> Stifling gentle sympathy;
> Disease untrac'd and ling'ring pain,
> That felt the wild magician's charm in vain
> Here did th' inglorious native wear away
> The blissful night, the prowling day
>
> .   .   .   .   .
>
> Whose darken'd mind in mercy found no joy,
> Who vengeful—conquer'd only to destroy.

In Zoffany's *Death of Cook* the heroic, suffering Cook and the idealized savage who murders him confront one another, both noble beings, in a moment of classic tragedy. But in Fitzgerald's poem the noble savage, we might say, by the very act of killing the hero of empire has transformed himself into 'the inglorious native'. As incidents occurred involving the death of famous navigators, European writers and artists began to take a less friendly attitude to the native peoples of the Pacific. The guilt for individual atrocities was laid upon the native character in general. Certainly broad distinctions such as the gentility of the Society Islanders and the ferocity of the New Zealand Maoris continued to be drawn. But the death of commanders like Marion du Fresne and Cook, the massacre of the men of Furneaux, and later those of La Pérouse, did much to bring about some fundamental revisions in European thought concerning the nature of 'savages' in general. Three years after the appearance of Fitzgerald's poem Julien Crozet delivered a fierce tirade upon the savage character in his *Nouveau voyage à la mer du Sud*. Crozet had seen his captain, Marion du Fresne, butchered by the Maoris on the New Zealand coast in 1772. The incident, not unnaturally, helped him to form very strong views about the nature of savages:

The Children of Nature are now so much praised and extolled as having more virtues and less vices than those who are called cultured, because their upbringing has cultivated their minds to a higher perfection. For my part, I contend that among all created animals there is nothing more savage and dangerous than the natural and savage peoples themselves. I would rather meet a tiger or a lion, since I expect to distrust them and to protect myself from such wild beasts. My opinion is founded on what I have seen myself.

I have followed the profession of the sea from my young days, and have never possessed the happy leisure to be able to give my life to the reflections with which Philosophers are educated; but I have journeyed through a great part of the world, and have found that when reason among the peoples of Nature, as among animals, is not facilitated and perfected through a good upbringing, then they are given to the passions of rapacity, violence, and treachery....

I endeavoured to stimulate their curiosity, to learn the emotions that could be awakened in their souls, but found nothing but vicious tendencies among these Children of Nature: and they are all the more dangerous in that they greatly surpass Europeans in physical strength.

Within the same quarter of an hour I have found them to change from childish delight to the deepest gloom, from complete calmness to the greatest heights of rage, and then burst into immoderate laughter the moment afterwards. I have noticed them change towards each other, one moment caressing, and menacing the next; but they were never long in the same mood, and always struck me as having dangerous and deceitful tendencies.[29]

One of the interesting features of Crozet's description is that it contains a description of the emotional volatility of native peoples which agrees substantially with picture drawn by the champions of soft and sentimental primitivism. But whereas they interpreted emotional volatility as evidence of natural virtue Crozet interpreted it as evidence of natural viciousness. Crozet's statement thus becomes an important landmark in the transition from the European concept of the noble savage to its opposing concept, the ignoble savage.

But the image of the noble savage was never entirely eradicated from European thought, for the belief in the natural goodness of savages was, at bottom, a belief in the natural goodness of man. Anders Sparrman records how Crozet once told Jean Jacques Rousseau himself the details of the Marion massacre and something of the true character and behaviour of the New Zealand savages. 'Is it possible', Rousseau replied, 'that the good Children of Nature can really be so wicked?'[30]

Since European thought was so preoccupied with the philosophy of nature during the eighteenth century, the arts and crafts of the Pacific made nothing like the impression the peoples themselves did. The very idea of art, implying industry, was not easily to be incorporated within the Arcadian dream of islanders who gained their bread and milk without toil from the trees. Neither in the poetry nor in the paintings and engravings evoked by the early voyages are the people of the Pacific imaged as craftsmen. At most their arts appear as attributes of dress, or separately as ethnographical illustrations. The only native art that gained wide attention from Europeans from the beginning was the dance, for the dances were interpreted not as evidence of native artistry but of savage freedom.

A genuine interest in the primitive arts of the Pacific developed, however, from an interest in curiosities, an interest present at all times in the history of travel but specially cultivated by the English virtuosi of the seventeenth and eighteenth centuries. Native artefacts were collected by Banks and his party on the *Endeavour's* voyage, and drawings made of them. 'I was highly entertained at Oxford with a sight of some curiosities you sent from Otahieta and new Zealand', wrote Falconer to Banks on 16 January 1773.[31] Zoffany was greatly interested in curiosities from the Pacific and the Orient and made a large collection of them. Indeed, there appears to have been some agreement between him and Banks, when preparations were being made for the second voyage, that the painter should receive not only a thousand pounds for the voyage but also 'a third share of all curiosities'.[32]

To say that an object was 'curious' was to express an interest in it without passing an aesthetic judgement. Thus Parkinson speaks of New Zealand paddles as 'curiously stained',[33] fish-hooks and whistles as 'curiously carved',[34] and Maoris as 'curiously tattooed'.[35] Similar comments were made by Banks and Cook in their journals of the

85. Long hand club (*Tiaha*), Museum für Völkerkunde, Vienna. (Previously in the Leverian Museum, London.) From Kaeppler (1978), p. 192

86 (far right). Wood carving (possibly from a canoe), New Zealand, length 11½ in., width 2½ in. Göttingen (OZ 323). From Kaeppler (1978), p. 201

first voyage. Travellers, for all that, could not but help admiring many of the objects they observed and collected, so that phrases in which aesthetic approval, however qualified, is implicit arise simultaneously. So Parkinson found the head of a canoe 'singularly carved',[36] certain native carved work 'very ingeniously wrought',[37] canoes that were 'carved with great ingenuity and painted very neat', and a flaxen garment 'ornamented with a beautiful wrought border'.[38]

Cook was among those who found something to admire in Polynesian carving. Concerning Tahitian canoes he wrote: '. . . they have high curved sterns the head also curves a little and both are ornamented with the image of a Man carved in wood, very little inferior work of the like kind done by common ship carvers in England'.[39] In his view the carving upon New Zealand canoes was 'neither ill designed nor executed'.[40] Parkinson was more specific:

> The men have a particular taste for carving: their boats, paddles, boards to put on their houses, tops of walking sticks, and even their boat valens, are carved in a variety of flourishes, turnings and windings, that are unbroken; but their favourite figure seems to be a volute, or spiral, which they vary many ways, single, double, and triple, and with as much truth as if done from mathematical draughts: [Plate 85] yet the only instruments we have seen are a chizzel, and an axe made of stone. Their fancy, indeed, is very wild and extravagant, and I have seen no imitation of nature in any of their performances, unless the head, and the heart shaped tongue hanging out of the mouth of it, may be called natural. [Plate 86][41]

During the second voyage, although opinions vary from one observer to another, comment upon the whole was more favourable, and value judgements more frequently made. George Forster, for example, writes concerning Maori art: 'All their

124

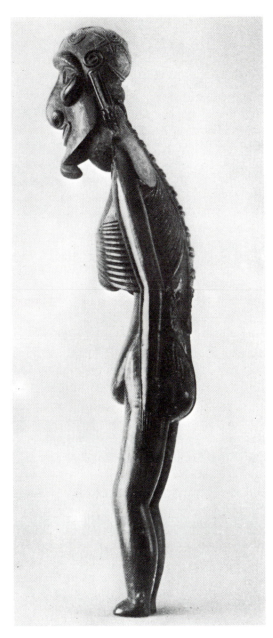

tools were very elegantly carved and made with great attention.'[42] Their cloaks 'had elegant borders' and they 'might have passed for the work of a much more polished nation'.[43] The clubs of the Cook Islanders were 'as highly polished as if our best workmen had made them with the best instruments'.[44] The craft work of the Cook Islanders revealed that they 'want neither taste to design, nor skill to execute whatever they take in hand'.[45] And, on the third voyage, William Anderson describes the New Zealand canoes as being ornmented 'in such a manner as not only shows much design' but 'also great labour and patience in the execution'.[46]

At Easter Island, platforms of masonry were found not inferior to the best plain pieces of English masonry.[47] Small pieces of carving seen there were considered to be both well designed and well executed.[48] (cf. Plates 87, 88) Neither Cook nor George Forster, however, was impressed by the grotesque features of the large statues (Plate 89). 'The eyes, nose, and mouth were scarcely marked on a lumpish ill-shaped head; and the ears, which were excessively long ... were better executed than any other part, though a European artist would have been ashamed of them.'[49] As might be expected the travellers found it easier to accommodate their critical judgements to the

non-representational carving than to any work which involved unnatural proportions in the human figure. When George Forster wrote about the figurehead on a Maori canoe, for example, he called it: 'A misshapen thing, which with some difficulty we perceived was meant to be a human head, with a pair of eyes of mother of pearl, and a long tongue lolling out of its mouth'.[50] But even when proportions were unnatural, comment was not always uncompromising. George Forster wrote that the wooden figurines of Easter Island were 'wrought in a much neater and more proportionate manner than we could have expected, after seeing the rude sculpture of the statues. They were made to represent persons of both sexes; the figures not very pleasing, and the whole figure much too long to be natural; however, there was something characteristic in them, which showed a taste for the arts.'[51]

The music and song of the peoples of the Pacific were not in general commented upon so favourably as the glyptic arts. A New Zealand wind instrument 'made a very uncouth kind of braying'[52] while a trumpet from a large whelk produced 'a hideous bellowing'.[53] Tahitian music, consisting of but three or four notes 'without variety or order, was only a kind of drowsy hum, which could not indeed hurt the ear by its discordant sounds, but made no pleasing impression upon our minds'.[54] Nor was the music of the Cook Islands much better. A musical instrument was found which had a range of four or five notes. 'Its resemblance to the syrinx, or Pan's flute of the civilized Greeks, dignified it more than any music it contained.'[55] On the third voyage Anderson was not so severe: ... 'they produce a pleasing, yet simple, music, which they vary much more than one would think possible.'[56] James Burney, son of a musician and musicographer, predictably paid more attention to the music he heard in the Pacific when serving as second lieutenant on *Adventure* on Cook's Second Voyage. The musice of the Society Islands did not impress him at all and he had nothing to say about it. Maori music he found rather better, though there was 'no great variety' in it, the flutes being 'more curious for their carving then for any music that can be got out of them'. Songs he heard at Queen Charlotte Sound were better than elsewhere and he wrote a tune he heard down on a stave, noting that the first two bars were repeated continuously 'till their words are expended' and then closed with the last bar. 'Sometimes they Sing an underpart which is a third lower except the 2 last notes which are the same.'[57]

Tongan music was the most interesting of all.

> ... they sing in parts, keeping the Same time and varying 4 notes without ever going beyond them. So many singers & so few notes you always hear the whole together. the difference of Words and Voices make some variety. the Singers (that I heard) all were women, one confined herself entirely to the Lower Note which acted as a Drone. they sing low and ended with the minor Chord it put me in mind of the Church singing among the Roman Catholics—instruments, Flutes (Nosy) and Reed Organs.[58]

And again he noted down the tune on a stave.

It was, however, as already mentioned, the Polynesian dances which made the most lasting impression upon the minds of the voyagers. By means of detailed accounts, engraved illustrations, and through popular poetry and drama they became widely known throughout Europe, until more than any other single activity they came to symbolize the island life itself (Plates 91A, 91B).

The curiosities collected on Cook's voyages provided some of the first items for many European collections of Pacific ethnography. Through Cook, Banks, Solander, and the Admiralty, the British Museum acquired a large collection. John Reinhold Forster presented some of his collection to the University of Oxford. Anders Sparrman left material to the Academy of Sciences, Stockholm. James Patten, the surgeon on the *Resolution*, left a large collection to Trinity College, Dublin. James King[59] also left a collection of curiosities to Trinity College.[60] John Webber bequeathed his collection to the Museum of Bern. Private collectors quickly entered the field acquiring items, directly or indirectly, from seamen returning from the Pacific. The most notable of these early collectors was Sir Ashton Lever (1729–88), a virtuoso who began collecting minerals and items of natural history. But Cook's voyages directed his attention to the arts of the Pacific. Anticipating wide public interest he moved his collection from Alkrington Hall, Manchester, to London in 1744 (Plate 90). A *Companion to the Museum* was published in 1790. The preface states that the *Companion* was published because of repeated requests from 'many Persons of the most distinguished Learning and Abilities, Admirers of the Works of Nature, in its almost infinite Variety of Forms and Properties, and those curious works of Art, which display the inventive Genius as well of the untutored Indian, as of the more polished European or Asiatic'.[61]

The Pacific island material was the *pièce de résistance* of the Museum, if we have regard for its size and position in the Museum. After passing through a hall, flanked by hexagonal pillars from the Giant's Causeway, the visitor first viewed specimens of Pacific art in an arched passage which led into the Sandwich room. Here examples of the arts of the peoples of the Pacific ranging from Nootka Sound to Dusky Bay and from Easter Island to New Caledonia were displayed to the public.[62] The way in which many of the items were described in the *Companion* reveals how taste in England was gradually being accommodated to forms of art which were, as Hawkesworth put it when describing Maori carving, 'not in the likeness of anything that is known on our side of the ocean, either "in the heaven above, or in the earth beneath, or in the waters that are under the earth"'.[63]

The *Companion to the Leverian Museum* describes a war club from the Cook Islands as being 'made of wood almost equal in hardness to the Brazilian, and superior in beauty to mahogany'. The carving 'by dint of industry and ingenuity is perfectly uniform in pattern, and highly ornamental'. The opinion of Captain Cook is quoted in connexion with a pouch from Prince William Sound: 'the ornamental part of some of these, may be put in competition with the most delicate manufactures found in any part of the known world.'[64] Captain King is quoted on Sandwich Island matting: 'whether we regard strength, fineness, or beauty, they certainly excel the whole world.'[65] The curiosities of the Pacific were coming to be acknowledged as works of art of considerable value in their own right.[66]

The Pacific did not, of course, apart from the statues of Easter Island, possess great

90. *The Leverian Museum*, artist unknown, pen and watercolour, $9\frac{1}{4} \times 6\frac{7}{8}$ in. Fuller Collection, Bishop Museum Library, Hawaii. From Kaeppler (1978), p. 14

91A. *A Night Dance by Men, in Hapaee*, engraving after Webber by W. Sharp, in Cook and King, *Voyage to the Pacific Ocean* (1784), pl. 16

91B. *A Night Dance by Women, in Hapaee*, engraving after Webber by W. Sharp, in Cook and King, *Voyage to the Pacific Ocean* (1784), pl. 17

monuments of antiquity to challenge the knowledge of the archaeologist. In this regard the area forms a contrast with the Near East which began to receive increasing attention from European travellers at the time the Pacific was being opened up by explorers and traders.[67] In the challenge to neo-classical values the cultural impact of the two areas upon Europe was, in a sense, complementary. The Near East gradually undermined the authority of classical models by revealing monumental art which antedated that of Greece and Rome, while the Pacific drew attention to forms of art produced by people living a life more primitive and closer to nature than the Greeks and Romans. It is to be remembered that in the eighteenth century much of the appeal of the Greek as opposed to the Roman was itself grounded in an enthusiasm for the simple, bare, monumental, and primitive. Johann Winckelmann, although the prophet of neo-classicism, had stimulated an interest in the origin of art by treating the arts themselves as products of history susceptible to growth, change, and decay, and laid stress upon the importance of considering the nature of materials used by artists and the climatic conditions of the area, in studying the formation and the perfection of art. 'There is no sufficient reason', he wrote, 'for assigning any particular country as the land of its birth, for every nation has found within itself the seed of those things which are indispensable.'[68] Here was a clear suggestion that the arts could be studied with reference to such factors as geology, natural history, and climate, as a guide. And where better could such factors be studied than where man existed in a 'natural uncultivated state'?

There was only one region left now, claimed John Douglas, writing in the preface to the official account of the third voyage, where it was possible to find man living in a state of nature, since all other primitive people revealed the results of contact with more advanced societies. Only the Pacific islands were 'fit soil from whence a careful observer could collect facts for forming a judgment, how far human nature will be apt to degenerate, and in what respects it can ever be able to excel.'[69]

Examples of the natural degeneration of human nature were found readily enough in such practices as cannibalism, infanticide, and what contemporary Europeans interpreted as free-love. Examples of natural excellence were to be found in the arts and crafts of the native peoples. Consequently Douglas proceeded to ask a question that has continued to fascinate art critics down to the present day:

> ... can we, without astonishment, observe to what a degree of perfection the same tribe (and indeed we may here join, in some of those instances, the American tribes visited in the course of the present voyage) have carried their favourite amusements, the plaintive songs of their women, their dramatic entertainments, their dances, their Olympian games, as we may call them; the orations of their chiefs; the chants of their priests; the solemnity of their religious processions; their arts and manufactures; their ingenious contrivances to supply the want of proper materials, and of effective tools and machines; and the wonderful productions of their persevering labour under a complication of disadvantages; their cloth and their mats; their weapons; their fishing instruments; their ornaments; their utensils; which in design and in execution, may vie with whatever modern Europe, or classical antiquity can exhibit?[70]

Perhaps, after all, the labours of the scholars are being misdirected. Perhaps the clue to the origin of art and indeed of civilization, suggests Douglas, is not to be found by digging up the buried monuments of Greece and Italy but by studying life as lived in the islands of the Pacific:

It is a favourite study with the scholar to trace the remains of Grecian or Roman workmanship; he turns over his Montfaucon with learned satisfaction ;and he gazes with rapture on the noble collection of Sir William Hamilton. The amusement is rational and instructive. But will not his curiosity be more awakened, will he not find even more real matter for important reflection, by passing an hour in surveying the numerous specimens of the ingenuity of our newly-discovered friends, brought from the utmost recesses of the globe, to enrich the British Museum, and the valuable repository of Sir Ashton Lever? If the curiosities of Sir Ashton's Sandwich-room alone, were the only acquisition gained by our visits to the Pacific Ocean, who that has the taste to admire, or even eyes to behold, could hesitate to pronounce, that Captain Cook had not sailed in vain? The expense of his three voyages did not, perhaps, far exceed that of digging out the buried contents of Herculaneum. And we may add, that the *novelties* of the Society or Sandwich Islands, seem better calculated to engage the attention of the studious in our times, than the *antiquities*, which exhibit proofs of Roman magnificence.[71]

Douglas's enthusiasm for the arts of the Pacific could be dismissed as the enthusiasm of an editor determined to make the most of his material—but not justly. Years before Douglas's remarks appeared in print the Society of Dilettanti itself, one of the centres of classical scholarship in Britain, had revealed an interest in the novelties of the Pacific. On 22 August 1775 Thomas Jones had called on William Hodges, his old fellow-pupil in Richard Wilson's studio. Jones informed Hodges that he had been approached by 'Mr. Stewart (the Athenian, as he was called) in the name of the Dilettanti Society, to go out with Captain Cook in his next voyage'. Jones had been trying to gain his parents' consent to study in Italy. They refused until they heard about Stuart's proposal whereupon they relented immediately and Jones left—for Italy.[72]

The primitive arts of the Pacific, it may be said then, though appealing first to Europeans as curiosities came to acquire an ethnographic interest because of the light they could throw on the nature of primitive societies. In that interest lay the seeds of the aesthetic appeal of Pacific primitive art for Europeans. We might well proceed to ask what was the quality of the appeal of these arts in the field of taste in England during the last two decades of the eighteenth century.

Although Canon Douglas makes occasional parallels with classical art when speaking of the arts of the Pacific, he was well aware that their appeal lay elsewhere. They appealed to the imagination rather than the intellect, and their recognition as objects of beauty and elegance forms a part of the history of the romantic movement. It is significant that Douglas, in writing about the appeal of Pacific Art, should quote Thomas Warton, a pioneer in romantic criticism:

> . . . in an age (says Mr. Warton), advanced to the highest degree of refinement, that species of curiosity commences, which is busied in contemplating the progress of social life, in displaying the gradation of science, and in tracing the transition from barbarism to civility. . . . We look back on the savage condition of our ancestors with the triumph of superiority; and are pleased to mark the steps by which we have been raised from rudeness to elegance. . . . In the meantime, the manners, monuments, customs, practices, and opinions of antiquity, by forming so strong a contrast with those of our own times, and by exhibiting human nature and human inventions in new lights, in unexpected appearances, and in various forms, are objects which forcibly strike a feeling imagination.[73]

130

92. *The Natche, a ceremony in honour of the King's son, in Tongataboo,* engraving after Webber by S. Middiman, the figures by Hall, in Cook and King, *Voyage to the Pacific Ocean* (1784), pl. 22

Warton's mention of antiquity here is not a reference to classical antiquity but to the antiquity, as he says, 'of our ancestors'. He is referring to the emergence of the northern nations of Europe from barbarism. And Douglas proceeded to point out that the '*manners, monuments, customs, practices, and opinions* of the present inhabitants of the Pacific ... form the *strongest contrast* with those of our own time in polished Europe.' The appeal, that is, of the arts of the Pacific will be similar in nature and perhaps stronger in its impact upon the imagination than the arts of the barbarian tribes of northern Europe: 'A *feeling imagination* will probably be more struck with the narration of the ceremonies of a Natche at Tongataboo [Plate 92], than of a Gothic tournament at London; with the contemplation of the colossuses of Easter Island, than of the mysterious remains of Stonehenge.' Thus, whereas Europeans first tended to interpret life in the Pacific (following the reports of travellers like Bougainville and Banks on Tahiti) in terms of classical antiquity, the appreciation of the life and the arts of the Pacific became increasingly an aspect of the romantic movement. The change is apparent in portraiture. Reynolds's *Omai* is a thoroughly neo-classical version of the noble savage. But John Webber's *Poedooa* (Colour Plate 13) is a highly romantic image of a firm-breasted young Raiatean girl bare to the waist,[74] who wears the flowers of the cape jasmine in her hair and a Gioconda look upon her face. She represents both the mysteries of the East[75] and the sensual pleasures of Tahiti, the sailor's paradise.

Indeed, even at the beginnings of Pacific exploration travellers did not always turn to the Greeks to find parallels to describe Polynesian society. For Parkinson, the Scot, the Tahitians were 'in constitution, what the ancient Britons were before civilization'.[76] Sparrman, the Swede, wrote how he recognized among the Maoris of New Zealand 'many of the methods of war and murder of our Gothic Viking forefathers with their swords, fires, and burnings'.[77] It was the arts of the peoples of the Pacific, however, which became most closely associated with romantic taste. As Warton's border ballads harkened back to the childhood of the British nations so, in a sense, the songs of the Polynesians hearkened back to the childhood of the human race. 'They are the first rude beginnings of arts', wrote J. R. Forster, 'and for that very reason they are in more general use, than the same arts are among us.'[78] 'The Lovers of music will easily conceive', wrote his son, of the music of the Cook Islanders, 'that this divine art is certainly in its infancy among the inhabitants.'[79] Such music therefore could throw light on the origin of music itself. Payne Knight, as we have seen, believed that Polynesian society threw light on the nature of Greek society in its golden age. Similarly Southey, thinking of the *Iliad* not as a classical masterpiece but as a series of border ballads,[80] claimed that 'the people to whom the poem relates seem to have been as nearly as possible in the same stage of barbarism or civilization (call it what you will) as the South Sea Islanders when the missionaries became acquainted with them.'[81] Even Australian aborigines came to be compared with Gaelic bards. 'Their poets', wrote Thomas Watling, 'neither having the advantage of writing or printing, are necessitated to travel . . . to extend their reputation. It is but lately that an itinerant sable *Ossian* called this way, and held forth to some hundreds of his countrymen, who after kindly entreating, escorted him to some other bourne, to further promulgate his composition.'[82] And as with music so with sculpture. To George Forster the workmanship of the statues of Easter Island 'spoke the arts in their infancy'.[83] Holding a similar opinion Payne Knight used descriptions in Cook's voyages to present a picture of the origin of sculpture among mankind in his *Progress of Civil Society* (1796):

> Awaked, the fleeting image still he saw,
> And marked each lineament with pious awe;
> Then strove, with rude design and infant art,
> In mimic form, its semblance to impart:
> With sharpen'd flint the features coarsely hew'd
> In the soft crumbling stone or mouldering wood;
> And bade rough trees in shapes of limbs arise,
> And gems and corals sparkle in the eyes;
> Rich plumes and furs the head and body deck,
> And pearly bracelets dangle round the neck.

While Péron, the French naturalist, confronted with the carvings of Tasmanian aborigines, wrote in his journal: 'I recollected those famous Ruric characters, formerly used by the nations of the north of Europe, and which, like these, consisted of a succession of figures roughly designed, of circles, squares, triangles, etc. which were nevertheless, by different combinations, capable of transmitting all the ideas of the people who made use of them.'[84]

In such ways the music, poetry, sculpture, and social institutions of Pacific peoples became associated in the minds of many European travellers with the customs of their own ancestors. It is no accident, therefore, that the only type of play which foreshadowed the exotic pantomimes, *Omai* and the *La Mort du Capitaine Cook*, in the matter of realistic costuming and setting were precisely those that sought to recall as Warton put it 'the savage condition of our ancestors', namely the national history play.[85] Both appealed strongly to patriotic sentiment, both appealed not to the intellect but to the 'feeling' imagination; and both eschewed the elevated timelessness of the classical stage, either by appealing to an historical reality, as in the case of the history play, or to a geographical reality, as in the case of the exotic pantomime.[86]

5. European Reactions to the Pacific, 1788–1802

In 1783 the East India Packet *Antelope* under the command of Henry Wilson, after leaving Macao on 20 July 1783, ran into a storm and was wrecked on one of the Palau Islands. He and his ship's company were befriended by the natives of one of the neighbouring islands who, under their chieftain Abba Thule, did all they could to assist the shipwrecked men while they built a schooner. After a stay of four months Wilson sailed for Macao in his new vessel. He took with him Lee Boo, the son of Abba Thulle who wanted him to see the world and be educated in England. Both Lee Boo and Wilson became known to George Keate (1729–97), a *littérateur* and virtuoso who was a member of the Royal Society and the Society of Antiquaries. Keate immediately saw the literary possibilities in Wilson's story and prevailed upon the captain to allow him to write a faithful account of it from his journals and communications. Consequently in 1788 Keate's *Account of the Pelew Islands* appeared.

Keate's *Account* invites comparison with Hawkesworth's *Voyages*, for both are travel books by literary men and present an idealized picture of Pacific island natives. But Keate, with the accumulated knowledge of Cook's three voyages behind him, was not disposed as Hawkesworth was, to see all natives as varieties of the noble savage. The comparisons and distinctions made by men like John Douglas and the Forsters were not lost upon him. For Keate the value of the Pacific Islander consisted no longer in his being an exemplar of natural virtue, but in his being a picture of man 'in a variety of lights' that were particularly well suited for philosophical speculation. Whereas, argued Keate, all civilized men are much of a muchness, 'in countries, which science or the gentle arts, have never reached, we observe a wonderful disparity'.[1] Keate, that is, echoes the reason put forward by Lord Monboddo and John Douglas for greater scientific attention to Pacific peoples. Some native peoples, Keate claimed, are treacherous, barbarous, and inhuman. This is a notable departure from Hawkesworth's indiscriminate championship of primitive peoples. Hawkesworth, as we have seen, was disposed to interpret the Fuegians as fine specimens of hard primitivism; to Keate they were no more than degraded brutes. He adopted J. R. Forster's idea that the power of harsh climates degraded native peoples from an 'original happiness', and remarked that civilized man should be thankful he was not destined 'to be an inhabitant of Terra del Fuego, or to add one to the number of the forlorn savages of the Northern Pole'.[2] But despite the concessions which Keate makes, in his introduction, to Douglas's ethnological programme and to Forster's climatic determinism, his *Account* provides remarkable evidence of the hardihood and the resilience of the belief in the noble savage in the face of evidence accumulating from successive voyages.

Keate wrote his book, he tells us, to present 'a new people' to the world, a people who were 'an ornament to human nature'; and to contravert the opinion that the inhabitants of the Palau Islands were inhuman and savage.[3] In their relations with Wilson and his shipwrecked crew Keate's islanders reveal all that is admirable in natural good sense: their manners are refined, their feelings sensitive, and they exercise the most delicate consideration for the feelings of their unfortunate guests. Therefore, Keate concludes, the school of nature is still the best school. The islanders acting from impulse alone are quite unconscious of deceitfulness in others. How much better this is than the suspicion and distrust natural to men reared in civilized societies! Thus Keate reveals the stress being placed upon sensibility by the fashion of the times. He finds the islanders noble not because of their admirable physique, or their freedom from social constraints, but because they possess good sense and good hearts. Keate's savage of sensibility is typified for us in his description of Abba Thule. What is stressed now is not the physical aspect of native life but the moral and spiritual qualities of the native, such as generosity of feeling and nobility of soul:

> With regard to the excellent man, who ruled over these sons of Nature, he certainly, in every part of his conduct, shewed himself firm, noble, gracious, and benevolent; there was a dignity in all his deportment, a gentleness in all his manners, and a warmth and sensibility about his heart, that won the love of all who approached him.—Nature had bestowed on him a contemplative mind, which he had himself improved by those reflections that good sense dictated, and observation confirmed.... Placed as he was by Providence in its obscurer scenes, he lived beloved by his *Chiefs*, and revered by his people; over whom, whilst he preserved a dignity that distinguished his superior station, he reigned more as the father than the sovereign.—The eyes of his subjects beheld their naked prince with as much awe and respect, as those are viewed who govern polished nations, and are decorated with all the dazzling parade and ornaments of royalty; nor was the purple robe, or the splendid diadem necessary to point out a character, which the masterly hand of Nature had rendered so perfect![4]

Keate informs us that there was a draughtsman on board the *Antelope* besides 'two or three young men acquainted with drawing'. The draughtsman was Arthur William Devis (1763–1823) a history- and portrait-painter[5] who, after first receiving tuition under his father Arthur Devis (1711–87) studied at the Academy and came under the notice of Reynolds. At the age of twenty he was appointed by the East India Company to accompany Wilson in the *Antelope*.[6] Devis made many sketches on the island, principally portraits of the natives.[7] His portrait of Abba Thulle was engraved for Keate's *Account* (Plate 93). In it, as in Keate's verbal description of the man, is to be traced a movement away from physical beauty to the expression of nobility of character in the representation of the noble savage. The eyes are alert and deepset in shadow beneath a large brow, the mouth large and sensuous, the chin finely moulded, and the hair swept back in disordered freedom from the face. Devis is more concerned with expressing the intelligence and sensibility of the native than with his physical manliness. His portait of *Ludee, one of the Wives of Abba Thulle* (Plate 94), is both sentimental and erotic and may be compared with the palpable eroticism which characterized the depiction of native women a decade before, as for example in John Webber's study of Poedooa.

Just as Hawkesworth appears to have been influenced in his interpretation of Pacific people by his work in translating Fénelon's *Télémaque*, so Keate appears to have been influenced in his interpretation of the Palau Islanders by the intimate acquaintance which he had formed with Voltaire during the 1750's. Voltaire's *L'Ingénu* displays many of the qualities that Keate attributes to Abba Thulle and Prince Lee Boo, and passages in *L'Ingénu* find their echo in Keate's *Account*. Voltaire thus describes the education of the Huron:

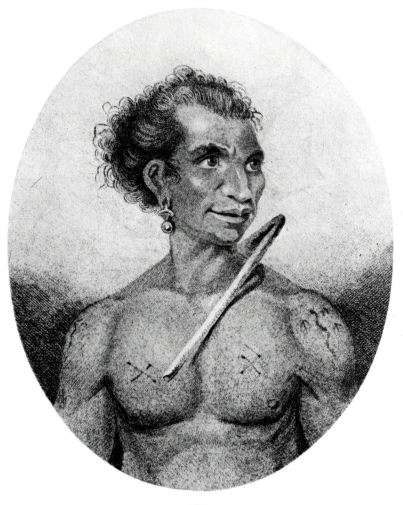

93. *Abba Thulle King of Pelew*,
engraving after Arthur W.
Devis by H. Kingsbury, in
George Keate, *Account of the
Pelew Islands* (1788), f.p. 55.
Copyright The Society of
Antiquaries, London

94. *Ludee, one of the Wives of
Abba Thule*, engraving after
Arthur W. Devis by H.
Kingsbury, in George
Keate, *Account of the Pelew
Islands* (1788), f.p. 187

The ingenious youth was making a rapid progress in the sciences, and particularly in the science of man. The cause of this sudden disclosure of his understanding was as much owing to his savage education as to the disposition of his soul; for having learned nothing in his infancy, he had not imbibed any prejudices. His mind, not having been warped by error, had retained all its primitive rectitude. He saw things as they were; whereas the ideas that are communicated to us in our infancy make us see them all our life in a false light.[8]

In a similar fashion Keate contrasts the schooling of nature with the schooling of civilization:

... the eye of philosophy will candidly view and discriminate between the two parties; the people of Pelew, tutored in the school of Nature, acted from impulse alone, they were open and undisguised; unconscious of deceit themselves, they neither feared nor looked for it in others.—Our countrymen—born and brought up in a civilized nation, where Art assumes every form and colouring of life, and is even perfectioned into a science, were fashioned by education to suspicion and distrust, and awake to all their busy suggestions.—Such is the fatal knowledge the world teaches mankind, fencing too often the human heart against the inlets of its own happiness, by weakening confidence, the most valuable bond of society![9]

And when Voltaire's Jansenist was locked up in the Bastille with the Huron he commented: 'have I consumed fifty years in instruction and not attained to the degree of natural good sense of this child, who is almost a savage'.[10] This may be compared with Keate's comment upon Lee Boo when he dined with him at Captain Wilson's: 'he adapted himself very readily to whatever he saw were the customs of the country, and fully confirmed me in an opinion which I have ever entertained, that *natural* good manners is the *natural* result of *natural* good sense'.[11] A detailed study of Voltaire's *L'Ingénu* and Keate's *Account* will elicit similar parallels.

Keate's book is notable in two other respects. First, it is written in a serious and somewhat moralizing vein, in which a pietistic note is clearly discernible. Captain Wilson, unlike some of his more famous predecessors in the Pacific, proves to be an exemplary Christian. Prayers were heard and read, we are told, with real devotion each Sunday by the shipwrecked company. Immediately after the disaster the men agreed to Wilson's suggestion that all the liquor on the wreck should be staved in order to minimize the danger of unfortunate incidents with the natives. Keate, furthermore, refrains from discussing the sexual habits of the natives or of any encounters between the sailors and the native women that might give cause for criticism. Indeed there was nothing in the book to offend even the most prudish taste (which was something new in Pacific voyage literature) while at the same time the story was—and is—a splendid yarn of danger and adventure in the South Seas. It is not surprising therefore that the book proved to be most popular. A popular version, *The Interesting and Affecting History of Prince Lee Boo*, ran through twenty editions from 1789 to 1850. A version of the story appeared on the stage, and Coleridge recorded the deep impression which the melancholy tale of the young prince's death in England made upon him in his youth.[12]

Keate's book is also notable because it provides further evidence of the growing interest in the arts of the Pacific. Keate himself was a great collector. Thomas Martyn wrote concerning his collection: 'For elegance and brilliancy in effect no museum exceeds that of George Keate, in which all the varieties in shells, corallines, gems and minerals, with a rich assortment of every species of semi-transparent or opaque fossil bodies, and specimens of the most exquisite and costly works of art, are, by the unrivalled taste of the possessor, and happy skill of the architect, most effectually and beautifully displayed.'[13] Keate was not only a virtuoso but also a gentleman of taste. It is of interest, therefore, to note that the majority of the engraved plates in his *Account* are devoted to the native 'ornaments' brought back by Wilson; the artefacts of the Palau Islanders being sympathetically described in detail in the text (Plate 95).

Although it occurs rather late in the history of the idea (and he himself was already sixty when he wrote it) Keate's *Account* is the most thoroughgoing and elaborate presentation of the noble savage in the literature of the South Seas, just as Sherwin's engraving, *The Landing at Middleburgh*, is the most elaborate example in the visual arts. But the book had no successor during the eighteenth century. Indeed the whole primitivistic interpretation of Pacific peoples was being challenged from many directions at the time the *Account* was published. There was, for example, the growing insistence by scientists and philosophers that particularized and factual accounts of native peoples must be assembled. There was, too, the wide publicity given to massacres and atrocities perpetrated upon navigators by hostile natives. And there was, above all, the austere religious temper of evangelical thought growing more powerful among all classes of English society year by year, a temper that was disposed to take neither a lenient view of cannibalism, infanticide, and what appeared to be the licentious dances and sexual orgies of native savages, nor of the parodies of such things which pamphleteers and popular versifiers had made capital use of during the 1770's. English society was slowly but surely ceasing to be diverted, instructed, and amused by savages. That something of a similar nature was taking place in French thought is to be gathered from a study of the published accounts of the disastrous voyage of La Pérouse.

Among the thousands of Europeans who enjoyed reading Cook's *Voyages* was Louis XVI, King of France. So great was his interest that he had a special edition of South Sea voyages prepared for the education of the Dauphin.[14] The appearance of the official account of Cook's third voyage inspired Louis to plan a French scientific voyage to embrace 'the discoveries which remain to be made, or to be perfected, in the

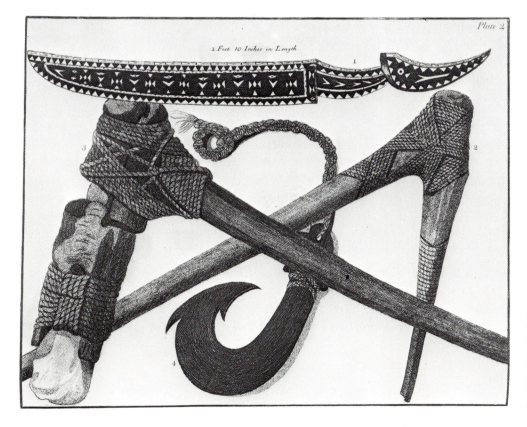

95. *Artefacts from the Pelew Islands: 1. a State Sword; 2. a Hatchet; 3. a moveable Hatchet; 4. a Fish Hook*, engraved after I. Plott from the originals by H. Kingsbury, in George Keate, *Account of the Pelew Islands* (1788), f.p. 175

different parts of the globe'. La Pérouse sailed from Brest on 1 August 1785 and after extensive work in the north-west and north-east portions of the Pacific covering a period of four years, and a visit to Botany Bay, nothing more was heard of him until Peter Dillon arrived in Calcutta in 1827 with the story of the wreck of the French vessels on the reefs of Vanikoro.

One of the significant aspects of La Pérouse's voyage is to be found in the increased attention his official instructions required him to pay to the detached and objective observation of native peoples. Cook had been advised: 'to observe the genius, temper, disposition and number of the natives and inhabitants where you find any'.[15] But nothing like the empirical and objective study which the scientists who accompanied him had brought to the study of plants and animals was brought (as we have seen) to the study of man. The Forsters, it is true, had made a notable beginning, but from the official point of view the study of native peoples was still largely prudential. The Admiralty advised Cook to study natives in order to establish good relations with them. Consequently although objective accounts of natives certainly were written there was a tendency to judge them according to their attitudes to European voyagers and in the light of European values. Adam Ferguson, in his *Essay on the History of Civil Society*, published two years before the *Endeavour* sailed to the Pacific, had noted how the study of man lagged behind the study of other sciences:

> In every other instance . . . the natural historian thinks himself obliged to collect facts, not to offer conjectures. When he treats of any particular species of animals, he supposes, that the present dispositions and instincts are the same they originally had, and that their present manner of life is a continuance of their first destination. He admits that his knowledge of the material system of the world consists in a collection of facts, or at most, in general tenets derived from particular observations and experiments. It is only in what relates to himself, and in matters the most important, and the most easily known, that he substitutes hypothesis instead of reality, and confounds the provinces of imagination and reason, of poetry and science.[16]

Then in 1773, Lord Monboddo expressed a similar point of view: 'it is really surprising', he wrote, 'that in an age, in which natural history has been so diligently cultivated, this part of it (i.e. the study of man in a state of nature), so much more interesting to us than any other, should have been neglected'.[17] The numerous accounts and engravings which had been in circulation since the early 1770's, the appearance of actual natives, such as Aotourou and Omai in Europe, of the Pacific islands upon the stage and in popular poetry, the continual discussion among philosophers concerning the nature of savages, and the growth of ethnographical collections, all helped to promote the demand for more particularized, more objective, and more precise information about the peoples of the Pacific.

Philosophers who desired to promote the objective study of man became increasingly aware of the great need for an accurate graphic survey of the world's peoples, a survey from which all traces of distorting idealism had been shorn. Herder, at the conclusion of Book VI of his *Ideen zur Philosophie der Geschichte der Menschheit* in which he had dealt with the social organization of the peoples of the world, put the problem with great emphasis:

> O for a magic wand, which, at once transforming into faithful pictures all the vague verbal descriptions that have hitherto been given, might present man with a gallery of figures of his fellow creatures! But we are far from the accomplishment of

138

such an anthropological wish. For centuries the Earth has been traversed with sword and the cross, by toymen and brandy merchants: no one thought of the peaceful pencil, and it has scarcely entered the minds of the numerous herd of travellers, that words do not paint forms, particularly that which is of all the most delicate, the most various, and ever changing. For a long time men sought after the wonderful and dealt in fiction: then they occasionally idealized, even when they gave figures; without considering, that no faithful zoologist idealizes, when he delineates foreign animals. And is human nature alone unworthy of that accurate attention, with which plants or animals are drawn? Yet, in modern days the laudable spirit of observation has begun to be excited towards the human species, and we have delineation of some nations, though but few, with which those of de Bry, or le Brun, not to mention the missionaries, will bear no comparison; it would be a valuable present to the world, if anyone, who has sufficient abilities, would collect such scattered delineations of the varieties of our species as are authentic, and thus lay the foundations of a perspicuous *natural philosophy* and *physiognomy of man*. Art could not easily be employed in a more philosophical pursuit....[18]

In the light of this growing interest in anthropological studies it is not surprising that La Pérouse's instructions for the observation of native peoples were more precise and detailed than Cook's:

... he will observe the genius, character, manners, customs, bodily constitution, language, government and number of the inhabitants.... He will direct natural curiosities, both of land and sea, to be collected; to be arranged in order; and a descriptive catalogue of each kind to be drawn up, in which will be mentioned the places where they were found, the uses to which they are applied by the natives of the country, and, if they be plants, the virtues ascribed to them.... In like manner he will order the garments, arms, ornaments, utensils, tools, musical instruments, and everything used by the different people he shall visit, to be collected and classed; and each article to be ticketed, and marked with a number corresponding to that assigned it in the catalogue.[19]

By such means the art of native peoples was not to be left to the haphazard collecting of earlier voyages. This increased attention to the study of man is also revealed in the instructions concerning the employment of draughtsmen. La Pérouse's artists, like those of Cook, were expected to provide views of coasts and to record the 'remarkable situations' encountered by the voyagers. But their obligations in the matter of depicting native peoples were drawn up in considerably more detail than any instructions delivered to Cook. Duché de Vancy, the landscape and figure draughtsman, assisted by the Prevosts (uncle and nephew), who acted as natural-history draughtsmen, were required to prepare 'portraits of the natives of the different parts, their dresses, ceremonies, buildings, boats and vessels, and all the productions of the sea and land ... if he shall think that drawings of them will render the descriptions more intelligible.'[20]

The great bulk of the drawings made by La Pérouse's artists, however, perished with them following the wreck of the *Boussole* and *Astrolabe* at Vanikoro. The few drawings made by the artists of the expedition in the form of the engraved plates in the *Atlas* to the voyage prepared by Milet-Mureau are an inadequate record. They reveal little real advance in objective portrayal. But though the *Atlas* fails to record a more scientific approach to the drawing of natives, it does provide further evidence of the shift from an attitude of trust to one of distrust in the native character. A great fund of goodwill still existed for the native peoples of the Pacific when La Pérouse left on his expedition and his instructions were most solicitous of their well-being, for it was an expedition conceived in the highest ideals of the Enlightenment. 'His majesty will consider it as one of the happiest events of the expedition, if it should terminate without costing the life of a single individual.'[21] So read the instructions. But it is clear that La Pérouse, though he carried out his instructions to the letter in his contact with the natives, distrusted them almost as much as Crozet did. He made his first contact with them at Easter Island and left a description far from sympathetic:

> No person who reads the narratives of modern navigators can imagine the Indians of the South Sea to be in a savage state. On the contrary, they must have made very great progress in civilization, and I believe them to be as corrupt as the circumstances in which they are placed will allow them to be. My opinion . . . is not founded on the various thefts they committed, but the manner in which they effected them. The most daring rascals of Europe are less hypocritical than the natives of these islands. All their caresses were false. Their physiognomy does not express a single sentiment of truth. The object most to be suspected is he who has just received a present, or who appears to be the most correct in rendering a thousand little services.[22]

The engraving *Insulaires et Monumens de l'Île de Pâques* (Plate 96), said to have been based on a drawing by de Vancy, affords a parallel with La Pérouse's remarks. Designer and engraver have represented the natives within the conventions of soft primitivism. The classicizing element is retained in the elegant features, serene expressions, pale skins, and draperies; the erotic element is preserved in the bare breasts and scanty clothing of the women. But the theme is the cunning and aptitude for theft of the natives. They are, in short, drawn as La Pérouse described them, as hypocrites; noble in appearance but far from noble in deed.

96. *Insulaires et Monumens de l'Ile de Pâques*, engraving after Duché de Vancy by Godefroy, in *Atlas du Voyage de la Pérouse* (1797), pl. xi

La Pérouse's misgivings deepened into very real dislike after the massacre of his companions; de Langle, the Commander of the *Astrolabe*, Lamanon, the naturalist, and ten others at Samoa. The description of Manu'a which La Pérouse wrote shortly after the affair is of more than passing interest because it is probably the first account which seeks to contrast the beauty of the Polynesian islands with the ferocity of the inhabitants—a contrast to be repeated again and again by missionaries and travellers in later years:

> This charming country unites the advantages of a soil fruitful without cultivation, and a climate requiring no clothes. The cocoa, plantain, guava, orange, and bread-fruit tree, bestow on these fortunate people abundance of wholesome nourishment; and fowls, hogs, and dogs, which live on the surplus of their produce, afford them an agreeable change. They were so wealthy, and had so few wants, that they despised our clothes and instruments of iron, and would accept only beads: abundantly supplied with articles of real utility, they desired nothing but superfluities..., What imagination would not conceive this delightful place the abode of felicity! These islanders, we were continually saying, must be the happiest people upon earth: surrounded with their wives and children, they must pass their days serene and tranquil in the bosom of repose: they have no other care but that of bringing up birds, and, like the first man, of gathering without labour the fruits that hang over their heads. But we were mistaken: this charming abode was not that of innocence. We saw no weapons, it is true: but the bodies of these Indians, covered with scars, proved that they were often at war, or quarrelling with one another; and their features announced a ferociousness not perceptible in the countenances of their women. Nature, no doubt, left this impression on the persons of these Indians, as a warning, that man, scarcely emerged from the savage state, and living in anarchy, is a more malignant being than the wildest beast.[23]

The island paradises of the Pacific that was to say, from being the abode of innocent joy they were to Bougainville, Wallis, and Banks had become for La Pérouse, as for Crozet, the abode of treachery and crime. What at first seemed to reflect an image of the Garden of Eden had turned out to be a bower of Armida.

The engraving *Massacre de Mm de Langle, Lamanon et dix autres individus des deux equipages* (Plate 97) by Nicholas Ozanne, reflects La Pérouse's hostility, and in so diong makes a notable departure from the pictorial convention of the noble savage. La Pérouse had contrasted the fertility of the island with the ferocity of its inhabitants; and the engraving depicts a scene of unmitigated violence occurring upon a beautiful tropical beach abounding in coconut palms, bananas, and bread fruit. La Pérouse had described the Samoans physically as 'about five feet ten inches, and their muscular limbs of colossal proportions gave them an idea of their own superiority, which rendered us by no means formidable in their eyes'. Ozanne depicts them as muscular but squat in physique. They are not now posed in the manner of ancient marbles, their movements being depicted as swift, angular, and without grace. Both in their proportions and their movements they are no longer invested with the neo-classical dignity of the noble savage. Expressions are violent, the mouth open, the eyes deep-set and dark, the hair frizzed out on all sides; while instead of the classically draped *tapa* cloth the men are seen clothed in light grass skirts which give them a shaggy, wild, and unkempt appearance. By way of contrast it is to be noted that the idealized family on the extreme left, and the woman and child on the extreme right, both appear to be looking upon the affray with considerable distaste. Both these groups, in the greater paleness of their skins, the elegance of their hair, the drapery about their loins, and their palpable nudity, provide a note both idyllic and erotic amid the scene of violence. They belong to the conventions of soft primitivism from which the engraving as a whole makes such a notable departure. For Ozanne has sought to depict the Polynesian as a violent, treacherous, and somewhat contemptible foe. The engraving consequently occupies an important place in the European iconography of Polynesians. Further evidence that the last decade of the century represents a transitional phase in French thought—as in English—when the natives of the Pacific were being regarded with mixed feelings is provided by the fictitious *Découvertes dans la mer du Sud. Nouvelles de M. de la Pérouse. Jusqu'en 1794.*[24] Abandoned upon a Pacific island after the wreck of their vessel, the author describes the feelings of the company at the thought of a possible encounter with natives:

> Nous avions trouvé dans nos relâches sur les terres de la Mer du Sud, des habitans doux et hospitaliers; mais nous savions aussi qu'il ne falloit pas trop compter, sur l'esprit inconstant des sauvages, nous avions dans la mémoire les relations des différens navigateurs qui avoient voyagé avant nous dans ces parages; nous savions qu'ils avoient recontré des peuplades antropophages, la mort de Cook, celle de M. Marion Dufresne, celle des dix hommes de l'équipage du capitaine Fourneaux, et tous les les événemens funestes arrivés depuis, dont nous avions eu connoissance au Brésil, se retraçoient avec horreur dans nos esprits: la nuit fut cruelle, nous la passâmes dans plus vives agitations.[25]

97. *Massacre de Mm de Langle, Lamanon et dix autres individus des deux équipages*, engraving after Ozanne by Déquevauviller, in *Atlas du Voyage de la Pérouse* (1797), pl. 66

Sure enough in the morning they found themselves surrounded by natives who turned out to be cannibals. When upon the point of being roasted and eaten they were saved by the timely arrival of another portion of the ship's company who had become separated from them earlier. Despite this experience the noble desire not to use force except in the direst of emergencies, so carefully written into La Pérouse's instructions, remained the guiding principle of the little band. When it became necessary to use

force to protect themselves they were very unhappy: 'Cette journée fut pour nous à tous égards une journée triste: on nous avoit attaqués, nous avions repoussé la force par la force, mais nous avions versé du sang humain, cette idée douloureuse frappoit les moins sensibles.'[26] But shortly afterwards at a ceremonial reception in their honour they were able to save some natives from being killed and eaten as part of the festivities: '... cela nous consoloit un peu des meurtres que nous avions commis la vieille.'[27] In such stories we may witness the intrusion of the image of the ignoble savage into accounts which also derive much from the sentimental attitudes still current. 'Quelque soit l'idée qu'on se forme de la férocité des sauvages, ils sont hommes, comme nous; leur cœur n'est inaccessible ni au sentiment de l'honneur, ni aux impressions de la reconnaissance.'[28]

Crozet and La Pérouse came to detest the natives of the Pacific for what they considered to be their cunning, ferocity, and treachery. But in England, from the time of Cook's first return from the Pacific, there were those who were appalled by the stories they read of sexual promiscuity, human sacrifices, and infanticide. The way in which the fashionable sections of English society had treated Omai, first making a social lion of him and then sending him back to Huahine laden with presents but still a pagan, outraged evangelical opinion. The satirical poets, as already indicated, touched on the matter more than once, and George Forster thought it necessary to criticize Omai's reception in England in the foreward to his *Voyage*.

In 1780 a pamphlet was printed by J. Bell of London entitled *A Letter from Omai to the Right Honorable the Earl of (xxxxxxxx).*[29] *Translated from the Ulaietean tongue In which, amongst other things, is fairly and irrefragably stated, the Nature of Original Sin: Together with a Proposal for Planting Christianity in the Islands of the Pacific Ocean.* It is of more than passing interest because it reveals how the conventional figure of the noble savage used throughout the eighteenth century to criticize the shortcomings of civilized society could be used for the special purpose of attacking both the Methodists and the Established Church. In the *Letter* Omai thanks his lordship for all the favours he received from him and his friends during his stay in England:

> And after thanking you for the powder, shot, gun, crackers, sword, feathers, and watch, let me thank you also for my conversion to Christianity: I ought perhaps to have mentioned this before the sword and the crackers, but as the fire and sword have commonly taken the lead, I will not dispute their title to it.[30]

Omai complains that he had been attacked while in England by a Methodist preacher who had told him that had he not been fortunate enough to hear the name of Christ while in England he would be damned for all eternity. As a consequence he made some study of theology and came to the conclusion that his Tahitian brethren would not be eternally damned, 'any more than many of the people of Europe will be saved, who, from bare hearsay, promise themselves security'.[31] His Tahitian brethren, he claims, will be saved, either by the good works they perform, or by the mediation of Christ, since they are not in a position to be saved through faith. Those who preach 'the efficacy of faith without works', said Omai, 'do much harm to the common people of England'.[32] Having attacked the Methodists, Omai then puts forward a scheme for planting Christianity in the South Seas, suggesting that a number of the friends of Lord Sandwich in high places in the Church would be more honourably employed in preaching Christianity in the Pacific. 'As religion increases with us, we shall want more teachers—as it decreases with you, you will want fewer.'[33] The *Letter* is also of interest because in the year after Cook's death when so much was being written in his praise it sounds a critical note on his activities in the Pacific which, though unfair, indicates that the adulation of Cook if widespread in the years after his death was certainly not unanimous:

> I cannot conclude my letter, without saying how much real concern I feel for the unfortunate fate of poor Captain Cook, who was certainly very cruelly and inhumanly butchered, for nothing more than ordering his crew to fire on a banditti of naked savages; who seemed to look as if they had a right to the country in which he found them.[34]

Although this pamphlet is written in the vein of the satirical *Omai* poems it deals with an issue they had avoided. The question so many Englishmen were beginning to formulate for themselves was not the question of the philosophers and deists, whether man living in a state of nature attains thereby a natural virtue; it was the far more uncompromising question of the evangelists: 'Can savages, however virtuous, enter the kingdom of Heaven?'

Thomas Haweis, a founder of the (London) Missionary Society, was one of the many who answered the question firmly in the negative. He tells how reading Cook's voyages in his youth led him to conceive of missionary enterprises in the South Seas. Haweis became the trustee and executor of Selina Hastings, the Countess of Huntingdon (1707–91), who more than anyone else introduced the moral earnestness of Methodism among the circles of the English nobility and gentry. Later he became the manager of her Trevecca College, from whence evangelists were sent to many parts of the world. Haweis preached the first sermon to the Missionary Society on 22 September 1795. In that sermon we meet with sentiments already expressed in La Pérouse's reflections upon the Samoans, but now they are combined with a sense of moral and religious urgency:

> A new world hath lately opened to our view, call it Island or Continent, that exceeds Europe in size: New Holland; and now become the receptacles of our outcasts of society.—New Zealand, and the innumerable islands, which spot the bosom of the Pacific Ocean, on each side of the Line, from Endeavour Straits to the Coasts of America, many of them full of inhabitants,—occupying lands, which seem to realize the fabled Gardens of the Hesperides,—where the fragrant groves, which cover them from the sultry beams of day, afford them food, and clothing; whilst the sea offers continual plenty of its inexhaustible stores; and the day passes in ease and affluence, and the night in music and dancing. But amidst these enchanting scenes, savage nature still feasts on the flesh of its prisoners—appeases its Gods with human sacrifices—whole societies of men and women live promiscuously, and murder every infant born amongst them.[35]

To Haweis, as to La Pérouse, the natural beauties of Tahiti offered a sharp contrast to its spiritual and moral degradation. 'Yet untutored offspring of fallen nature! how are you to be pitied', he exclaimed in his sermon. If Tahiti preserves an image of the Garden of Eden, it is an Eden not where man lives in a state of innocence but as Eden after the Fall. Just how much Haweis and the men who founded the Missionary Society detested noble savagery and the sentimentalism associated with it is revealed in his thoughts concerning Omai:

> The foolish Omai was an expense more than would have maintained a mission to the island. Not so much as an attempt was made to give him any knowledge tending to the saving of his soul. He was led away to stare, and be stared at, at our public places, and be as abandoned as those who frequent them; and in the presence of all

the officers his introduction at Huaheine, the place of his settlement, at his return was celebrated by an offering to the Eatoa![36]

The missionary enterprise helped to bring together and co-ordinate much of the dissatisfaction with the sentimental primitivism that accounts of Tahiti had stimulated. The evangelists had no doubts about the superiority of Christian civilization over all other forms of society, and they considered it a pressing obligation upon Christians to make the Gospel known in the South Seas.

The missionary ship *Duff*, under Captain Wilson, was sent out to Tahiti in 1796, the year following the establishment of the Missionary Society. The Tahitian chieftain Pomare agreed to cede the district of Matavai to the missionaries for their use. Three years later the Directors of the Society appointed a committee to consider a suitable memorial for presentation to Captain Wilson for his services in helping to establish the first mission in the South Seas. It recommended 'that an artist of the first eminence should be engaged to make a representation of the interview which took place with the Chiefs of the Island of Otaheite soon after the arrival of the *Duff*'.[37] Some specific instructions were laid down for the guidance of the painter. Wilson and his nephew were to figure prominently, and the portrait of 'the meritorious individual Mr. Robson'[38] was to be included. Another group was to show the various chiefs and their attendants 'and convey as accurate a representation as possible of their appearance'. The view was to be set in Matavai, contain a view of the missionary houses, the surrounding country, the harbour, and the *Duff* lying at anchor. The committee felt that these instructions were sufficient for the painter to begin with. Subordinate parts of the picture 'were to be determined by a committee after consulting with the artist and others on the subject'. Three hundred guineas were set aside for the execution of the painting,[39] and the commission fell to Robert Smirke (1752–1845).

Smirke made a preliminary sketch in oils for the painting (Plate 98) which may be profitably compared with the finished painting (Plate 99). The sketch reveals that the large standing figure of the native on the extreme left was originally drawn in the manner of a resting Hercules figure. In the finished painting the figure was made more deferential and there too, but not in the sketch, the native woman, to his left, holds a hand before her breasts with becoming modesty, while the two naked young Tahitians, to his right in the sketch, have been reduced to one in the finished painting, and placed modestly behind a drape slung over the roped enclosure, to cover his nakedness. The witch-doctor is shown blind, and the whole native group represented not so much as noble savages (though they are all fine physical specimens) but as docile children awaiting the blessing of a higher civilization. This central theme suitably conveyed, Smirke did what he could to present the costumes and setting as realistically as possible. Pomare and his wife are shown correctly upon the backs of their attendants—a position that a history-painter of an earlier generation would have avoided. The ship's officers, the missioners and their wives are shown in the dress of the day, while the coconut palm, the banana, and the bread-fruit serve to typify the vegetation and symbolize the island's fertility. The Directors were keen that the picture should be shown at the Academy—Smirke exhibiting it in 1799. In July of the same year the Directors came to an agreement with the printseller, Jeffries, that an engraving be made. Jeffries arranged for Bartolozzi to make a line engraving of the painting and obtained the copyright from the Directors in return for the first 100 coloured prints and the first 300 plain. It was agreed that the engraving should be 'in the manner of line and chalk and of the size of that of the Death of General Wolfe'.[40]

By such means the Missionary Society brought its work before the notice of the

145

public. During the succeeding years the missions to the Pacific gradually substituted for the noble savage of the eighteenth century a strikingly contrasting type; an individual thoroughly treacherous and deceitful in his native state who could yet be transformed into a Christian citizen obedient to the laws of God and the laws of Europeans as a result of the intercession of the Holy Spirit in Christian conversion. The power of evangelical thought at this time is indicated by the fact that the engraver who helped to transform Buchan's Fuegians into noble savages, happy and contented in their natural state (Plate 31), lived to depict Tahitians as 'untutored offspring of fallen nature' anxiously awaiting the Christian revelation. And in this Bartolozzi symbolizes the changing sentiment of the times. Many who in their youth had wept like Coleridge over the tomb of Prince Lee Boo, paradigm of the natural virtues, came in the end to give their pennies to the missionary societies to save the peoples of the Pacific from their natural vices, and to agree, with Coleridge, that 'Christianity brings immense advantages to a savage'. John Sterling recorded how the poet came to see the life of the islanders from the missionaries' point of view:

98. Robert Smirke, *Sketch for the Cession of Matavai*, pen and oil, 22 × 30 in. (1798). Nan Kivell Collection 21, National Library of Australia, Canberra

> The missionaries have done a great deal for us in clearing up our notions about savage nations. What an immense deal of harm Captain Cook's *Voyages* did in that way! Sailors, after being a long time at sea, found a fertile island, and a people of lax morals, which were just the things they wanted; and of course there never were such dear, good, kind, amiable people. We know now that they were more detestably licentious than we could have imagined. And then the romance of the Pelew Islanders! There scarcely ever existed such a set of blood-thirsty barbarians. Savages have a notion of higher powers than their own all around them; but that is a part of superstition not religion.[41]

So for the deistic picture of the noble savage who apprehended the Deity through the processes of natural revelation there came to be substituted the evangelistic picture of an ignoble and degraded brute who might be saved from eternal damnation only by concerted missionary activity.

99. Robert Smirke, *The Cession of Matavai*, canvas, 118 × 76 in. (1799). Livingstone House, London. By permission of the London Missionary Society

But the older tradition lingered. The beauty of Tahiti and the charm of its peoples had been a prime cause of the mutiny on the *Bounty*, and the pristine beauty of the island itself continued to make a deep impression upon newcomers. The paintings which James Tobin made in his journal on the *Providence*, on Bligh's second voyage (1791–4), echo the mood of the Tahitian landscapes of William Hodges. Tobin was not a professional artist, and his drawings are of interest in enabling us to gauge the scope of the visual interests of a British naval officer voyaging in the Pacific during the last decade of the century.[42] Like Hodges he was interested in atmospheric conditions. He depicts, for instance, the condition of wind, cloud, and water under a gale, off Table Bay. He was interested, too, in curiosities of natural history such as barnacles found on a spar, or a Tasmanian anteater. And, apart from the coastal profiles normally feature in sailors' log-books, he makes a practice of drawing landscapes as settings to interesting items of natural history or ethnography. He draws a native *mia-mia* in Tasmania in great detail, paints the vegetation carefully, and adds detailed description in his journal. In painting a view of Adventure Bay he makes a feature of the bird-life of the region. His work thus testifies to that mergence of two areas of interest and feeling concerning nature already discussed above, the interest in natural history and the enjoyment of landscape as a whole. Scientific interests predominate in Tobin's drawings except when he comes to depict the landscape of Tahiti. In both his descriptions and paintings of that island the lineaments of the Arcadian dream of

147

100. George Tobin, *On the Matavai River, Island of Otahytey*, watercolour, $8\frac{1}{4} \times 6\frac{3}{4}$ in. (1792), from Sketches on H.M.S. *Providence*, 138. Mitchell Library, Sydney, A.563. By permission of the Trustees of the State Library of New South Wales

Wallis, Bougainville, Banks, and Diderot are preserved. The paintings suggest the green tropic richness of island vegetation and the life of ease and pleasure which had so attracted the *Bounty* mutineers (Plate 100). But Tobin's vision was romantic. It was the sublime elements of the scenery—the Matavai river impeded by huge boulders, cataracts falling from great heights, the mountains clothed with trees to their summits and half hidden in mists—that struck his imagination most forcibly. Even his Tahitian women are no longer classicistic in style, they are small, exotic creatures—inhabitants of a Tahitian dreamland.

Further evidence of the persistence of the vision of an earthly paradise in the minds of British seamen may be gained from the journal of George Hamilton. As surgeon on the *Pandora*, sent out under Edward Edwards to arrest the *Bounty* mutineers, Hamilton had visited Tahiti a year prior to Tobin. He left a description which reveals that, however evangelists might rage in pious protest, Tahiti was still for seamen, what it had been for Bougainville, *le mirage océanien*:

> This may well be called the Cytheria (*sic*) of the southern hemisphere, not only for the beauty and elegance of the women, but their being so deeply versed in, and so passionately fond of the Eleusinian mysteries; and what poetic fiction has painted of Eden, or Arcadia, is here realised, where the earth without tillage produces both food and cloathing, the trees loaded with the richest of fruit, the carpet of nature spread with the most odiferous flowers, and the fair ones ever willing to fill your arms with love.[43]

Hamilton's *Journal* thus reveals how Tahiti continued to exemplify the life of soft primitivism at the level of popular thought. But the changing spiritual temper of the times in art, religion, and politics made the ideal of such a life increasingly unpopular.

148

In France, particularly, the republican virtues championed during the Revolution had brought the ideals of hard primitivism back into official favour. Savages were endowed with the virtues that good republicans aspired to. Simple in his needs and desires, self-disciplined, courageous, and with a great capacity for endurance, the savage became a symbol of revolutionary freedom and ideal perfectibility.[44] This attitude to Pacific peoples, springing directly from the ideals of the Revolution, is graphically portrayed in Labillardière's *Relation du voyage à la recherche de la Pérouse* (1800). Jacques Julian de Labillardière was the naturalist on the *Recherche*, commanded by Bruni D'Entrecasteaux. The expedition (1791–3) was sent to the Pacific to search for La Pérouse. The figures of the natives which appeared in Labillardière's *Relation* were engraved from drawings made by Piron, the artist on the *Recherche*. There is no sentiment, no sensuousness, no sense of luxury, no aura of soft primitivism clinging about the dry, wiry natives which appear in this book. Instead they have been invested with a good deal of the heroic stoicism which Jacques Louis David, at that time the dominant influence in French art, expressed in his republican history pieces. The engraving of the *Sauvage des Îles de l'Amirauté* (Plate 101) is, in its torso, a close imitation of the *Doryphoros*, Polykleitos' ideal warrior, even to the emphasis upon the pelvic girdle, the hollow at the side of the gluteal muscles and the roll of flesh above the knee. The *Femme du Cap de Diemen* (Plate 102) combines in part the gestures of a *Venus de Medici* and a *Wounded Amazon*, while the *Sauvage de la Nouvelle Zélande*[45] is clearly based on the head of Jupiter.

The unknown English translator of Labillardière's *Relation* wrote a preface to his translation that echoes the spirit of heroic humanism present in the engravings. The

101. *Sauvage des Îles de l'Amirauté*, engraving after Piron by Copia, in Labillardière, *Relation du voyage à la recherche de la Pérouse, Atlas* (1797), pl. 3

102. *Femme du Cap de Diemen*, engraving after Piron by Copia, in Labillardière, *Relation du voyage à la recherche de la Pérouse, Atlas* (1797), pl. 6

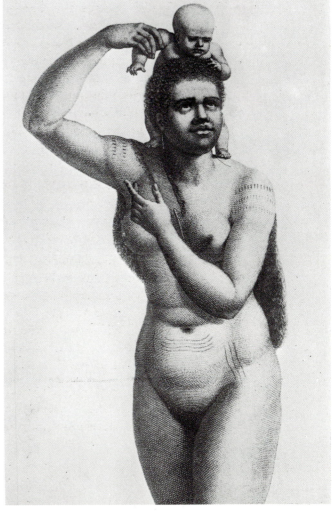

ideas which he expressed have much in common with Adam Ferguson. In his *History of Civil Society*, Ferguson depicted man as a social being capable, no matter what his condition, of overcoming the limitations imposed by environment, and of reaching out towards a state of perfection. Books of travel, says the translator of Labillardière, are of value not only to the navigator, geographer, and naturalist, but also the moral philosopher who 'loves to trace the advances of his species through its various gradations from savage to civilized life'.[46] From them he can gather the evidence he needs to trace the social, intellectual, and moral progress of man. Travellers have revealed the life of savages in such diversity that the philosopher can only conclude that even in a state of nature man is a rational being, placed in different physical circumstances. Even in his most degenerate condition he is yet much higher than the brutes, so that we learn nothing from comparing him with beasts. He is, on the other hand, a creature who is

> Everywhere adapting means to ends, and variously altering and combining those means, according to his views and wants. Man, even when pursuing the gratification of animals instincts, too often miserably depraved, shows himself to be possessed of nobler faculties, of liberty to chuse among different objects and expedients, and of reason to direct him in that choice. There is sufficient variety in human actions to show that, though Man acts from motives, he acts not mechanically, but freely; yet sufficient similarity of conduct, in similar circumstances, to prove the unity of his nature. Hence there appears no ground whatever for supposing, that one tribe of mankind is naturally of an order superior to the rest, or has any shadow of right to infringe, far less to abrogate, the common claims of humanity.[47]

This is all very close to Ferguson in thought. Environment does not set a limit to man's achievements but provides him with possibilities. Yet history records the decline and fall of empires. Did it not follow, therefore, man being a creature infinitely resourceful, that the decline of societies in one part of the world heralded the rise of new societies elsewhere? And where more likely than in the islands and countries of the Pacific where the natives, though still primitive, recalled in so many ways the lives, manners and customs of the ancestors of the European nations?

> Without obtruding our own sentiments on the reader, we may be permitted to ask, ... whether ... the advantages of civilisation may not, in the progress of events, be transferred from the Europeans, who have but too little prized them, to those remote countries which they have been so diligently exploring? If so, the period may arise, when New Zealand may produce her Lockes, her Newtons, and her Montesquieus; and when great nations in the immense regions of New Holland, may send their navigators, philosophers, and antiquaries, to contemplate the ruins of *ancient* London and Paris, and to trace the languid remains of the arts and sciences in this quarter of the globe. Who can tell, whether the rudiments of some great future empire may not already exist at Botany Bay?[48]

Pacific peoples, as we have seen, had come to be identified in romantic thought with the barbarian peoples from whom sprang the nations of northern Europe. Both were taken to be exemplars of the virtues of hard primitivism. This strand of thought became associated with ideas concerning the perfectibility of man, on the one hand, and reflection upon the decline of the ancient empires of the Mediterranean and the Near East, on the other. The conjunction of the two strands of thought led to a theory of social undulation in which the Pacific came to be considered a likely theatre for the emergence of new civilizations as those of the West declined. These ideas had been developed fully in Claret Fleurieu's edition of Marchand's *Voyage autour du monde*, the English translation of which had appeared a year prior to the translation of Labillardière's *Relation*. It is quite likely that Labillardière's English translator drew upon Fleurieu for his thoughts on social undulation.

The voyage of Etienne Marchand (1790–2) was a commercial venture to the north-west coast of America to obtain furs, during which a number of new islands in the Marquesas was discovered. Fleurieu used the voyages as a peg on which to hang his own immense erudition in the history of voyages. He also collated a great deal of information provided by earlier voyages, and subjected his material to detailed critical examination wherever it was found to be conflicting. In the course of propounding a theory concerning the origin of the Indians of the north-west coast of America, Fleurieu propounded an undulation theory. The arts, manners and customs of these Indians, Fleurieu claimed, revealed distinct traces of a more advanced civilization. 'Many of these carvings are well proportioned' he wrote, speaking of their totem poles, 'and executed with a considerable degree of ingenuity, which appears rather extraordinary amongst a people so remote from civilized refinement.'[49] Quoting from Dixon's *Voyage* (1789) in support of his argument he proceeded to point out that 'architecture, sculpture, painting, and music are found united, and in some measure naturalized, in a country whose inhabitants, in other respects, still appear in the state of savages'.[50] After tracing other elements of civilization in the manners and customs of the people he proceeds to argue that they are the degenerate ancestors of people once living within the frontiers of the Mexican Empire who were forced to move northwards following the dispersion brought about by the Spanish conquest. In the course of three centuries, Fleurieu claimed, they degenerated from the civilized state achieved within the Mexican Empire. From this particular argument Fleurieu proceeded to generalize from the parallels between primitive man and the ancestors of the European nations to the history of society in general:

If we are not disposed to challenge all the testimonies of antiquity, we cannot refuse to believe that the Old World has had its infancy and its adolescence: and, observing it in its progressive career, we may consider it as in its maturity, and foresee, in an unlimited time, its decrepitude and its end.... Read what travellers and historians have related to us of the New World; you will there find the man of the Old one in his infancy; among the small scattered nations, you will fancy that you see the first Egyptians, wild and savage men, living at random, ignorant of the conveniences of life, even of the use of fire, and not knowing how to form arms for defending themselves against the attack of beasts: in the Pesserais of *Tierra del Fuego*, the savage Greeks, living on the leaves of trees, and, as it were, browsing on grass, before Pelasgus had taught the Arcadians to construct huts, to clothe themselves with the skins of animals, and to eat acorns; in the greater part of the savages of Canada, the ancient Scythians, cutting off the hair of their vanquished enemies, and drinking their blood out of their skull ... in Mexico, you will recognize the Cimbri and the Scythians, burying alive with the dead king, the great officers of the crown: in Peru, as well as in Mexico, and even among the small nations, you will find Druids, Vates, Eubages, mountebanks, cheating priests, and credulous men: on every part of the continent and in the neighbouring islands you will see Bretons, the Picts of the Romans, and the Thracians, men and women, painting their body and face, puncturing and making incisions in their skin....

The picture which the New World exhibited to the men of the Old who discovered it, therefore offered no feature of which our own history does not furnish us with a model in the infancy of our political societies.[51]

It was a simple step to argue that the New World of America and the Pacific would repeat the history of the Old. Like Monboddo and Douglas, Fleurieu stressed the great importance of studying primitive peoples intensively as soon as Europeans came in contact with them. By separate intensive studies only of peoples still living in a state of nature would it be possible to trace the progress of man from savagery to civilization:

> It is by partial studies, it is by contemplating the men of every country under his first cover, and, as it were, in his original dress, that we shall be able to succeed in graduating the scale of human intelligence, by ascending from the stupid *Pesserais*, who knows only how to shiver on the *Tierra del Fuego*, or the wild Hottentot, who differs little from the *man of the woods*, to the genius who created the Iliad, or him who anatomized light, and submitted to calculation the laws of gravity.[52]

The ideas of social progress and undulation expressed by Fleurieu and Labillardière's English translator found a prominent place in William Lisle Bowles's poem, *The Spirit of Discovery or the Conquest of Ocean*, published in 1804. The reading of voyage literature had suggested to Bowles the possibility of an epic on the history of discovery. The poem was originally intended to consist of six books, but he reduced it to five eventually because 'the great subject of the Discovery of America is in the hands of such poets as Mr. Southey and Mr. Rogers'. For Bowles, a keen evangelist, the rise and fall of empires was seen in a theological and moral context. Navigation, which shall be the means whereby the knowledge of God will be finally spread throughout the whole world, derived, Bowles claimed, from Noah's ark. Britain through her perfection of the art of navigation will be the instrument whereby all the nations of the earth will be brought to embrace Christianity, if, Bowles warned, she does not sink like Tyre under the weight of her sins. If she does, because of such evils as the slave trade, then a new nation may rise in the south.

> My heart has sigh'd in secret, when I thought
> That the dark tide of time might one day close,
> England, o'er thee, as long since it has clos'd
> On Ægypt and on Tyre: that ages hence,
> From the Pacifick's billowy loneliness,
> Whose tract thy daring search reveal'd, some isle
> Might rise in green-haired beauty eminent,
> And like a goddess, glittering from the deep,
> Hereafter sway the sceptre of domain
> From pole to pole; and such as now thou art,
> Perhaps NEW-HOLLAND be.

Bowles, like other evangelical poets, criticizes the belief in the natural virtue of savages and champions the idea of progress and the missionary enterprise. He also uses detailed descriptions of exotic landscape drawn from travel literature in order to figure forth an allegory of the moral world through which man gropes towards the light of Christianity. In this, Bowles's *Spirit of Discovery* may be compared with a greater poem, Coleridge's *Ancient Mariner*:[53]

> They who in darkness walk'd, and in the shade
> Of death, have seen a new and lovely light.

As in the umbrageous forest, through whose boughs,
Mossy and damp, for many a league, the morn
With languid beam scarce pierces, here and there
Touching some solitary trunk, the rest
Dark waving in the noxious atmosphere:
Through the thick-matted leaves the serpent winds
His way, to find a spot of casual sun;—
The gaunt hyenas thro' the thickets glide
At eve. Then, too, the crouched tiger's eye
Flames in the dusk, and oft the gnashing jaws
Of the fell crocodile are heard. At length,
By man's superior energy and toil,
The sunless breaks are cleared; the joyous morn
Shines through the op'ning leaves; rich culture smiles
Around; and howling to their distant wilds
The savage inmates of the woods retire.
Such is the scene of human life, till want
Bids Man his strength put forth; then slowly spreads
The cultur'd stream of mild humanity,
And gentler virtues, and more noble aims
Employ the active mind, till beauty beams
Around, and nature wears her richest robe,
Adorned with lovelier graces.

That was one way in which the Christian apologist could interpret exotic landscapes and primitive peoples in conformity with the moral and theological precepts of Christianity. No older vision of a Golden Age or pastoral Arcadia lingers, for Bowles, amid the moral gloom of the pagan lands even when they are endowed with the sunshine of the tropics and the bounty of Pacific islands. But Bowles's way was not the only way. For Chateaubriand, perhaps the most influential Christian apologist of the day, the image of Tahiti as *le mirage océanien* still lingered. But in that mirage, supremely beautiful as it was, death was the only reality: Chateaubriand wrote the fifth chapter of his *Génie du Christianisme* on the theme of Tahiti to stress the power of death over mortal man even in the most lovely places upon Earth. 'L'homme ici-bas ressemble à l'aveugle Ossian, assis sur les tombeaux des rois de Morven: quelque part qu'il etende sa main dans l'ombre, il touche les cendres de ses pères.' And as with Ossian, so too even with the pleasure-loving Tahitians:

Sous ces ombrages ignorés, la nature avait placé un peuple beau comme le ciel qui l'avait vu naître: les Otaïtiens portaient pour vêtement une draperie d'écorce de figuier: ils habitaient sous des toits de feuilles de mûrier, soutenus par des piliers de bois odorants, et ils faisaient voler sur les ondes ce doubles canots aux voiles de jonce, aux banderoles de fleurs et de plumes. Il y avait des danses et des sociétés consacrées aux plaisirs; les chansons et les drames de l'amour n'étaient point inconnus sur ces bords. Tout s'y ressentait de la mollesse de la vie, et un jour plein de calme, et une nuit dont rien ne troublait le silence. Se coucher près des ruisseaux, disputer de paresse avec leurs ondes, marcher avec des chapeaux et des manteaux de feuillages, c'était toute l'existence des tranquilles Sauvages d'Otaïti. Les soins qui, chez les autres hommes, occupent leurs pénibles journées, étaient ignorés de ces insulaires: en errant à travers les bois, ils trouvaient le lait et le pain suspendus aux branches des arbres.

Telle apparut Otaitï à Wallis, à Cook et à Bougainville. Mais, en approchant de ces rivages, ils distinguèrent quelques monuments des arts, qui se mariaient à ceux de la nature: c'étaient les poteaux de Morai. Vanité des plaisirs des hommes! Le premier pavillon qu'on découvre sur ces rives enchantées est celui de la mort, qui flotte au-dessus de toutes les félicités humaines.[54]

So Chateaubriand returned to the theme of *Et in Arcadia Ego* used by poets and artists repeatedly to symbolize that self-conscious awareness of the transience of life which has always haunted the European imagination. Chateaubriand's book was one long argument for the superiority of Christianity over all other religions; here the *Et in Arcadia Ego* theme, classical in its origins, is found once again, used to underline a Christian truth. The dolorous shepherds who, in Poussin's painting, bend in wonder over the tomb they have stumbled upon in their blissful Arcadia have become Polynesians whispering into the ears of the dead in a South Sea island paradise. But the moral is the same: upon earth all pleasures are transient and death the only reality. The idea was first figured forth in its Tahitian setting somewhat tentatively, as we have seen, in Woollett's engraving after Parkinson, '*Ewharra' in Huaheine* (Plate 36). It was upon this very plate that Chateaubriand assuredly drew when he began to write his own essay on transience, for he concludes it with a passage clearly based on his impression of the engraving:

Arrivé au lieu du repos, on ne descend point le corps dans la terre, mais on le suspend dans un berceau qu'on recouvre d'un cannot renversé, symbole du naufrage de la vie. Quelquefois une femme vient gémir auprès du Morai; elle s'assied les pieds dans la mer, la tête baissée, et ses cheveux retombant sur son visage: les vagues accompagnent le chant de sa douleur, et sa voix monte vers le Tout-Puissant avec la voix du tombeau et celle de l'océan Pacifique.[55]

15. The Port Jackson Painter, *A Woman meeting her Husband*, watercolour, 6⅝ × 11 in. (*c.* 1790). Banks MS 34, Botanical Library, British Museum (Nàtural History)

16. The Port Jackson Painter. *Ban nel lang meeting the Governor by appointment after he was wounded by Willa ma ring in September 1790*, watercolour, 9¼ × 15½ in. (*c.* 1790). 'Watling' drawings 49, British Museum (Natural History)

17. St.-Sauveur, *Tableau des découvertes du Capne Cook et de La Perouse*, hand-coloured etching (1797)

s du Cap.ne Cook, & de la Pérouse

Guillaume.-4. Hab.ts de l'Ile de Paques.-5. Hab.ts de la Baije de Norton.-6. Hab.ts des Iles Sandwick
de Castries.-10. Hab.ts de la Baye ou Port des François-11. Hab.ts de Maouna.-12. Hab.ts de Macao
Hab.ts de la Baye des Manilles.-16. Hab.ts des Iles Pelow.-17. Hab.ts d'Oonolaska.-18. Hab.ts d'Ulietea
ts de la Nouvelle Caledonie.-22. Hab.ts d'Otaiti.-23. Hab.ts d'Anaamoka.-24. Hab.ts de Hapaïe

an.ij de la Republique Françoise *Par Jacques Grasset S.t Sauveur* Ancien Vice Consul de France en Hongrie.
queu.n M.on de France. Et a Bordeaux chez la C.en S. Sauveur sous le peristile de la grande Comedie.

Phelipeau Sculp.
Ecrit par Malbeste

18. Ferdinand Bauer, *Eucalyptus capitata*. Eucalyptus Lahmanni. Schau., watercolour, 14¼ × 21¾ in. (*c.* 1810). Ferdinand Bauer drawings of Australian plants, Box 2.f.55, Botanical library, British Museum (Natural History)

6. Settlement at Port Jackson, 1788–1800

THE British occupation of Australia began with the foundation of the penal settlement at Sydney Cove, Port Jackson, in January 1788 by Captain Arthur Phillip. Sir Joseph Banks, whose evidence before a committee of the House of Commons was largely responsible for the choice of Botany Bay as the location of the new settlement, was alive to the fact that it opened a new region for science and for the collection of natural curiosities. As President of the Royal Society he took an official interest in all information that contributed to knowledge and as adviser to the King on the management of the Royal Garden at Kew he was particularly anxious to gain seeds and plants from New Holland.[1] The early Governors of the Colony—Phillip, Hunter, King, and Bligh—were aware of the bent of Banks's interests and appreciated the value of doing what they could to satisfy them: while he acted as their unofficial representative to Government they did all they could to satisfy his unflagging interest in the natural productions of the newly settled country.[2]

Phillip sent many personal letters to Banks describing the land, its plants, animals, and native peoples. He accompanied these descriptions from time to time with drawings. On 3 December 1791, for instance, he enclosed a drawing of a waratah in one of his letters and informed Banks that he had 200 drawings of plants and animals prepared for his inspection.[3] It is not clear who made these drawings for Phillip. The Admiralty certainly did not consider it necessary to appoint a professional artist to a fleet of convict transports. Nor did the fleet contain a convict artist.[4] There were, however, two men with considerable proficiency in drawing who were well able to produce illustrations of the plants and animals, and to record their impressions of the native people and the scenery of New Holland, namely George Raper,[5] a midshipman on the *Sirius*, and an artist who, until he is identified, may conveniently be called the Port Jackson Painter,[6] since the great bulk of his work is concerned with subjects to be identified with the environs of Port Jackson. Three other men also made drawings worthy of mention during the first four years of settlement: Lieutenant William Bradley and Captain John Hunter (both of the *Sirius*), and Arthur Bowes, assistant surgeon on the *Lady Penrhyn*. The work of Raper, Bradley, Hunter, and the Port Jackson Painter has certain similarities both in subject-matter and in style, similarities which are best understood in the light of the development of naval draughtsmanship and natural-history illustration in England during the second half of the eighteenth century.

The Port Jackson Painter was the most accomplished of this circle of naval draughtsmen, his style influencing the work of the others. His known work consists of over 250 water-colour drawings. These include coastal profiles, drawings of birds, snakes, insects, fish, and mammals collected in the neighbourhood of Port Jackson or Norfolk Island, together with drawings of aborigines both as individuals and in groups, and several illustrations of incidents associated with the first years of the Colony, that is between 1788 and 1792. The Port Jackson Painter's repertoire is thus closely related to the graphic work of the exploring expeditions. Other features of his work also link him with the traditions of naval cartography and illustration. He frames his drawings, for instance, by means of a triple-banded border, the external bands being of one colour (often pink or grey), the reserved band so created being tinted with another colour of lighter tone. And he made maps and charts of harbour surveys. Some personal mannerisms of style help to identify his work. He rarely fails to adopt a formula for the coloration of the skies of his drawings which makes use of a gradated wash of cobalt through lemon-yellow to pink-madder; the sequence being reversed when treating water reflections—a common feature of his work. Foreground waves are indicated by means of a characteristic horizontal hatching. Both aspects of the painter's style are revealed in his water-colour *Ban nel lang meeting the Governor by appointment after he was wounded by Willa ma ring in September 1790* (Colour Plate 16). Figures are usually well-proportioned but crudely drawn; frontal or almost frontal shoulders and breasts are commonly conjoined to profile heads, buttocks, and legs, giving the figure a twisted and primitive appearance. Heads are usually drawn in full face or profile, the three-quarter view being rarely attempted. There is a tendency to silhouette, especially in portraits (Plate 104), but in figure work the contours of the breasts and the pelvic girdle, and the navel, knee, and calf-muscle are usually clearly indicated (Colour Plate 15). The hallmark of the painter's style is the irregular, sinuous, brushwork used to depict the markings upon the bark of trees, and varied foreground features, such as rocks and water (Plate 103).

It is to be noted that the Port Jackson Painter working in a tradition of topography relatively untouched by the neo-classical tradition of the Academy rarely attempts to make his aborigines affect the proportions and the gestures known to eighteenth-century artists through their acquaintance with ancient marbles. That he was not, however, entirely immune from the devices of neo-classicism is revealed by his tondo of a wounded aborigine (Plate 105), which is drawn in the pose of the Dying Gaul. But this is exceptional. For the most part the Port Jackson Painter sought, as honestly as his skill would allow, to present the characteristic features of the aborigines he chose to represent with their ritual painting and cicatrization, and their daily activities of food

103. The Port Jackson painter, '*The Hunted Rushcutter*', watercolour, 6¾ × 11¾ in. (*c.* 1790). Banks MS. 34. British Museum (Natural History)

104. The Port Jackson painter, *Gna-na-gna-na*, watercolour, 10 × 7¾ in. (*c.* 1790). 'Watling' Drawings 26.49, British Museum (Natural History)

105. The Port Jackson painter, *A Native wounded while asleep*, watercolour, 6¾ diam. (*c.* 1790). 'Watling' Drawings, 61 British Museum (Natural History)

106. Port Jackson painter, *Snake*, watercolour, $11\frac{1}{2} \times 8$ in. (*c.* 1790). Banks MS 34.79, Botanical Library, British Museum (Natural History)

107. Port Jackson painter, *Black Swan*, watercolour, $9 \times 7\frac{1}{2}$ in. (*c.* 1790). 'Watling' Drawings, 87.283. British Museum (Natural History)

gathering. But the approach is by no means objective; into the ethnographical record there has crept an amused superiority not altogether untempered by a certain tenderness of feeling. This latter quality echoes that sentimentality with which the savage was endowed in such current works as Keate's *Account of the Pelew Islands*. Certainly it is not without significance that the Port Jackson Painter never portrays his natives in attitudes of extreme violence. Even in such illustrations as the '*Hunted Rushcutter*' (Plate 103), there is no attempt to present the aborigine as a ferocious brute; curiosity and amusement are the feelings evoked, not derision and scorn.

The work of the Port Jackson Painter is seen at its best in his illustrations of natural history. His drawing of a *Snake*, for example (Plate 106), is distinguished by its breadth of design and its feeling for the lissom vitality of the reptile. His *Black Swan* (Plate 107) unites grace of line with a fine economy of pattern.

The work of George Raper both in its subject-matter and its style is closely related to the work of the Port Jackson Painter.[7] Raper uses the triple-banded border, frequently gradates his skies from cobalt through yellow to crimson, and uses horizontal hatching to represent waves upon foreground water. His colours, however, in his views are usually paler and cooler than those of the Port Jackson Painter, being more in the nature of tinted drawings. Both painters worked frequently upon similar subjects and Raper appears to have copied the work of his companion on at least two occasions: namely, a view of the wreck of the Sirius and a drawing of aboriginal implements.[8] Raper's work lacks the vitality and scope of the Port Jackson Painter but his natural-history drawings, particularly those of fish and flowers, are finely executed.

The work of William Bradley, apart from his charts, is known only from the twenty-nine water-colour illustrations in his MS. journal, another two water-colours in the

Mitchell Library[9] and a small one in the Nan Kivell Collection have been ascribed to him.[10] Bradley did not cover so wide a range of subjects as the Port Jackson Painter but like him drew coastal profiles and harbour views on the voyage out, recorded incidents, such as the *First Interview with the Native Women of Port Jackson*[11] and the *Wreck of the Sirius at Norfolk Island*[12] together with nautical *mirabilia* such as *Waterspouts off the Coast of Java* (Plate 108), and *Ice Islands observed off Cape Horn*. His style, like his subject-matter, is related to the work of the Port Jackson Painter, but his minute figures and hesitant treatment reveal his limitations as a draughtsman. There is, however, a certain visual fantasy in such paintings as *Fortified Bay on the W. Side the entrance of Rio Janeiro*[13] which is not to be attributed entirely to his deficiencies in draughtsmanship. Bradley's *View in Broken Bay, New South Wales, March 1788*,[14] with its foreground embellishments consisting of contrasting native and European groups, its harbour containing native canoes and European vessels against a background of virgin bushland, is the forerunner of a type of view to be repeated again and again by artists working in the Colony during the succeeding fifty years.[15]

Paintings completed by members of the Port Jackson circle soon found their way to England together with specimens of the local plants and animals. 'Our ship', wrote James Hardy Vaux, 'was . . . literally crowded, so as to resemble Noah's Ark. There were kangaroos, black swans, a noble emu, and cockatoos, parrots, and smaller birds without number . . . all . . . except one cockatoo, which was carefully nursed by its mistress, and half a dozen swans, fell victims to the severity of the weather. . . . On their arrival in England, they were sent by Captain King as a present to the Royal Menagerie in Kew Gardens.'[16] The natural curiosities aroused the interest of the British public far more than the story of the foundation of the penal settlement. Early

108. William Bradley, *Waterspouts off the Coast of Java, near Batavia, 24 Sept. 1791*, watercolour, $5\frac{1}{4} \times 7\frac{1}{2}$ in. MS *Journal*, f.p. 290 Mitchell Library, Sydney. By permission of the Trustees of the State Library of New South Wales

publications were designed largely to meet the current interest in books of travel which had been greatly augmented by the success of Cook's *Voyages* and to satisfy the interests of scientists and virtuosi in the natural productions of the country. It is significant that John Stockdale, the publisher of the *Voyage of Governor Phillip to Botany Bay* (1789), in an advertisement prefaced to the book, asks his readers to excuse the delay in publication on the grounds that, although the government was kind enough to communicate Phillip's official papers to him for publication these unfortunately contained 'little information on subjects of natural history, and many other points, concerning which the curiosity of every reader would naturally be excited'[17] The publication of the book was, in consequence, delayed as it was found that the ships returning from Sydney were bringing interesting new information which made it necessary to engrave new plates. Before the book was published John Latham (1740–1837), the leading English ornithologist of his day, had already in his possession a considerable number of original drawings of Australian birds, and was able to furnish Stockdale with drawings and descriptions. Drawings made in the Colony appear to have circulated among some members of the Royal and the Linnean Societies interested in the plants and animals of New Holland. At the time, for instance, that John Latham produced his *General History of Birds* (1821–8) a collection of drawings of birds of New South Wales were in the possession of John Francillon, a London silversmith who acted as an agent for the disposal of John Abbott's drawings and specimens.[18] These drawings may have been the copies or they may have been the original drawings which came into the possession of James Lee, the Hammersmith nurseryman who had employed Sydney Parkinson as a natural-history draughtsman before Banks took him to the South Seas. Lee was a close friend of Banks and introduced many exotic plants into England including the fuchsia. Lee's drawings are probably the originals from which the collection of 214 paintings of birds and mammals of New South Wales, now known as the Lambert[19] drawings, were copied.

The piecemeal arrival of drawings in England, their passing from hand to hand, their duplication by careful copying by professional draughtsmen, and their subsequent dispersal into public and private collections in England, Australia, and New Zealand, makes the identification of original drawings by members of the Port Jackson circle of draughtsmen a complicated and hazardous matter. But their history does serve to underline the fact that they were essentially scientific documents and indicates how far the interest shown in Australia among educated people in Britain during the first years of settlement was directed towards the natural curiosities of the country.

Further evidence of the nature of educated interest in Australia during its first years is contained in the second illustrated book to be published concerning the settlement at Port Jackson. The title of John White's *Journal of a Voyage to New South Wales with 65 plates of Non-descript Animals, Birds, Lizards, Serpents, Curious Cones of Trees, and other Natural Productions* (1790) makes it quite clear that the book is concerned with a voyage and natural history, and not with the problems of establishing a penal colony.[20] In a letter prefaced to the book White reveals that it was undertaken at the request of Thomas Wilson, a member of the Linnean Society, and expresses the hope that it will lead to the promotion of Wilson's favourite science. White proceeds to thank those scientists such as George Shaw, the zoologist, James Edward Smith, the botanist, and John Hunter, the famous surgeon and anatomist, all of whom had helped him to describe 'so great a variety of animals presented for the first time to the Naturalist'. A number of artists were employed in England to make finished drawings for the *Journal*. Although some of these drawings may have been made from dried

109. *The White Fulica*
(White Gallinule), engraving in John White, *Journal of
a Voyage to New South Wales*
(1790)

specimens most of them appear to be redrawn from originals executed in the
Colony—fifteen of the engravings certainly have been made from originals by the
Port Jackson Painter. Some of the engravings in White depict the animal in its natural
landscape setting. The engraving of *The White Gallinule* (Plate 109), a kind of moorhen
of Lord Howe Island, that became extinct possibly before white settlement in 1834, is
shown in its appropriate habitat. Indeed the background is suggestive of the contours
of Mounts Lidgbird and Gower at the south-east end of the island.

Another book also undertaken at the persuasion of Thomas Wilson was James
Edward Smith's *Specimen of the Botany of New Holland* (1793–4). Smith was the founder
and first president of the Linnean Society of London and a close friend of Banks. He
made his mark in the scientific world when, as a young medical student, he induced
his father to purchase for him the great collection of Carl von Linné.[21] Smith's book
reveals that five years after the foundation of the Colony a considerable interest in the
cultivation of Australian flowers had already developed in England. The intention of
the book was 'to inform the cultivators of plants concerning what they had already
obtained from New Holland', and to point out things worthy of acquisition. The
illustrations in the book were taken from coloured drawings made in the colony and
sent by John White to Thomas Wilson who communicated them later to Smith along
with the dried specimens. The finished drawings were painted and engraved by James
Sowerby (1757–1822)[22] who was at that time, in co-operation with Smith, producing
their monumental *English Botany* (1790–1814). *A Specimen of the Botany of New Holland*
reveals that certain London nurserymen, notably Grimwoods of Kensington, and
Lee and Kennedy of Hammersmith, had been cultivating for some time previously
Australian plants brought home by returning vessels. Indeed we are told that in 1789
many Australian plants were to be seen 'in the highest perfection' at the

Hammersmith nursery and that James Lee regretted that 'the discovery of those countries was not made at a period of his life, when he could have gone personally to reap the glorious harvest'.[23] Professional botanists were also eager to collect specimens from New Holland. On 10 June 1793 John Sibthorp, Sherardian Professor at Oxford, wrote to Banks: 'The Pacquet from New South Wales arrived yesterday full of Curiosities, fresh and in high Preservation. I could discover curious Banksia amongst them and with the assistance of Gärtner whose figures many of them are drawn from Specimens in your Museum. I shall be able to make out most of the Genera. I write to Governor Philips this Evening to thank him for the favour—but it is to your kindness that I am primarily obliged.'[24]

The nobility and gentry interested in horticulture, at the time a more than usually fashionable pursuit, were equally interested in New Holland's exotic plants. At Nyn Hall, Barnet, the dowager Lady de Clifford, Smith tells us, had a waratah growing in her garden, though up to the time of publication it had not flowered.[25] Lord Viscount Lewisham was more fortunate, his *pimelia linifolia* had flowered in February 1794. A year previously *pimelia* had flowered at Sion House. *Mimosa* had been raised in plenty from seeds brought from Port Jackson and, writes Smith, 'is now not uncommon in our greenhouses'.[26] Smith's interest in the plants of New Holland was echoed two years later by Francis Bauer when he published his *Exotic Plants Cultivated in the Royal Garden at Kew (1796)*, a magnificent folio of coloured engravings of flowers mainly from Australia and the Cape. 'The settlement of a colony on the coast of New South Wales', he wrote in the opening paragraph of the preface, 'has offered to us a fresh store of botanical wealth, in a climate nearly congenial to our own; and of this a large share has been transmitted to Kew, by Arthur Philip, Esq. the Governor.'[27] And with what excitement and enjoyment the flowering of such rare exotic specimens was attended may be estimated from a letter which the Duchess of Portland sent, about this time, to Banks:

The Duchess of Portland presents her Compts to Sir Joseph Banks—hopes he will excuse the trouble she is now giving him—The Dchss of P. understands The *Nymphaea Nelumbo*[28] was introduced into England by Sir Joseph Banks, and that it never has yet Flowerd in this Country—The Dchss of Portland came to town from Bulstrode last Night, and left her plant [bearing that name] in a very prosperous way towards Flowering very fine; and from its forward appearance should imagine it might blow in a few days—The Dchss thought it possible Sir J. Banks might have some Curiosity upon this subject, which is her reason for giving him this information—at the same time she should be much Obliged to him if he would let her know what Colour she may expect the Flower to be.[29]

The plants and animals of Australia then, excited attention because they were viewed as remarkable curiosities. Smith complained about those horticulturists who claimed that 'the vegetable productions of New Holland, however novel and singular, are deficient in beauty'.[30] Yet the opinion was widespread. The strangeness of the plants placed difficulties in the way of classifiers. Dr. Solander's notebooks classifying the plants he collected with Banks at Botany Bay are a mass of erasures and revisions. Until the definitive work of Robert Brown had been completed, early workers on Australian botany busied themselves correcting the mistakes of their predecessors. The intractability of the new material had one important consequence for botanical theory, for it led Brown to adopt the natural system of Jussieu in the place of the sexual system of Linnaeus, a decision which led to the general acceptance of the natural system among British botanists.

The situation was if anything more difficult when it came to the classification of animals. Australian animals perplexed Dr. George Shaw (1751–1818) when he came to describe them for John White. Shaw was one of the most esteemed zoologists of his day, a founder of the Linnean Society (1788), a member of the Royal Society (1789) and an assistant keeper of the British Museum (1791), yet when he came to discuss the classification of the kangaroo he was initially beset by grave doubts:

> The kangaroo, the most extraordinary and striking animal which the Southern Hemisphere has yet exhibited to our view, may admit of being arranged differently by systematic naturalists. If we take into consideration the very remarkable particularity of the abdominal pouch with which the female is provided, we may with Gmelin, Schreber, Pennant, and others, rank it in the genus *Didelphis*, or *Opossum*: but if we advert to the form, structure and situation of the teeth, we shall find them so totally different from the animals of that genus as to preclude all possibility of an association with the *Delphides*. In the mean time, if external form or habit alone were regarded, we might consider the kangaroo as a gigantic kind of *Jerboa*, since it has the same length of hind-legs, the same brevity of fore-legs, and the same springing motions and shape; yet the teeth are almost as different from those of the *Jerboa* as from those of the *Opossum*. In fact, we need not have the slightest hesitation in forming for the kangaroo a distinct genus with the characters above prefixed.[31]

In a more general way it can be argued that the wealth of new material which arrived in such abundance from the Pacific during the last two decades of the century exposed not only the systematics of the biological sciences but also traditional European ideas concerning the nature of the universe to novel and difficult questions, and was one of the factors which led to the collapse in scientific circles of the chain of being as an acceptable explanation of universal nature.[32] That cosmology was fittingly expressed by Linnaeus, the most influential naturalist of the century, in the following fashion:

> If we consider the generation of Animals, we find that each produces an offspring after its own kind . . . and that from each proceeds a germ of the same nature with its parent; so that all living things, plants, animals, and even mankind themselves form one 'chain of universal Being', from the beginning to the end of the world: in this sense truly may it be said, that there is nothing new under the sun.[33]

Now James Edward Smith not only bought Linnaeus's library, he also did much, like Banks and James Lee, to spread his ideas in England. That he accepted the idea of the great chain of being in the form in which Linnaeus enunciated it is revealed by a reflection which he appends to his remarks upon the first plate of his book on Australian plants:

> It is the peculiar privilege of reasoning man not only to extend his enquiries to a multiplicity of attainable benefits to himself and to his species, beside the mere animal necessity of food, but also to walk with God through the garden of creation, and be initiated into the different plans of his providence in the construction and oeconomy of all these various beings: to study their dependencies upon one another in an infinitely complex chain, every link of which is essential; and to trace all those various uses and benefits to every branch of the animal creation. . . . In this point of view no natural production is beneath the notice of the philosopher, nor any enquiry trifling under the guidance of a scientific mind.[34]

But natural philosophers more than once complained that the Australian section of the garden of Creation appeared to be planned upon principles not easily reconciled with the idea of a chain of universal being. Smith himself outlined the theoretical difficulties presented by the natural productions of the country:

> When a botanist first enters on the investigation of so remote a country as New Holland, he finds himself as it were in a new world. He can scarcely meet with any certain fixed points from which to draw his analogies; and even those that appear most promising are frequently in danger of misleading him. Whole tribes of plants, which at first sight seem familiar to his acquaintance, as occupying links in Nature's chain ... prove, on a nearer examination, total strangers, with other configurations, other oeconomy, and other qualities; not only the species that present themselves are new, but most of the genera, and even natural orders.[35]

And to Captain John Hunter, who published his *Journal of the Transactions at Port Jackson and Norfolk Island* in the same year that Smith began publishing his *Specimen of the Botany of New Holland*, the animals of the country constituted an even greater scientific problem than the plants. The logic of the great chain of being rested upon the inviolability of the species. Each link in the chain was an entity, distinct in essence from every other, no matter how close one link might approximate in its structure and biological functions to another. In seeking for an explanation, however, for the novel forms of animal life peculiar to Australia, Hunter ignored the presuppositions of the prevalent theory:

> It would appear, from the great similarity in some part or other of the different quadrupeds which we find here, that there is a promiscuous intercourse between the different sexes of all those different animals. The same observation might be made also on the fishes of the sea, on the fowls of the air, and, I may add, the trees of the forest. It was wonderful to see what a vast variety of fish were caught, which, in some part or other, partake of the shark: it is no uncommon thing to see a skait's head and shoulders to the hind part of a shark, or a shark's head to the body of a large mullet, and sometimes to the flat body of a sting-ray.[36]

It would be a mistake to dismiss Hunter's extraordinary notions as being of no account on the grounds that they are nothing more than the chance reflections of a seaman possessing no professional knowledge of natural history. Within twelve months of their publication Hunter's remarks were being used by Erasmus Darwin to support a crucial aspect of the first fully formulated theory of organic evolution. The theory was enunciated in the chapter on generation in Darwin's *Zoonomia*, published in 1794. Therein Darwin claimed that the great multiformity of species now existing upon earth all originated from a single living filament and that the original natural orders which evolved from it produced the present great variety of species as a result of the promiscuous intercourse of a smaller number of original species generating new forms—some of which proved to be fertile. The notion of primeval promiscuity is at the heart of Erasmus Darwin's evolutionary theory. Yet, the only specific example he provides to prove that such promiscuity occurred in the early days of life upon the planet is the passage from Hunter quoted above:

> Such a promiscuous intercourse of animals is said to exist at this day in New South Wales by Captain Hunter. And that not only amongst the quadrupeds and birds of different kinds, but even amongst the fish, and, as he believes, amongst the vegetables. He speaks of an animal between the opposum and the kangaroo, from the size of a sheep to that of a rat. Many fish seemed to partake of the shark; some

with a skate's head and shoulders, and the hind part of a shark; others with a shark's head and the body of a mullet; and some with a shark's head and the flat body of a sting ray. Many birds partake of the parrot; some have the head, neck and bill of a parrot, with long straight feet and legs; others with the legs and feet of a parrot, with the head and neck of a sea-gull.[37]

Since this is the only example Darwin cites it provides reason to speculate upon the possibility of the example itself having played some part in the formation of this aspect of Darwin's theory. In any case it is clear that reflection upon the curious productions of Australasia was continuing to minister to the emergence of evolutionary thought.

There is no more remarkable evidence of the change which took place in European attitudes to primitive peoples between the end of the seventeenth and the end of the eighteenth centuries than that afforded by the contrast between Dampier's and Cook's reflections upon the nature of the life of the Australian aborigine. It was not that they were incapable of writing an objective and factual account of the aborigine as they saw him (for both men were outstanding observers), but they drew quite different inferences from somewhat similar observations. In the account of his first voyage to New Holland, Dampier drew a graphic and most repulsive image of the aborigine:

> The Inhabitants of this Country are the miserablest People in the world. The Hodmadods of Monomatapa, though a nasty People, yet for Wealth are Gentlemen to these; who have no Houses and skin Garments, Sheep, Poultry and Fruits of the Earth, Ostrich Eggs, etc. as the Hodmadods have: and setting aside their Humane Shape, they differ but little from Brutes.[38]

Dampier's picture impressed itself upon the European mind; Cook when observing aborigines upon the eastern coast was careful to indicate where his own observations agreed and where they differed from Dampier's observations of aborigines on the north-west coast. But after the carefully written account of them which appears in his *Journal*, Cook began to reflect upon the simple and austere life of the aborigine:

> From what I have said of the Natives of New-Holland they may appear to some to be the most wretched people upon Earth, but in reality they are far more happier than we Europeans; being wholly unacquainted not only with the superfluous but the necessary Conveniences so much sought after in Europe, they are happy in not knowing the use of them. They live in a Tranquillity which is not disturb'd by the Inequality of Condition: The Earth and sea of their own accord furnishes them with all things necessary for life, they covet not Magnificent Houses, Household-stuff etca, they live in a warm and fine Climate and enjoy a very wholsome Air, so that they have very little need of Clothing and this they seem to be fully sencible of, for many to whom we gave Cloth etca to, left it carelessly upon the Sea beach and in the woods as a thing they had no manner of use for. In short they seem'd to set no Value upon any thing we gave them ... this in my opinion argues that they think themselves provided with all the necessarys of Life and that they have no superfluities.[39]

Such philosophizing on the nature of happiness was for Cook most unusual, and when we find a similar passage also appended to Banks's account of the aborigines[40] we may not unreasonably assume that in this instance Banks's opinions carried weight with Cook. On the other hand we have Cook's explicit statement that the reflections are his own opinions and have no reason for assuming that Banks convinced Cook against his own better judgement. It is significant that Cook never at any time went out of his way to describe the Society Islanders as noble savages however much Banks enthused about life in Tahiti. Cook did not respond sympathetically to the luxury and indolence of Tahitian life but his comments upon the Australian aborigine suggest that he was responsive to those aspects of primitivistic thought which viewed the life of nature as a renunciation of the luxuries and excesses of civilization in which the virtues of endurance and courage were called into continuous operation by the vicissitudes of daily life. In his approach to the Australian aborigine we find Cook, in short, responsive to the philosophy of hard primitivism while remaining suspicious, as the Forsters were, of the soft primitivism exemplified by life in the Society Islands.

Courage was the cardinal virtue of hard primitivism, and it was the courage of the Australian aborigines which first impressed itself upon Cook's company. There was the remarkable case of the two natives who disputed the landing at Botany Bay. 'As soon as we approached the rocks two of the men came down, each armed with a lance about 10 feet long, and a short stick . . . resolved to dispute our landing to their utmost, though they were but two, and we thirty or forty at least.'[41]

For Lord Kames, writing his *Sketches of the History of Man*, this was an example of 'true heroic courage'. Their acts suggested, he continued, that 'the people in that part of New Holland must be a very different race from those whom Dampier saw'.[42]

The plate in Parkinson's *Journal* entitled *Two Natives Advancing to Combat* (Plate 110) had already pictured the aborigines as classical heroes in which the foremost native is drawn in the pose of the Borghese Gladiator, holding a shield and spear which owe far more to classical antiquity than to New Holland. But whether this classicizing of the Australian aborigines began with a lost drawing by Parkinson or was introduced by some unknown draughtsman in developing Parkinson's field sketches for Chambers's engraving is not known. In any case the engraving gave powerful support to the view embraced by both Cook and Kames which saw the aborigine as an exemplar of a harsh but virtuous primitive life.

Despite such endeavours to idealize the aborigine the factual accounts which Cook and Banks brought back bore out much of what Dampier had written. For those who did not choose to regard a lack of material wealth as one of the necessary conditions of happiness, the new knowledge of the aborigine brought back by the *Endeavour*'s company only reinforced earlier opinions. In the field of natural philosophy and reflective thought the general tendency was to regard the New Hollander as brutish rather than heroic: instead of fostering poetic parallels from Theocritus and Vergil he stimulated thought concerning that aspect of the chain of being which presupposed a link between the higher primates and man. For the greater part of the century writers cited the Hottentot as the lowest link in nature's chain,[43] but Dampier's account had presented the New Hollander as a rival candidate for the position. Lord Monboddo, for instance, found the New Hollanders added force to his theory that man and the anthropoid apes belonged to the same species. Man in his original condition, Monboddo claimed, associated in groups like beavers, living together in huts and cabins while carrying on their hunting and fishing in common. 'The huts of the New Hollanders', he pointed out, 'are not near so well built as those of beavers, and serve only as a cover to the head and shoulders, as I am informed by the travellers who have lately been in that country.'[44] In Monboddo's opinion the New Hollanders could never have invented the art of speech for themselves because of the very low and barbarous state in which they live. A similar belief in the low position which they

110. *Two of the Natives of New Holland, Advancing to Combat*, engraving after Parkinson by T. Chambers, in Parkinson, *Voyage to the South Seas* (1773), pl. xxvii

occupied in nature's chain was expressed by George Shaw in his *Zoology of New Holland* (1793) when he wrote, 'the wretched natives of many of those dreary districts seem less elevated above the inferior animals than in any other part of the known world'.[45]

Nevertheless, during the late 1780's and early 1790's, it was still possible to present the Australian aborigine as an idealized figure possessing proportions, attitudes, and expressions derived from classical art. The pictorial interpretation of the aborigine in the neo-classical manner initiated by the engraving in Parkinson, discussed above, is continued by engravings in Phillip's *Voyage* and Hunter's *Journal*. The presence of noble savages in these books is at first surprising when we have regard for the attitudes adopted by men like Monboddo and Shaw, which are fairly typical of the literary reaction to the aborigine, and because drawings by members of the Port Jackson circle of draughtsmen were probably available to the publishers; drawings in which, as we have seen, the aborigine was not rendered as an example of noble savagery. The

111. *Natives of Botany Bay*, engraving after Robert Cleveley by T. Medland, in *The Voyage of Governor Phillip to Botany Bay* (1789), pl. 6

112. *Hut in New South Wales*, engraving after Robert Cleveley by T. Medland, in *Voyage to Governor Phillip to Botany Bay* (1789), pl. 9

publishers, it seems, while utilizing original natural-history illustrations drawn on the spot, rejected similar drawings of native people. The rejection was due, doubtless, to a question of taste. Both Phillip's *Voyage* and Hunter's *Journal* were expensive quartos handsomely produced by subscription and designed to interest virtuosi and men of taste for whom the image of the native as a noble savage still held a strong quasi-aesthetic appeal.[46] Consequently illustrations of aborigines by Robert Cleveley engraved by Thomas Medland for Phillip's *Voyage* are not based upon drawings sent from Sydney but upon neo-classical prototypes of the noble savage as used by

Cipriani, Bartolozzi, and Sherwin for the illustration of Cook's *Voyages*. In this regard the curly hair, pale skin, and dignified posture based on classical models with which Cleveley has endowed his natives (Plate 111) may be contrasted with the frizzy hair, dark skin, and somewhat comical posture of the natives in the Port Jackson Painter's *Woman Meeting her Husband* (Colour Plate 15). In Cleveley's *Hut in New South Wales* (Plate 112) a native family is placed in an idealized parkland setting beside a *mia mia* commodious and dignified enough for a noble savage to live in, while a *putto* holding an enormous *womerah* serves as a piccaninny, and a coconut palm symbolizes the South Seas.

When Hunter's *Journal* was published three years later, however, the pictorial convention of the noble savage was rapidly declining from the eminent position it had held during the 1770's. The engraving made from Hunter's own drawing of a *Man of the Islands called Lord Howe Group* (Plate 113) is, within the restricted limits of Hunter's ability, a straightforward ethnographical statement reproduced, appropriately, together with the sailing-craft of Lord Howe. That the engraver followed Hunter's drawing faithfully may be seen by comparing the engraving with the original in the Nan Kivell Collection.[47] Nevertheless, the publisher has included one example of a typical noble savage family, the *Family of New South Wales* (Plate 114), engraved by William Blake from a sketch traditionally attributed to Governor King, a wash drawing in the Mitchell Library (Plate 115). If so then Blake has, like so many other engravers, elevated the conception and refined the drawing. Engraved some four years after he had published the *Little Black Boy* in his *Songs of Innocence* the engraving is, in some ways, the poem's visual equivalent. Unlike Cipriani and Sherwin, for whom the noble savage was little more than a special application of the elevated style suited to history painting, Blake was personally interested in the moral status of the life of savages and the problem it posed Christian theology. That pagans deprived of Revelation should suffer eternal damnation was a belief morally repugnant to him.

113. *Man of the Islands called Lord Howe Group*, engraving, in Hunter, *Historical Journal* (1793)

114. *A Family of New South Wales*, engraving by William Blake said to be after a sketch by Governor King, in Hunter, *Historical Journal of the Transactions at Port Jackson* (1793), f.p. 414

115. *Family of New South Wales*, artist unidentified, traditionally attributed to Governor P. G. King, wash drawing, $9\frac{1}{4} \times 6\frac{1}{4}$ in. (date not known). Banks papers, xv, A 20–23, Mitchell Library, Sydney. By permission of the Trustees of the State Library of New South Wales

116. *Man of the Island of Tanna*, engraved after Hodges by J. Basire, in Cook, *Voyage Towards the South Pole* (1777), pl. xxvi

117. *Woman of the Island of Tanna*, engraving after Hodges by J. Basire, in Cook, *Voyage Towards the South Pole* (1777), pl. xlv

Blake's little Black Boy though he never hears the name of Christ is capable of dimly apprehending, by means of his awareness of nature's plenitude, the beneficence of God. Something of Blake's deep sympathy for primitive people, so apparent in his poem, has entered into the engraving. The infant on its mother's shoulders and the boy striding behind are no longer artificial *putti* but little black children whose innocence is, for Blake, touched with a profound melancholy. Although it comes towards the end of the history of the type there is no finer pictorial expression of the idea of the noble savage in visual art than Blake's engraving; and it is a measure of the gulf between practical observation and the creative imagination that it should be based upon the representation of a people Dampier called the most miserable in the world.

This was not the first occasion, however, when Blake came into contact with drawings of Pacific people. As an apprentice in Basire's studio of some four years' standing he would certainly have seen the drawings by William Hodges which came into his master's hands in 1776 to engrave for the official account of Cook's Second Voyage. In some of these engravings, such as *Man of the Island of Tanna* and *Woman of the Island of Tanna* (Plates 116, 117), it is not too fanciful to glimpse, in their wiry linearity and characteristic intensity, the presence of Blake's own hand.

It is possible to trace the collapse of the noble savage as a pictorial convention, after 1795, in Blake's own work. Three years after he engraved *A Family of Botany Bay* he assisted in the illustration of Captain J. G. Stedman's *Narrative of a Five Year's Expedition against the Revolted Tribes of Surinam*. In the engraving entitled *Family of Negro Slaves from Loango* (Plate 118) a graceful and dignified young negro, drawn nude but for a loincloth, stands in a pose recalling the *Doryphoros*, and holds a basket of fish in one hand and a large fish in another. An embodiment of youthful masculine beauty it may be compared with the striding male figure in *A Family of New South Wales*. In

118. *Family of Negro Slaves from Loango*, engraving by William Blake, in J. G. Stedman, *Narrative of a Five Years' Expedition against the Revolted Tribes of Surinam* (1796), pl. 68

sharp contrast, however, is a clothed female figure, with a baby strapped to her back, who smokes a pipe with one hand and holds a lighted taper with the other. This figure with its grotesque pose, pouting mouth, dullwitted expression, and clinging children could almost be taken as a parody upon the woman and children in *A Family of New South Wales*. Its affinities are clearly not with the noble savage type but with caricature and comic draughtsmanship. Here, then, in the same engraving the noble savage is confronted by the comic savage, a graphic type to become far more common in the succeeding century; and it is in line with the later development that the comic figure should be depicted clothed and smoking a pipe, and bearing the marks of degeneration consequent upon contact with Europeans.

The changing attitude to the savage revealed in Blake's engravings may be studied also in Watkin Tench's *Complete Account of the Settlement at Port Jackson*, published in 1793. It was, as we have seen, a critical time for the conception of the noble savage. On the one hand, George Keate's *Account of the Pelew Islands* was enjoying wide popularity, on the other, evangelical opinion soon to give rise to a number of missionary societies, was becoming increasingly critical of glowing accounts of pagan savages. Tench's book reflects the cross-currents of the time. His long and detailed account of the young aborigine Arabanoo who, after being forcibly captured, made such a favourable impression upon the official members of the Colony, is clearly written under the influence of Keate's *Account*. Tench noted the gentleness and humanity of Arabanoo's disposition; his extraordinary courteousness to the laides of the settlement; his countenance, which 'under happier circumstances ... would display manliness and sensibility'.[48] He noted an occasion when Arabanoo performed an act of 'attentive benevolence' for one of his own countrymen, and how he displayed symptoms of disgust and terror at the sight of a flogging.[49] Such language and sentiments are very close to those of George Keate, and the parallel was further enhanced by the fact that both Arabanoo and Prince Lee Boo died of smallpox. Tench at the conclusion of his story calls for the sympathy of his readers: 'I feel assured that I have no reader who will not join in regretting the premature death of Arabanoo'[50] and proceeds to give an account of Arabanoo's character which pictures him, like Lee Boo, as a savage of unusually fine sensibility:

> The character of Arabanoo, as far as we had developed it, was distinguished by a portion of gravity and steadiness, which our subsequent acquaintance with his countrymen by no means led us to conclude a national characteristic. In that daring, enterprising frame of mind, which, when combined with genius, constitutes the leader of a horde of savages, or the ruler of a people, boasting the power of discrimination and the resistance of ambition, he was certainly surpassed by some of his successors, who afterwards lived among us. His countenance was thoughtful, but not animated: his fidelity and gratitude, particularly to his friend the governor, were constant and undeviating, and deserve to be recorded. Although of a gentle and placable temper, we early discovered that he was impatient of indignity, and allowed of no superiority on our part. He knew that he was in our power; but the independence of his mind never forsook him. . . . He did not want docility. . . . He was, perhaps, the only native who ever attached to us from choice; and who did not prefer a precarious subsistence among wilds and precipices, to the comforts of a civilized system.[51]

Although Tench's language is so like Keate's it is clear that he does not attribute the fine feelings of his hero, as Keate does, entirely to the life of nature. For Tench, Arabanoo had great potentialities of character which were being developed by his contact with Europeans. By giving this twist to his presentation of a savage of sensibility, Tench is able to include a good deal of primitivistic sentiment in his book, while preserving a position from which he can attack the noble savage as a philosophical conception. This he proceeds to do in another part of his book:

> A thousand times ... have I wished, that those European philosophers, whose closet speculations exalt a state of nature above a state of civilization, could survey the phantom, which their heated imaginations have raised: possibly they might then learn, that a state of nature is, of all others, less adapted to promote the happiness of a being, capable of sublime research, and unending ratiocination: that a savage roaming for prey amidst his native deserts, is a creature deformed by all

those passions, which afflict and degrade our nature, unsoftened by the influence of religion, philosophy and legal restriction: and that the more men unite their talents, the more clearly the bands of society are drawn; and civilisation advanced, inasmuch is human felicity augmented, and man fitted for his unalienable place in the universe.[52]

And yet, despite all this, some pages earlier in his book, Tench, in describing a kind action on the part of some wild natives who assisted his party to cross a creek, writes 'let him whose travels have lain amongst polished nations, produce me a brighter example of disinterested urbanity, than was shown by these denizens of a barbarous clime, to a set of destitute wanderers, on the side of the Hawkesbury'.[53] Tench does not, of course, contradict himself, for his reflections are founded upon both specific instances and more general observations; but there is clearly an inconsistency of attitude, a receptiveness to conflicting opinions about the nature of life among primitive people which is so much a feature of the period in which he wrote. In the end, when summing up the position the aborigine held in the scale of civilization, Tench came to conclusions similar to those of Dampier, Monboddo, and George Shaw:

> If they be considered as a nation, whose general advancement and acquisitions are to be weighed, they certainly rank very low, even in the scale of savages. They may perhaps dispute the right of precedency with the Hottentots, or the shivering tribes who inhabit the shores of Magellan. But how inferior do they show themselves when compared with the subtle African; the patient watchful American; or the elegant timid islander of the South Seas.[54]

The inconsistency of sentiment, if not of logic, in Captain Watkin Tench's descriptions of the Australian aborigine serves to remind us that two quite contradictory attitudes to nature run through much of eighteenth-century thought. On the one hand it was claimed that all our misfortunes are due to our departure from nature's laws, while on the other it was claimed that man could only raise himself above the brute creation by improving upon nature. The contradiction was often more apparent than real depending upon the particular meaning of the word nature concerned.[55] Nevertheless, the two attitudes did arise from a real division in eighteenth-century thought.[56] Whereas the discovery of the Society Islands ministered, as Gilbert Chinard has shown,[57] to the first attitude, the discovery of Australia (and New Zealand) ministered rather to the second. This is not surprising. The Society Island were naturally fertile, capable of sustaining a form of society which Europeans found congenial: by comparison Australia (and New Zealand) were infertile, 'barbaric coasts'. Settlement upon them therefore tended to stimulate that aspect of eighteenth-century thought which found the ordering of nature and a belief in the idea of progress acceptable. The frame of mind which saw Australian nature as something to be worked upon and made congenial for human occupation was expressed from the beginning. It was stated in detail in Phillip's *Voyage*:

> There are few things more pleasing than the contemplation of order and useful arrangement, arising gradually out of tumult and confusion; and perhaps this satisfaction cannot anywhere be more fully enjoyed than where a settlement of civilised people is fixing itself upon a newly discovered or savage coast. The wild appearance of the land entirely untouched by cultivation, the close and perplexed growing of trees, interrupted now and then by barren spots, bare rocks, or spaces overgrown with weeds, flowers, flowering shrubs, or underwood, scattered and

119. Henry Webber, *Hope, Art, Labour and Peace at Botany Bay*, medallion, 2¼ in. diam. Designed by Henry Webber and made by Josiah Wedgwood from clay sent from Sydney in 1788. The Wedgwood Museum, Barlaston

120. *Liberty presenting Art, Labour and Peace with the bonnet rouge*, Sevres porcelain medallion (*c.* 1796). The Wedgwood Museum, Barlaston

intermingled in the most promiscuous manner, are the first objects that present themselves; afterwards, the irregular placing of the first tents which are pitched, or huts which are erected for immediate accommodation, wherever chance presents a spot tolerably free from obstacles, or more easily cleared than the rest, with the bustle of various hands busily employed in a number of the most incongruous works, increases rather than diminishes the disorder, and produces a confusion of effect, which for a time appears inextricable, and seems to threaten an endless continuance of perplexity. But by degrees large spaces are opened, plans are formed, lines marked, and a prospect at least of future regularity is clearly discerned, and is made the more striking by the recollection of former confusion.[58]

Pleasure at witnessing the imposition of order upon untamed nature was not an inappropriate sentiment to express upon the occasion of the foundation of a penal settlement and few reflections are more commonly expressed by travellers in New South Wales during the following fifty years. It was a short step from expressing pleasure at the emergence of order from the wilderness to prophecies concerning the future of the Colony. The Society Islands had inspired poets and painters to reflect upon the past glories of the Golden Age, and Botany Bay inspired George Forster[59] and Erasmus Darwin to rhapsodize upon the glories to come. Josiah Wedgwood had fashioned a medallion from clay sent from New South Wales by Phillip which depicted 'Hope encouraging Art and Labour, under the Influence of Peace, to pursue the employment necessary to give security and happiness to an infant settlement.' The designer was Henry Webber, John Webber's brother. An engraving of the medallion was used as a frontispiece to Phillip's *Voyage* (Plate 119), and this was accompanied by a dedicatory poem by Erasmus Darwin, entitled *The Visit of Hope to Botany Bay*.[60] The subject must have been congenial enough to Darwin with his progressivist and evolutionary ideas soon to blossom in the *Economy of Vegetation* and *Zoonomia*. Interpreting Wedgwood's medallion he introduced the allegorical figure of Hope who stands high upon a rock overlooking Sydney Harbour. Calming the waves and stretching her hands over sea and land she delivers a prophetic message, telling how broad streets will extend their stately walls about a city planned with circle and crescent, and how villas will crown the landscape, and farms, orchards, spires, and quays rise as commerce expands and the city grows. The vision of Darwin's Hope was essentially municipal and agricultural. But it was not long before the same design was being used a political symbol. Henry Webber's design was produced by Wedgwood in the year the French Revolution began, and about seven years later the French porcelain manufactury at Sevres, looking for a suitable design to symbolize the new spirit of liberation, copied the design closely. But on this occasion Hope is replaced by Liberty who, presents a Phrygian cap or *bonnet rouge*, at the end of her sceptre, to Peace, Art and Labour, and behind them, on a cracked and broken Ionic column (Louis XVI had been excuted three years before), is hung a shield askew, containing the royal emblem, a triple *fleur-de-lis* (Plate 120).[61]

At Sydney Cove, however, the new delight in civic order gave rise to prophetic pronouncements, and it was not very long before the prophecies became variants of those notions of social undulation given currency, at this time, by Fleurieu and others. So for James Tuckey, writing his *Account of a Voyage to Establish a Colony in Bass's Strait* (1805), Australia, like Rome—the parallel was to be pointed by others also—will use the outcasts of other societies to build an empire which will emerge in the South as the empires of the North decline:

> When I considered the motives; when I contrasted the powers, the ingenuity, and the resources of civilised man, with the weakness, the ignorance, and the wants of the savage he came to dispossess, I acknowledged the immensity of human intelligence.... These thoughts naturally led to the contemplation of future possibilities. I beheld a second Rome, rising from a coalition of banditti. I beheld it giving laws to the world, and superlative in arms and in arts, looking down with proud superiority upon the barbarous nations of the northern hemisphere....[62]

Such ideas, so congenial to the ambitions of colonial nationalism, were to be expressed again and again, throughout the century.

If the ordering of the Australian landscape gave early observers pleasure, so also did those aspects of it which reminded them of England. Hawkesworth, one of the few sources of information concerning New South Wales available to members of the first fleet, paraphrasing Cook and Banks, wrote of the landscape of New South Wales: 'it is upon the whole rather barron than fertile', but continued with approval, 'yet the rising ground is chequered with woods and lawns'.[63] Parkinson, the other available authority, wrote more enthusiastically: 'The country looked very pleasant and fertile; and the trees, quite free from underwood, appeared like plantations in a gentleman's park.'[64]

The opinion that the land in the neighbourhood of Port Jackson was in many places like an English park, with the authority of Parkinson to back it, was expressed by several members of the first fleet. Describing the entrance to Sydney Harbour, Hunter wrote: 'Near, and at the head of the harbour, there is a very considerable extent of tolerable land, and which may be cultivated without waiting for its being cleared of wood; for the trees stand very wide of each other, and have no underwood: in short, the woods on the spot I am speaking of resemble a deer park, as much as if they had been intended for such a purpose.'[65] Elizabeth Macarthur applied this particular description more generally. In a letter to her friend Miss England she remarks that 'the greater part of the country is like an English park, and the trees give it the appearance of a wilderness or shrubbery, commonly attached to the habitations of the people of fortune'.[66] This view that the Australian landscape was like an English nobleman's park is also suggested in early pictorial representations of it. The Port

Jackson Painter places his amiable aborigines in a countryside composed of gentle lawn-like foregrounds which slope down to a lake-like harbour backed by evenly rounded hills which are dotted with isolated clumps of trees and fringed with long belts of timber. It is all rather like a whimsical antipodean commentary upon the landscaping of Capability Brown whose taste and methods had transformed so many of the country seats of England during the 1750s and 1760s.[67] Cleveley's designs for the engravings in Phillip's *Voyage* are also park-like in character but, unlike the Port Jackson Painter, he makes a concession to the exotic nature of the scenery by introducing the coconut palm and the grass tree.

Despite such homely comparisons observers were, of course, well aware of the essential difference between English and Australian scenery. Men became aware of an element of deceit in this apparently beautiful park. It was a curious land in which the exotic brilliance of the plants, birds, and insects detracted from the barrenness of the soil and the vagaries of the climate. Above all it was difficult to cultivate. James Edward Smith, as we have seen, claimed in 1793 that the most promising Australian plants could prove to be extremely misleading to the botanist. Already in the first months of settlement observers were extending a similar criticism to the land in general: the nobleman's park was an enchanted park in which things were not what they seemed. So it appeared to Arthur Bowes as his ship sailed into Port Jackson on 26 January 1788:

> ... the finest terras's, lawns, and grottos, with distinct plantations of the tallest and most stately trees I ever saw in any nobleman's grounds in England, cannot excel in beauty those w'h nature now presented to our view. The singing of the various birds amongst the trees, and the flight of the numerous parraquets, lorrequets, cockatoos, and maccaws, made all around appear like in enchantment; the stupendous rocks from the summit of the hills and down to the very water's edge hang'g over in a most awful manner from above, and form'g the most commodious quays by the water, beggar'd all description.[68]

A somewhat similar view was taken by Lieutenant Southwell in a retrospective description of the Sydney harbour which he wrote in his MS. journal a few months later. By then, however, the enchanting beauty had begun to appear as something of a delusion:

> ... nothing can be conceived more picturesque than the app'e of the country while running up this extra [ordinary] harbour. The land on all sides is high, and cover'd with an exuber'n of trees; towards the water, craggy rocks and vast declivity are everywhere to be seen. The scene is beautifully height'ed by a number of small islands that are dispers'd here and there, on which may be seen charm'g seats, superb buildings, the grand ruins of stately edifices, etc. etc., which as we pass'd were visible, but at intervals the view being pr'ty agreeably interrupted by the intervention of some proud eminence, or lost in the labyrynth of the inchanting glens that so abound in this fascinating scenery. 'Tis greatly to be wish'd these appearances were not so delusive as in reality they are.[69]

There were of course neither charming seats nor superb ruins, but the strangeness of the scenery lent itself to fanciful description. When the young convict Thomas Watling[70] sailed up Sydney harbour a few years later, he too, culling his imagery from English poetry and French romance, saw the landscape as an enchanted and deceitful garden:

The flattering appearance of nature may be offered as the best apology for those mistaken eulogisms lavished by a late eminent circumnavigator upon this place. Perhaps nothing can surpass the circumambient windings, and romantic banks of a narrow arm of the sea, that leads from this to *Parramatta*, another settlement fourteen miles off. The poet may there descry numberless beauties; nor can there be fitter haunts for his imagination. The elysian scenery of a Telemachus;—the secret recesses for a Thompson's musidora;—arcadian shades, or classic bowers, present themselves at every winding to the ravished eye.—Overhead the most grotesque foliage yields a shade, where cooling zephyrs breathe every perfume. Mangrove avenues, and picturesque rocks, entwined with non-descript flowers:—In short, were the benefits in the least equal to the specious external, this country need hardly give place to any other on earth.[71]

For Watling, then, the beauties of Australia were so delusive that even Cook was misled by them. He is a valuable commentator, so far as the study of the history of ideas concerning Australian nature is concerned, for he sought not only to describe individual plants and animals but also to give his general impressions of the country. On one occasion he wrote:

Returning then back to general observations; and supposing you to have heard something of the swiftness, meekness, and singular formation of the Kangaroo, of the Opossum, Guanoe, Lizards, etc., I may say, that not only these, but the whole appearance of nature must be striking in the extreme to the adventurer, and at first this will seem to him to be a country of enchantments. The generality of the birds and the beasts sleeping by day, and singing or catering in the night, is such an inversion in nature as is hitherto unknown.[72]

One reason then for the country's apparent enchantment is its inversions. Watling has here given the medieval notion of antipodal inversion, so frequently used by critics of European social institutions in their descriptions of Austral Commonwealths for the purposes of political satire, a biological twist—and in this form it was to gain wide currency among observers of the Australian scene throughout the greater part of the succeeding century.

The view that Australia was a land of enchanted wonders was taken up by Thomas Pennant in attempting to describe the habitations of the aborigines. 'Their habitations', he wrote, 'were little wigwams, made of sticks covered with bark; others reminded you of those of the *Dryads* of the poets: they formed a hollow in vast trees of the country, to the height of six or seven feet, which they effected by fire; they left so much untouched that the trees grew most luxuriantly, and gave the image of Tasso's enchanted groves.'[73]

The fanciful and romantic observations of the first observers were not borne out by closer examination. A growing distaste for the country begins to set in almost immediately after the first favourable impressions are recorded in January 1788. The reason is to be sought for partly in the material circumstances of the observers; surrounded by the poverty, hunger, and loneliness of the first critical years of settlement, all of which produced an overpowering longing to return home among all members of the settlement, convicts and officials alike, and partly in the visual monotony of the Cumberland Plain[74] in its virgin state. For Watling, and doubtless for others also, homesickness induced a melancholy that coloured, as he admitted in one of his letters to his aunt, both his verbal and visual accounts of the Colony:

In my saddest hours, and God knows there are many of them, I have observed you are then most busy with my memory. Melancholy's sombre shadow louring over my soul, endears the fleeting moment by impelling me to write to you. Indeed, it is solely owing to this despondent state of mind, that ought I have produced for these last four years proceeds. When this gloom frowns dreadful over the vista of my being, I but too much indulge the dreary prospect—exploring the wide domain of adversity terminated only by the impending darkness:—hence it is, that whatever flows from my pen, or is laboured by my pencil, affects, in some degree, the tone of mind that possesses me at the period of its production.[75]

Southwell had called the country surrounding Sydney Harbour picturesque, and Watling, too, speaks of 'picturesque rocks' seen on his trip to Parramatta. But Watling did not consider Australian landscape in general to be picturesque. The landscape would suit a poet's imagination but it was no place for a painter. This he makes quite clear in one of his letters:

My worthy friend, Mr. H—, may reasonably conclude, that these romantic scenes will much amuse my pencil; though therein he is much mistaken. The landscape painter, may in vain seek here for that beauty which arises from happy-opposed off-scapes. Bold rising hills, or azure distances would be a kind of phaenomena. The principal traits of the country are extensive woods, spread over a little-varied plain.[76]

This was, after all, quite an accurate description of the Cumberland Plain, a region which lacked the type of picturesque beauty that appealed so much to writers like William Gilpin. It is quite possible that Watling had some acquaintance, either directly or indirectly, with the works of Gilpin, for Gilpin makes a distinction between romantic and picturesque very much like Watling's distinction. Arthur's Seat, to take an example, was, for Gilpin, romantic but not picturesque, since it was 'odd, mis-shapen and uncouth',[77] words that recall to some extent Watling's description of the scenery and natural productions of Australia.

Nevertheless, as Watling was aware, picturesque landscape was never meant to be a faithful representation of a scene from one point of view. They were composite, contrived landscapes wherein motifs from several sketches were assembled according to the rules of picturesque beauty. So he was prepared to qualify his remark that Australian landscape was unpaintable:

I however confess, that were I to select and combine, I might avoid that sameness, and find engaging employment. Trees wreathing their old fantastic roots on high; dissimilar in tint and foliage; cumbent, upright, fallen, or shattered by lightning, may be found at every step; whilst sympathetic glooms of twilight glimmering groves, and wildest nature lulled in soft repose, might much inspire the soul—all this I confess. . . .[78]

In other words a little judicious selection might make it possible to compose a wild landscape in the manner of Rosa, or a moonlight scene, then so fashionable in England. Although only a few of his sketches and but one well-documented landscape in oils have been preserved it is possible to observe Watling in the process of carrying out his suggested programme. This may be done by comparing his wash drawing *Taken from the Westside of Sydney Cove behind the Hospital* (Plate 121) with the painting he composed from it, *Sydney in 1794* (Plate 122).

We need not doubt that Watling's drawing, though generalized and lacking in

182

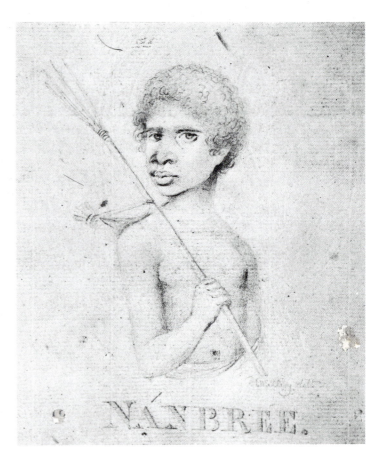

123. Thomas Watling, *Nanbree*, pencil, $7 \times 5\frac{1}{4}$ in. (*c.* 1794). 'Watling' drawings 43, British Museum (Natural History)

detail, is a fairly faithful statement. It contains an horizon line which curves evenly in one arc, a line that Gilpin condemned as unpicturesque in his appreciation of landscape forms. 'Indeed', says Gilpin, 'a continuity of line without a break, whether it be concave, straight or convex, will always displease, because it wants variety.'[79] In the painting, Watling altered the horizon line. It is varied in clarity, softened by atmosphere, broken by trees and cottage smoke, and transformed into a shallow serpentine curve. In the drawing the greater part of the foreground is bathed in an even raking light. Describing his own method Gilpin wrote: 'in general, we are perhaps better pleased with a *dark* foreground. It makes a kind of graduating shade, from the eye through the removed parts of the picture; and carries off the distance better than any other contrivance.'[80] In the painting Watling has darkened the foreground so leading the eye to the Cove, the subject of the painting. Against this dark foreground he has placed a near building on the right in the light. Here, too, Watling is working in conformity with Gilpin's suggestions, who wrote: 'In a landscape ... when a building, or other object of consequence appears in the foreground, and the distance is of little value, the light ... may then fall on the foreground.'[80] Watling has suppressed several foreground details to be seen in the drawing, after the manner of Gilpin, who, speaking of his own work, wrote: 'in most of these sketches the foreground is just washed in'.[81] In the place of the foreground details in his sketch Watling has added two important pictorial embellishments which help to typify the locality of the scene, a naval and military officer conversing, and a group of natives seated around a camp fire amid bushes to the left.[82] To complete the picturesque treatment Watling has added a large tree of indeterminate species on the left—a casuarina presumably—and his personal version of a clump of eucalypt on the right,

184

to form a *coulisse*, in the normal manner of picturesque landscape. Gilpin, for instance, had written, 'call for an ancient oak to give the foreground grandeur when we want the magnificence of its shadowing form to mantle over a vacant corner of a landscape'.[83]

From these alterations, *Sydney in 1794*, emerges as a product of a composite vision. Sufficient topographical facts have been preserved in the mid-distance for the painting to be a useful illustration of Sydney Cove after six years of settlement: in other respects the picture conforms to a pattern that might have been used by any itinerant landscape-painter in England possessing some proficiency in oil-painting and some acquaintanceship with the picturesque travel-books of the day. Watling was certainly aware of the travel-books for he wanted to publish one himself on New South Wales. In a projected advertisement which he had sent to his aunt in which he called himself 'Principal Limner in New South Wales' he proposed 'the Execution of a Picturesque Description of that Colony; in an highly-finished Set of Drawings, done faithfully upon the Spots, from Nature, in Mezzo, Aqua-tinta, or Water Colours'[84]. The project, however, came to nothing.

Finally, it must be observed that in Watling's work there is evidence that the status of the aborigine was in transition. Watling, himself subject to the barbarous penal code of the time, had no sympathy with the enlightened policy which Phillip sought to institute in the settlement's dealings with the aborigines. For Watling there was no nobility in the savage and he considered official policy to be hypocritical and singularly unchristian:

> ... our governors ... have carried philosophy, I do not say religion, to such a pitch of refinement as is surprising. Many of these savages are allowed, what is termed, a

124. Thomas Watling, *A Group on the North Shore of Port Jackson New South Wales*, pen and wash, 10 × 16¾ in. (*c.* 1794). 'Watling' Drawings 35, British Museum (Natural History)

125. *The tooth evulsion ritual.* Engraving after Thomas Watling, in David Collins, *Account of the English Colony in New South Wales* (1798–1802), i, between pp. 572–3

126. *A Night Scene in the Neighbourhood of Sydney,* engraved by T. Powell after William Alexander, probably from sketches by Watling sent from Sydney, in David Collins, *Account of the English Colony in New South Wales,* ii (1802), frontispiece

freeman's ration of provisions for their idleness. They are bedecked at times, with dress which they make away with the first opportunity, preferring the originality of naked nature.... This you will suppose not more than laudable; but is there one spark of charity exhibited to poor wretches, who are at least denominated christians? No, they are frequently denied the common necessaries of life! wrought to death under the oppressive heat of a burning sun; or barbarously afflicted with often little merited arbitrary punishment—this may be philosophy, according to the calculation of our rigid dictators; but I think it is the falsest species of it I have ever known or heard of.[85]

Indeed Watling's opinion of savages was rather like that of Crozet's already mentioned: 'Irascibility, ferocity, cunning, treachery, filth, and immodesty, are strikingly their dark characteristics—their virtues are so far from conspicuous, that I have not as yet been able to discern them.'[86] And yet despite such opinions Watling's pencil portraits of individual natives, as in his drawings of *Bi-gong* and *Nanbree* (Plate 123), are rendered with sensitivity and discernment. His opinions of aborigines did not lead him to make caricatures of them. This may well have been due to a natural honesty of observation, but it must also be remembered that Watling worked for men like David Collins and John White who took a somewhat more favourable view of the natives, while admitting the lowly level of their culture. But Watling, of course, in depicting aborigines no longer uses the ennobling poses of antique sculpture, nor does he adopt the mock-heroic sentiment present in the drawings of the Port Jackson Painter. In such wash drawings as *A Groupe on the North Shore* Watling depicts aborigines in poses observed to be typical of them (Plate 124). Collins's *Account* includes appendixes dealing with the manners and customs of the aborigines. They are illustrated by eight engravings depicting details of an initiation ceremony and one of a native burial. These, from the style, are by Watling, and it is to be noted that Collins writes: 'I was fortunate enough to attend them (i.e. the ceremonies described) ... attended by a person well qualified to make drawings of every particular circumstance that occurred.'[87] These drawings, intended to convey ethnological information such as the tooth evulsion ritual, have no trace of the precepts of neo-classical composition (Plate 125). By 1798 man himself in the Pacific region was becoming an object for depiction by natural-history draughtsmen. And yet when Collins produced the second volume of his *Account* in 1799 he used as a frontispiece an engraving from a drawing by William Alexander, which is almost certainly based upon a sketch by Watling. But on this occasion the aborigine is once again seen through a veil of romantic feeling as the happy exemplar of the simple life (Plate 126).[88] The noble savage was not extinct: he was too much a phoenix of the European imagination for that.

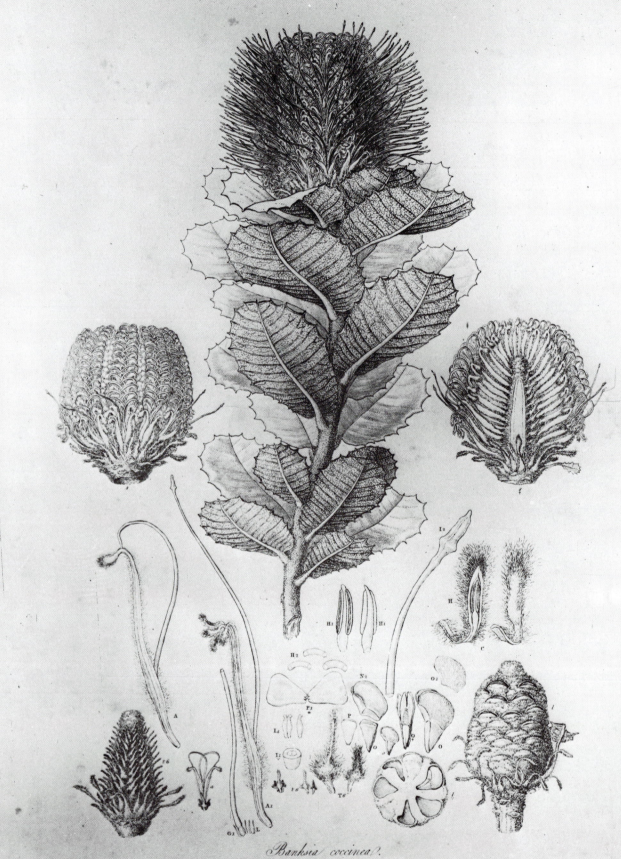

Banksia coccinea.

Brown prod. fl. nov. holl. p. 394. n. 17.

Ferd. Bauer.

7. Exploration in the South Seas and Typical Landscape, 1800–20

MATTHEW FLINDERS accompanied Bligh's second voyage to the Society Islands and later gained considerable experience in charting Australian waters. After returning from service in New South Wales in 1800, Flinders sought and gained the patronage of Sir Joseph Banks, who entered upon the project of charting the Australian coast thoroughly, with a characteristic enthusiasm. Nor, on this occasion, did the Navy Board show any disposition to thwart the wishes of Sir Joseph, since 1778 the President of the Royal Society. When Banks wrote to the Board asking whether a proposal of his for an alteration was likely to be approved Nepean, the Secretary, replied: 'Any proposal you may make will be approved, the whole is left entirely to your decision.'[1] Consequently the hand of Banks is very much in evidence both in Flinders's instructions and in the choice of the scientific personnel for the voyage. Whereas Cook's last voyage and that of Vancouver[2] had revealed a tendency on the part of the navy to provide scientists and artists from within its own ranks, Flinders's voyage conforms to the pattern of Cook's first two voyages in which the navy made use of professional supernumeraries. This pattern, adopted by the French and Russian voyages to the Pacific, owes its origin to Banks's successful achievements during Cook's first voyage, and the influence, both direct and indirect, which he was able to bring to bear upon the organization of scientific expeditions by virtue of the pre-eminent position he held in the scientific councils of Europe.

Flinders left Spithead in the sloop *Investigator* on 18 July 1801 with the object of making a thorough exploration of the coasts of Australia. He was instructed to send to the Secretary of the Navy Board full accounts of his proceedings, copies of surveys and drawings he had made together with 'such papers as the Naturalist and Painters may think proper to send home'.[3] As in the case of the *Bounty*, *Porpoise*, and *Guardian*, the *Investigator* was fitted up with plant cabins and provided with a gardener in order to preserve plants collected on the voyage for shipment to the Royal Gardens at Kew. Banks selected Robert Brown as Flinders's botanist. Brown had studied medicine at Edinburgh, and in 1795 obtained a double commission of ensign and assistant surgeon in a Fifeshire Regiment. His interests, however, centred upon botany. He had already become well known for his published work when he met Banks in 1798. Ferdinand Bauer was chosen as botanical draughtsman. He and his brother Francis were among those botanical artists attracted to England by the fame and patronage of Banks. Ferdinand accompanied John Sibthorp upon his tour of Greece in 1786 and returned to Oxford with him where he made the finished drawings for Sibthorp's *Flora Graeca* (1806–40). Then in the autumn of 1800 at the age of forty Bauer accepted the commission of botanical draughtsman to the *Investigator* at the rate of £300 per annum.

Both Brown and Bauer established themselves as masters in their own particular fields and achieved a partnership in the pursuit of botanical science which has probably never been equalled. In 1810 Robert Brown produced the first-fruits of his

127. *Banksia coccinea*, engraving after Ferdinand Bauer, in his *Illustrationes Florae Novae Hollandiae* (1813)

voyage with Flinders, the first volume of his *Prodromus Florae Novae Hollandiae*, which has been described by Joseph Dalton Hooker, himself one of the finest of British botanists, as 'the greatest botanical work that has ever appeared'.[4] After his return to England, Bauer began to illustrate Brown's work in his *Illustrationes Florae Novae Hollandiae* (1813). Unable to find artists and engravers capable of engraving the plates successfully he undertook the work himself. But war and a decline in the interest in botanical publications which set in about 1810 made it necessary for him to abandon the work after the fifteenth plate had been issued. Returning to Vienna, Bauer completed his drawings of Australian plants there. Goethe, ever alive to the claims both of art and science, became an admirer of Bauer's work and claimed that it revealed how it was still possible to serve both art and science at the same time.[5] Bauer's drawings reveal a complete mastery of the problems of botanical draughtsmanship. A botanist of considerable ability himself he sought in his drawings to reveal both the beauty of a plant and its scientific structure. Although he laboured with infinite care upon detail he never lost sight of a plant as a unified whole, so that he avoided both the dryness of science and the sweetness of sentiment. It must be noted, too, that he made a practice of drawing not only leaf and flower, to which many botanical draughtsmen confined their attentions, but also included sections and diagrams of buds, see-pods, petals, and the roots of plants (Plate 127). In his magnificent drawings of Australian animals, at once aesthetically and scientifically convincing, it is as if the eye of Dürer were looking at a strange new world once again. Nor is not at all surprising why Goethe was so pleased with Bauer's work (Plate 128). Bauer's drawings reveal, too, how the scientific scrutiny of appearance was leading scientific draughtsmen increasingly towards the depiction of structure, and hence to graphic penetration beneath the surface of things (Colour Plate 18).[6]

William Westall (1781–1850) accepted the post of landscape-painter to the expedition at a salary of £315 per annum, being recommended by Benjamin West. He was at the time a probationer at the Academy and doubtless owed his appointment to William Daniell who was first offered the position but whose engagement to Westall's sister had caused him to withdraw. On the *Investigator* Westall found himself in a position similar in some respects to that in which Hodges had found himself twenty-eight years before. Flinders, like his hero Cook, made use of his landscape-painter in the drawing of coastal profiles. Brown and Bauer, like the Forsters and Wales, were outstanding men in their field of science. But there was a difference. On the *Resolution*

128. Ferdinand Bauer, *Platypus*, watercolour, $5\frac{1}{2} \times 18\frac{1}{2}$ in. Ferdinand Bauer drawings, Zoological Department, British Museum (Natural History)

Entrance of Port Phillip taken May 3. 1802 at 9ʰ 20ᵐ a.m.

Point Nepean

Entrance   North 5 miles

Cape Schanck taken May 3. 1802 at 11ʰ a.m.

129. *Coastal views of the
Entrance of Port Phillip and
Cape Schanck*, (with Arthur's
Seat at extreme left) en-
graved after William
Westall, in Flinders, *Voyage
to Terra Australis, Atlas*
(1813)

the study of the atmosphere, as we have seen, influenced Hodges's approach to his art. On the *Investigator* Westall's art appears to have been influenced more by his companions' study of botany and geology. It is probable that in the highly detailed rendering of vegetation to be observed in Westall's Australian landscapes (more closely finished even than the work of John Webber) we have the result of his association with Brown and Bauer; and in the detailed study of terrain something of Flinders's interest in geology and coastal survey.

An extract from Flinders's *Voyage to Terra Australis* will serve to show how Flinders made use of Westall in providing coastal profiles. It was at a time when the *Investigator* was leaving Port Phillip:

When the entrance was cleared, and five miles distant, Mr. Westall took a view of it, which will be an useful assistance in finding this extensive, but obscure port; and at 11 o'clock, when we bore away eastward to pass Cape Schanck, he sketched that cape and the ridge of hills terminating at Arthur's Seat. ... It will always be desirable for vessels to get sight of this cape, before they run far into the great bight for Port Phillip; and if the wind blow strong from the southward, it will be unsafe to run without having seen it.[7] [Plate 129]

A study of the original water-colour drawings made on the Australian coast and now in the National Library of Australia reveals that Westall exercised considerable artistic skill in making such profiles. More elaborate than the profiles drawn by either Hodges or Webber—who did not regard such drawings as a major item of their work— Westall's coastal profiles reach the high-water mark of profile drawing so far as the Pacific is concerned. To the accurate statement of detail and clarity of contour so necessary to this practical art Westall has added a feeling for atmosphere, and an aerial perspective that suggests the mass and depths of headlands, and the relative distance of hinterland hills and mountains.

That Westall's drawings were in fact as useful to navigators as Flinders intended them to be is revealed in his son Robert Westall's account of an incident which occurred at the Royal Geographical Society years afterwards:

After the celebrated voyage of the *Adventure* and the *Beagle* (1826–1836) Captain King was at the Society where he gave an account of their voyage, and stated that he could not refrain from mentioning the great assistance that these engravings were to the expedition on several occasions, from their fidelity to nature. On their first approach to Australia, in the neighbourhood of King George's Sound, during a heavy gale, they doubted whether they could make the harbour, but as they approached the coast they so readily recognized the entrance by the aid of the illustration that they sailed straight in without hesitation instead of being beaten

191

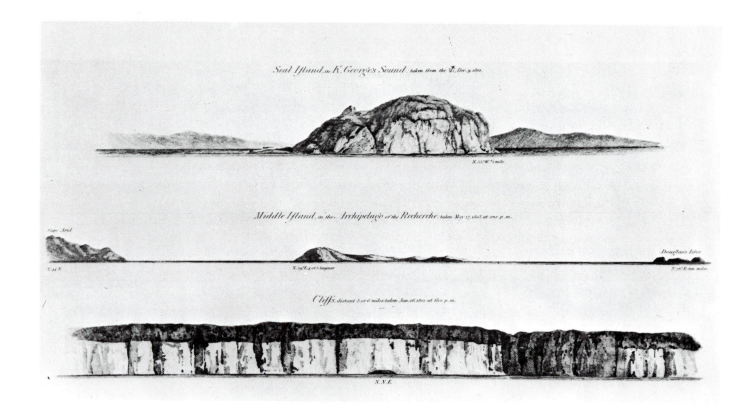

Seal Island in K. George's Sound, taken from the S. Dec. 9 1801

Cape Arid   Middle Island in the Archipelago of the Recherche, taken May 17, 1803 at one p.m.   Douglas's Isles

Cliffs, distant 5 or 6 miles, taken Jan. 26. 1802 at five p.m.

N.N.E.

130. *Coastal views of Seal Island in King George's Sound; Middle Island in the Recherche Archipelago, and of Cliffs taken on 26 January 1802, between Recherche and Nuyt's Archipelagos*, engravings after William Westall in M. Flinders, *Voyage to Terra Australis*, Atlas (1813)

about at sea. Captain King was much pleased on being told that Mr. Westall was present, and at the close of the meeting warmly thanked him for the assistance received from the thoroughly artistic accuracy of his work.[8] [Plate 130]

Flinders realized that coastal profiles could be made to reveal not only the elevation of a coastline, its bays, harbour, headlands, and such like; it could also be used to give some indication of the geological structure of the coastlines surveyed. That he desired Westall's drawings to reveal such facts is clear from a passage in his *Voyage*, written on 26 January 1802 when the *Investigator* was on the southern Australian coast between Recherche and Nuyt's Archipelagos:

Abreast of our situation at half-past two, the level bank again closed in upon the shore, and formed cliffs very similar to those along which we had before run thirty leagues. Their elevation appeared to be from four to six hundred feet, the upper third part was brown, and the lower two-thirds white; but as we advanced, the upper brown *stratum* was observed to augment in proportional quantity. We could not distinguish as before, the smaller layers in the two *strata*; and from the number of excavations in the white part, apparently from pieces having fallen down (see Mr. Westall's sketch), I was led to believe that the lower portion of these cliffs to be grit stone, rather than calcareous rock.[9] (Plate 130)

An examination of the engraving by Westall in Flinder's *Atlas* to the voyage reveals that the artist has brought out the cardinal features described. In general Westall's work looks heavy in treatment because he makes it carry so much information concerning rock structure, land forms, and vegetation (Plate 131). This is particularly true of his treatment of foregrounds. The series of field drawings which Westall completed on the *Investigator*, in possession of the National Library of Australia, are less laboured and much more attractive. They include many fine drawings of Australian plants (Plate 132), figure studies of Australian aborigines (Plate 133) and one of the earliest recordings of an aboriginal cave painting (Plate 134).

192

It was, however, no part of Westall's original plans when he joined the *Investigator* to make only drawings useful to scientists and navigators. He had gone to the South Seas in search of the exotic. But he found New Holland very much below his expectations. A letter which he wrote to Banks from Canton indicates that he had but a hazy idea of the purpose of the voyage and of the size of the Pacific:

> I am sorry to say the voyage to New Holland has not answered my expectations in any one way, for though I did not expect there was much to be got in New Holland, I should have been fully recompenced, for being so long on that barrin coast, by the richness of the South Sea Islands which on leaving England I had reason to suppose we should have winter'd at instead of Port Jackson. *I was not aware the voyage was confined to New Holland only had I known this I most certainly would not have engaged in a hazardous voyage where I could have little opportunity of employing my pencil with any advantage to myself or my employers.*[10]

Westall's purpose in writing to Banks was to seek permission to go on to Ceylon, where he felt that he would find the kind of scenery congenial to his art:

> ... a Country where I could scarcely fail of success: for the rich picturesque appearance of that Island; every part affording infinite variety, must produce many subjects to a painter extremely valuable. And as no painter has yet been there what

131. William Westall, *View of Port Bowen* (now Port Clinton) *in Queensland*, canvas, 34 × 49½ in. (exh. in R.A. 1812). Admiralty House. By permission of the Lord Commissioners of the Admiralty

I should acquire would be perfectly new, and probably interesting from the island being one of the richest in India and lately acquired.[11]

Westall, then, agreed with Thomas Watling; the scenery of New Holland was not suited to landscape-painting. If he did not go to Ceylon, he complained to Banks, he would be forced to return to England 'with subjects which, when executed can neither afford pleasure from exhibiting the face of a beautiful country nor curiosity from their singularity, New Holland in its general appearance differing little from the northern parts of England'.

Flinders returned to Sydney, after circumnavigating Australia, on 9 June 1803. Having found the *Investigator* unseaworthy he decided to return home on the *Porpoise*. But the *Porpoise*, and the *Cato* which accompanied it, were wrecked on a coral reef off the Queensland coast on 17 August. All the plants and dried specimens were lost. But Brown and Bauer fortunately had remained at Sydney with the bulk of their great collection. Westall managed to preserve his drawings. After eight weeks on the reef, the shipwrecked party was rescued by schooners sent from Sydney. Westall proceeded in the *Rolla* to China which was reached on 14 December 1803. He had no desire to return immediately, hoping to find in the East the scenes he had sought in vain with Flinders. Shortly after arriving he obtained permission to go up the river above Canton with a number of scientists.

On one occasion, whilst sketching in an island garden, a mandarin's barge landed a number of ladies and gentlemen of rank, they went to an open summer house, and learning that a foreignor was in the grounds, desired Mr. Westall to be sent for. When introduced to the party he was looked upon with great curiosity; the ladies, in particular minutely examining his attire, and laughing heartily at its

132. William Westall, *Grass Trees (Xanthorrhoea)*, pencil, 10 × 7 in. (1802). National Library of Australia

133. William Westall, *A native of Port Jackson*, pencil, 12½ × 10½ in. (1802). National Library of Australia

novelty. Although at the time he felt abashed at being thus exhibited yet the scene made a lasting impression on his mind, and, on retiring, while the party recreated themselves with music and singing, he made a sketch of the subject before him. The extreme beauty and delicacy of the females, the richness of their costumes, combined with a charming peep of the Canton river, the magnificent exotic trees and plants of the garden—conspicuous among them the feathery bamboo and the lofty palm, garlanded with wild undergrowth of the richest fruit and flowers—formed a composition which could scarcely be excelled in loveliness. Of this incident he afterwards painted a large picture which was exhibited at the Royal Academy in 1814.[12]

It was for such scenes as this, of course, that Westall embarked with Flinders. From the China records at the India Office we learn that he was anxious to proceed thence and to parts of India which 'have hitherto been but little visited of artists' in order to make up 'the deficiency of his drawings . . . which the barren coast of New Holland afforded him no opportunity of doing', and applied to the President of the East India Company, on 25 January 1804, for permission to travel thither and sought introductions 'to the Governments to which he might proceed, to facilitate his object'.[13] The Company approved his project and recommended that letters be written to the Governors of Madras, Bombay, Ceylon, and Prince of Wales's Island (Penang). Westall left Macao on 6 February on board a vessel which formed part of the fleet under Commodore Dance and arrived at Bombay on 30 April 1804. Here he visited the Mahratta Mountains and made drawings of the cave temples at Kurlee and Elephanta. He declined an invitation to accompany Wellesley's army to

134. William Westall, *Copy of an Aboriginal painting at Chasm Island* (near Groote Eylandt), pencil and wash, $10\frac{1}{2} \times 14\frac{1}{2}$ in. (1803). National Library of Australia

135. William Westall, *View of Wreck Reef Bank taken at Low Water*, canvas, $23\frac{1}{2} \times 33\frac{3}{4}$ in. (*c.* 1812/13). National Maritime Museum, London. On loan from the Ministry of Defence—Navy

Seringapatam, and by 19 February 1805 was home again in England. Madeira, however, had attracted him on the voyage out, and thence he returned in the same year; but, being affected by sunstroke and headaches, he left the island for Jamaica. By 1806 he was home again and (apart from a visit to France in 1847) did not travel again.

In 1808 Westall held an exhibition in Brook Street, London, showing scenes in the lands where he had travelled. He also exhibited ten foreign views at the Gallery of the Associated Artists in the same year. As his exotic scenes did not sell well he exhibited drawings he had made in Worcestershire and the Wye Valley in the following year. The Australian scenes, however, were not forgotten. On 7 June 1809 Joseph Farington recorded in his diary that Banks was busy pressing Westall's claim for finishing pictures 'of the places he visited in the South Seas' with the Admiralty. 'Sir Joseph', wrote Farington, 'said that the French, when they made voyages of discovery published and preserved all that related thereto, but that we sent artists out and on their return hesitated to make use of the fruits of their labours.'[14] Lord Mulgrave thereupon, according to Farington, asked Banks whether he would take upon himself the responsibility of having the necessary drawings and pictures painted. Banks said that he would and Westall was asked to be moderate in his charges. A week later Westall informed Farington that he had been commissioned to paint a series of pictures from the drawings he had made on Flinders's voyage. Then in the year following Flinders himself returned home after a long imprisonment by the French in Mauritius, and a start was made with the publication of his voyage. Westall prepared drawings to illustrate the voyage and also painted several oils for the Admiralty. Three of these paintings, were exhibited in the Academy of 1812. The finest of these was his *View in Sir Edward Pellew's Group, Gulf of Carpentaria* (Colour Plate 21), which for its sustained and uncompromising high tonality throughout is a remarkable painting for its time. The painting also testifies to Westall's interest, at this time, in aboriginal ethnography. In the central foreground Westall has painted a small bark shelter containing two *rangga*, the decorated stones used by the Aborigines of the Gulf in the totemic 'maraiin' ceremony.[15]

Westall's son records that these paintings attracted considerable attention because of their novelty:[16] 'They were all views of places, for the most part for the first time visited by Europeans. In the foregrounds were displayed the magnificent and gorgeous foliage of the flora of the country, painted with great attention to their botanical character.' This explicit statement confirms what is already apparent from an examination of the paintings, that they are not simply topographical transcripts of nature, but landscapes in which typical specimens of Australian flora have been introduced into the foreground in order to characterize the country depicted. The oil-paintings which he executed for the Admiralty reveal greater fluency of treatment and a keener desire to render the truths of light and atmosphere than is to be found in the sketches made upon the *Investigator*. Freed from the need to document geological and botanical facts that pressed upon him during the voyage, Westall was able to bring a greater sense of breadth and unity to his work. The paintings gained Westall some recognition, and in the same year he was elected an Associate of the Academy. The year before he had begun to make an annual visit to the Lake District, a practice he continued for many years. There he became a friend of Wordsworth, Southey, and Sir George Beaumont. At Cole Orton, Beaumont's residence, he mingled with a circle of painters which included Constable, Wilkie, Collins, Haydon, and Mulready. Yet the memory of Australia and its 'barrin coast' never entirely escaped him for when he died in 1850 he was working on a painting of *Wreck Reef a few days after the Wreck of the Porpoise and the Cato*: an experience he had lived through forty-seven years before (Plate 135).[17]

The voyage of the *Géographe* and the *Naturaliste* (1800–4) under the command of Nicolas Baudin was a scientific one like the voyage of the *Investigator*. But whereas, apart from charting, the main contribution of Flinders's voyage was to the study of botany, the main contribution of the French voyage was to zoology. The expedition, sponsored by the *Institut National* and dispatched by the order of Napoleon, left Havre in October 1800. The scientific contingent was a much more ambitious affair than the *Investigator*'s, consisting of four astronomers and hydrographers, three botanists, five zoologists, two mineralogists, four artists, and five gardeners. But Baudin was a poor navigator, paid little attention to the health of his men, and was quite out of sympathy with the work of the scientists. Consequently many of the latter remained at Mauritius when the expedition arrived there, including three of the artists, Milbert, Lebrun, and Garnier. As a result the task of preparing the graphic records of the voyage fell to Nicholas Petit, a portrait-painter, and Charles Alexandre Lesueur (1778–1846), a young man who had gained the humble post of *novice-timonier* after a competitive examination. Lesueur formed a close friendship with François Péron (1775–1810) whose original application to accompany the expedition had been refused on the grounds that the scientific party was complete. But he gained an interview with Antoine de Jussieu (1748–1836), one of the committee who selected the naturalists, and was asked to prepare a memoir for submission to the *Institut*. In his memoir he set forth the desirability of including a medical naturalist in the party for the purposes of making researches in anthropology. On the basis of his memoir Péron was given a place among the zoologists of the expedition. Throughout the voyage Péron and Lesueur worked as a team and at its conclusion were charged with the responsibility of publishing the voyage.

Although Lesueur had not been appointed as an artist his great abilities were soon recognized from drawings he made of fish and 'phosphorescent animals' before the expedition reached Mauritius. Throughout the voyage, though circumstances forced him to make a wide range of drawings, he continued to specialize in the illustration of marine fauna—in which he developed great skill. Zoophytes, particularly, constituted a special interest for the scientists. Péron records the excitement which attended their study: 'The amazing number of these animals, their strange and whimsical forms, the beauty of their colours, the facility of their motions, and the agility of their evolutions, furnished an agreeable spectacle to all our ship's crew, and to myself, and my friends Lesueur and Maugé their number and diversity afforded an inexhaustible fund of pleasure, and were the subject of philosophical enthusiasm.'[18] (Colour Plates 19, 20, 22) The expedition specialized in zoological research and brought back an enormous collection of specimens, which a committee consisting of Laplace, Bougainville, Fleurieu, Lacépède, and Cuvier were asked to examine and report upon. The report spoke of the work performed by Péron and Lesueur in glowing terms:

> Of the five zoologists appointed by the government, two remained at the Isle of France. Two others perished at . . . Timor. Péron alone was left; but supported by his invigorated ardour, and the efforts of his coadjutor Lesueur, a zoological collection was made, the extent and importance of which become more and more manifest. It is composed of more than one hundred thousand specimens of animals, several of which will constitute new genera; and the new species, according to the report of the Professors of the Museum, are upwards of two thousand five hundred. If we call to mind that the second voyage of Cook, fruitful as were its discoveries, made known not more than two hundred and fifty new species, and that all the united voyages of Carteret, Wallis, Furneaux, Mears, and even Vancouver, did not produce as great a number,—it results that Péron and Lesueur alone have discovered more new animals than all the travelling naturalists of modern days.[19]

Thus while Brown and Bauer were making a collection pre-eminent in the history of botany, Péron and Lesueur were engaged upon making a collection pre-eminent in the history of zoology. The committee proceeded to give full recognition to the scientific value of the drawings made by Lesueur:

> A description, nevertheless, how complete soever it may be, can never give a sufficiently just idea of those singular forms, which have no precise point of comparison in objects previously known. Correct figures alone can supply the imperfection of language. Here, the labors of which it is our duty to render an account, acquire a new interest. Fifteen hundred drawings or paintings, executed by M. Lesueur, with extreme precision, reproduce the principal objects which were collected by his careful industry, and that of his friend. All these drawings, either made from living animals or recent specimens, form the most complete and the most precious series of the kind that we have any knowledge of. . . . The history of Man is not less indebted to him. All the details of the existence of the natives have been designed by him with the most scrupulous accuracy. All their musical instruments, those of war, of hunting, of fishing, their domestic utensils; all the peculiarities of their clothing, of their ornaments, of their habitations, of their tombs; in a word all that their rude ingenuity has been able to accomplish, is found united in the productions of this skilful and indefatigable artist. The principal site of the coasts explored by the expedition: different views of the town of Sydney, the capital of the English colony of New South Wales, its plan, etc., give to the Atlas of the History of the voyage . . . a new character of importance.[20]

It is significant that Lesueur used a form of landscape art for the purposes of ethnographical illustration. Landscape was used to convey certain facts about the construction of native canoes and their form of navigation (Plate 136). He drew native dwellings amid typical vegetation, in order to reveal the form of their construction, adding a native group together with a heap of shells (to indicate their diet) in the foreground. Lesueur was not original, of course, in thus using landscape for the purpose of ethnographical illustration, but his work does provide a clear example how the study of ethnology, like the study of botany and geology, could influence an artist's approach to painting. The combined effects of these sciences was leading the landscape painting of the expeditions away from the neo-classical and the picturesque towards a form of landscape best described as typical.[21] During the first decade of the nineteenth century this form of landscape began to receive some theoretical attention.

Lesueur's work was admirably supported and complemented by that of his friend, Nicolas-Martin Petit, the one remaining portrait and figure painter to Baudin's expedition after the more senior artists remained at Mauritius. Little is known about Petit, who died accidentally in Paris in 1805 shortly after his return home from the voyage; even the date of his birth or where he studied remains unknown. But it is clear that he was trained in portrait and figure work, which is in the neo-classic mode of the time and not without a touch of the elongated Mannerist affection present in much French neo-classical draughtsmanship of the time of the Empress Josephine. Nevertheless Petit was no unthinking exponent of that noble savage primitivism which characterizes the work of Piron, the artist on D'Entrecasteaux's voyage ten years before. Petit did his very best, within the conventions of neo-classicism, to draw what he saw to be characteristic and typical. As Dr Plomley has observed, his portraits of Tasmanians appear to have been honestly observed and may be taken as 'fairly true representations of his subjects': the broad nose and prominent nostrils, wide mouth and full lips, the sunken eyes, and the forehead' overhanging the root of the nose so as to produce a marked notch' (Colour Plate 23). In his work the physiognomical distinctions between Tasmanians and the Aborigines of the Australian mainland are clearly distinguished (Colour Plate 24).[22]

Baudin's expedition might have done even better had it been able to carry out the high ambitions of the ethnographical programme that had been originally prepared for it. This reflected the interests of the *Société des Observateurs de l'Homme*, founded in Paris in 1799, the members of which included the zoologist Cuvier and the botanist Jussieu. The member of the society that prepared the memoir for the voyage concerning the observation and study of natives peoples was Joseph-Marie Degérando (1772–1842), philosopher and a pioneer social anthropologist whose ideas were well in advance of his time. In order to study man adequately Degérando insisted it was essential that his whole way of life be studied and the first essential therefore was to study the native language and understand it; a programme for the future, but one quite impossible for Baudin's men to carry through. Quite apart from the internal dissensions that developed, and the zoologist Peron's inadequacies as an ethnologist, even the elementary problem of establishing contact with native people for any extended length of time presented insuperable difficulties. So Degérando's programme had to lie forgotten for the greater part of a century before it began to be implemented. With the decline of the high ideals and ambitions of the Enlightenment in France, as elsewhere in Europe, observers contented themselves with the acquisition of knowledge that was readily useful for the prosecution of European interests.[23]

The early years of the century found European artists travelling and working in

136. *Terre de Diémen: Navigation*, engraving after Lesueur, in F. Péron, *Voyage ... aux Terres Australes* (1807). Atlas by Mm. Lesueur and Petit, pl. xiv

many distant parts of the world. The effect of Cook's voyages upon the imagination of the young contributed not a little to this diaspora. For many young artists Banks's version of the grand tour, with its possibility of adventures in distant colonies and the prospect of painting scenes never painted before, held more attractions than the visit to Italy. For more than one artist the Pacific voyage was the prelude to world travel. Hodges travelled extensively in India and later in Russia. Westall travelled in China, India, Madeira, and the West Indies. Lesueur, after a period in France, travelled to the United States in 1815 where he earned a high reputation both as a scientist and a scientific draughtsman.[24] The example of such men inspired others. It was Hodges who encouraged Zoffany to visit India, and it was doubtless the considerable success which he met with there under the patronage of Warren Hastings which encouraged Thomas Daniell (1749–1840) to travel to India with his nephew William (1769–1837).[25] The Daniells remained in India for ten years. By means of the camera obscura and by preparing and selling their aquatints while upon their travels, the Daniells succeeded in financing their movements themselves. The success of their publications prepared the way for the travelling artists of the nineteenth century who, freed from the binding commissions of scientific voyages, were able to freelance their way around the world. During the early decades of the century the Daniells produced many illustrated publications dealing with India, Ceylon, China, and South Africa. Julius Caesar Ibbetson visited China with Cathcart's Embassy as early as 1788, and William Alexander went there with Staunton's Embassy in 1797. For Alexander, as for Hodges and the Daniells, voyaging aroused an interest in the exotic landscape and determined much of his career. In 1798 he published *Views taken during the Voyage to China*. In 1804 he illustrated Sir John Barrow's *Travels in China*, and in 1806 his *Voyage to Cochin China*. In 1805 Alexander had published his own *Costume of China*.

The growing interest in views taken in distant lands was promoted by such publishing houses as Havell & Son, and Rudolph Ackermann. Daniell and Robert

Havell (*fl.* 1800–40) established the Zoological Gallery in Oxford Street, opposite the Pantheon. Here works of art were published and an agency formed for the sale of specimens and items of interest to the natural historian. Masters of aquatint engraving, the Havells produced some particularly fine books on exotic birds, notably Audebert's *Oiseaux dorés ou à reflets metalliques* (1802), and Audubon's *Birds of America* (1827–38); and also books of exotic landscapes, such as Daniell's *Views of India*, J. Baillie Fraser's *Views in the Himala Mountains*, and Salt's *Views in Africa*. Rudolf Ackermann set up his publishing house and print shop in the Strand in 1795, and published many illustrated books of foreign travel, such as Vidal's *Buenos Aires and Monte Video*, Forrest's *Ganges and Jumna*, Grindlay's *India* (1826–1830), and *The World in Miniature* (1821–6).[26]

Such publications made more apparent than ever before the great diversity of scenery throughout the world and this led to reflection upon the true object of landscape-painting. Out of these reflections emerged the idea of the typical landscape. It is first met with as an idea subsumed by, but by no means logically related to, the idea of the picturesque. To understand the position it will be necessary to review briefly the course of the picturesque mode of perception to the end of the eighteenth century.

From about 1730 onwards, under the inspiration of such poets as Thomson and Dyer, connoisseurs and people of taste in England came to judge natural scenery increasingly according to picturesque standards. Towards the end of the century this new point of view was formulated into theories of picturesque beauty by such men as Uvedale Price, Payne Knight, and Repton. Earlier writers, like Gilpin, were content to define the picturesque as 'that kind of beauty which would look well in a picture' and leave it at that. In 1794 Price claimed the picturesque to be an aesthetic category distinct from both the sublime and the beautiful, and distinguished by roughness, sudden variation, and irregularity. Payne Knight, however, in his *Analytical Enquiry into the Principles of Taste* (1805) claimed that the picturesque was nothing less than the 'true visible appearance of things',[27] and that it was the manner of imitating nature appropriate to painting. This went to the heart of the matter; but it was Price's definition which entered into general currency, for it helped to systematize a good deal of general opinion concerning the nature of the picturesque. When Jane Austen,[28] Hazlitt,[29] and Coleridge[30] speak of the picturesque they follow Price rather than Knight, considering it to be a quality of the appearance of some things rather than to be the painterly mode of perception. Now in the many attempts to define the term, the exotic is never named as a crucial factor in the creation of picturesque beauty. And rightly so. Yet the exotic certainly helped to nourish picturesque taste, as it had helped to nourish the rococo. Buildings, landscapes, peoples, costumes, and even customs deriving from distant or little-known countries were so frequently called picturesque that the terms became virtually interchangeable. It is true that, having regard for Price's definition which may be taken to express (though more systematically) the general view, exotic things frequently exhibited roughness, sudden variation, and irregularity. But the term picturesque was widened to cover exotic things not intrinsically picturesque. In 1808 Samuel Daniell published *A Picturesque Illustration of the Scenery, Animals and Native Inhabitants of the Island of Ceylon*, thus using the term to cover Cingalese things in general regardless whether the items depicted were intrinsically picturesque. And Thomas Watling, as we have seen, contemplated in 1793 a 'picturesque description' of New South Wales although he had explicitly claimed that Australian scenery was romantic and not picturesque. It is clear, of course, that such usages of the term—a fashionable one—lent respectability to such undertakings. But what is far more significant is the fact that the term picturesque was being used to embrace the growing interest in the exotic. Payne Knight pointed out that 'Hindoo domes' were perfect examples of Edmund Burke's theory of beauty. But, he added, 'I do not believe that Mr. Burke or his commentator (i.e. Price) ever found such a building beautiful'.[31] In fact when such buildings as Sezincote and the Brighton Pavilion came to be built they were erected by architects imbued with ideas of picturesque beauty. Now exotic architecture made common ground with the theory of the picturesque on the question of suitability. Picturesque architecture was architecture that was suited to its surroundings, architecture, in other words, which harmonized with its landscape setting. It is not without significance that the nursery of exotic architecture in England was Kew, the great nursery for exotic plants. Where else was it more suitable to erect a Moorish building, a Turkish mosque, and a Chinese pagoda than at Kew, where the plants of such countries could be found growing? The belief that certain types of building were suited to certain types of scenery promoted reflection upon the qualities that characterized, or were typical of, a given landscape. Payne Knight claimed that English landscape possessed qualities of its own. Because of these qualities it should never—on the grounds of good taste—be embellished with Grecian temples:

> In the rich lawns and shrubberies of England they (i.e. Grecian temples) lose all that power to please which they so eminently possess on the barren hills of Agrigentum and Segesta or the naked plains of Paestum and Athens. But barren and naked as these hills and plains are, they are still, if I may say so, their native hills and plains—the scenery in which they sprang; and in which the mind therefore contemplates them connected with numberless interesting circumstances, both local and historical—both physical and moral, upon which it delights to dwell. In our parks and gardens on the contrary, they stand wholly unconnected with all that surrounds them—mere unmeaning excrescences; or, what is worse, manifestly meant for ornament, and therefore having no accessory character, but that of ostentatious vanity: so that, instead of exciting any interest they vitiate and destroy that, which the naturalised objects of the scenery connected with them would otherwise excite. Even if the landscape scenery should be rendered beautiful by such ornaments its beauty will be thought of as a vain and affected coquette; which although it may allure the sense, offends the understanding; and, on the whole, excites more disgust than pleasure.[32]

It was not a far cry from criticism of classical buildings placed in English settings to the criticism of English landscape-paintings executed according to Italianate models. In his *Essay on Painting* published in the same year as Payne Knight's *Analytical Enquiry*, Edward Dayes cast doubts upon the value of the Italian tour for young artists and pointed out that English scenery has its own peculiar beauties that artists should attend to:

> The vast importation of fine pictures has, in a degree, removed the necessity of the young artist going to Italy; and, in any case, he should by no means be sent there too young. . . . Almost all our landscape painters bring away as much prejudice as spoils them through life; for it is by no means uncommon to see the air of that climate brought into all their English scenes. . . . We mean the introduction of Italian skies, without considering climate. . . . Countries, as well as men, have their own peculiar character, and should, no doubt, be equally attended to.[33]

Recognition that each country has a peculiar type of landscape could be used to justify a theory of landscape art in which each region of the earth produced its own

202

typical form of beauty. This step was taken by Alexander von Humboldt, who was greatly influenced in his reflections upon the art of landscape by the writings of George Forster and the paintings of Hodges.

When George Forster returned home from Cook's second voyage he remained a few years in England and wrote his account of it. He then accepted the chair of natural history at Cassel, frequently visiting Göttingen for books and scientific materials, where he formed a close friendship with Humboldt. It was Forster who inspired Humboldt to prepare himself carefully for a career of scientific travel, the career in which he ultimately distinguished himself so greatly. In 1790 he paid a brief visit to England with Forster and it was probably at this time that he saw paintings by William Hodges in the home of Warren Hastings. Writing, years later, in his *Cosmos*, Humboldt himself described the influence which Forster's writings and Hodges's' paintings had upon his own career:

> The lessons of experience . . . tell us how often impressions received by the sense from circumstances seemingly accidental, have so acted on the youthful as to determine the whole direction of man's course through life.... If I may have recourse to my own experience, and what awakened in me the first beginnings of an inextinguishable longing to visit the tropics, I should name George Forster's descriptions of the islands of the Pacific—paintings by Hodge (*sic*) in the house of Warren Hastings, in London, representing the banks of the Ganges—and a colossal dragon tree in an old tower in the Botanical Gardens of Berlin.[34]

Humboldt was not merely reminiscing; he proceeded to analyse how written description, landscape-painting, and botanical illustration could be used to give Europeans a better idea of the multiformity of nature. But the basic principles of the ideas which he developed so fully in the *Cosmos* had been foreshadowed years before in his *Ideen zu einer Physiognomik der Gewächse* (1806) and incorporated in his *Ansichten der Natur* (1808). In this latter work, Humboldt sought to provide accurate and compelling views of certain natural regions, such as the steppes of central Asia and the jungles of South America. He sought not so much to provide new information as to capture the imagination of his readers and bring home to them a sense of the wonder and excitement which he had himself felt in the presence of nature in her most exotic and majestic forms. His attempt was well received; the *Ansichten* went through three editions in his lifetime and was translated into most European languages. Charles Darwin read Humboldt and so did John Ruskin. It has been said of him thay by 1810 he was, with the exception of Napoleon, the most famous man in Europe.

To Humboldt the world consisted of climatic zones more or less distinct from each other. In the *Ansichten* he sought to outline the general character of each zone. To him nature in her noblest form was to be found only in the tropics where in mountainous regions the traveller could pass in survey at successive altitudes all the vegetal forms of the earth and study the stars of both the northern and southern heavens. Organic development, fecundity, and vitality, increase, he claimed, as one moves from the poles to the equator. Nevertheless, each climate has a beauty peculiar to itself; to the tropics belong variety and magnitude in vegetation; to the north the aspects of its meadows and the periodic renovations of the seasons. The primeval force of nature tends, however, to bind all animal and vegetable life to fixed and recurring types. Consequently, every region of the earth has a certain natural physiognomy. This very fact, argued Humboldt, provided a new field for the landscape-painter. It was not merely a matter of portraying specific types of vegetation. 'The azure of the sky, the lights and shadows, the haze resting on the distance, the forms of animals, the succulency of plants and herbage, the brightness of the foliage, the outline of the mountains, are all elements which determine the total impression characteristic of each district or region.'[35] In his chapter on the 'Physiognomy of Plants' in the *Ansichten*, Humboldt describes the sixteen dominant forms of plant life that determine the physiognomy of the tropics. The systematizing botanist has to separate into distinct groups many plants which the student of the physiognomy of nature will combine, for determinations of natural physiognomy must be guided solely by those elements of magnitude and mass from which the total impression of a region gains its character. 'When plants or trees present themselves in masses, the outlines and distribution of the leaves and the form of the stems and of the branches are blended together. The painter (and here the artist's delicate tact and appreciation of nature are demanded) can distinguish in the middle distance and background of a landscape groves of palms or pines from beechwoods, but he cannot distinguish the latter from woods consisting of other deciduous forest trees.'[36]

Humboldt's conception of landscape as the portrayal of characteristic types of scenery determined by the principles of climate was based upon a personal knowledge and deep appreciation of many distinct climatic regions. He therefore was able to present the problem of landscape-painting in a new light. Until the end of the eighteenth century, reflection upon landscape-painting rested largely upon the pre-supposition that all landscapes derived either from the coniferous and deciduous forests of northern and central Europe or from the evergreen landscapes of the Mediterranean. To take one example of many: Uvedale Price has much to say upon the relative merits of spring and autumn scenes in the inspiration of the landscape-painter.[37] He did not concern himself with landscapes in which seasonal transitions are a minor, or even negligible, element of their appearance.[38] But to Humboldt such a landscape type—tropical landscape—was the noblest of all; and a landscape-painter could serve no higher purpose than to bring its beauties (manifest in its plant groups) to the notice of the European public:

> It would be an enterprise worthy of a great artist to study the aspect and character of all these vegetable groups, not merely in hot houses or in the descriptions of botanists but in their native grandeur in the tropical zone. How interesting and instructive to the landscape painter would be a work which should present to the eye, first separately and then in combination and contrast, the leading forms which have been enumerated! . . . It is the artist's privilege, having studied these groups, to analyse them: and thus in his hands the grand and beautiful form of nature which he would portray resolves itself, (if I may venture on the expression) like the written works of men, into a few simple elements.[39]

Perhaps it might be possible, Humboldt points out, by means of the combined efforts of the painter and the poet to give Europeans some idea of the glowing richness of nature in the tropics:

> . . . many . . . of the enjoyments which Nature affords are wanting to the nations of the North. Many constellations, and many vegetable forms,—and of the latter, those which are most beautiful (palms, tree ferns, plantains, arborescent grasses, and the finely divided feathery foliage of the Mimosas) remain forever unknown to them. Individual plants languishing in our hot-houses can give but a very faint idea of the majestic vegetation of the tropical zone. But the high cultivation of our languages . . . and the imitative art of the painter, open to us sources whence flow abundant compensations, and from whence our imagination can derive the living

204

image of that more vigorous nature which other climes display. In the frigid North, in the midst of the barren heath, the solitary student can appropriate mentally all that has been discovered in the most distant regions, and can create within himself a world free and imperishable as the spirit by which it is conceived.[40]

Thus Humboldt would transform the painting of nature in her exotic forms from being an item of scientific topography and documentation to an expressive form of landscape art, essential, in his view, to the nourishment of the European imagination.

It is no part of the plan of this book to trace in detail the influence of Humboldt's writings on landscape-painting in Europe itself. A few indications must suffice. Karl Gustav Carus's *Neun Briefe über die Landschaftsmalerei* (1831) contained an appendix *Andeutungen zu einer Physiognomik der Gebirge*, which appears to have been directly influenced by Humboldt's *Ideen zu einer Physiognomik der Gewächse*. Dr. Badt has shown how Carus's writings influenced landscape-painters on the Continent.[41] In England the influence of Humboldt's writings may be discerned in the suggestion that the new Houses of Parliament at Westminster should be decorated not only with murals celebrating the history of the nation[42] but also with large pictorial maps befitting the legislative centre of 'an empire over which the sun never sets'. The suggestion was made in a published letter written by Saxe Bannister, a former Attorney General of New South Wales, to Sir Charles Eastlake, Secretary to the Commission of Fine Arts. One of the series of such maps was to present:

> ... pictures of the whole globe; the forests of the Canadas in some of their wild characteristics, in contrast with the houses and the harvests so rapidly thinning those forests:—the fisheries of Greenland, the fur-hunting of Hudson's Bay, and the scene of the lost, as well as the track of successful explorers of the frozen north:—the West Indian Islands brilliant in natural beauties, and struggling to produce results worthy of the sublime cause of negro emancipation:—the free, peaceful, and christian settlements of Western Africa in contrast with its man hunts, and slave marts:—the sheep walk, and the mission house, which, led by wise, humane policy, would extinguish barbarism in South Africa:—the mines and stock stations already pushed deep into the Australias, with the encampment of the explorer on their splendid plains, or frightful stony deserts:—the infinitely varied works of nature and of man, savage as well as civilized, in New Zealand, in Ceylon, in the Asiatic Archipelago, in China, and in the South Sea Islands.[43]

To support his argument Bannister quoted from Humboldt's *Cosmos*, at the time widely read in England. The pictures were intended to be grand enough to decorate a palace and to be able to instruct the rulers of the Empire by giving them 'an acquaintance with the entire globe'. Bannister had in mind a form of art which Hodges had suggested years before, one which would combine the dignity and moral value of history-painting with that enjoyment of nature implicit in landscape-painting. But the suggestion came to nothing.

The influence of Humboldt is also discernible in the writings of Ruskin. In an appendix entitled 'Plagiarism' placed at the end of the third volume of *Modern Painters* (1856) Ruskin felt it necessary to defend himself against the charge of indebtedness to Humboldt for ideas in his chapters on landscape.[44] Of direct borrowing there was perhaps none; but Ruskin read and admired Humboldt's writings and quoted him frequently.[45] Several of his quotations come from Humboldt's *Personal Narrative of Travels to the Equinoctial Regions of America*, in the 1814 English translation by Helen Maria Williams. It is unlikely that Ruskin knew of Humboldt's *Ideen zu einer*

Physiognomik der Gewächse when he published his first long essay 'The Poetry of Architecture', in Loudon's *Architectural Magazine* (1837). But his interesting attempt to distinguish the peculiar beauties of the cottage architecture of the different nations of Europe by relating them to their physical environment, echoes on a miniature scale the ideas which Humboldt had applied to the whole globe. The division which Ruskin makes of scenery into four main types, green, blue, grey, and brown, in this essay[46] is the first of his many attempts to deduce the aesthetic appeal of a scene from its physical characteristics. In the final volume of *Modern Painters* (1860) he discusses 'the climates or lands into which our globe is divided ... with respect to their fitness for art',[47] dividing them into Forest Lands, Sand Lands, Grape and Wheat Lands, Meadow Lands, and Moss Lands. The strong suspicion that Humboldt is at the back of Ruskin's mind in making such a division is reinforced by the fact that the first division, Forest Lands, is illustrated by a quotation from Humboldt.

Ruskin's relation to Humboldt is, however, but one indication of his lifelong interest in science, and his lifelong endeavour to reconcile his deep interest in natural history, with his interest in art. Ruskin's early passion for geology—he was reading books on geology at the age of nine, and explored the caves at Matlock at the age of ten—need not be elaborated here, nor, for that matter, his wide reading and deep knowledge in those other sciences of visible nature, botany, zoology, and meteorology.

Humboldt's writings stimulated an interest in travel unequalled since the publication of the *Voyages* of Cook. 'Who is unacquainted with the colossal labours of a Humboldt?' wrote Otto von Kotzebue in the introduction to his *Voyage of Discovery into the South Sea and Behring's Straits, for the purpose of exploring a North-East Passage* (1815–18). And it came about that Humboldt, himself greatly inspired to travel by two members of Cook's second voyage, was to stimulate and influence later voyagers to the Pacific, not least of whom was Charles Darwin. The young landscape-painter who travelled with Kotzebue, Louis Choris, was another who was acquainted with Humboldt's ideas and they influenced his approach to landscape-painting.[48]

Kotzebue informs us that Choris, who had already accompanied the naturalist Marshall von Biberstein, as painter, in a tour of the Caucasus, offered himself as an artist to the expedition. Upon the return of the expedition his work was well received by the artists and by the Academy of St. Petersburg. Only a few of the drawings, however, were included in Kotzebue's account of his voyage, mainly portraits. Choris informs us that his drawings were shown to many people distinguished in arts and letters in Paris and that they encouraged him to publish them. 'Fort de leur suffrage, il entreprit ce travail, bien persuadé qu'il n'existe aucun livre de ce genre qui offre une si grande variété d'objets dessinés, et surtout un recueil si nombreux de portraits des divers peuples qu'il a vus. Il s'était surtout attaché à rendre fidèlement les traits caractéristiques, la couleur, en un mot, la physionomie de ces peuples.'[49] Choris did not succeed, if we may judge by his published work, in rendering the native peoples of the Pacific more faithfully than many of the artists who had preceded him to the Pacific, but he had the advantage of a public becoming more accustomed to books illustrating exotic lands and peoples (Plate 137). Unlike earlier artist-travellers to the Pacific, whose published views constituted an integral part of the official publication of the voyage which they accompanied, Choris was able to publish his drawings separately. The first of these he called *Voyage pittoresque autour du monde* (1822). Although entitled a *Voyage pittoresque* the contents embraced the scope of the drawings normally undertaken by an artist attached to a scientific voyage; it included portraits, landscapes, some coastal profiles, together with ethnographical and natural-history

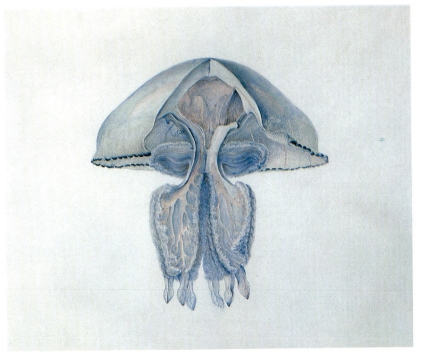

19. Charles-Alexandre Lesueur, Antamomical section of *Meduse Scyphomeduse—Rhizostoma Cuvieri* (Rhizostoma Octopus—Linne), water-colour on vellum, $5\frac{1}{8} \times 5\frac{1}{2}$ in. (1788), Lesueur Collection 70056, Musée d' Histoire Naturelle, Le Havre

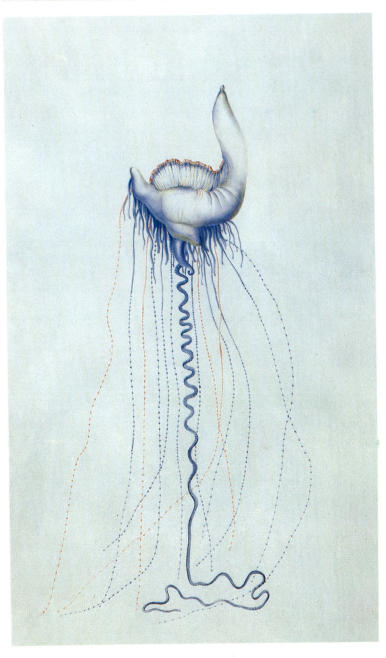

20. Charles-Alexandre Lesueur, *Physalia*, water-colour on vellum, $11 \times 5\frac{1}{2}$ in. Lesueur Collection 70067, Musée d' Histoire Naturelle, Le Havre

22. Charles–Alexandre Lesueur, *Dasyurus viverrinus* (Quall) (detail), Australian native cat, gouache on vellum, $9\frac{7}{8} \times 15\frac{3}{4}$ in. (*c.* 1801–3). Lesueur Collection, Musée d'Histoire Naturelle, Le Havre

21 (preceeding pages). William Westall, *View of Sir Edward Pellew's Group, Gulf of Carpentaria* (detail), canvas, $24\frac{3}{8} \times 34\frac{1}{4}$ in. (*c.* 1812). Admiralty House, London

137. Louis Choris, *Danse des femmes dans les Îles Sandwich*, lithograph, in *Voyage Pittoresque autour du Monde*, Paris, 1822, pl. XVI

drawings. Cuvier and Adalbert von Chamisso (1781–1838)[50] co-operated in the description of the scientific plates. In Choris's publication, therefore, an attempt is made to merge the interest of a picturesque travel book and the work of artists attached to scientific voyages. For Choris as for the Daniells, *pittoresque* and *picturesque* have nothing of the precise meaning which Price and Payne Knight sought to give them, and his use of the word is a further indication of its widening connotation to embrace exotic illustration in general. In 1826 Choris brought out another book of drawings based on work executed on Kotzebue's first voyage, entitled *Vues et paysages des régions équinoxiales*. It owed its origin to Humboldt. 'Cette entreprise m'a été inspirée par la lecture de l'immortal ouvrage de M. le baron de Humboldt, *les Tableaux de la Nature*.'[51] In the introduction Choris quotes Humboldt's remarks on the value of a work which would represent the sixteen principal types of tropical vege-tation, and proceeds to write with great enthusiasm concerning the supreme beauty of tropical landscape:

> Les paysages situés sous le beau ciel des Tropiques, avec leur végétation gigantes-que, presque toujours verte, presque toujours chargée de fleurs et de fruits, ne ressemblent en rien aux paysages de nos pays, où les longs hivers suspendent et paralysent les ressorts d'une nature qui semble fatiguée et vieille. Quel immense intervalle dans le chaîne végétale, entre le palmier des contrées équinoxiales et les lichens des régions voisines des pôles![52]

In his description of the sixteen vegetable groups of tropical nature Humboldt gave pride of place to the palms and the bananas. To him the palm was the most beautiful of all plants:

... the loftiest and noblest of all vegetable forms, that to which the prize of beauty has been assigned by the concurrent voice of nations in all ages; for the earliest civilisations of mankind belonged to countries bordering on the regions of palms, and to parts of Asia where they abound.... In receding from the equator and approaching the temperate zone, palms diminish in height and beauty. The indigenous vegetation of Europe only comprises a single representative of this form of plants, the sea-coast Dwarf-palm or Chamaerops.[53]

The banana was likewise of great beauty and had also, like the palm, ministered to the growth of civilization:

In all parts of the globe the palm is accompanied by that of Plantains or Bananas.... Groves of plantains and bananas form the ornament of moist places in the equatorial regions ... like the farinaceous cereals of the north, they have followed man from the infancy of civilisation. The aboriginal site of this nutritious plant is placed by some Asiatic fables or traditions on the banks of the Euphrates, and by others, with more probability, at the foot of the Himalaya. Grecian fables named the fields of Enna as the happy native land of the cereals; and if in northern climes, where corn is cultivated in immense unbroken fields, their monotonous aspect adds but little to the beauty of the landscape, the inhabitant of the tropics, on the other hand, in rearing groves of plantains wherever he fixes his habitation, contributes to the adornment of the earth's surface by the extension of one of the noblest and beautiful forms of the vegetable world.[54]

Whereas Hodges had sought to make tropical landscape conform to the taste of his time by adapting it to the Italianate landscape, Humboldt, himself inspired by the paintings of Hodges, asserted that the noblest forms of landscape are to be found in the tropics. Writers like Douglas and Fleurieu had found in the Pacific many correspondences with the life and customs of the racial ancestors of the European nations; Humboldt asserted that the palm and the banana, among the noblest forms of vegetable life, had fostered civilization itself from its infancy. The exotic strangers were found once again, upon examination, to trace their descent from the gods.

8. British Reactions to Australian Nature, 1800–21

No graphic work of any consequence clearly attributable to the last three years of the eighteenth century is at present known, and no trained artist appears to have been working in Sydney during the time between the departure of Thomas Watling and the arrival of John William Lewin on 11 January 1800. Lewin was one of those young men talented in drawing who were brought to the practice of scientific draughtsmanship to satisfy the increased demand for illustrated texts concerned with botany, zoology, entomology, conchology, and so on. Some idea of the background of Lewin's training (and further evidence of the way in which the South Seas continued to stimulate scientific draughtsmanship) may be obtained by first paying some attention to the interests and career of Thomas Martyn.

Martyn was a natural-history draughtsman who in 1782 purchased a large collection of shells, which contained many new species, from some naval officers recently returned from the Pacific. This purchase suggested to him the idea of bringing out, in sections, a great illustrated catalogue of all the shells of the world. Unlike earlier books on conchology every item was to be illustrated with the greatest precision and in the greatest detail in colour. Since the most beautiful, most rare, and most sought-for shells came from the South Seas, Martyn decided that his first volume should be devoted to *Figures of Non-Descript Shells, Collected in the different Voyages to the South Seas Since the Year 1764*. In publishing his work in 1784 Martyn explained his new graphic method: 'the long descriptions and details of the generation and properties of Shells, given by most writers on Conchology, are wholly omitted here; and the utmost care has been taken that each figure, by being an exact and faithful transcript from nature, shall be sufficiently explanatory of the subject which it represents'. Here is to be observed a further application of the principle of using drawings to supplement scientific records which Falconer discussed in correspondence with Banks sixteen years before. It is not surprising, therefore, to find Martyn proudly informing his readers that 'this performance has already received from the approbation of many noble and learned persons, and more particularly Sir Joseph Banks; a sanction too given in a manner the most flattering'.[1] Martyn, however, experienced difficulty in finding artists skilled enough to carry out his work; miniature-painters were too expensive to employ and others could not render the minute detail required. So he hit upon the idea of founding an Academy for illustrating and painting in natural history, in which he could train boys with talent in the practice of the art. The Academy never seems to have been much more than a means of getting a good deal of illustrative hack-work completed cheaply. Martyn's practice was to draw and etch the outline and main contours of a shell which was then coloured by his assistants. Always keen to receive flattery from important people, Martyn sent free copies of his *Universal Conchologist* to most of the crowned heads of Europe and was the happy recipient of medallions from the Pope, the Emperor of Germany, and the King of Naples. In

138. *Freckled Ear (Navosa)*,
from Thomas Martyn, *The
Universal Conchologist* (1789),
pl. 63

replying to Martyn on behalf of the German emperor, the Baron Ignatius Born
complimented Martyn upon the magnificence of his publication: 'Natural history',
he said, 'would make a rapid progress, if we could have paintings of all the organised
bodies in nature executed with equal accuracy and fidelity.... But we want artists,
who are at the same time connoisseurs in natural history, to execute the whole with
proper precision.'[2] Martyn's book included, among others, shells from the South Seas
from the cabinets of the Duchess of Portland, Sir Ashton Lever, and George Keate
(Plate 138).

John William Lewin (1770–1819) was the kind of artist the Baron Born had in
mind, uniting an interest in art and natural history. He came of a family of ornithologists and artists. His father, William Lewin, a Fellow of the Linnean Society, was the
author of the *Birds of Great Britain*, published in seven volumes from 1789 to 1794, and
in a second edition in eight volumes from 1795 to 1801. For this work William Lewin
had the help of his three sons, John William, Thomas William, and Thomas. John
William, therefore, doubtless gained his training in natural history, in drawing, and
in engraving in his own home at Darenth, Kent, and later at Hoxton, London.
Ornithology was one of the Duchess of Portland's many interests and the Lewins
appear to have been acquainted with her.[3] Such an acquaintanceship would certainly have helped John William to obtain the recommendation which the Duke of
Portland, then Home Secretary, sent to Governor Hunter on 6 February 1798
advising him to expect the arrival in the Colony of 'Mr. Lewin ... a painter and
drawer in natural history ... desirous of pursuing his studies in a country which
cannot fail to improve that branch of knowledge.'[4] Lewin undertook before departing
to collect insects in the South Seas for Dru Drury (1725–1803), the son of a silversmith
of Cheapside and a member of an old City family who had assembled during his
lifetime the finest entomological collection in England. Some idea of the collection
may be obtained from a printed description of it which Drury published in 1788 with
a view to sale:

There may be in Holland collections more numerous, having in many instances a greater number of single species, yet no collection abounds with such a wonderful variety in all the different genera as this. All the specimens of which it is composed, are in the highest and most exquisite state of preservation, such an extensive collection can be supposed to be; and a very considerable are *unique*, such as are not to be found in any other cabinet whatever, and of considerable value; many of which, coming from countries exceedingly unhealthy, where collectors, in procuring them, have perished by the severity of the climate, give but little hope to expect that any duplicate will ever be obtained during the present age.[5]

Drury's circle of friends included: Sir Joseph Banks; James Edward Smith (who praised Drury's work highly in the first Presidential address to the Linnean Society);[6] Moses Harris, an artist friend of Thomas Martyn deeply interested in science and invention; John Latham, the ornithologist; James Lee, the horticulturalist; John Francillon, the silversmith who possessed many paintings by members of the Port Jackson circle; and Alexander Macleay, the Secretary of the Linnean Society, who later became Colonial Secretary in New South Wales under Governor Darling's administration. In order to augment his collection Drury printed *Directions for collecting Insects in Foreign Countries* which he circulated widely among travellers embarking for distant regions. He also published *Thoughts on the Precious Metals, particularly Gold, with directions to travellers, etc. for obtaining them, and selecting other natural riches from the rough diamond down to the pebblestone*. The directions were extremely varied ranging from clothing and diet to crystallography.

Although the men who collected for Drury were freer agents than the naturalists attached to scientific voyages, Drury's instructions to travellers paralleled those issued by the navy (often by the good offices of Banks) to commanders for the guidance of their scientific personnel. Indeed they may have been prompted by Banks's practice. When Lewin sailed for Sydney he took Drury's instructions for collecting insects with him. Drury also provided him with equipment for collecting: a gun, a mahogany cabinet glazed, corked, and papered with twenty-four drawers, a magnifying glass, and fifty-two copper plates for etching. Altogether they amounted in value to $51\frac{1}{2}$ guineas, which Lewin undertook to repay with a collection of insects from New South Wales as soon as possible.[7] Thomas Mersham, author of *Entomologica Britannica*, and Alexander Macleay, Secretary of the Linnean Society, also jointly advanced money to Lewin when he arrived in Sydney expecting the value to be returned to them in insects.[8] It is not surprising that the interest in the plants of New Holland both as a scientific and as a fashionable pursuit should be so closely followed by the study of insects. In his inaugural address to the Linnean Society, James Edward Smith noted the connexion between the two sciences. 'No branch of natural history, after botany,' he observed, 'has for some years past had more attention paid to it than enthomology. . . . Botany necessarily leads to the study of insects.'[9]

Shortly after Lewin's arrival in Sydney, Governor King sent Lieutenant Grant to explore Bass Strait. Seeking to provide Grant with what naturalists were available in the Colony, King arranged for George Caley, Banks's resident plant collector, to accompany Grant in the *Lady Nelson*, and for Lewin to embark in the second vessel, the *Bee*. But the voyage was a failure for Lewin—the *Bee* having to put back to Port Jackson in the face of strong head winds. Then in June and July 1801 Lewin travelled with Grant on a voyage to the Hunter River, and made some drawings there. In November he sailed in the *Norfolk* to Tahiti apparently to search for pearls on lines recommended by Drury. But the voyage proved disastrous, and after his return in the

139. John William Lewin, *Sphinx Oldenlandiae*, engraving, in *Prodromus Entomology*, London (1805), pl. 3

Porpoise in December 1802 Lewin did not put to sea again, but took up residence at Parramatta, making excursions into the country from time to time in order to collect specimens. Lewin soon found, however, that Drury's instructions for collecting insects were of little help in the new country and informed him so in a letter:

> ... I must inform you about this country and you will find that Insects is not to be got here as att home for in all my trialls with the Sheet by beating I never could get Ither Caterpillars or full Boddyed Moths for the trees are so exceedingly high that it is but few that you can reach with a long pole and I have not found it answer by beating the Shrubs or underwood and I was at a loss to know where to look for the larvae of the moths for a great wile after I came here for I never could find any in all my different travels into the country but now my surprise is at an end and dare to say yours will be the same when I inform you I dought not but will be greatly pleased to hear that I have twenty Drawings with the larvae and chrysalis and moths compleat for engraving which feed by night and secret themselves by knawing a hole ither in the Body of the tree, or else the Branches & there lie hide all the Day ...[10]

Lewin remained at Parramatta until 1808, a good deal of his time being spent in preparing the drawings and engravings for his *Prodromus Entomology* (1805) (Plate 139) and his *Birds of New Holland* (1808) which were published in London with the help of his brother Thomas. The preface to the *Prodromus* reveals that Lewin was hoping to

216

raise sufficient funds by the publication of the book to return to England. The preface to his *Birds*, also written by his brother Thomas, stated that the volume 'is the beginning of a work which is intended to comprehend the whole of the Birds of New Holland as they come to hand'. Neither book, however, aroused much attention in England. There were sixty-seven subscribers to the *Birds* among people in New South Wales, but only six from England. The Australian shipment of the *Birds* appears to have been lost, and this probably accounts for the existence of a Sydney edition of the *Birds*, published in 1813 perhaps to satisfy some of the local subscribers to the original edition. But by 1813 Lewin was finding natural-history painting a most precarious profession to practise in the young Colony; and the London edition of the *Birds* could not have appeared at a time less propitious.[11] In England the demand for illustrated books on natural history had definitely declined. Robert Thornton had to suspend the publication of his luxurious *Temple of Flora* (which had been appearing in parts since 1797) in 1807. Thornton blamed heavy taxation and the war, but the market for such books was probably already overloaded.[12] In 1808, Sir Joseph Banks, then sixty-five years of age, wrote a long letter to his collector Caley in which he complained about the declining interest in botany. 'I cannot say that Botany continues to be quite as fashionable as it used to be. The immense number of new Plants that have every year accumulated seem to deter the people from making Collections as they have little hopes of making them perfect in any branch.[13] Lewin appears to have appreciated that there was a general decline in interest in natural-history drawing. In 1808 he moved to Sydney and here began to paint topographical views of the town. But to understand Lewin's contribution to landscape-painting in New South Wales, it is desirable, first, to refer to the work of two other painters John Eyre and George William Evans.

Colonial topography in Australia first appears in the work of Eyre and Evans during the early years of the nineteenth century. John Eyre, the son of Thomas Eyre, a woolcomber and weaver of Coventry, was born about 1771, and was apprenticed to his father in 1784,[14] receiving the freedom of the city in 1792.[15] In February 1799, however, he was apprehended and committed to Coventry gaol on a charge of housebreaking. Convicted at the Assizes on 23 March 1799 Eyre was ordered to be transported for seven years. He left England in the *Canada* on 21 June 1801, arriving at Sydney on 14 December.[16]

From the topographical views which he executed in the Colony, John Eyre appears to have had some training in the elements of perspective and drawing before he was transported, although by trade a woolcomber and weaver. There were, however, people in Coventry in Eyre's time capable and willing to teach apprentices the elements of topographical painting. Eyre may have received some such training as that provided by Joseph Barnes who, in 1811, published at Coventry the second edition of his *Young Artist's Companion containing Plain and Easy Directions for the Acquirement of the Art of Drawing, Calculated to Enable Youth, with a little attention and practice to become proficient in the very useful and ornamental accomplishment.*[17] The preface explains that the author had been induced to publish 'at the request of several of his friends, whose children have experienced many great advantages in the course of their practice by strictly following the directions it contains, many of them have become proficients in a short time.' Evidence that the book was directed largely to apprentices is contained in a letter prefacing the book:

> Boys of a steady and sprightly genius want some innocent relaxation; and what
> can be thought of that combines in itself so many excellences as drawing? In very

many trades and professions it is requisite and essential; it induces youth to habits of attention and application, and by filling up that time aggreeably, which might otherwise run to waste, it causes them to bear confinement without disgust.... These are habits of the first importance to a tradesman.[18]

Little is known of John Eyre's life in New South Wales. Although his sentence would not have expired until 1806 he received a conditional pardon on 4 June 1804.[19] On 1 July 1804 he advertised to buy water-colours in the *Sydney Gazette*. Years later, on 5 January 1811, there is a reference to his appointment to paint the numbers on the houses on the east side of the Tank Stream, and of being paid 6*d*. per house from the Police Fund. On 15 August 1812 he advertised his intention of leaving the Colony 'at the earliest opportunity'.[20]

Eyre's work is confined mainly to views of Sydney painted in water-colour. They are purely topographical in intention and seek to provide an unambiguous account of the position and appearance of the principal Sydney buildings. They mark therefore in their treatment a distinct break with the picturesque compositions of Thomas Watling. Eyre seeks only to be informative; he had been paid 6*d*. for every house he had numbered in the town and his pictures suggest a desire to identify and distinguish every one of them. His *View of Sydney from the West Side of the Cove* (Plate 140) may be taken as typical of his work. He preferred a rocky foreground, which, though stylized, adequately suggests the sandstone ridges shelving Sydney Cove, and in it he usually introduced a native group. All buildings are drawn with precision and the vessels in the Cove rendered with a primitive insistence upon detail. The peculiar character of the local vegetation received little attention being reduced to a conventional formula; except when, upon occasion, he does endeavour to represent the slender trunks and typical branching of eucalypt saplings. Broad washes of colour are united with a primitive delight in detail; boats are seen lengthwise or end-on, each with its own reflection in the glassy waters of the Harbour. Apart from the conventionalized native group[21] which serves as a normal embellishment to colonial views, Eyre's pictures of Sydney are devoid of people; or, apart from an occasional flock of birds or a pennant flying from a mast, of any sense of atmosphere. Such views are essentially documentary panoramas and were used by D. D. Mann in his *Present*

140. John Eyre, *View of Sydney from the West Side of the Cove*, watercolour, 13½ × 25½ in. (*c.* 1805). Dixson Gallery, Sydney. By permission of the Trustees of the State Library of New South Wales

Picture of New South Wales (1811) as aids in describing Sydney's buildings.[22] Absalom West also used fourteen paintings by Eyre to illustrate his *Views in New South Wales* (1812–14). West's *Views* were the first to be published in the Colony: the first twelve being issued for £3 the set in 1812, and the second set were included with the first and offered for £9 the twenty-four in 1814. The publications of both Mann and West are best considered in the light of the interest in colonial and exotic topography which marked the early years of the century in Britain. West's *Views*, though engraved largely for the local colonial market, were probably suggested by Mann's earlier work, and many of the views found their way to England. Whereas Watling followed the picturesque precepts of such men as Gilpin, Eyre's work is modelled upon the smooth, factual style expounded in such books as Edward Dayes's *Instruction for Drawing and Colouring Landscapes* (1805) and exemplified in aquatint by such publishing houses as Robert Havell & Son.

George William Evans was the second topographical artist at work in Sydney during the first decade of the century. Born at Warwick in 1778 he revealed a talent for drawing in his youth and was articled to an engineer and architect. He is said to have run away to sea in 1796 and married the Captain's daughter of the vessel that took him to the Cape—upon arrival there. He secured a post in the Government Dockyard, but sailed for New South Wales shortly after 25 March 1802 when the Cape was handed back to the Dutch, arriving in Sydney on 15 October 1802. At first a storekeeper at Parramatta, he was appointed Acting Surveyor-General on 10 August 1803 during the absence of Charles Grimes. He began painting topographical views about this time. The styles of Eyre and Evans are so close and their subject-matter so similar that it is most probable the style of one influenced the style of the other, but it is not possible to be sure in which direction the influence flowed. Eyre was the older man, had arrived before Evans, and there is evidence to suggest that he may have been painting in the Colony before Evans. On the other hand Evans was a free man, had been trained professionally as a draughtsman, and his earliest work can be dated earlier than anything certainly by Eyre. Evans, in any case, was the first of many land surveyors responsible for the production of topographical landscapes in Australia during the following fifty years. After Flinders's *Voyage* marine exploration became less important and land exploration more important. The change is reflected in graphic art by the replacement of the naval draughtsmen of the first years of settlement by military draughtsmen and land surveyors after the turn of the century.

Hitherto all engraved views of the Colony had been published only as illustrations to books. At this time, however, engraved views of Sydney, published separately, began to appear. The first was that engraved by W. S. Blake from a painting sent to London in 1800 (Plate 141). Drawn in the precise topographical manner, the town, with the sun rising above the Sydney Heads, wears a neat and prosperous air and recalls the eulogy written by Péron upon the progress of the town when he visited it in 1802.[23] Dedicated to Governor Hunter, one of the purposes of the engraving may well have been to show the growth of the town during his administration. The second, separately published, engraving was an aquatint by F. Jukes, after a painting by Edward Dayes, who drew it from a sketch which had been painted in the Colony by an unknown artist and sent to London on 17 November 1802. It was printed on 10 April 1804. There is a marked similarity between the foreshortened vessel on the extreme left of the aquatint and the vessel in a similar position in Eyre's *West View of Sydney Cove*. This suggests that the original painting from which Dayes worked may have been drawn by Eyre. It is possible that the view engraved by W. S. Blake was composed from a drawing or drawings by Watling.

The Australian aborigine, as we have seen, was one of the natural curiosities of the country, and as the interest in curiosities steadily declined after 1800 local artists became less interested in depicting natives. Whereas such artists as the Port Jackson Painter and Thomas Watling made many studies of native groups and many portraits of individual natives, after 1800 the aborigine is relegated increasingly to fulfil the function of a pictorial embellishment to topographic landscape, providing a local touch and pointing the contrast between primeval life and the busy progress of the town. Travellers like Jacques Arago and Charles Darwin noticed the startling contrast afforded by the spectacle of naked savages carrying on their disputes in the streets of a modern town. Topographical views of Sydney and nearby towns executed during the first quarter of the century rarely failed to note the contrast between the life of nature and the progress of civilization. Figures of natives gathered around a fire, seated before a *mia mia*, or wandering in search of food, become stereotypes and are found in drawing after drawing.[24] Watling had first adopted the practice of using aborigines to provide foreground motifs in his views, and the practice is continued in the work of Eyre, Evans, and later artists like James Taylor, James Wallis, and Joseph Lycett. The growing delight in urban progress, and the concurrent reduction of interest in the savage as a symbol of the desirable life of nature implicit in colonial topography, finds a close parallel in remarks made by Sydney Smith when reviewing Collins's *Account* in 1803 for the *Edinburgh Review*:

> To introduce an European population, and, consequently, the arts and civilisation of Europe into such an untrodden country as New Holland, is to confer a lasting and important benefit upon the world ... how absurd are those systems which proscribe the acquisitions of science and the restraints of law, and would arrest the progress of man in the rudest and earliest stages of his existence! ... we must have recourse to matter of fact, and judge of the rude state of society, not from the praises of tranquil *literati*, but from the narratives of those who have seen it through a nearer and better medium than that of imagination.[25]

The conventionalization of the aborigine so apparent in the topographical views is

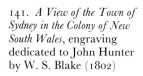

141. *A View of the Town of Sydney in the Colony of New South Wales*, engraving dedicated to John Hunter by W. S. Blake (1802)

142. T. R. Browne, *Hump-back'd Maria, a female well-known about Sydney*, watercolour, $11\frac{1}{2} \times 9\frac{1}{2}$ in. (1819). Nan Kivell Collection 149B, National Library of Australia

apparent also in the drawings of individuals and native groups of the period. Very little original work of this type was produced by local artists between 1800 and 1810, but by 1812 a T. R. Browne is known to have been working at Newcastle. Most probably a convict, Browne helped to illustrate the manuscript assembled by Lieutenant Thomas Skottowe with drawings of plants, animals, and natives of New South Wales.[26] In Browne's drawings of aborigines—both in Skottowe's manuscript and in other drawings—the tenderness of feeling in Watling's native portraits and the kindly sentiment in the work of the Port Jackson Painter have vanished. The figures have been reduced to a comic formula which is itself paralleled in the nick-names used as titles to the drawings: 'Hump-back'd Maria' (Plate 142), 'Long Jack', and 'Pussy Cat'. The natives are no longer seen as individuals but as grotesque caricatures; the type forms, in distorted silhouettes, being reshuffled and reassembled from group to group. Browne's comical aborigines seem to have met with local favour for he made a number of sets of them, and his drawings were apparently copied by at least one imitator.[27]

The contrast between primitive and civilized life so often presented by the topographers was at times adapted to present the native as a humble and docile child of nature awaiting the blessings of civilization and Christianity, as Smirke had done in his *Cession of Matavai*. John Lewin presented the aborigine in this manner in a transparency which he executed as a decoration for a ball held at Government House on the occasion of the Queen's birthday in 1811. The design has not survived, but some idea of it may be gained from a description in the *Sydney Gazette*:

In the center of the ball-room were the Royal initials in chrystal, beautifully worked, suspended between festoons of leaves and flowers extending across the room, the north end of which was covered with a transparent painting (executed by Mr. Lewin in a highly finished style) the subject local, and the design particularly appropriate, being the representation of our Native Race in their happy moments of festivity, contrasting in silent admiration their amusements to the recreations of a polished Circle; and instead of expressing dissatisfaction at the humility of their condition, earnestly anticipating the blessing of civilisation while a striking full-sized figure, drawn in one of the most animated attitudes of the *corrobori* pointed with his waddy at the Church of St. Phillip, of which an accurate perspective view was given, as symbolical of the Christian Religion inviting them to happiness. Each of the portraits bore so accurate a resemblance to some familiar native as scarcely to leave a doubt that the representation was taken from the life, in whatever attitude the Artist considered best adapted to his subject; the whole of the scene receiving a warmth of colouring from the judicious representation of their fires, and the softness of expression produced by the reflected rays of the rising moon. As this part of the preparation was unexpected, the admiration was the more nervous, and none forebore the meed of praise to the performance.[28]

It may be doubted whether Lewin's part in the preparations was not known beforehand by Michael Massey Robinson,[29] who on the same evening recited his *Ode for the Queen's Birthday* and on this occasion referred for the first time in his poetry to the 'aboriginal question' at some length. The close similarity between the *Sydney Gazette*'s description of the aborigines in Lewin's transparency and those described by Robinson in his poem for the occasion clearly suggests that there was some collaboration between painter and poet. Like a topographical draughtsman, Robinson first describes a cultivated landscape symbolizing civilized progress and places the native in it by way of sharp contrast:

> Oh! Pow'r Supreme! Whilst thy benignant Hand,
> Dispenses Blessings o'er this grateful Land,
> Bids cultur'd Hills and waving Vallies smile,
> Rewards fair Industry and sweetens Toil,
> Bids rising Genius bend to Wisdom sage,
> Whilst Learning opens her instructive Page,
> May Reason muse . . . and, in the Solemn Pause
> Indulge a Sigh in suff'ring Nature's Cause.
> —Not with presumptuous Thought thy Pow'rs scan,
> But urg'd by Kindred Ties from Man to Man,
> With sympathetic Energy retrace,
> The lorn Condition of yon sable Race,
> For Ages doom'd in Indolence to roam,
> The rocks their Refuge, and the Wilds their Home!

The state of the aborigine is then depicted as a wretched one which only the light of religion can improve:

> Lost to each social Interchange of Thought,
> Their Youth neglected, and their Age untaught,
> Unless with bar'brous Yell to Wound the Ear,
> And with grim Antick hurl the trembling Spear,
> Unless the FINNY Victims to beguile,
> And snatch subsistence from the Scanty Spoil!

222

Hap'ly whilst calm Religion's genuine Voice
In other Climes bids other Tribes rejoice,
Pours into darken'd Minds her lurid Rays,
And bids the wondering Savage live to Praise,
'Ere many circling Years have onward roll'd
May call these Wand'rers to the 'promised Fold',
And from the Dawn o' Reason's genial Ray
Bid their Night yield—to intellectual Day.

The theme of Lewin's painting and Robinson's poem must have met with the Governor's approval, for some time later he informed Bathurst that 'it seems only to require the fostering Hand of Time, gentle Means, and Conciliatory Manners to turn these poor Un-enlightened People into an important Degree of Civilisation'.[30]

The topographical views of Sydney executed by Evans and Eyre were taken from the heights fringing Sydney Cove and look in towards the heart of the expanding town. Even when topographers moved further afield to draw such houses as Woolloomooloo and Ultimo, or the settlements along the Hawkesbury, interest remained centred upon the manifestations of civilization amid the primeval wilderness. The signs of human occupation invariably gave travellers a sense of genuine relief. The experience of Péron while travelling along the road from Sydney to Parramatta was similar to that of many who came after him, though expressed in a language more resounding than most:

Cependant les forêts s'entr'ouvrent çà et là; des défrichemens plus ou moins étendus s'offrent au voyageur; il découvre de jolies habitations ombragées par des arbres élégans; il contemple, avec une douce émotion, ces champs nouveaux, où la foible graminée du Nord s'élève sur les débris des puissans Eucalyptus: il retrouve avec plaisir, sur ces bords lointains, les animaux les plus utiles de sa patrie; les taureaux y bondissent avec une vigueur égale ou même supérieure à celle que développoient leurs pères au milieu des froids pâturages de l'Hibernie; la vache,

143. *A View of Hunter's River, near Newcastle, New South Wales*, engraving after I. R. Browne by W. Preston, in West, *Views in New South Wales* (1812–14), pl. v

plus féconde, donne aussi plus de lait dans ces climats moins rigoureux que les nôtres; le cheval de l'Angleterre s'y présente avec la même force, avee la même fierté qu'aux rives de la Tamise; et le cochon de l'Europe s'améliore par ses croisemens multipliés avec ceux des îles de la mer du Sud, qui lui sont supérieurs pour la taille et pour la qualité de la graisse et de la chair.[31]

In such descriptions, the attitudes expressed in *The Voyage of Governor Phillip*, and by Erasmus Darwin were carried on into the nineteenth century. The bushland itself, however, continued to repel. Watling, as we have seen, complained about the monotony of immense forests extending over a 'little varied' plain, but he contrived to make his views picturesque by selection and combination. The less complicated vision of the topographers, however, presented the landscape of the Cumberland plain in all its natural monotony. Similarly, T. R. Browne's *View of Hunter's River* (Plate 143) renders the natural vegetation with a monotonous uniformity of both shape and tone. The eye is hemmed in by a close, grey horizon, the only variety being provided by columns of smoke from native fires rising from the blanket of the forest. A literary equivalent may be found in Robinson's *Odes*. For Robinson the bushland is a dark and savage wood into which only human occupation and cultivation can bring a 'social light'. Although the idea of human progress under the aegis of an enlightened Britain was a cardinal theme for Robinson, as it was for William Lisle Bowles, we may find vestiges in the work of both men of old European fears of the forest. For them nature is still an allegory (slowly unfolding itself through the ages) of the will of God; a long journey through a dark wood to a paradise garden. Robinson was no great poet but it is well to remember that he imaged Australian nature against a background of traditional Christian thought:

> Time was, when o'er THIS dread expanse of land
> No TRAIT appear'd of Culture's fost'ring hand:
> And, as the wild Woods yielded to the Blast,
> Nature scarce own'd the unproductive Waste.
> O'er rugged Cliffs fantastic Branches hung,
> 'Round whose hoar Trunks the slender Scions clung,
> Impervious Mountains met the ling'ring Eye,
> Whose cloud-cap't Summits brav'd the Sky.
> Rocks, whose repulsive Frown access defied,
> And Bays, where idly ebb'd the slumb'ring Tide—
> Unless some Straggler of the NATIVE RACE,
> In crude Canoe exposed his sooty Face;
> With lazy Motion paddled o'er the Flood,
> Snatch'd at the spear-struck Fish—and hugged his Food.
>
> But when BRITTANNIA's Sons came forth, to brave
> The dreary Perils of the length'ning Wave;
> When her bold Barks, with swelling Sails unfurled,
> Trac'd these rude Coasts, and hail'd a new-found World.
> Soon as their Footsteps press'd the yielding sand,
> A sun more genial brighten'd on the Land:
> Commerce and Arts enrich'd the social Soil,
> Burst through the gloom and bade all Nature smile.

The 'impervious mountains' to the west were as monotonous to look at as the enclosed plain. 'They resemble a vast curtain, which limits the horizon on the northwest', wrote Péron, 'no break, no peak, varies the outline; an horizontal line, above which is distinguished another regular tier of mountains of a browner shade, deepens the melancholy of these mountains.[32] But Péron was not immune to the fascination of Australian scenery, and in the end it became for him an item of considerable philosophical interest. Somewhat prone to hasty generalization he seized upon the current notion of antipodal inversion in order to explain the peculiarities of Australian nature. His speculations began when he sought to explain the remarkable contrast between the fertility of Timor and the barrenness of the neighbouring shore of Australia:

> The dismayed and astonished navigator turns away his eyes, fatigued with the contemplation of these unhappy isles and hideous solitudes, surrounded as he views them with continual dangers; and when he reflects that these inhospitable shores border those of the archipelago of Asia, on which nature has lavished blessings and treasures, he can scarcely conceive how so vast a sterility could be produced in the neighbourhood of such fecundity. In vain would he seek the cause from the ordinary laws of nature, the true principle of a contrariety which he cannot discover, nor even conjecture; but this is not the only phenomenon in the natural construction of New Holland, and we shall find the same subjects for astonishment and meditation in each of the various parts of the history of this vast continent.[33]

In Australia, Péron proceeded to find inversions and contrarieties of nature in a great many phenomena for which a rational explanation was not immediately available. For instance the fact that Sydney, backed by an enormous chain, as he said, of impassable mountains should be parched by hot westerly winds during summer months struck him as most odd:

> ... all the western and north-western parts of this portion of New Holland, are occupied by a very extensive chain of mountains, the height of which appears to be equal to that of the most elevated chains already known. Who would not be induced to think, from such a constitution, that the winds which pass over these mountains must be characterized by a colder temperature? This consequence is so natural and so conformable to all the principles of natural philosophy, that it would seem not to admit of any kind of modification; and nevertheless, it receives, in the case in question, the most decided and absolute exception, as if the atmosphere of New Holland, as well as the animals and the vegetables of this singular continent, has its peculiar laws, which differ from all the principles of our sciences and all the rules of our systems.[34]

Péron also discussed the irregular flooding of the Hawkesbury River and came to the conclusion that it could not be explained by meteorological phenomena normal either to equatorial or temperate regions. While agreeing that the floods were most probably due to heavy rain in the catchment area of the river he claimed that such floods were quite unpredictable according to the known laws of meteorology:

> ... how wonderful must these heavy rains appear which can suddenly occasion the waters of a small streamlet to rise the height of from 30 to 50 feet, which happen at the most opposite seasons, occur so frequently in a year, and in a manner so independent of the atmosphere, of the course of the winds, or of tempests ... It must be allowed that, in this, as in many other phenomena New Holland defies our conclusions from comparisons, mocks our studies, and shakes to their foundations

the most firmly established and most universally admitted of our scientific opinions. As we proceed in speaking of this continent, justly denominated by the English the unequalled and wonderful, we shall find still other and not less inconceivable examples of these apparently whimsical freaks of nature.[35]

Péron's book did much to popularize the notion that Australian nature was whimsical and freakish in its operations. James O'Hara took up the idea again in his *History of New South Wales* (1817), though his description of the peculiarities of Australia probably owed more to Hunter's *Journal* than to Péron:

> Nature may be said to have in this country indulged in whim. She sometimes mimicks herself in giving to smaller animals, such as the native rat, the general form and characteristics of the kangaroo; she gives to a great variety of species, the false belly of that animal; in numerous instances, animals were discovered which might at first sight be considered monstrous productions, such as an aquatic quadruped, about the size of a rabbit, with the eyes, colour and skin of a mole, and the bill and web-feet of a duck, a parrot with the slender legs of a sea-gull, a skate with a head like that of a shark.... The whole animal creation appeared to be different from that of every other region: nor less so the vegetable; every tree and shrub, perhaps without exception, was of a species peculiar to the soil, and another Flora diffused an endless variety of unknown tints and forms.[36]

Such a theme possessed literary possibilities and Sydney Smith made the most of them when he had occasion to review O'Hara's book in the *Edinburgh Review*:

> ... in this remote part of the earth, Nature (having made horses, oxen, ducks, geese, oaks, elms, and all regular productions for the rest of the world) seems determined to have a bit of play, and to amuse herself as she pleases. Accordingly, she makes cherries with the stone on the outside; and a monstrous animal, as tall as a grenadier, with the head of a rabbit, a tail as big as a bed-post, hopping along at the rate of five hops to a mile, with three or four young kangaroos looking out of its false uterus, to see what is passing. Then comes a quadruped as big as a large cat, with the eyes, colour, and skin of a mole, and the bill and webfeet of a duck—puzzling Dr. Shaw, and rendering the latter part of his life miserable, from his utter inability to determine whether it was a bird or a beast. Add to this a parrot with the head of a seagull; a skate with the head of a shark; and a bird of such monstrous dimensions, that a side-bone of it will dine three real carnivorous Englishmen;—together with many other productions that agitate Sir Joseph, and fill him with mingled emotions of distress and delight.[37]

The attitude of amused wonder which Sydney Smith adopted towards the oddities of Australia found expression also in the poems published by Barron Field[38] in his *First Fruits of Australian Poetry* (1819). Although his first poem, *Botany Bay Flowers*, borrows heavily from Shakespeare, echoes Marvel, and affects the botanical conceits of Erasmus Darwin, it does express the genuine interest in natural curiosities which excited many of the first visitors to New South Wales. Australian nature is seen as it had been seen by Bowes, Southwell, and Watling, as a brilliant and fantastic, but enchanted, garden. The flowers and insects were so curious and colourful that the land was a fit home for the Queen of the fairies:

> ... here
> Queen Mab would have no cause to fear
> For her respectable approach,

Lest she could not set up her coach.
Here's a fine grub for a coach-maker,
Good as in Fairy-Land Long Acre;
And very-long-indeed-legg'd spinners,
To make her waggon-spokes, the sinners!
And here are winged grasshoppers;
And, as to gnats for waggoners,
We have mosquitoes will suffice
To drive her team of atomies.
If therefore she and her regalia
Have never yet been in Australia,
I recommend a voyage to us,
On board the Paper Nautilus;
But I incline to the opinion
That we are now in her dominion . . .

But the land of faery was for Field, as for Watling, a melancholy land also: outside the small cultivated areas of the settlement lay 'desart forests' and a 'barren wood'; and Field in a conceit most fittingly topsy-turvey, expressed the hope that Oberon, King of Fairies, might squeeze the juice of the *epacris* into his eyes,

To take from eyes all error, that when next
They wake, all this may seem a fruitless dream.

For Field, like Watling, was thoroughly homesick. In his second, and better, poem, *Kangaroo*, Australia is once again a land of monstrous prodigies and antipodal inversions—a topsy-turvey land where all things are exceptional and upsidedowned-ness is the order of the day. So hopelessly desolate a country, Field observes, could never have formed a part of the original creation. The land, surely, must have been created upon the occasion of the Fall of Man. The kangaroo, of all its living creatures, is its one saving grace:

Kangaroo, Kangaroo!
Thou Spirit of Australia,
That redeems from utter failure,
From perfect desolation,
And warrants the creation
Of this fifth part of the Earth,
Which would seem an after-birth,
Not conceiv'd in the Beginning
(For GOD bless'd His work at first,
And saw that it was good),
But emerg'd at the first sinning,
When the ground was therefore curst:—
And hence this barren wood!

Now Field was particularly well versed in seventeenth-century literature (it was his lifelong interest) and the view of Australian nature which he presents here bears a kinship with the views expressed by such men as Godfrey Goodman (and echoed by John Donne and others) that nature had also fallen from its state of primal beauty when man fell from Grace. But for Field, Australian nature did not fall, it 'emerg'd at the first sinning'. It was in short something separate and distinct from the primal creative intention. Similarly, the kangaroo was not created in the normal way by God when he created the other animals, it was rather, a 'divine, mistake', having been made playfully by nature (here the creative force of God) when the Deity was at rest on the Seventh Day after having completed the more serious and normal work of the Creation. It was an animal

> Join'd by some divine mistake,
> None but Nature's hand can make—
> Nature, in her Wisdom's play,
> On Creation's holiday.

Together with such echoes from the theological cosmologies of the seventeenth century, Field also echoes the ideas of his contemporaries; namely that the animals of Australia were not the products of distinct acts of Creation but were anomalies or, as Erasmus Darwin called them, 'animal mules' produced as the result of the promiscuous intercourse of original genera:

> She had made the squirrel fragile;
> She had made the bounding hart;
> But a third so strong and agile
> Was beyond ev'n Nature's art;
> So she join'd the former two
>   In thee, Kangaroo.

And yet the animal, for all its contradictions, was, said Field, like a discord resolved into a harmony:

> For howsoe'er anomalous,
> Thou yet art not incongruous,
> Repugnant or preposterous.
> Better-proportion'd animal,
> More graceful or ethereal,
> Was never follow'd by the hound,
> With fifty steps to thy one bound.
> Thou can'st not be amended: no;
> Be as thou art; thou best art so.

For Field then, Australian nature had produced its own peculiar masterpiece, its own typical form of beauty.

Freakish and unattractive forms of nature hemmed in the young settlement on all sides. The roads were lined by long avenues of eucalypt and the cleared land as yet consisted only of isolated pockets of settlement set amid the grey monotony of the forest. The same monotonous vegetation could be seen growing to the very tops of the impenetrable mountains to the west. 'All agree', wrote Péron, giving the view of the aborigines, 'in the impossibility of clearing this western barrier.' Before 1813, the unconquered mountain chain, to the west of Sydney provided the most obvious example of the inscrutability and hostility of nature in Australia.

The barrier was penetrated in 1813 by Gregory Blaxland, William Lawson, and William Charles Wentworth. In search of pastures for their expanding flocks, the explorers not unnaturally assessed the country with the eyes of graziers. They had no time to admire views. The mountains themselves they found rough, infertile, and inhospitable. They were followed by George William Evans,[39] surveyor and topographical draughtsman, to report upon the new land discovered beyond the mountains. Evans found the mountains as disagreeable as Blaxland's party did. It was the rich pastoral country beyond the mountains that excited the imaginations of the first explorers as it did those of many settlers who came after them. And to Cox, the roadmaker who followed them, the mountains were a series of engineering problems to be overcome.

But with the completion of the road some appreciation of the local mountain scenery begins to appear in the diaries of travellers. It is present in the diaries kept by Governor Macquarie and Major Antill when the Governor made a progress over the mountains in 1815 in order to 'appreciate the importance of the Tract of Country laying Westward of them'. This progress had the touch of a grand tour about it.[40] Macquarie and his party halted to admire the magnificent prospects stretching before them from various vantage points along the route, the Governor finding appropriate names for views which impressed him. It is not without significance that the first view which impressed the company was of the settlements along the Nepean as seen from the high scarp of the mountains. Purely mountain scenery, however, in which no signs of human habitation mingled was also found to possess its attractions:

> On the S.W. side of the King's Table Land, the Mountain terminates in abrupt precipices of immense depth, at the bottom of which is seen a glen, as romantically beautiful as can be imagined, bounded on the further side by Mountains of great magnitude, terminating equally abruptly as the others; and the whole thickly covered with timber ... to which the Governor gave the name of 'The Prince Regent's Glen.'[41]

And somewhat further along the road the party encountered another spectacle to give pause to travellers in search of the picturesque:

> Proceeding hence to the 33rd mile on the top of a hill, an opening presents itself to the S.W. side of Prince Regent's Glen, from whence a view is obtained particularly beautiful and grand—Mountains rising beyond mountains, with stupendous masses of rock in the foreground, here strike the eye with admiration and astonishment. The circular form in which the whole is so wonderfully disposed, induced the Governor to give it the name of 'Pitt's Amphitheatre'.[42]

John William Lewin accompanied the Governor as the artist of his party. Since 1808 he had turned his attention from natural-history draughtsmanship to the painting of views. But in these views there remains the natural-historian's insistence upon the careful scrutiny of detail. In the landscapes which he painted upon Macquarie's Progress, he dispensed with the stereotyped foreground motifs common to early colonial views and with the contrivances of picturesque composition. While his landscapes are of no great artistic merit in themselves, they do provide yet another example of a natural-historian's mode of vision being brought to bear upon the problems of landscape painting. Furthermore, the works which Lewin painted on the Progress are of considerable historical importance, since in them we may trace the rude yet distinct beginnings of an Australian school of landscape painting. Lewin in most of his water-colours dispensed with the picturesque *coulisse* of foreground trees first applied to Australian scenery by Thomas Watling. Instead, foregrounds are usually treated as open spaces containing a few details such as rocks, fallen timber, and local plants or animals (Plate 144). Vegetation is no longer a prominent foreground feature; usually the tree forms are depicted in the middle distance (Plate 145). For Lewin the horizon is no longer, as it was for the first topographers working in Australia, an unbroken line of grey forest. It takes on a variety of forms, at times it is an

144. John William Lewin, *Campbell River*, watercolour, 8¾ × 10¾ in. (1815). Mitchell Library, Sydney. By permission of the Trustees of the State Library of New South Wales

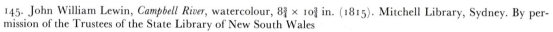

145. John William Lewin, *Campbell River*, watercolour, 8¾ × 10¾ in. (1815). Mitchell Library, Sydney. By permission of the Trustees of the State Library of New South Wales

146. John William Lewin, *Evans Peak*, watercolour, 8¾ × 10½ in. (1815). Mitchell Library, Sydney. By permission of the Trustees of the State Library of New South Wales

147. John William Lewin, *Sidmouth Valley*, watercolour, 8¼ × 10¼ in. (1815). Mitchell Library, Sydney. By permission of the Trustees of the State Library of New South Wales

irregular sandstone buttress, or thickly forested scarp, thrown sharply against the sky (Plate 146), at times it is an irregular line of misted vegetation seen through the open tracery of the closer trees, or a faint blue hill-top in the distance. Lewin drew the eucalypt with an eye to the fact that it does not completely shroud the background against which it is drawn, and that its foliage is carried upon branches often widely dispersed (Plate 147). He grasped, in short, the open nature of the tree, and he observed many features of its growth missed by earlier artists: the variety of colour in the trunk of the tree; the nature of the bark, hanging in long strips and clinging in the fork of branches; the strange angles and twisted appearance of saplings affected by storms and fires in growth. He noted, too, how one part of a tree will carry new leaves while another part only carries dead branches, how young suckers spring up at the roots of trees, and how stumps blackened with bush fires put out new foliage. Only the characteristic colour of the vegetation eluded him, as it eluded so many others, prior to the emergence of the *plein air* and impressionist painters of the last two decades of the century. Lewin, as we have seen, began as a natural-history draughtsman and first drew Australian vegetation (in the form of details of branches) as a setting for his drawings of birds and insects.

The subject-matter which came to Lewin's hand during Macquarie's Progress contained much that was to become typical of Australian life during the remainder of the century: the encampment, with an open fire attended by a few stockmen, explorers, travellers, or drovers, their horses at grass and a flock of sheep, or herd of cattle nearby, resting; the settler's hut and stockyards in a wooded valley; a bullock team on the road; the flat yellow sweep of a plain high with grass, some gum-trees along a water-course with blue hills and a pale-blue sky beyond. Such pictorial emblems of the expanding frontier recur again and again throughout the century.

The Blue Mountain crossing was also noted in contemporary verse. Robinson was not given to referring to local events in his highly artificial *Birthday Odes*, but the mountain crossing was such a significant event in the life of the Colony that it found a mention in his *Ode for the Queen's Birthday, 1816*. Robinson however made no attempt, as Lewin did, to describe any of the typical features of the landscape described. He still saw nature through the eyes of such picturesque poets as Thomson and Dyer, and his mountain scenery echoes descriptions of Welsh and Scottish highlands to be found in Collins and Gray. In a study of the history of European attitudes to nature in Australia his work is of importance in showing how traditional fears of forests and wild mountainous regions were carried over into verse written in the Colony, as may be seen in his description of the Blue Mountains:

> Where yon Blue Mountains, with tremendous Brow,
> Frown on the humbler Vales that wind below,
> Where scarcely human Footsteps ever trac'd
> The craggy Cliffs that guard the ling'ring Waste.
> O'er the Wild Surface of the Western Plains,
> Aerst the lorn Range of Isolated Trains:
> Where from the Birth of Time the slumbering Soil
> Had born no Traces of the Peasant's Toil—
> Behold, where Industry's encourag'd Hand
> Has chang'd the lurid Aspect of the Land;
> With Verdure cloathed the solitary Hills,
> And pour'd fresh Currents from the limpid Rills;
> Has shed o'er darken'd Glades a social Light,
> And BOUNDLESS REGIONS OPEN TO OUR SIGHT!

To Robinson the virgin forest was still the abode of melancholy; the cultivated landscape the harbinger of social happiness. Nor was this view confined to convicts and other exiled Englishment. The native-born Australian, William Charles Wentworth, adopted a similar point of view in his *Statistical, Historical and Political Description of the Colony of New South Wales* (1819). This book, written while Wentworth was a student at Cambridge, even though it echoes for the first time the voice of the Australian abroad homesick for the bush, still describes the local landscape in picturesque terms and reveals a preference for the cultivated landscape. Wentworth, however, showed a genuine enthusiasm for Australian landscape even if he was unable to observe it with the same clarity as Lewin.[43] Although a member of the first party to cross the Blue Mountains, they inspired in him the same sensations of melancholy which we find in the poetry of Robinson. In a long description of the environs of Sydney he has occasion to describe the view to the west:

> If you afterwards suddenly face about to the westward, you see before you one vast forest, uninterrupted except by the cultivated openings which have been made by the axe on the summits of some of the loftiest hills, and which tend considerably to diminish those melancholy sensations its gloomy grandeur would otherwise inspire. The innumerable undulations in this vast expanse of forest, forcibly remind you of the ocean when convulsed by tempests; save that the billows of the one slumber in a fixed and leaden stillness, and want that motion which constitutes the diversity, beauty and sublimity of the other. Continuing the view, you arrive at that majestic and commanding chain of mountains called 'the Blue Mountains' whose stately and o'ertopping grandeur forms a most imposing boundary to the prospective.[44]

The virgin Australian landscape, then, still inspired melancholy feelings even among the native-born. Doubtless Robert Brown's description of Australian vegetation and his explanation of the monotonous colour of the vegetation, which he published in a botanical appendix to Flinders's *Voyage*,[45] encouraged such attitudes. For Brown was read and quoted by many on this question, including Humboldt. Moreover, the enthusiastic descriptions of the pastures beyond the mountains were counterbalanced by descriptions of the land found farther still to the west. In his *Journal of Two Expeditions to the Interior of New South Wales* (1820) John Oxley recounted disappointment after disappointment, telling of dry creek beds, rotten swampy country, hostile natives, and insect pests. In his clear impersonal account of the country was to be found further corroboration of Watling's view that the Australian landscape was a 'weary prospect': 'One tree, one soil, one water, and one description of bird, fish, or animal prevails alike for ten miles and for one hundred. A variety of wretchedness is at all times preferable to one unvarying cause of pain and distress.'[46] Such comments were more damning indictments than Watling's sophisticated distaste, for they made no attempt to pass judgement upon the landscape in aesthetic terms but condemned it outright for its monotony.

9. *Colonial Interpretations of the Australian Landscape, 1821–35*

BEFORE 1821 very little settlement had taken place beyond the sandstone highlands enclosing the Cumberland Plain. Governor Brisbane, who succeeded Macquarie in 1821, removed restrictions on the settlement of the country beyond the mountains and made the Hunter Valley availabe to settlers by moving the convict establishment at Newcastle to Port Macquarie. Settlement also fanned out southwest beyond the Cow pastures and the Bargo Brush from Wingecarribee to the Limestone Plains, and to the south in the Illawarra-Shoalhaven District.[1]

This rapid expansion of the frontier brought a greater variety of scenery before the notice of travellers and artists, and their reactions, accordingly, were more varied. The alluvial flats of the Hawkesbury and Hunter rivers, the sandstone scarps of the Blue Mountains, the cedar brush of the Illawarra and Port Stephens, and the grass plains of the Bathurst and south-western districts, all began to contribute to the complex of ideas coming to be associated in these years with Australian landscape.

The increase in migration to Australia meant that a new interest was being taken in the Colony, in England. The first men to describe or depict the Australian scene, from John White and the Port Jackson circle of naval draughtsmen to Barron Field and John William Lewin (before 1808), had sought in their work to satisfy the curiosity of English virtuosi and naturalists for whom local officials frequently acted as agents. But the death of Sir Joseph Banks in 1820 marks a change in patronage as in government. After 1820, artists and travellers in describing the Australian scene have the practical interests of prospective migrants very much in mind. Interest in natives and natural curiosities no longer occupy pride of place in books about Australia. And because information was now directed towards a different class of persons, such books became less expensive, less sumptuous, and less well produced.

Some convict artists were still at work, particularly in Tasmania. But the typical draughtsman is now no longer a convict convicted of forgery or a naval officer, he is a military surveyor, a travelling artist, or a professional artist-migrant. It may be said in general that the formal quality of landscape-painting in the Australian colonies at this time was determined by a desire partly for topographical accuracy and partly for the traditional respect for picturesque beauty. But there is a considerable difference between the picturesque compositions of the period and the picturesque painting of the last decades of the eighteenth century. For, within a picturesque framework, far more attention was now given to local peculiarities of terrain, vegetation, and atmosphere. The work of Lewin in this regard is continued. Foregrounds, instead of being embellished with native groups, now begin to feature typical scenes of colonial life, and artists begin to appreciate the variety of landscape afforded by the Colony.

The topographical painting begun by Eyre and Evans is continued in the work of two men who arrived in the Colony during the Macquarie administration: James Taylor, and Joseph Lycett, both of whom published drawings after 1821.

Major James Taylor arrived in Sydney in August, 1817 with the 48th

234

(Northamptonshire) Regiment, and left the Colony six years later.[2] Taylor made
finished drawings from sketches executed by G. W. Evans on John Oxley's exploration of the western rivers of New South Wales in 1817–18.[3] He is best known,
however, for his panoramic view of Sydney published in aquatint by Robert Havell
(Plate 148). Closely finished in the topographical manner, the panorama seeks to
convey a clear picture of the progress of the settlement, and the scenery and life typical
of Port Jackson. It has been put together, therefore, with much the same intention as
the pictures drawn for the mechanical panoramas introduced into London by Robert
Barker and Robert Burford. As published, Taylor's panorama consists of three parts
which join together. Taylor contrives to appeal to the variety of interests which the
Colony had aroused in England since its establishment. The officers of the 48th
Regiment who walk in the grounds of the Military Hospital, and the Hospital itself
with its convalescents in their long gowns, help to signify the rise of the civilized arts in
the distant Colony, and are sharply contrasted with native groups beside their
primitive dwellings. The natives themselves afford a further contrast between cultivated society and wild nature, since those in and near the precincts of the Hospital
are clothed sufficiently not to give offence whereas those beside their own dwellings in
the open fields still go stark naked. Similar contrasts are pointed by the cultivated
European flowers in the hospital garden and the native flowers beyond, and between
the cleared pastures of the foreground and the monotonous brush of the Cumberland
Plain looking towards the Blue Mountains in the distance.

The second topographical artist of the period was Joseph Lycett, a convict who, like
Thomas Watling, was transported for forgery. He arrived in Sydney in 1814.

148. *The Town of Sydney in New South Wales* (detail) (1823), engraved by Robert Havell and Sons, London, after James Taylor. (The central section of a pan-oramic view in three sections.)

235

Employed in the police office upon arrival he was again apprehended forging notes in 1815; the *Sydney Gazette* of 3 June 1815 announced:

> Among those in custody on multifarious charges is a Mr. Lycett, who, unfortunately for the world as well as for himself, had obtained sufficient knowledge of the graphic arts to aid him in the practice of deception, in which he has outdone most of his predecessors. The bills of Mr. Thrupp he has imitated by a means that had not in this Colony been before resorted to by the ingenious—The printing type used in such bills had been so well imitated in copper plate as to deceive the eye upon a slight glance.

For this he was sent to Newcastle, the place of secondary punishment, where about a year later Captain James Wallis was appointed Commandant. Lycett came into Wallis's employ. He planned a church at Newcastle for him and painted the altar piece. It is highly likely too that Lycett also executed the original drawings from which engravings by another convict named Preston were made at Newcastle, the copper being taken from ships' bottoms. Twelve of these engravings were later published by Ackermann in Wallis's *Historical Account of New South Wales* (1821). The drawings for these engravings have been attributed to Wallis for no better reason than that they appear in a book which he compiled. But there is no evidence that he made any other drawings in his lifetime and no originals, except one to be discussed shortly, are known which relate to Preston's engravings. It seems likely that Wallis employed Lycett to make drawings for him as John White had, a few years earlier, employed Watling. It might well have been one of the reasons why Wallis recommended a conditional pardon for Lycett in 1819, which allowed him to return to Sydney.

Wallis's *Account* was yet another book produced in response to the growing popular interest in the Colony and the cognate interest in exotic scenery. The publishers offered the engravings as evidence of social progress. 'They will serve to show and convince from what slender beginnings, and in how few years, the primeval forest . . . may be converted into plains covered with bleating flocks, lowing herds and waving corn; may become the smiling seats of industry and the social arts, and be changed from a mournful and desolate wilderness, into the cheerful village, the busy town, and the crowded city.'[4] And the publishers again made the claim, that the Colony 'at no very remote period' would 'become the mistress of the Southern hemisphere'.[5] The engravings themselves reveal however that the men involved in their production were as interested in the 'mournful wilderness' as in the 'cheerful village'. Aborigines are introduced as foreground *staffage* but occasionally, as in *Corroboree*, they attain the individuality of portraits. More attention is given to the character of the local vegetation than we find in the work of Eyre and Evans, and there is a special interest in cloud formation. That both Wallis and Lycett were attracted by the primitive character of the Corroboree and sought to appeal to the romantic susceptibilities of the time is indicated by the description which accompanies the illustration of the dance.[6] The subject was one which appealed strongly to romantic taste and colonial artists returned to it time and again throughout the century.[7]

The painting in the Dixson Gallery, Sydney, entitled *Corroboree at Newcastle* (Plate 149) relates closely to the engraved *Corroboree* in Wallis's *Views*, and we may assume that either the engraving was developed from it, or from a lost drawing from which the painting was also developed, and that the artist in all probability was not, as has been traditionally believed, Wallis, but his convict assistant, Lycett. It is perhaps the earliest painting of an Australian subject in which a romantic attitude to nature is clearly and unambiguously expressed. Lycett has made the most of the romantic

possibilities of the subject: the glowing light of the fires is reflected from the painted bodies of the natives and the exotic trees; the moon breaks through a tracery of cloud to illumine the distant bay. Yet romantic interests have not obscured an insistence upon topographical detail. Both the eucalypt at the right and the dying tree at the left are faithfully depicted, as are the dark shapes of the casuarina silhouetted against the moonlit harbour, with the peak of Nobbies in the distance.

In or about 1820 Lycett was employed by Governor Macquarie to paint views of New South Wales and Van Diemen's Land. Three of these were sent by Macquarie to Bathurst and probably helped to gain him his full pardon. He left Sydney on the *Shipley* on 8 September 1822.[8] On arrival in London, Lycett began to prepare his *Views in Australia* for publication, issuing them in thirteen monthly parts from July 1824 onwards. The *Views* were dedicated to Earl Bathurst and the public was asked to 'behold the gloomy grandeur of solitary woods and forests exchanged for the noise and bustle of thronged marts of commerce; while the dens of savage animals, and the hiding places of yet more savage men, have become transformed into peaceful villages or cheerful towns'.[9] It was also claimed that the *Views* would convey 'to Australians of the year 4000 more correct ideas of its aboriginal state than it is in the power of the most eloquent historian to impart'.[10] Unfortunately for this proud claim a comparison of some of Lycett's finished drawings and the engravings which he himself made from them reveals that he was prepared to deviate quite considerably from the 'aboriginal state' of nature he had observed in the Colony, in order to make his engravings conform to English contemporary taste in landscape painting. One of the thirteen original paintings by Lycett, acquired by the Mitchell Library from the Earl of Derby's Library, was painted in 1823, and nine of them resemble engraved plates published in Lycett's *Views*. The one signed original drawing must have been painted in England after Lycett's return; and since all the thirteen paintings are of uniform size and scale upon similar paper, and are all in a similar condition of

149. Joseph Lycett, *Corroboree at Newcastle* (previously attributed to James Wallis, canvas, 28 × 48 in. (*c.* 1817). Dixson Gallery, Sydney. By permission of the State Library of New South Wales

preservation it is probable that all thirteen were painted in England, and are finished drawings made from Australian sketches. Assuming this to be so, it is puzzling to find that the engravings reveal a considerable departure in the character of the vegetation depicted from the relevant original drawings. The alterations have been so comprehensive as to change completely the visual effect of the scenery represented.

If we compare the water-colour painting *Salt Pan Plain, Van Diemen's Land* with the engraving of it (Plates 150, 151), we notice that Lycett, like Watling before him, has altered his engraving in order to bring it into line with the precepts of picturesque composition. The single eucalypt on the extreme left of the painting has been transformed into two trees of indeterminate species in the engraving, while the open tracery of the foliage of the tree against the sky has been transformed into opaque, laterally disposed foliage somewhat similar to an oak, and the leafless branches reduced to a minimum. The heavy foliage thus created is made to throw a shadow across a ridge of rocks bearing Australian plants in the foreground. What appear to be casuarinas have been introduced into various parts of the foreground to give variety of shape and colour to the vegetation. Thus although it has been found necessary to alter the character of the eucalypt, by endowing it with opaque and laterally disposed foliage and using it for the purpose of casting heavy foreground shadows, it is to be observed that a variety of Australian plants have been introduced for the purpose of providing picturesque variety, while retaining the Australian character of the scene.[11] Likewise, typical figures of bushrangers, hunters, swagmen and landowners are often introduced.

One problem, however, remains. An alteration between a sketch made on the spot and a finished drawing may be simply explained as a desire on the part of the artist to compose his landscape according to some precept of pictorial beauty. But the differences we have been examining occur between finished drawings which, on the evidence, Lycett executed in England, and his engraved views. It seems reasonable to suppose that the finished drawings were prepared for engraving and then rejected for another set of drawings.[12] The divergence between the original drawings however and the engravings requires an explanation.

An answer may perhaps be found in the views expressed by Barron Field concerning nature in Australia when he crossed the Blue Mountains in October 1822. Field left the Colony in February 1824 and published his *Geographical Memoirs* in London during the following year. The book included an account of his Blue Mountain crossing, and it is to be noted that the *Historical Account of New South Wales* published with the last set of Lycett's *Views* refers to Field's book in favourable terms. It is possible that either Lycett or his publisher were in touch with Field after his return to England. Field would certainly have been interested in any projected publication relating to the Colony particularly as he was himself preparing a similar book for the press at the time. Furthermore, the fact that Field had approved, edited, and written an introduction for a book by another convict, James Hardy Vaux, in 1819, would make him a likely candidate for either Lycett or Lycett's publisher to approach for support, or for an opinion upon the *Views*, the first of which were published in July 1824. Even if it is impossible to establish beyond doubt any direct connexion between Lycett's alterations and Field's expressed opinions concerning the Australian landscape, the *Views* afford us a valuable visual commentary upon Field's opinions, which we shall now examine.

Field's *Geographical Memoirs* provide us with a more detailed account of those reactions to Australian nature which he had begun to express in his poems. The curious forms and exotic colour of the flowering shrubs appealed to him but he found

150. Joseph Lycett, *View of the Salt Pan Plain, Van Diemen's Land, from the hill above Antills Ponds on the road from Hobart Town to Port Dalrymple*, watercolour, 20 × 14 in. (*c.* 1824). Dixson Library Sydney. By permission of the Trustees of the Public Library of New South Wales

151. Joseph Lycett, *Salt Pan Plain, Van Diemen's Land*, engraving, in *Views in Australia* (1824)

Australian nature in its more general aspects to be most unattractive; in Australia, he said, 'Nature is prosaic, unpicturesque, unmusical'.[13] He enlarged upon this view in *Geographical Memoirs* in a Journal of a tour across the Blue Mountains which he made in 1822. At the end of the first day of the tour he wrote:

> On the banks of the Nepean, I saw almost the only deciduous native tree in the territory, namely, the white cedar (melia azedarach), the common bead-tree of India, beautiful in itself, and congenial to me from that singularity. All the other indigenous trees and shrubs, that I have seen, are evergreens; the eternal eucalyptus with its white bark and scanty tin-like foliage, or the dark casuarina tall, and exocarpus funeral; all as unpicturesque as the shrubs and flowers are beautiful:—the various, justly called proteaceous, banksia, and the hesperidean mimosa, the exquisite epacris, the curious grevillea, xanthorrhoea, the sceptre of Flora, telopea the magnificent, and thysanotus the lovely. New South Wales is a perpetual flower garden, but there is not a single scene in it of which a painter could make a landscape, without greatly disguising the character of the trees. They have no lateral boughs, and cast no masses of shade; but, in return, it is to this circumstance, which causes so little vegetable putrefaction, that the healthiness of the climate is mainly to be attributed.[14]

As we have seen, Lycett did alter the character of the trees in his engravings, providing them with laterally disposed and opaque foliage capable of casting masses of shade. Field proceeds to inquire into the reason for the unpicturesque nature of the Australian forests. He agrees substantially with Watling that the unpicturesqueness is due to a lack of variety in the landscape, and with the reasons given by Robert Brown (whom he quotes) for this lack of variety. But Field also suggests that the unpicturesqueness may simply be due to the fact that most Australian trees are evergreens:

> . . . no tree, to my taste, can be beautiful that is not deciduous. What can a painter do with one cold olive-green? There is a dry harshness about the perennial leaf, that does not savour of humanity in my eyes. There is no flesh and blood in it: it is not of us, and is nothing to us. Dryden says of the laurel,
>
> > From winter winds it suffers no decay;
> > For ever fresh and fair, and every month is May.
>
> Now it may be the fault of the cold climate in which I was bred, but this is just what I complain of in an evergreen. 'For ever fresh', is a contradiction in terms; what is 'forever fair' is never fair; and without January, in my mind, there can be no May. All the dearest allegories of human life are bound up in the infant and slender green of spring, the dark redundance of summer, and the sere and yellow leaf of autumn. These are as essential to the poet as emblems, as they are to the painter as picturesque objects; and the common consent and immemorial custom of European poetry has made the change of the seasons, and its effect upon vegetation, a part, as it were, of our very nature. I can therefore hold no fellowship with Australian foliage, but will cleave to the British oak through all the bareness of winter. It is a dear sight to a European to see his young compatriot trees in an Indian climate, telling of their native country by the fall of their leaf, and, in due time, becoming a spring unto themselves, although no winter has passed over them, just as their fellow-countrymen keep Christmas though in the hottest weather, and, with fresh fruits about them, affect the fare and sometimes the fireside of old England.[15]

240

It would be a mistake to view Field's opinions merely as the prejudices of an homesick English exile. At the time in which he wrote the superiority of the deciduous forests of northern Europe, as material for the imagination of poet and painter, over other forms of landscape was being challenged by the widely read and extremely influential writings of Humboldt. A few years before Humboldt had written, as we have seen, championing the tropical forests and claiming that 'many of the enjoyments which Nature offers are denied to the nations of Europe'. Field was acquainted with the writings of Humboldt, and the views which he expressed are best understood as a criticism of the views being put about by Humboldt and his followers.[16]

Field's poor opinion of Australian scenery asserted itself when he described his crossing of the mountains. Although he commented briefly upon the grandeur of the views he spent no time describing them, and, when we consider the rapid time he made between Springwood and the bottom of Cox's Pass, very little time observing them. When he quotes Wordsworth—'the power of the hills was upon me'—we gain the impression that he is affecting a romantic sentiment he does not feel very strongly. The true sentiments of Field emerge rather in such comments as those he wrote on the evening of 9 October when safely at the bottom of Mount York:

> The ridge of mountains (or rather rocks), along which this passage could alone be effected, is very difficult and desolate. The trees (still eucalyptus) are stunted and burnt. . . . The King's Tableland is as anarchical and untabular as any His Majesty possesses. The Prince Regent's Glen below it (if it be the glen that I saw) is not very romantic. Jamison's Valley we found by no means a happy one. Blackheath is a wretched misnomer. Not to mention its awful contrast to the beautiful place of that name in England, *heath* it is *none*. *Black* it may be when the shrubs are burnt, as they often are. Pitt's Amphitheatre disappointed me. The hills are thrown together in a monotonous manner, and their clothing is very unpicturesque—a mere sea of harsh trees; but Mr. Pitt was no particular connoisseur in mountain scenery or in amphitheatres.[17]

Field, who had been dramatic critic for *The Times*, and a friend of Coleridge and Wordsworth, certainly did consider himself a connoisseur of mountain scenery and found no difficulty in passing judgement upon nature's handiwork when it did not reach picturesque quality—just as one might upon a poorly constructed play.

Field, furthermore, despite his associations with Lamb, Leigh Hunt, and the Lake Poets, preferred the wit and verbal dexterity of the seventeenth century to the emotional freedom of the Romantic Revival. One consequence of this was a preference for the pastoral landscape of the seventeenth century to romantic scenes of wild nature. It is likely that Field's comments upon Blue Mountain scenery are an oblique criticism of the more receptive attitude adopted by Governor Macquarie and his *entourage* when they crossed the mountains in 1815. Field disliked Macquarie, and this may explain the cutting edge of his pen when he comments upon the Governor's naming of Blue Mountain prospects and localities. Yet, at bottom, we have in Field an example of a highly intelligent, coherent, but *retardataire* taste seeking to accommodate itself to the novel problems in the appreciation of landscape and natural history posed by Australian nature.

An indication that Field's comment on the Blue Mountains is not to be dismissed as an exile's prejudice may be once again tested by comparing the remarks of this Englishman in Australia with a description of the mountains which that Australian in England, William Charles Wentworth, wrote into his poem *Australasia* a year after Field passed over them. Despite the fact that in Wentworth's poem the voice of colonial nationalism is heard clearly for the first time his attitude to the Blue Mountains does not differ decisively from Field's:

> How mute, how desolate thy stunted woods,
> How dread thy chasms, where many an eagle broods,
>
> How dark thy caves, how lone thy torrents roar,
> As down thy cliffs precipitous they pour.

The fact of the matter was, of course, that neo-classical taste (and the taste of both Wentworth and Field was essentially neo-classical) never enthused greatly over mountain scenery. And when the mountains in question were as forbidding in shape and vegetation as the Blue Mountains, it was especially difficult to appreciate them according to any received canon of natural beauty. But men like Field and Wentworth were able to react with genuine enthusiasm to the gentle curves and blue distances of the savannah lands beyond the mountains, for they brought to mind pastoral imagery deeply woven into the texture of European poetry and painting—and they represented potential pastoral wealth.

Until 1820 reflection upon nature in Australia had been very largely based upon the experiences of the colonists settled around Sydney Harbour and the Cumberland Plain, these reflections not being modified to any great extent by the reports of navigators and descriptions of Van Diemen's Land. The result of these reflections, as we have seen, was to establish two prevailing attitudes to Australian nature, attitudes that are at times closely blended: firstly, the belief that the natural productions of Australia were novel creations and that the characteristic features of Australian nature were contrariety and eccentricity; and secondly, the belief that Australian scenery was visually monotonous and induced feelings of melancholy. Now these two views were based initially upon a limited knowledge of the Australian continent. After 1820 new types of landscape came increasingly within the experience of the colonists, explorers, and travellers. The new frontiers helped at times to reinforce the traditional views, at times to modify them.

The most striking contrast afforded by the new country opened up for settlement was that between the brushlands of the Cumberland Plain and the barren ridges of the Blue Mountains, on the one hand, and the grassy, almost treeless plains of the Bathurst district, on the other. So different were the two types of landscape that Barron Field who had expressed his dislike of Australian scenery while riding to the Nepean and crossing the mountains, found himself enjoying the landscape of the Bathurst Plains immensely a few days later. The change came at the end of the tiresome mountain journey, and his enthusiasm may be taken as evidence of his neo-classical predispositions:

> Mount York . . . redeems the journey across the Blue Mountains, for it leads you to the first green valley. The earliest burst of Christian trans-alpine country, as seen from the beginning of this mountain, is very beautiful. The sight of grass again is lovely. The view from the commencement of Cox's Pass down to it, is finer still. This *Big Hill* as it is alone called, should have been named Mount Pisgah, for it affords the first view of the promised land of Australia. . . . After three days' starving . . . your cattle now get plenty of green grass. Encamp then at the first bite; for there is water enough, and the station under Mount York is very picturesque into the bargain, *que ne gâte rien*.[18]

So Field found the picturesque at the foot of the mountains whereas Macquarie and

242

23. Nicholas-Martin Petit, *A Group of Tasmanian Aborigines*, watercolour, $9\frac{1}{2} \times 12\frac{5}{8}$ in. (1802). Muséum d' Histoire Naturelle, Le Havre, 20024-2

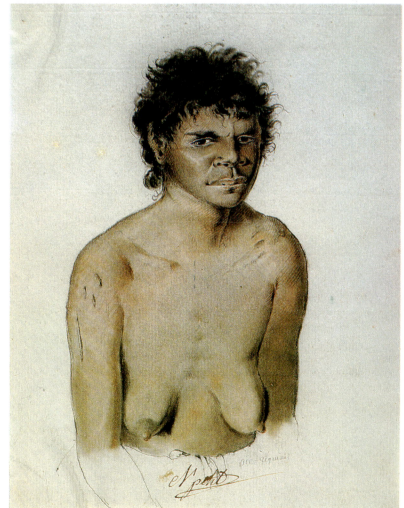

24. Nicholas-Martin Petit, *A Young Australian Aboriginal Woman*, inscribed 'Oïe-réquiné', pastel, $18\frac{1}{2} \times 12\frac{1}{4}$ in. (1801–3). Muséum d' Histoire Naturelle, Le Havre, 20035

26. Augustus Earle, *Solitude—Watching the horizon at Sun Set, in the hopes of seeing a vessel—Tristan De Acunha, in the South Atlantic* (detail), watercolour, 6¾ × 10 in. (1824). Nan Kivell Collection 12.3. National Library of Australia, Canberra

25 (preceeding pages). John Glover, *My Harvest Home*. canvas, 30 × 46½ in. (1840). Tasmanian Museum and Art Gallery, Hobart. By permission of the Trustees

his party had found it amongst them; a situation quite in keeping with the changing taste of the time, with Field's conservative taste, and with the increasing imprecision of the word itself. It was not, however, picturesque beauty which appealed to Field most but the quiet dignity of the pastoral, with its homely and classical associations, which he found as he moved westwards. The fact might have given him pause for a further reflection upon antipodal contrariety. On 12 October he travelled from O'Connell Plains, on the Fish River, to Bathurst. He had been delayed by rain in the morning but the evening—and he preferred evening as he tells us to 'the wild freshness of morning' (a choice essentially Augustan)—proved beautiful. He found himself for the first time since his arrival in the Colony travelling in a land his heart could warm to:

> I could hardly believe I was travelling in New Holland this day; so different—so English—is the character of the scenery—downs, meadows, and streams in the flat—no side scenes of eucalyptus.... The scarcity of wood now takes away the American log-appearance of the cottages; they build of turf here, and roof with straw or reeds, instead of wooden shingles. You may see as far as the eye can reach. Stockmen, cattle and sheep occasionally form your horizon, as in Old Holland—A Paul Potter or Cuyp effect rare in New Holland. At sunset we saw wooded hills, distant enough to display that golden blue or purple which landscape painters love. The smoke of the little village of Bathurst is seen for miles off, which that of no other town in Australia is. These things may seem trifling to an English reader; but by an American or Australian, accustomed to travel through the eternal shadow of monotonous woods, the charm of emerging into anything like European scenery will be duly appreciated.[19]

But it was not only the pastoral character of the country which appealed to Field, he also appreciated its potential productiveness. 'This', he wrote a few days later, 'is truly a land flowing with milk and honey.'[20] And Wentworth, writing a year later in Cambridge, also remembered the view from Mount York as a glimpse into a promised land:

> And, as a meteor shook athwart the night,
> The boundless champaigne burst upon our sight,
> Till nearer seen the beauteous landscape grew,
> Op'ning like Canaan on rapt Israel's view.

Biblical references were frequent, for as Field put it, the wilderness had given way to a Christian country. 'I congratualte you,' the Rev. Samuel Marsden had said to Thomas Hawkins and his family when he met them at the foot of Mount York on their way to Bathurst, 'you are all going to the land of Goshen.'[21] And two years later the Bathurst Plains presented a spectacle to another traveller which reminded him of the idealized pastoral landscapes of Claude Lorraine:

> The river Macquarie ran close to us, at the bottom of these little farms, broad, clear and rapid, and excited the most lively sensations, like the Niger of Africa, by reason of its unknown course. The fatigues of the journey were now over, and we were really in a christian country—the climate mild and delightful—the prospect cheerful and extensive—the sheep returning to the fold seemed healthy and happy, and awakened thoughts of abundance—of content—of thankfulness. The gorgeous sun was setting in a robe of gold, over that undiscovered country west of the Macquarie, and the scene was altogether worthy of a Claude.[22]

Something of the impact which this new country made upon early travellers is preserved for us in such a painting as John William Lewin's *Two Kangaroos in a Landscape* ((Plate 152). Painted in 1819 in the year of the artist's death it does convey some impression of the rich luxuriance of the grass, the open park-like character of the land with its dispersed clumps of trees and the distant blue hills which so delighted Field and reminded him of home. After the Western District and the country to the south-west of the Cow pastures (later known as the county of Argyle) had been opened up, writers and artists began once again to compare Australian scenery to an English park, as they had done during the first days of settlement. In his *Two Years in New South Wales* (1828) Peter Cunningham discusses the advantages accruing to a settler upon such land where so little clearing needs to be done. 'In several places such as the Goulburn plains, there is a goodly proportion of land without a single tree, while in other parts, such as Eden Forest, these are so sparingly scattered as to resemble more a nobleman's park, than a natural forest, all self-sown.[23] And on another occasion he describes the country between Wilson's Promontory and Western Port as resembling 'the park of a country seat in England, the trees standing in picturesque groups to ornament the landscape'.[24]

A good deal of game was to be had in these open forest lands. From Blaxland's *Journal* (1813) onwards,[25] explorers, travellers, and settlers continually provided accounts of hunting kangaroos and emus. 'It is really delightful to ride through these open spots, where there is scarcely a tree you would wish to see cut down, so much do they beautify the prospect;—while, if a kangaroo or an emu should start up in your path, you enjoy a clear and animated view of the chase, until the dogs finally surround and seize upon their victim'[26] (Plate 153). After 1820 emu and kangaroo hunts begin to appear increasingly as a pictorial embellishment in illustrations of Australian landscape: the hunter and his dogs begin to replace the aboriginal group as an

152. John William Lewin, *Two Kangaroos in a Landscape*, watercolour, 15 × 21¾ in. (1819). Nan Kivell Collection 139a, National Library of Australia, Canberra

153. *Kangaroo Hunt*, un-identified artist, water-colour, $10\frac{1}{2} \times 15\frac{1}{2}$ in. Nan Kivell Collection 557, National Library of Australia

emblematic foreground group. The change may be witnessed in Lycett's *Views* where in cases such as his *Distant View of Sydney*[27] we have the native group, the old symbol of the primitive life of Australia, and in others, such as his view of *Liverpool*, the European hunter, the new symbol of the adventurous life of the pioneer.

The hunter as an emblem of Australian colonial life is closely associated with the bivouac or encampment scene. Prior to the rapid expansion to the north, west, and south of the county of Cumberland, which began to take place in the 1820's, travellers did not have occasion to sleep out in the open to any great extent. But with the rapid spread of settlement after 1820, bivouacking, as it was first called, became a normal and significant aspect of colonial life. It was for many, after a long day in the saddle, or driving a bullock dray over primitive roads, the one period in the day when the traveller had a moment to enter a note in his journal, talk, or perhaps sing a song with his companions, consider what lay ahead and reflect—if he was given to reflection— upon the nature of things, particularly things Australian. The camp fire began to play an important part in the growth of new attitudes and new sentiments in the Australian colonies. We can assess its growing significance by comparing the descrip- tions and reflections of three travellers across the Blue Mountains. The first is by Major Henry Antill upon the occasion of the first encampment of the Macquarie Progress at Springwood on the evening of the 26 April 1815:

... this being our first encampment, it may not be amiss to describe our situation. We were encamped in an extensive forest of large lofty trees mostly of stringy and iron bark. Our party was formed into different groups, each having a large fire of its own, without which, from the coldness of the nights at this season of the year, it would be impossible to sleep in comfort. These different fires had, from the background where I was, a very beautiful effect, and enabled me to observe the

249

scene before me. Some were busily employed cooking; others were smoaking; making their huts, or cutting down timber for fuel, and reminded me by their very occupations of what I had read of a camp of gypsies or the *bivouacs* of a Continental army. I remained here a short time, and then retired to rest for the night in my hammock, swung between two poles, and covered with a tarpaulin, by the side of a comfortable fire large enough to roast an ox.[28]

The second description is by Barron Field upon the occasion of his second encampment in the Blue Mountains (a little beyond the present town of Katoomba) on the evening of 8 October 1822:

I could not sleep for thinking of our situation, and walked forth from my tent. The air was refreshing. All were asleep from fatigue, with large fires of piled wood at their feet, the gleams on which (for they had been suffered to go down) gave a picturesque effect to the tent and cart, and to the tethered horses, which were patiently standing on the bleak and bare hill. A little more than thirty years ago, this land was inhabited by savages only, and these hills had, from the beginning of time, formed an impassable barrier between their tribes. The spirit of British government had now come from the antipodes, and, with nothing but a colony of convicts, had, in that short time, penetrated upwards of a hundred miles into the interior of the country, and established a township there, to which the unarmed might travel as safely as from London to Bristol. The very sleeping grooms beneath me had been thieves and robbers, and the blasted heath looked like New Hounslow; but our persons and property were inviolate.[29]

The third description is by Mrs. Elizabeth Hawkins upon the occasion of the first encampment of her family in the Blue Mountains on the evening of 12 April 1822:

It was a lovely moonlight night, and all was novelty and delight to the elder children. Immense fires were made in all directions. We gave them their supper, and after putting the younger ones to bed, I came from the tent, in front of which was a large fire, our drays and carts close in view. The men—nine in number—were busily employed in cooking in one place, our own men roasting a couple of fowls for our next day's journey; at another the men (convicts), not the most prepossessing in their appearance, with the glare of the fires and the reflection of the moon shining upon them, in the midst of a forest, formed altogether such a scene as I cannot describe. It resembled more a party of banditti, such as I have read of, than anything else. I turned from the view, took the arm of Hawkins, who was seated at the table with the storekeeper, and went to the back of the tent. Here we saw Tom and the three eldest girls trying who could make the best fire, as happy as it was possible for young hearts to be. Then I seemed to pause. It was a moment I shall never forget. For the first time for many a long month I seemed capable of enjoying and feeling the present moment without a dread of the future. 'Tis true we had in a manner bade adieu to the world, to our country and our friends, but in our country we could no longer provide for our children, and the world from that cause had lost all its charm. You, Bowling, and all my friends and acquaintances, I thought of with regret, but the dawn of independence was opening upon us. Hawkins was again an officer under Government, a home to receive us, and the certainty under any circumstances of never wanting the common necessities of life. You, my dear Ann, must have suffered in mind what we long had suffered, to form an idea of what we then felt. After a little while we returned to the table. These were moments of such inward rest that Hawkins took up a flute belonging to one of the party, and calling Eliza to us, she danced in a place where perhaps no one of her age had ever trod before.[30]

Antill was mainly concerned with the novel pictorial features of the scene and the sensation of physical well-being he clearly derived from the occasion; for Field also the scene was picturesque and memorable, and symbolized the progress of civilized society and the spread of British law into a howling wilderness; but for Mrs. Hawkins the bivouac situation provided an occasion for a moment of decision when old loyalties were painfully relinquished and new ones fashioned. For her, as for so many who came after her, the evening encampment witnessed the gradual transformation of the exile into the pioneer.

Artists, likewise, began to react to the significance of the bivouac situation as soon as settlement began to spread widely over the country. The first water-colour which John William Lewin painted upon the Macquarie Progress was one which illustrated Antill's description of the encampment at Springwood (Plate 168). He depicts a portion of the party settling down for the night. The raking light of the late afternoon sun penetrates the tall forest timber suffusing the scene with rosy tones, and camp fires are being lit. This is most probably the earliest illustration of those bivouacking, camp-fire, boiling-the-billy scenes that were to achieve an almost iconographic significance in the later years of the century as they came to symbolize the free and adventurous life of the Colonies and to play a part, eventually, in the *mystique* of colonial nationalism.

The changing content of Australian colonial art, in consequence of the rapid extension of the rural frontier after 1821, may be best observed in the work of the two most important artists working in Australia during the period under consideration, Augustus Earle and John Glover.

Earle was born in 1793 and was the son of James Earle (1761–96),[31] an American artist who had gone to England as a young man, probably with his brother Ralph (1751–1801) where, after a period of study, he had gained some attention as a portrait-painter, and had exhibited at the Academy for nine years. Augustus studied at the Academy where two of his fellow-students, the Americans C. R. Leslie and S. F. B. Morse, became his intimate friends.[32] In 1813 Morse and Earle made a sketching trip together. 'With their sketch books and drawing apparatus, they visited the sea-shore and towns adjacent making pedestrian excursions into the country in search of scenery.'[33] In 1815 Earle obtained a passage on a store ship bound for Sicily and Malta,[34] possibly through the influence of his half-brother, Captain W. H. Smyth, who commanded a gun-boat in Lord Exmouth's squadron. It was in this gun-boat that Earle visited many parts of the Mediterranean, including Malta, the ruins of Carthage and Ptolemaia, Sicily (where he ascended Etna), and Gibraltar (where he drew caves and Moorish ruins). In 1817 he returned to England.

In March 1818 Earle left for America where he resided with a Mr. Cummings in New York, practised his profession and encouraged the youthful attempts at drawing of Thomas S. Cummings, later well known as a miniature-painter.[35] In July 1818, however, Earle was residing in Philadelphia and exhibited two pictures at the Pennsylvania Academy of Fine Arts.[36] On 11 February 1820 he embarked on the *Warrior* and reached Rio de Janeiro on 2 April. In June he visited Chile, and by 18 July had reached Lima, where he remained practising as a painter until 10 December 1820, when he left Callao on the *Hyperion* bound for England.[37] While on board he made several water-colour paintings illustrative of naval life. His *Divine Service on Board a British Frigate H.M.S. Hyperion*, in the Nan Kivell Collection, probably formed

154. Augustus Earle, *A North-Easter, Tristan D'Acunha*, watercolour, 7½ × 13 in. (1824). Nan Kivell Collection 12.13, National Library of Australia

the basis for his *Divine Service, as it is usually Performed on Board a British Frigate at Sea*, which Earle exhibited at the Royal Academy seventeen years later.[38] Earle did not return to England, transhipping from the *Hyperion* to the *Arna* bound for Rio, where he continued to work for several years. He seems to have travelled about the country considerably. He was in Pernambuco in 1821 at a time when the country was disturbed by the conflict between the patriots and the Portuguese. His *Gate of Pernambuco in Brazil* was painted in Brazil and sent to London where it was exhibited in the Academy of 1824.[39] Early in that year Earle received letters of introduction to Lord Amherst, recently appointed Governor-General of India, and decided to leave Rio. On 17 February 1824 he embarked on the *Duke of Gloucester*, an overladen and wornout Margate hoy bound for Cape Town. The vessel encountered very bad weather and was driven to the island of Tristan da Cunha on 6 March, but was unable to anchor until 21 March. On the 29th the *Duke of Gloucester* left the island suddenly, having obtained a consignment of potatoes, leaving Earle ashore. Here he was forced to remain for several months.[40]

In his account of his residence on Tristan da Cunha Earle reveals that he visited the island for the purpose of adding valuable drawings to his sketch-book. On 20 March 1824 he wrote:

> I determined to return in the boat with the man when they left our vessel [i.e. the *Duke of Gloucester*]. I did so, and took with me my dog, gun, boat cloak, and sketch book, hoping to be able to add a few interesting drawings to my portfolio, as this was a spot hitherto unvisited by any artist.[41]

To visit spots unvisited by artists was the purpose of Earle's extensive travels. During a period of approximately twenty years he wandered about the world perhaps more extensively than any artist before him, and succeeded in making a reasonable living partly because, being fully trained at the Academy, he could turn his hand to portraiture, landscape, and subject painting at will, and partly because he was a person of considerable ingenuity and resource.

252

Earle's sojourn on Tristan da Cunha provided him with an excellent opportunity of making sketches of the wilder aspects of nature which he also described in his account of his residence on that island.[42] He made drawings of the heavy seas, rocky coastline (Plate 154), and the mountains of the interior, and also painted many genre studies such as the killing of albatross in the mountains, catching and flinching sea-elephants and rafting their blubber on to boats off-shore. In one, Earle depicted himself with his dog watching for a ship to take him off the island. (Colour Plate 26). Such paintings were full of the spirit of adventure and it is not surprising that when Earle came to exhibit some of them in Sydney a year later a correspondent of the *Sydney Gazette* should write: 'Mr. Earle's representations ... of romantic scenery in Tristan da Cunha ... were much admired here, as they partook of the manner of Wilkie, and had something congenial to colonial taste in their character and execution.'[43]

On 29 November 1824 Earle was taken off the island by the *Admiral Cockburn* bound for Tasmania, and arrived in Hobart on 18 January 1825. There are few paintings by Earle of Tasmanian subjects and he does not appear to have remained there for any length of time. He was there long enough, however, to note the park-like quality of the scenery, for to his *June Park, Van Diemen's Land*[44] he adds the note: 'the grand appearance of the Country in its natural state. Perfect Park Scenery.'

By 31 October 1825 Earle was in Sydney for on that date he was engaged to decorate the dining-room for the farewell banquet to Governor Brisbane.[45] The transparency was still in vogue and Earle's choice of a suitable subject for the occasion

155. Augustus Earle, *Captain John Piper*, canvas, $17\frac{1}{2} \times 12\frac{1}{8}$ in. (*c.* 1825–6). Australian National Gallery, Canberra

156. Augustus Earle, *Mrs. John Piper*, oil on cardboard on wood panel, $18 \times 12\frac{1}{4}$ in. (*c.* 1825–6). Australian National Gallery, Canberra

253

reveals an ironic sense of humour. It is described by the correspondent of the *Sydney Gazette* mentioned above:

> When Sir Thomas dined with the Emancipists, Mr. Earle painted for them a transparency, representing Diogenes with a lanthorn in his hand, searching through 'this varsal worlde' for an honest man and at length finding one in the person of Sir Thomas. The representation was too childish to have been the offspring of Mr. Earle's refined taste, though it may of his sportive fancy. But even the execution of it was not worthy of him in consequence, perhaps, of the hurried manner in which it was got up. It bore no resemblance to a great philosopher and honest man. Sir Thomas's infant daughter screamed with horror when told that the 'honest man' was her father. It seemed rather a caricature representation of an honest guardian of the hours, in the height of his zeal to preserve the peace, clapping his lanthorn to the face of a drunken pickpocket.[46]

Despite this apparently unsuccessful piece of work Earle became well known as a portrait-painter in Sydney. He is recorded as having painted a large and a small portrait of Governor Brisbane; a portrait of Sir Ralph Darling, Brisbane's successor; and portraits of John Mackaness, the Sheriff; Dr. Robert Townson, a naturalist; Coulson, the Paymaster of the 3rd Regiment; James Dunlop, associate-astronomer to Brisbane, and a half-length portrait of Mrs. Blaxland. His full-length portraits of Captain John Piper and of his wife Mary Ann Piper, and also the separate studies of their heads (Plates 155, 156), which appear to have been separate commissions, are excellent examples of his work. He also executed a small portrait of Darling which was engraved as a frontispiece to Howe's Almanac for 1827.[47]

A pupil and an exhibitioner at the Royal Academy, Earle mingled among the best Sydney colonial society with ease and travelled about the Colony on his painting excursions like a gentleman. His self-portrait 'presents the spectator with a full view of the fire of genius that animates the countenance of the original', wrote the *Gazette* correspondent. In July 1826 he advertised the opening of his art gallery in which he exhibited his paintings.[48] The gallery was 'much visited by the youth of the Colony, and must have a considerable influence in promoting good taste among the rising generation'.[49] In the month following he announced his intention of opening a school of painting at his rooms at 10 George Street where artist's materials were also available for sale.[50] In August also Earle obtained a lithographic press locally and began publishing a set of Australian views, and on 23rd, the following observation appeared in the *Gazette*.

> The lithographic press is constantly employed by that indefatigable artist, Mr. Earle. Several prints have emanated from the press, and it is thought that the *Australian* and *Monitor* will institute proceedings at law against Mr. Earle for having the temerity to knock off circulars. As for ourselves, we are regardless of this infringement upon the profession of typography, so long as the artist encrouches not upon the newspaper line.

Earle travelled a good deal about the Colony, his 'extensive peregrinations' included a journey across the Blue Mountains to Bathurst and the Wellington Valley, a journey in 1826 to the Hunter River, Port Stephens, and Port Macquarie, and a journey the following year to the Illawarra District. By keeping to his plan of visiting places never before visited by artists Earle travelled more extensively in New South Wales than any previous artist and, in consequence, the paintings which he made from his sketches cover a correspondingly greater variety of scenery. In his *Waterfall in*

254

157. Augustus Earle,
Waterfall in Australia, canvas,
28 × 33 in. (*c.* 1826). Nan
Kivell Collection 9,
National Library of
Australia, Canberra

Australia (Plate 157) he depicts himself preparing to draw one of his aboriginal guides
who is posed picturesquely before a waterfall in the Blue Mountains. To the right, four
other members of his party cling to precarious footholds as they seek to examine the
yawning gulf below. Earle's interest in the structure of rock is manifest here as it is in
his Tristan da Cunha paintings. And when he arrived at Wellington Valley he made
several sketches showing himself and his party examining Mossman's Cave by the
light of torches (Plate 158).

   Earle was the first artist of any consequence to visit the Illawarra District. After
1819 cattle grazing and cedar-getting developed, at first slowly, in the region, but it
began to receive increasing attention from travellers during the 1820's who wrote
most favourably of its sub-tropical scenery and luxuriant vegetation. Barron Field,
Peter Cunningham, and Alexander Harris[51] all wrote glowing descriptions of the
district. The scenery was utterly different from the monotony of the Cumberland
Plain and the pastoral park-lands beyond the Blue Mountains. It was not Paul Potter,
but Humboldt, who sprang to mind as Field rode through the district in the spring of
1823, exactly a year after he had crossed the Blue Mountains:

   The vines or lianas wreathed the trees, like the boa constrictor, and festooned the
   way, as if they were placed for one of Astley's[52] equestrians to leap from the horse

255

over them, or hung dangling like the ropes in a belfry. The valley reminded me of Humboldt's descriptions of South American vegetation.[53]

Peter Cunningham, travelling through the Illawarra a few years later, expressed a similar opinion:

> The tall fern, cedar, and cabbage trees; the numerous creeping vines, climbing up and throwing their fragrant tassels of flowers downwards from the tops of the less lofty trees; the luxuriant growth of every vegetable product; with the red-crested black cockatoos, and large crested blue pigeons peculiar to this district, make you fancy yourself transported to some far-distant tropical region.[54]

Earle visited the Illawarra in May 1827. The Nan Kivell Collection contains four of his water-colours of the thick brush country described by Field (Plate 159). These water-colours, or the drawings upon which they were based, provided Earle with material for a bivouac scene which he exhibited in the Academy of 1838, entitled *A Bivouac of Travellers in Australia, in a Cabbage-tree Forest, Day Break* (Plate 160). In this painting, the last Earle exhibited at the Academy, several strands of colonial iconography are interwoven: imagery associated with hunting is joined with images of noble savages and noble frontiersmen[55] all set in a landscape of precisely painted exotic vegetation that would have pleased the readers of Humboldt. The Illawarra also afforded Earle with an opportunity to paint further pictures of grottoes and other geological curiosities (Plate 161).

256

160. Augustus Earle, *A Bivouac of Travellers in Australia in a Cabbage Tree Forest, Day Break*, canvas, 46½ × 32¾ in. (*c.* 1838). Nan Kivell Collection 14, Commonwealth National Library, Canberra

Earle's water-colour technique consisted in laying-in his drawing with a fine brush, establishing his tones with washes of brown or lamp-black for foregrounds, greys for mid-distances, and mauves and blues for backgrounds. Over these he painted transparent washes of local colour in which brown, purple, rose, and green predominate, with yellow lights and occasional splashes of crimson at points of interest to bring the composition together. Earle's compositions, at their best, are broad and firmly constructed, with sharp tonal contrasts making effective patterns as in *A North-Easter, Tristan D'Acunha* (Plate 154). This painting also reveals his interest in the depiction of weather that is to be observed in so many of his paintings. In *Squall off Tristan D' Acunha* (Plate 162) Earle produced a piece of documentary naturalism comparable with but vastly different from the cloud studies of Dahl and Constable painted almost three years before.[56] He was also responsive to more subtle effects of atmospheric change. His *Port Jackson*[57] is, perhaps, the earliest attempt to portray the suffused rose and mauve tones of an afterglow over Sydney Harbour during a summer or early autumn evening—an effect greatly favoured by the Australian plein air and impressionist painters of the last two decades of the century.

Earle was assisted in his travels by the current interest in panoramas. In February 1827 he painted eight views from the top of Palmer's hill, Sydney, which he sent to Burford[58] who used them for painting his panorama of Sydney. Burford had the assistance of Lieutenant-Colonel Dumeresq in producing the panorama and naming the buildings. It was exhibited in London in 1828, and, according to the *Gazette* correspondent quoted above, was 'operating in the principal towns in Britain' in 1829.[59] Earle also painted scenes which were later made into a panorama of Hobart, and another was made by Daniell and Parris from drawings Earle made in Madras.

On 20 October 1827, Earle left Sydney in the *Governor Macquarie* for New Zealand, returning to Sydney in the *Snapper* on 5 May 1828. Five months later he left in the *Rainbow*, visiting the Caroline Islands, Guam, Manila, Singapore, and Madras. Just as he was establishing his reputation as an artist in Madras his health suddenly declined. He travelled to Pondicherry and took a passage on board the *Julie* which was condemned at Mauritius. Here he executed a series of panoramic views of the island, returning to England by the free-trader *Resource*, after an absence of over thirteen years.[60]

On 4 September 1830, almost two years after Earle had left Sydney, John Glover (1767–1849), at the end of a long and successful career as an artist, left Gravesend with his family in the *Thomas Lowry* to settle in Tasmania.[51] He was, at the time, sixty-three years of age and approaching the end of a career as a landscape-painter and teacher of art which, according to one account, had been so successful as to enable him to bring out £60,000 to the Colony. The account may be exaggerated but Glover certainly possessed considerable means when he arrived.

The exact reasons for Glover's migration have not been ascertained. Bred in the country, where as a child he had worked in the fields and had begun his career like Lewin drawing birds, it is likely that he felt the appeal of retiring to a farming life in a colony which might provide excellent prospects for his family.[62] Sales of his work had fallen off as a result of the slump following the end of the Napoleonic Wars, and it is likely that the economic crisis of 1825 had had a similar effect. At the time, Van Diemen's Land was receiving considerable publicity as a desirable home for migrants with capital intending to set up as free farmers. In 1825 the Van Diemen's Land Company received a charter, and the under-secretaries were receiving so many individual inquiries concerning Tasmanian land grants that a circular was made available at the Colonial Office.[63]

161. Augustus Earle, *A View of the Coast of New South Wales, Illawarra*, watercolour, 8 × 10½ in. (1827). Nan Kivell Collection 12.46, National Library of Australia, Canberra

162. Augustus Earle, *A Squall off Tristan D'Acunha*, watercolour, 6½ × 10 in. (1824). Nan Kivell Collection 12.4, National Library of Australia, Canberra

Glover desired both to set himself up with his family as a farmer and grazier and at the same time to continue his painting. James Backhouse, who visited Glover in 1833, informs us that he 'came to this country when advanced in life, to depict the novel scenery'.[64] And Louis Philippe, when Duc d'Orleans, is reported to have commissioned him to paint pictures of Tasmania, 'wishing to become familiar with its peculiar features' when he was told, during Glover's second visit to France, that the artist was proceeding thither.[65]

The *Thomas Lowry* arrived at Launceston on 18 February 1831 and Glover decided to cross overland from Launceston to Hobart in order to sketch and study the nature of the country.[66] By August 1831 he had purchased an old location, Ring Farm, at the Tea-Tree Brush, eighteen miles from Hobart, and sent his free man, Thomas Eley, there as a resident 'to superintend such assigned servants as might be sent there'.[67] At the same time Glover kept up a house in the town, and began immediately to paint landscapes of the local scenery. In his *Diary* G. T. W. B. Boyes, the Colonial Auditor, tells us of a visit he made to Glover on 9 September 1831:

> Walked with Hill up to Glovers. Saw his picture of Mount Wellington. Sun rising and Moon setting in its finished State. I like the twilight part of it very well—the depth of the Valley where the night damps are still lying while upon the ground the Vapour is escaping along the top of the mountains in the form of clouds before the approach of morning—with a very gaudy effect of Sunshine—where the Trees in the foreground are designed with hideous fidelity to Nature.

Glover, had he access to Boyes's *Diary*, might have been surprised to find criticism pursued so keenly in the small society of Van Diemen's Land. But Boyes, like Barron Field, was nothing if not a gentleman of taste, with a sharp and subtle pen for the weaknesses of his fellows, a man for whom the criticism of art and letters was a matter of some importance. His extensive reading list during a short return visit to England in 1832 included Payne Knight's *Analytical Enquiry into the Principles of Taste*; and like Barron Field he found the faithful imitation of Australian trees an offence to good taste. Glover himself was of a different opinion. He must have worked hard during his first few months in Hobart. Boyes records how he 'met Glover on the road buried in a painting'.[68] When the Colonial Solicitor, Alfred Stephen, left on the *Eliza* early in 1832 for England on two years leave of absence, he took with him in frames made of colonial woods two large views Glover had painted; one of them 'near Hobart Town looking up the country'.[69] These paintings Glover's son tells us 'were exhibited and admired at the Suffolk Street Exhibition'.[70] Glover had been a foundation member of the Society of British Artists when it was established in 1823 and had contributed regularly to the annual exhibitions until he migrated, and remained a member of the Society until his death. The sudden arrival of a famous artist into the small official circle of Hobart doubtless made some impression. He was immediately accepted. Boyes recorded on 5 April 1832 how he noticed Glover and his daughter at the Governor's levee upon the occasion of the Queen's birthday. Indeed it is possible that it was the influence of the Glover family which initiated the interest in landscape-painting in water-colours so fashionable in official circles in Tasmania during the 1830's and 1840's. Although Boyes made many sketches while serving in the administrative branch of the army during the Peninsular War[71] his diary does not reveal any indication that he began sketching in Tasmania until the arrival of the Glovers. From then on Boyes's references to his own sketching is frequent and continuous until his death in 1853. Furthermore, young John Glover described to his brother-in-law, how, on the voyage out he had found 'card playing every evening ... not my forte', and therefore kept to his sketch-book 'as long as I could find subjects to work from;

163. John Glover,
Tasmanian Landscape, pencil,
pen and wash, 7 × 10½ in.,
Glover sketch-book no. 102,
begun 19 December 1834.
Nan Kivell Collection 644,
National Library of
Australia, Canberra

164. John Glover, *Drawing*,
wash, 7 × 10½ in., Glover
sketch-book, no. 102, f. 112.
Nan Kivell Collection 644,
National Library of
Australia, Canberra

165. John glover, *Drawing*,
wash, 7 × 11½ in., glover
sketch-book, no. 102, f. 102.
Nan Kivell Collection 644,
National Library of
Australia, Canberra

and towards the end was establishing a little community of amateur artists, both ladies and gentlemen'.[72]

In 1832 Glover obtained an extensive grant of land at Mill's Plains on the northern slopes of Ben Lomond in the north-eastern part of the island. Here he built a large two-storied stone house near the rivulet Nile, a tributary of the South Esk, calling his property Patterdale, after Patterdale, in Cumberland, where he formerly lived. Once settled he continued to paint prolifically as he had done throughout life. In less than three years he was able to prepare sixty-eight paintings for exhibition and consign them to London. They were exhibited in Bond Street in 1835, the exhibition catalogue stating that they were 'descriptive of the Scenery and Customs of Van Diemen's Land'.[73]

In order to carry out his intentions as described in the catalogue Glover appears to have divested himself of certain stylistic mannerisms he had acquired during his career as an artist in England. His English landscapes tend to be eclectic, featuring the mannerisms of Claude, Rosa, and the Dutch; in Australia he became increasingly concerned with topographical clarity of vision. Glover was quite conscious of the novelty of the scenery and there is evidence that he felt a need to modify his style to cope with it, and to fulfil the programme he had set himself. The exotic birds of Australia still held a special interest for Europeans, and in painting the Blue Mountain parrot (*Trichoglossus moluccanus*), the cuckoo of Van Diemen's Land (probably *Cacomantis flabelliformis*), the Van Diemen's Land night jarr (*Aeogotheles cristata*), and the small owl of Van Diemen's Land (probably *Tyto castanops*) for his exhibition Glover returned to one of his earliest interests. According to a family tradition: 'He had an extraordinary influence over birds, and some of those which he tamed and allowed to fly away would come back from the woods at his call'.[74]

In returning to bird painting, Glover was doubtless also acknowledging the continued interest overseas in Australia's natural productions; and it was this interest also which most probably induced him to take special care in rendering the characteristic vegetation of Tasmania. One of his paintings in his 1835 exhibition, for instance, took as its subject the fern trees on the side of Mount Wellington (Cat. no. 4); to another, *The River Tamar, near George Town, Van Diemen's Land* (Cat. no. 19—quite possibly drawn from a sketch made on the day he set foot in Tasmania, judging by the subject) he adds the note: 'the high trees are Gums; the round and full, the She-oak; the small, the Whattle'. And to a view of his own homestead at Mill's Plains (Cat. no. 27) he notes: 'the taller trees are Gums, the lesser Whattle'. But Glover, apart from seeking to differentiate types of trees, sought also, as Lewin had done before him, to capture the visual character of the vegetation. And to quite a remarkable extent he succeeded.

By examining his sketch-books in the Nan Kivell Collection we may gain some idea of how Glover gradually overcame the difficulties associated with drawing the eucalypt. Although it is not possible to date the drawings accurately, a stylistic change is to be observed which moves from a mannered treatment of the tree, in which tapering branches twist in serpentine curves (differing little from trees in his Lake District drawings) (Plate 163), to a treatment in which the characteristic features of the tree is preserved (Plate 164). Like Lewin he perceived the open disposition of the foliage of the tree; and in his drawings, and most of his paintings, the trees of the mid-distance and background, and the horizon line itself, are not obscured by foreground trees (Plate 165). In this his Australian work differs from his English landscapes. That he was fully aware of the fundamental difference between European and Australian landscape is revealed by a note in the catalogue of his 1835 exhibition to his painting *Launceston and the River Tamar* (Cat. no. 36): 'There is a remarkable peculiarity in the

Trees in this Country; however numerous they rarely prevent you tracing through them the whole distant country.'

Glover sought also to give a faithful representation of life in the island, and certainly had the prospective migrant in mind. 'From the well-known character of the Artist's works for their fidelity and truth', the catalogue stated, 'it is presumed the pictures will become generally interesting.' Toward that end he painted a view of Hobart from his town house (Cat. no. 21) (Colour Plate 27), adding the note: 'the Geraniums, Roses, etc., will give some idea to what perfection Gardens may be brought in the country'. The picture is executed with an insistence upon detail and a bright prettiness of colour that affords a striking contrast to the generalized effects of light which characterize his English landscapes. Glover also painted *A View of the First Farm purchased by the Artist, near Brighton*, in order 'to give an idea of the style of living in Van Diemen's Land'. Other paintings helped to elicit aspects of the life of the pioneer. *The Cataract, near Launceston* (Cat. no. 32) carried the note: 'the Fire lighted by Captain Langdon as a Beacon to some lost friends who are on top of the Rock'. *Ben Lomond from Batman's Look-Out* (Cat. no. 15) carried the note: 'so named on account of Mr. Batman's frequenting this spot to entrap the Natives'.

Glover's Australian paintings are, however, not to be dismissed as having no other aim than topography. In his landscapes we witness an endeavour to accommodate the documentary prerequisites of exotic landscape to the vision of the masters Glover admired: at times to the pastoral idealism of Claude, at times to the pastoral realism of Paul Potter, and at times to the picturesque of Gaspard Poussin and Salvator Rosa. In this connexion it is to be borne in mind that Glover was sixty three years of age when he arrived in the Colony, and that his style had been formed in the last decades of the eighteenth century. Consequently, we possess in his Australian work a belated example of the Italianate landscape being accommodated to the scenery of Tasmania. We know that throughout life Glover greatly admired the paintings of Claude. It is said that he would have liked to have been known as the English Claude.[75] He owned two Claudes for which he paid £1,000 and £800 respectively. During the brief peace of 1814 he visited France where he attracted attention by setting up his easel in the Grande Galerie of the Louvre, between a landscape by Poussin and one by Claude, where he proceeded to paint a landscape of his own which, it is claimed, so delighted Louis XVIII when exhibited in the Salon of 1814 that he ordered a gold medal to be struck in its honour.[76] One of Glover's sketch-books of his Italian tour, in the Queen Victoria Museum, Launceston, reveals the close study he made of Claude's methods. On the back of one of these sketches he wrote:

> In the Claudes where not injured the illuminated atmosphere between the eye and objects very evident—except at the outside of the pictures which were made darker and clearer to improve the center—Nothing approaching to black admitted in the middle of the pictures thin and mellow as possible—figures standing before bright water kept clear and warm. Colour at top of the sky of the Evening painted raw and out of harmony in one small corner, to increase the beauty of the center, and perhaps to prevent the eye resting at the outside of the picture—Great part of the foreground of each evidently painted lower than nature to give value to the lights and distances—perhaps rather too much so, or perhaps they may have grown darker by time, being glazed—the great broad lights in the skies of both kept as clear as possible, the shadows of clouds but just distinguished—The diminution of strength of shadow in proportion to the distance attended to with great strictness.

It was not altogether inappropriate that Glover should seek to apply Claude's vision

166. John Glover, *Drawing*, wash, 7 × 10½ in., Glover sketch-book no. 102, f. 28. Nan Kivell Collection 644, National Library of Australia, Canberra

to the Tasmanian scene for he himself saw it as a kind of exotic pastoral Arcadia. George William Evans in seeking to describe the pastoral beauty of the Bathurst Plains, which, as we have seen, evoked images of ideal pastoral landscape in the mind of more than one traveller, compared them to the country to the eastward of Cori Linn at Port Dalrymple. Mill's Plains, the site of Glover's selection, was not far distant from Cori Linn and consisted of the same type of open forest country; well watered and rich in grass, it was ideal pastoral country. 'It is possible', wrote Glover in a catalogue note to a *View in Mill's Plains* (Cat. no. 49), 'almost everywhere to drive a Carriage as easily as in a Gentleman's Park in England.'

The Australian savannah however, was natural, not artificial; and to Glover, as to Barron Field and Samuel Marsden, it was something of a pastoral paradise. As the *Thomas Lowry* ascended the Tamar in February 1831, young John Glover observed with great satisfaction 'a rapid succession of little farmhouses, with pretty snug houses, all on rising ground, like so many little paradises, and immediately backed by undulating high hills, covered with woods'.[77] In the years following his father drew such scenes many times. A pious man, whose thoughts and reading turned increasingly towards religion in his later years, John Glover must have been reminded of the days of the patriarchs as he watched his flocks and herds multiply in the newly won pastures.[78] Indeed the country at times reminded him of the Garden of Eden: as on the occasion when he contemplated a 'Temptation' painting in an Australian

264

167. John Glover, *Drawing*, wash 7 × 10½ in., Glover sketch-book, no. 102. f. 29. Nan Kivell Collection 644, National Library of Australia, Canberra

setting. In one drawing he made a preliminary sketch of the subject (Plate 166). In others it is Claude's pastoral Arcadia that comes to mind; as when he sketches a large party, travelling with a flock of sheep (quite possibly the members of his own family), who have halted by the side of a stream which winds among a forest of young eucalypt (Plate 167). Although the vegetation is rendered faithfully enough, the subject has been invested with the dreamy pastoral poetry of Claude. Even so, Glover's pastoral interpretation of the Australian countryside differs radically from the more sophisticated pastorals he had painted in England. The artist appears to have been deeply impressed by the primeval beauty of his surroundings at Patterdale and there his work entered upon a final phase; a phase which depended less upon the picturesqueness and literary associations which mark so much of his English work, and relied more upon a clear perception of the characteristic features of the Australian scene. Consequently, what his work loses in elegance is more than compensated for by the surprising emergence, late in life, of a fresh, unaffected, and essentially empirical vision.

This immediacy of vision extended also to the work of his son John R. Glover. In *My Harvest Home* (Colour Plate 25), usually ascribed to John Glover, but more likely to be by John Glover junior (despite the fact that the subject is idealized by being painted against the golden glow of a Claudean sunset) the desire to document the local vegetation and the high cirrus clouds of an Australian autumn has remained, as indeed the necessity to portray faithfully harvesting in Tasmania for the prospective migrant has remained.[79] The resulting contrast between ideality and topography has invested the painting with unusual primitive charm. And we know that the atmosphere of rural plenty and physical well-being which the picture conveys was not merely a pictorial device but expressed the new experience of the Glover family as farmers in the antipodes. 'We sow, plant, fence and break up new ground in progressive order, and our crops, thank Goodness, turn out equal to most', wrote young Glover to his sister, 'our wheat in particular often surpasses most of our neighbours.... Mr. G(lover) continues painting.... This climate is certainly most salutory, and as to health, we all thank God, enjoy it with most beautiful equanimity.'[80]

If Mill's Plains reminded Glover of the pastoral landscape of Claude, the scenery of neighbouring Ben Lomond reminded him equally of the picturesque landscapes of Gaspard Poussin and Salvator Rosa. On the very first day of his arrival in Tasmania young Glover had noted the strong contrasts afforded by the great bare rocks that buttressed the hills: 'very like the management of Gaspard Poussin's landscapes; a good school for the chiaroscuro', he wrote to his sister.[81] On many occasions his father painted the wilder mountainous country, making frequent expeditions into the hills partly to explore, and partly to find material for paintings. On one such excursion Glover and his neighbour John Batman ascended to the top of Ben Lomond—the first white men to do so. The excursion is recorded by his son:

> The first material circumstance of 1833 was Mr. Glover's going to the top of Ben Lomond, with a party; which was on Jan 26. At one of our neighbouring settlers, a Mr. Batman, are kept a number of domesticated Sydney Natives, for the more particular purpose of sending them out to trace our wild ones if any should happen to be reported as being seen. These with other servants were sent forward a day previous, to make an accommodation ready. The grand party then followed and slept a night or two on the top, which is an immense flat surrounded by precipitous and romantically wild rocks. There are several small lakes on the top; of one of which Mr. Glover has made a painting, a romantic curiosity.... Mr. Glover went upon horseback, the only horse that has been so high.[82]

Glover's *Ben Lomond, Tasmania, with Hunting Party* (Plate 169) is one of several which he painted of the mountain. In it we may observe how Glover established a pictorial compromise between the traditional banditti scenes of Gaspard Poussin and Rosa on the one hand, and the claims of colonial documentation on the other. Both the hunt and the bivouac, as we have seen, had become, during the twenties, emblematic of Australian colonial life. The Glovers themselves on their very first night in Australia had, at the mouth of the Tamar, experienced the novelty and excitement of bivouacking out of doors:

> We had a grand corobbory on shore; myself [i.e. Glover's son] set foot on shore for the first time since I first went on board at Gravesend Sept. 1. A temporary tent was formed with a sail cloth; a glorious bonfire was kept up with wood on the spot in abundance; a calm moonlight night; some employed themselves in collecting wood and cutting down young trees, others with guns brought in birds, which were roasted over the glowing fire, potatoes roasted, etc. altogether a very pleasant commencement of the *bushing* system.[83]

In his *Hunting Party*, Glover has incorporated a similar scene. It is late afternoon and a hunter is bringing in his kill to the camp-fire. But the artist has chosen to romanticize the situation. His trees, especially those to the right, are of an indiscriminate pic-

168. John William Lewin,
Springwood, watercolour.
$8\frac{3}{4} \times 10\frac{3}{4}$ in. (1815).
Mitchell Library, Sydney.
By permission of the
Trustees of the State
Library of New South
Wales

169. John Glover, *Ben
Lomond, Tasmania, with
Hunting Party*, canvas
$30\frac{1}{4} \times 46$ in. (*c.* 1834). Nan
Kivell Collection 1109,
National Library of
Australia, Canberra

170. John Glover, *Western
View of Mountains*, canvas,
30×45 in. (1833).
Tasmanian Museum and
Art Gallery. By permission
of the Trustees

turesque species, and his Australian hunters and their women are clad in the plaids and kilts of Highlanders. A painting emerges which seeks once again to unite the picturesque with the topographical.

Although it is not possible to date Glover's Australian work precisely, the *Hunting Party* seems, on stylistic grounds, to be an early Australian work, so clearly do the tapering trunks, sinuous branches, and bunchy opaque foliage resemble the manner of tree drawing adopted in his Cumberland sketches. It is apparent, however, that Glover soon after settling at Mill's Plains became aware of the gulf between his own mannered representations of foliage and the true nature of the eucalypt. A study of his sketch-books in Australian collections, which cover both late English and early Australian work, reveals how Glover gradually broke with the formulae he had brought with him, to achieve (that which only Lewin's water-colours had foreshadowed) a faithful rendering of the formal features of Australian vegetation. The fruits of his studies are to be observed in his painting *Australian Landscape with Cattle* (Colour Plate 28). In this painting Glover has mastered the characteristic forms of the structure, ramifications, and foliation of the eucalypt, rendering it faithfully whether treated with detail in the foreground, or at various levels of generalization in the distance. In such paintings Glover mastered the formal and tonal problems involved in painting Australian open-forest vegetation naturalistically: only the colour eluded him.

Landscapes such as *My Harvest Home* and *Australian Landscape with Cattle* also mark a significant iconographic change in the treatment of Australian scenery. These landscapes no longer represent the exotic wilderness of an antipodean topsyturveydom where the trees are unpicturesque, the flowers botanical curiosities, and primeval man hunts the monstrous kangaroo; they are landscapes into which the European has entered, where sheep and cattle replace native animals, and the hunter's bivouac replaces the aborigine's corroboree. Glover was himself a squatter and he has depicted in the earliest landscapes authentically Australian, a squatter's Arcadia.

Glover did not refrain, of course, from depicting the aborigine. The natives were still too much a part of the colonial scene to be ignored in an exhibition, purporting to represent the life and scenery of Tasmania, destined for a London gallery. But we have no evidence that the Glovers had any affection for the natives, rather the reverse. 'The natives have been lately very troublesome and treacherous', wrote young Glover, 'spearing and murdering all they find in the least unprotected.'[84] The family was sceptical of George Robinson's efforts to pacify and protect the natives.[85] Glover's son had a simpler solution: 'the only alternative now is, if they do not readily become friendly, to annihilate them at once'. And that such a policy was put into practice by the squatters of Mill's Plains is indicated by the fact that John Batman kept domesticated natives to track the wild Tasmanian ones, and frequented 'Batman's Look-Out' on Ben Lomond to trap Tasmanian aborigines who worried settlers. Glover's attitude to the Tasmanian native is revealed quite clearly in his paintings of them. In his *Western View of Mountains* (Plate 170) they are represented as small, dark, naked, and unattractive little people who dance and leap with quick angular movements and grotesque gesticulations; he represents them, we might say, as the little black devils to be removed from his southern paradise.[86]

The attitude was widespread. As squatters pushed their runs deeper into the country they found the aborigines a nuisance and a menace to life and property. In the graphic arts a hardening, unsympathetic attitude is revealed in the grotesque comic figures of natives, published in Sydney during the 1830's. They follow the spirit of T. R. Browne's earlier caricatures. Indeed it may have been Browne who was

responsible for drawing the lithograph entitled *King Teapot and his Two Gins* (Plate 171) in 1833. The plump deformed 'king' and his emaciated wives are typical of the raw colonial humour of the time. Three years later W. H. Fernyhough (1812–49), a surveyor and architect, produced a series of lithographs which depicted well-known aboriginal personalities of New South Wales (Plate 173). Like the Port Jackson Painter he adopted a silhouette method of portraiture. But beyond that all similarity ceases. Clad in old European rags and divested of the last vestiges of that nobility with which the eighteenth century had clothed him, the aborigine was depicted as a monstrous and comical absurdity. But just how rapidly he had been degraded and debauched by contact with Europeans is better seen by comparing William Blake's noble family of New South Wales (Plate 114) with John Carmichael's ragged and besotted family of New South Wales, engraved half a century later (Plate 172).[87]

The emergence of pastoral imagery in colonial Australia made it possible to present a version of Australian nature more amenable to the European imagination. Nevertheless, during the height of the pastoral ascendancy the representation of Australia as a land of contrariety and antipodal inversion persists. The ideas of Péron and Field gain wide currency after 1820 and establish themselves in contexts particularly relevant to the times. The idea of inversion, as we have seen, arose from reflection upon the peculiarities of Australian plants and animals during the first years of settlement, but during the 1830's with the farming and grazing potentialities of the country receiving concerted attention, the notion of inversion is to be found expressed in pastoral and agricultural contexts. Thus Robert Dawson, writing in 1830, notes that the poorest soils contain more than three times the number of trees to be found in the rich soils. 'This', he remarks, 'like most other things in this strange country, is, I believe, nearly the reverse of what we find in England'.[88] And the blind traveller, Holman, noted in 1832 that whereas in England fertility 'diminishes as we ascend the height', in New South Wales, 'the summit is the most luxuriant part, exhibiting crops of the sweetest and most flourishing herbage'. And he concludes: 'It is to be remarked generally, of New South Wales, that nature has provided principles of fertility, exactly the reverse of those which observation has discovered to regulate the vegetable world of Europe.'[89]

As we have seen, European reactions to Australia after 1820 became, in general, more favourable, but reactions to the Australian aborigine, less favourable. Consequently it was possible to present the contrast between man and nature in Australia as another variation upon the theme of contrariety. Such a contrast is implied in Thomas Hervey's *Australia* (1825). Hervey gained most of his impressions of Australian landscape from reading Péron, and saw it as a utopia in which man alone existed in a degraded condition:

171. *King Teapot and his two Gins, Chief of the Bogan Tribe, as he appeared after having a Tightner*, lithograph, drawn by T. B. (1833)

172. *Male and Female Black Natives*, drawn and engraved by John Carmichael, published by J. Maclehose, Sydney (1839)

173. *Bill Worrell, Five Islands Tribe*, lithograph by W. H. Fernyhough published by T. G. Austin, Sydney (1836)

174. John Carmichael, *Sydney from Woolloomooloo Hill*, engraving, in *Select Views of Sydney, New South Wales* (drawn and engraved by J. G.), Sydney, 1829, pl. 4

Here man alone is not a favoured child;
Here—like a new-born world—where all seems rife
With boundless beauty bursting into life,
Here—'mid this clustering of all lovely things—
Man—like a blot upon the pageant, springs.

. . . . . .

Here nature, when she reared her mighty plan,
Sported with many things—but most with man!

This view was given a degree of permanence by being written into the 6th edition of the *Encyclopaedia Britannica* by Sir John Barrow in his article on *Australasia*. Secretary to the Admiralty for many years, Barrow had become known as an authority on South-East Asia because of his travels in China and the Eastern Seas. In Australia, Barrow claimed, following the current thought of the time, there was only one savage animal and that was man:

> ... in this great division of the globe, fully equal in extent to that of Europe, there is no quadruped larger than the kangaroo and there is none of a ferocious character.... Man only in Australasia is an animal of prey; and more ferocious than the lynx, the leopard, or the hyena, he devours his own species, in countries too where nature has done everything for his comfort and subsistence. The consequence is, that the population is so much checked and thwarted, that the number of all the natives who have been seen on the coasts of all the islands, would not in the aggregate amount to 20,000 souls. The only hope of improvement must depend on the future colonization of these healthful and fertile regions of the globe by some European power.[90]

The convict was used at times to point the same kind of contrast as the aborigine; for during the 1820's an increasing number of people both in Australia and England were coming to the conclusion that the convict was also a 'blot upon the pageant'. Convicts conspicuously replace aborigines as foreground motifs in John Carmichael's engraving of Sydney from Woolloomooloo Hill (Plate 174). Jane Roberts, sailing to

270

Tasmania in the early 1830's with colonial settlers returning home from holiday in England, notes how they praised the scenery and climate till it appeared like 'a fabled Elysium', and she pictured to herself 'a spot on which Nature in sportive mood, had lavished her choicest, her most opposite gifts'. But for her there was one great disadvantage: 'man was there, the cultivator of her soil, debased and shackled by his crimes, an involuntary servant to his fellow-man'.[91] To Wentworth, similarly, transportation was the great curse upon the brow of Australian nature, and he longs for the day when:

> No more the outcast convicts' clanking chains
> Deform thy wilds, and stigmatise thy plains.

In such ways the idea of contrariety accommodated itself to the new historical situation of the 1820's and 1830's. But in such forms it was little more than a gloss upon matters of immediate concern. The reason for its persistence and vitality as an idea is not to be found in the whimsical contexts in which it frequently appears but in the fact that it did express a fundamental European difficulty in understanding Australian nature. Until the appearance of the theory of organic evolution the productions of the country remained a problem for the systematizing philosopher and scientist.[92] In a long note to his poem, Thomas Hervey pointed out once again that: 'In Australia, nature, in her playfulness, has disappointed theories, and shown an utter disregard for received prejudices, even when supported by proverbs of 2000 years standing!' He proceeded to cite a long list of natural oddities in the usual manner. And the idea of inversion led him, as it had led others, to the idea of social undulation. But whereas in Wentworth's poem the idea of undulation had been used to express aspirations of colonial nationalism, Hervey's poem describes not a rise and fall of empires but a rise and fall of continents! The idea of Australia becomes associated with grandiose notions of evolutionary geo-physics. 'There is not', Hervey wrote in the Preface to his poem, 'a more sublime theory in geography than the one alluded to in this poem.' He had read accounts of the formation of coral reefs in Flinders's *Voyage*, and in a supplement to the *Encyclopaedia Britannica*.[93] We do not know yet, says Hervey, whether all the islands of the Pacific are formed from coral, though according to geologists the islands of Sunda, the Moluccas, and others in the Indian Ocean are gradually enlarging and consequently, he argues, the time must come when Australasia, Polynesia, and the islands of South-east Asia will form one vast continent with Asia. The result is certain: a world will be built from coral polyps, and the waters of the ocean in their search for a new bed will destroy one of the old continents. Hervey chooses Africa as the continent which the poet in a vision sees submerged beneath the waters as 'Notasia', the new continent, rises from the ocean.

Despite its extravagance the idea as expressed in Hervey's poem is of more than passing importance because we here meet again that evolutionary theory of the formation of continents elaborated by John Whitehurst and incorporated by Erasmus Darwin in his poem *The Economy of Vegetation*. Reflection upon the islands and continents of the Pacific was continuing to minister to the emergence of evolutionary thought.

10. Art, Science, and Taste in Australia, 1835–50

ROBERT BROWN'S *Prodromus Florae Novae Hollandiae* (1810) was largely responsible for continuing, in scientific circles, the interest in Australian botany begun by Banks. Australian plants also continued to fascinate English connoisseurs of horticulture during the 1820's. A long letter which Dr. Schultes, a professor of botany of Landshut, Bavaria, sent to Count Sternberg, the naturalist, describing a visit he made to England in 1824, provides an impression of the interest with which Australian plants were still being received into England.[1] Schultes informs us that Sir James Edward Smith's plant collection was especially rich in the productions of New Holland. Aylmer Burke Lambert's collection included Australian plants collected by Caley, Flinders, Captain P. P. King, Governor King, and John White. The Botanical Garden at Chelsea had received a large collection of Australian seeds from Barron Field shortly before Schultes's visit. He noted too that Colville's nursery at Chelsea, which specialized in rare plants, included much from New Holland. Many of the great nurserymen of London, Schultes observed,

> ... keep travelling botanists in their pay, who from the most remote parts of the globe must send them seeds, roots, and living plants. In China, the East Indies, the Cape of Good Hope, at Sierra Leone, New Holland, New Zealand, Paraguay, Chile, Mexico, and the most northern parts of America and Siberia, many of these enterprising individuals have collectors: so that Geography is often improved by the trade of horticulture.[2]

Schultes makes it clear in a revealing comparison between the flower markets of London and Paris that, in his opinion, the collection of rare exotics was a peculiarly English horticultural fashion:

> We have visited the celebrated flower-market of London; of which no German who has not seen it, could form a proper idea. What chiefly struck us is, that the greatest rarities and most trifling articles are here exposed for sale together, and that both are eagerly bought. Were such things to be carried to the *Marché aux Fleurs* at Paris, not a pennyworth of them would be sold. But by the two flower markets of these two principal cities of Europe, an estimate of the different characters of their inhabitants may be formed. The wealthy and respectable Englishman, who is a connoisseur, will purchase nothing that is common; for if pretty, he has it already in his garden;—and the poor Londoner who cannot afford to buy what is beautiful, will still obtain ... something green to decorate the window of his dark little attic, and give his last farthing for a bit of verdure. The opulent Frenchman, who values all objects only as they please the eye, without reference to their being common or scarce, is willing to pay a greater price for a lovely rose-bush, than for the rarest plant from New Holland or the Cape of Good Hope; and as to the poor artizan of the French capital, he only thinks of vegetable productions as they are fit for

272

175. *The Nerved-leaved Dryandra*, Robert Sweet, *Flora Australasica* (1827–8), f.p. 22

culinary uses; and whether they be blue or green to look at, is the same to him. Hence it arises that the Parisian flower-market offers a much more delightful vista than that of London, though it is much smaller and more poorly stocked.[3]

At Colville's nursery, Schultes met Robert Sweet, another writer on horticulture who, four years later, provided further evidence of the fashionable interest in Australia, in his *Flora Australasica: containing coloured figures and descriptions of some of the choicest species most proper for the conservatory or greenhouse, and many of which will endure the cold of our climate, in the open air, with a very little protection; with magnified dissections of their most essential parts, descriptions, and a full account of the best method of cultivation and propagation. The greater part are handsome evergreen shrubs, and many produce sweet-scented flowers; and as they are generally of free growth, and easily managed, they may be considered as the most desirable for cultivation* (1827–8). The title itself reveals clearly enough that the publication of the book was closely connected with the interests of English nurserymen specializing in Australian exotics (Plate 175). Delight in exotic flowers also determined the nature of a number of more scientific publications such as Sir William Jackson Hooker's *Botanical Miscellany: containing figures and descriptions of such plants as recommend themselves by their novelty, rarity or history, or by the uses to which they are applied in the Arts, in Medicine, and in Domestic Science* (1933). The two volumes are devoted almost entirely to exotic plants, and contain many references to Australian botany.

The interest in exotic botany was one aspect of the widening interest in exotic natural history in general. Interest in Australian zoology was not only catered for by

176. *The Kanguroo-Rat of New South Wales*, woodcut, $2\frac{1}{2} \times 3$ in., in Thomas Bewick, *General History of Quadrupeds* (1790).

such books as Lewin's *Birds of New Holland* (which appeared in a second edition in 1822, and a third in 1838), and George Gray's *Entomology of New Holland* (1833),[4] it featured also in illustrated compendia which specially catered for the popular interest in exotic nature: notably such books as Edward Donovan's *Naturalist's Repository or Miscellany of Exotic Natural History* (1834) and Dru Drury's *Illustrations of Exotic Entomology*, a second edition of which appeared in 1837. Curious and interesting Australian animals were also included in George Shaw's *Vivarium Naturae* (1789–1813), and Thomas Bewick's *General History of Quadrupeds* (1790) which frequently appeared in new editions during the first three decades of the nineteenth century (Plate 176).

Although British interest in the natural productions of Australia never ceased entirely there was a considerable slackening of local interest between 1810 and 1830. But the 1830's and early 1840's became a period of intense activity, and on this occasion visiting scientists were helped materially in their work by the presence in Australia of small but active circles genuinely interested in the advancement of science.

In New South Wales the most influential scientific circle was centred about Alexander Macleay and his son William. Both men had gained recognition for their contributions to science before settling in Australia. Alexander Macleay had been the Secretary of the Linnean Society from 1798 until 1825. In January 1826 he arrived in Sydney to become Colonial Secretary under Governor Darling. Before leaving England he had assembled a fine entomological collection which included many Australian specimens, and had assisted in supplying the scientific nomenclature for Lewin's *Prodromus Entomology* (1805). In Australia, Macleay extended his interests to ornithology and forwarded a large number of skins of Australian birds to the Linnean Society. His extensive garden at Elizabeth Bay, Sydney, became famous for its collections of rare and valuable plants and his home became a rendezvous for visiting scientists. His son, William, was well known as a naturalist in England, his name being associated with the advocacy of the quinary system of classification. Two other members of Macleay's circle included Captain Phillip Parker King, who had commanded the *Adventure* on its first surveying voyage of South America (1826–30), and Sir John Jamison, a surgeon and prominent pastoralist who employed his own collector, and sent notes and specimens to the Linnean Society and the Royal College of Surgeons.

274

A parallel development took place in Tasmania. In 1837 Sir John Franklin, who had sailed under Flinders and had had much experience in polar exploration, became Governor of the Colony, and, with the help of his wife, soon embarked upon the formation of a Tasmanian Natural History Society. In the first number of the Society's *Tasmanian Journal of Natural Science* the Rev. John Lillie set forth the interests of the Society as centreed upon the natural history and physics of Tasmania 'more particularly the departments of Zoology, Botany, Geology and Meteorology'. Lady Franklin, who was a most active patron of the Society, purchased the land and paid for the erection of a museum of natural history at Lenah Valley. The Society provided the nucleus for the Royal Society of Tasmania founded by Sir John Eardley-Wilmot. It was the first branch of the Royal Society to be established outside the British Isles.[5]

Now between 1835 and 1851 a number of distinguished scientists, including Charles Darwin, Count Paul E. de Strzelecki, Joseph Dalton Hooker, Thomas Henry Huxley, and John Gould, visited Australia. The local scientific groups were able to provide not only hospitality to such visitors, but, as in the case of Strzelecki and Gould, render considerable material help.

At the beginning of the first phase of British scientific exploration in the Pacific, Banks, as we have seen, helped to establish a close connexion between observation and draughtsmanship. During the second phase the value of the connexion continued to be recognized and maintained. Darwin, in a short autobiography, asserted that his own incapacity to draw was an irremediable weakness in his own work on the *Beagle*.[6] However, Sir William Jackson Hooker, Director of the Botanical Gardens at Kew, and John Lindley, Professor of Botany in the University of London, developed their abilities as draughtsmen to assist them in their work of accurately observing and describing flowers. It was an aspect of the value of drawing that John Ruskin was soon to repeat again and again in his books and lectures, an aspect fully appreciated by Joseph Dalton Hooker when he travelled under Sir James Clark Ross on the *Erebus*, and by Thomas Henry Huxley, when he travelled under Owen Stanley on the *Challenger*.

Hooker, who was appointed naturalist to Ross's expedition to the Antarctic (1839–43), maintained an interest in drawing and the pursuit of art throughout life. His father, Sir William Jackson Hooker, was an able botanical draughtsman; his grandfather owned a fine collection of paintings. 'I must say', he wrote to a friend while voyaging with Ross, 'that next to the want of Society, the want of music and painting is one of the most irksome which a sea Voyager is bound to endure.'[7] Drawing, however, in its more practical aspects, both as an adjunct to scientific observation and as a visual record of events, played an important part in Hooker's daily routine on board ship. He was constantly engaged while the vessel was at sea in a type of work in which Alexander Lesueur had excelled, the description and drawing of sea creatures that could not be easily preserved. In a letter which he wrote to his father he stressed the importance he attached to this branch of his work:

> Since leaving St. Helena, my time has been employed exactly as before; the net is constantly overboard, and catching enough to keep me three-quarters of the day employed drawing; the dissections of the little marine animals generally take some time, as they are universally microscopic. Though I never intend to make anything but Botany a study, I do not think I can do better than I am doing; it gives me a facility in drawing which I feel comes much easier to me, it pleases the Captain beyond anything to see me at work, and, further, it is a new field which none but an artist can prosecute at sea; the extent of this branch of Natural History is quite astonishing, the number of species of little winged and footed shells provided with

wings, sails, bladders or swimmers appears marvellous. The causes of the luminousness of the sea I refer entirely to animals (living). I never yet saw the water flash
without finding sufficient cause without electricity, phosphoric water, dead animal
matter, or anything further than living animals (generally *Entomostraca Crustacea* if
anybody asks you). These little shrimps are particularly numerous, especially two
species of them, thousands of one kind being caught in one night. . . . My collection
amounts to about 200 drawings, done from nature under the microscope.[8]

Hooker was a great admirer of the scientific draughtsmanship of Francis and
Ferdinand Bauer, and seems to have regarded Ferdinand's drawing of a *Banksia* as
one of the finest masterpieces of scientific draughtsmanship. 'As far as I could I
imitated Bauer's style of drawing dissections',[9] he wrote, on one occasion, to his
father.

A professional landscape-painter was not appointed to the Ross expedition.
Dayman, a mate on the *Erebus*, was the most capable draughtsman aboard, in
Hooker's opinion, but he left the vessel to take charge of the magnetic observatory in
Tasmania. And although Davis of the *Terror* was a tolerable artist and provided
material to illustrate the published account of the voyage, Hooker was called upon to
perform a good deal of work that would normally have fallen to a professional artist
had one been appointed, as, for example, the drawing of coastal profiles. 'Captain
Ross', Hooker once wrote to his father striking a note of complaint unusual for him,
'used often to make me sketch coastlines of hills and valleys of snow, which is most
miserable work.'[10] Nevertheless Hooker found, on occasion, scenes both curious and
dramatic in the Antarctic as Hodges had done before him, and sought to depict them
as well as he could for the information and entertainment of his friends at home. His
father, though he insisted that he should not lessen the value of his work in botany by
dissipating it through activity in allied sciences, encouraged this aspect of his work: 'I
rejoice', he wrote, 'that you make drawings of scenery. They will be invaluable.'[11]

In his landscape and seascape work, Hooker sought the same degree of accuracy
that he brought to the drawing of minute marine creatures drawn under a microscope. An Antarctic landscape, though it could entertain because of its curiosity and
the unusual beauties of nature it revealed, was a visual document that might well
reveal information of real worth to the professional geologist, meteorologist, botanist,
and zoologist. The contour of a mountain against the sky was to be rendered with as
much fidelity to fact as the structure of the leaf of a new species of plant. In a letter
home he writes:

> At present I am attempting a sketch of the ships off the Barrier and burning
> mountain in 78 degrees South for you, and should I succeed you shall have it; . . .
> There is a rather nice print published of Weddell's two ships bearing up in 74
> degrees 15 minutes by Huggins, which would be worth your buying; a few shillings
> would cover it, and the Icebergs in it give a very fair idea of those floating masses,
> though they are not flat-topped like most of those we have seen, nor is the colour at
> all good, as they should have a blue tinge.[12]

On another occasion he made a drawing as Hodges had done many years before of 'a
curious iceberg with a hole in it' and sent it to Walter Hood Fitch (1817–92), his
father's botanical draughtsman.[13] Describing it he writes:

> The berg is fair enough, but the sea will not do. He [i.e. Fitch] could copy it and
> with excellent effect; it was blowing hard and there were some black scudding
> clouds near the moon, which was reflected on the tips of the waves, close to the edge

276

of the berg. The water should be of an intense cobalt blue, and it should reflect a white glare on the sea. There are no harsh lines on an Iceberg; the shadows should be faint and the lights bright.[14]

Hooker later supplied several drawings which were vignetted by Fitch for publication in the official account of the expedition. Although Fitch's botanical work was beyond cavil, Hooker was critical of some of the vignettes. He found, for instance, that Fitch had 'refined upon Mount Sabine without improving it',[15] and in one copy of the account carefully pencilled in a more faithful outline of the mountain. Trained in visual documentation with its emphasis upon detail and precision it is not surprising to find that among his favourites at the Royal Academy in his later life were the landscapes of B.W. Leader.[16]

Thomas Henry Huxley, assistant-naturalist to the *Rattlesnake* on its surveying voyage in tropical Australia and the Louisiade Archipelago (1846–50), also made constant use of his abilities as a draughtsman to record scientific phenomena and the more notable events of the voyage. Like Hooker, Huxley made drawings (working with a microscope) of marine animals caught in the tow-net. These drawings were of great value to him in the basic work which he carried out into the structure of molluscs and coelenterates. In addition he made many ethnographical drawings in the Louisiade Archipelago. A competent figure-draughtsman, Huxley sought in his water-colours to provide an accurate record of the physical appearance of the natives of the region (Plate 177). His tropical landscapes, while composed with a natural feeling for composition which gives them considerable charm, never fail to provide an honest rendering of the characteristic features of the vegetation.[17]

The *Rattlesnake* was better provided with artists than was Ross's expedition. Captain Owen Stanley was himself a proficient topographical draughtsman.[18] And in New South Wales, Stanley met Oswald Brierly (1817–94) who accompanied the vessel as its artist. Neither science nor topography was Brierly's *metier*; he sought

178. Harden S. Melville,
Watering Gully-Cape Upstart,
in *Sketches in Australia and the
Adjacent Islands* (1849), pl. vii

rather in his paintings to represent the adventure and romance of life on the high seas.
Ships riding out heavy seas, or such paintings as *South Sea Whaling off Two-fold Bay*,[19]
full of spectacular excitement, are the kind of subjects he obviously enjoyed painting.
Yet in Brierly also, trained in naval architecture in his youth and following the
profession of marine painting throughout life, the detailed delineation, item by item,
of a ship's gear and rigging, always remains a paramount consideration. Whether the
subject was heroic adventure of sectional views of molluscs under a microscope, the
overriding consideration was the accuracy of the individual facts recorded. Brierly's
capacity for dramatic action and faith to ethnographic detail was combined in a
masterly fashion in his large watercolour painting in the National Library of
Australia entitled *First Arrival of White Men amongst the Islands of the Louisiade Archipelago*.
As Dr. Joppien has pointed out in his excellent discussion of the painting, it is one of
the few nineteenth-century paintings which continues and develops the theme of
cultural contact inaugurated in the painting of Hodges and Webber (Colour Plate
32).[20]

How close in intention the work of official artists to surveying voyages came to the
graphic work of the scientists who travelled with them is revealed in Harden S.
Melville's *Adventures of a Griffin* (1867). Melville accepted an appointment as topographical draughtsman under Captain Blackwood on the *Fly*, on its surveying voyage
from 1842 to 1846 in Torres Strait, New Guinea, and islands of the Eastern Archipelago. The book is no less valuable in being written for a juvenile audience for it
provides a graphic account of the life at sea of a young artist who had accepted an
appointment as ship's topographer. Quartered among the midshipmen he is drawn

Although the training of a scientist like Huxley and an artist like Brierly differed
considerably, there was little fundamental difference in their aesthetic attitude to
draughtsmanship when working together on the *Challenger*.

278

closely into both the seafaring and the scientific life of the ship, his draughtsmanship being at the service of all, whether to make an ethnographical drawing of a Bushman specially captured by the Captain for the purpose, to paint exotic flowers collected by the naturalists, or to paint typical landscapes (Plate 178), geological curiosities, and encounters with natives, for the published account of the voyage.

Although it was usually not possible, by the very nature of land exploration on the Australian continent, to organize expeditions on a scale commensurate with sea voyages engaged upon exploration and survey, the importance of making graphic illustrations of the new country opened up through exploration was recognized. Charles Sturt made drawings during his expeditions into southern Australia (1828–31) and central Australia (1844–6) which were later lithographed to illustrate the published accounts of his expeditions. They are essentially documentary drawings made to illustrate the nature of the terrain explored. Sturt's wide circle of scientific acquaintances included Robert Brown and John Gould, the ornithologist, and he was himself deeply interested in the study of geology. Accordingly the illustrations in his books are designed to meet the interests of such people. It is to be noted how clearly a drawing like the *Depot Glen* (Plate 179), for example, illustrates the geological structure of the scene depicted, a structure carefully described in the accompanying text.

The illustrations in Sir Thomas Mitchell's accounts of his Australian explorations perform a function similar to those in Sturt's. Mitchell was a proficient topographical draughtsman both in landscape and in figure drawing. Although the lithographs which illustrate both his books are poorly produced (and obscure to some extent the clarity of his work) he took care to see that his illustrations assisted the verbal account. To do this he occasionally adopted a common surveyor's practice. He extended the practice of naming outstanding landmarks along the upper and lower edges of panoramic drawings to the naming of items of botanical and geological interest. Thus his illustration of the *Western Extremity of Mount Arapiles*[21] has several brief notes at relevant positions along the upper and lower edges of the lithograph: 'an altered sandstone', 'casuarina', 'banksia', and the illustration of the *Fall of Cobaw*[22] has 'all granite'. Clearly the primary purpose of such illustrations was to convey topographical, geological, and botanical information.

179. Charles Sturt, *The Depot Glen in Lat 29.40 S, Long. 148 E*, watercolour, $6\frac{1}{2} \times 11\frac{1}{4}$ in. National Library of Australia

It would be a great mistake, however, to rule out the aesthetic factor as irrelevant when considering the work of such men as Sturt and Mitchell. During the period in which they worked it was possible for an artist who had been called upon to satisfy the illustrative requirements of science and exploration to transfer his attention to the service of taste, without involving any radical alteration either of his style or his interests. Similarly, explorers were not uncommonly men of taste and wide cultural interests who were interested in the nature of their own aesthetic reactions to new scenes. This is true of both Sturt and Mitchell.

At first greatly annoyed to learn that he had been posted to New South Wales, the country gradually gained a hold upon Sturt's affections. His descriptions, objective as they are in point of fact, also reveal his emotional reactions to the Australian landscape. 'He who has never looked on any other than the well-cultivated fields of England,' he wrote on one occasion, 'can have little idea of a country that Nature has covered with an interminable forest.'[23] His explorations took him into the dry western country and his accounts of it did much to strengthen the impression held since the first days of settlement, that the Australian forests were monotonous, and desolate, inducing melancholy. 'From this ground', he wrote describing a prospect viewed during his trip along the Murray, 'the view to the south, was over as dark and monotonous a country as could well be described.'[24] But the Australian climate, as distinct from the vegetation, gained his warmest praise, 'a climate, so soft that man scarcely requires a dwelling, and so enchanting that few have left it but with regret'. In such a climate, 'the spirit must necessarily be acted upon—and the heart feels lighter'.[25]

It is the same with Mitchell. Though both the verbal and visual descriptions of his explorations are mainly concerned with conveying information useful to scientists and prospective settlers, he is not unconcerned with his own personal reactions to the landscape. His journeys took him, for the most part, over better country than Sturt's, so his accounts are, on balance, more favourable. Mitchell frequently endows his illustrations with a romantic feeling which appealed so much to the sensibility of his time; rocky outcrops remind him of medieval castles, and the reasons he gives for exploring the interior of Australia read more like those of a gentleman of taste engaged upon a somewhat unusual grand tour than a man in search of new pastures for stock. Consider, for instance, the way he opens the preface to his *Journal of an Expedition into the Interior of Tropical Australia* (1848):

'Admiring Nature in her wildest grace', it has ever been the most attractive of the author's duties to explore the interior of Australia. There the philosopher may look for facts; the painter and the poet for original studies and ideas; the naturalist for additional knowledge; and the historian might begin at a beginning. The traveller there seeks in vain for the remains of cities, temples, or towers; but he is amply compensated by objects that tell not of decay but of healthful progress and hope;— of a wonderful past, and of a promising future.[26]

The tastes of the man of sensibility are also present in the explorer's views of new country his *Flood coming down the Macquarie*, dated precisely to 13 February 1846, for instance, together with its accompanying verbal descriptions clearly has geological and even meteorological interests to satisfy, but Mitchell, nevertheless, presented it as a moonlight scene by a waterfall, thus combining the romantic and the topographical, much in the same manner that Joseph Dalton Hooker sought to paint icebergs in the moonlight with all the precision of a botanical illustration.

Sir Thomas Mitchell was Surveyor-General of New South Wales from 1826 until his death in 1855.[27] During the second quarter of the nineteenth century the relation between land surveying and the practice of landscape-painting was a particularly close one, especially in colonies where large areas of land were being opened up for settlement. In Australia, as in America and New Zealand, surveyors frequently made drawings and paintings of the native peoples and of the new country encountered in the pursuit of their duties. The New Zealand Company, for example, employed William Mein Smith (1798–1869) and Samuel Charles Brees (1810–65), as surveyors. Both men made many paintings of New Zealand scenery. Charles Heaphy (1822–69), who was employed by the Company as its artist and draughtsman and who became the outstanding colonial artist of New Zealand, participated in survey work (Colour Plate 29).[28] He assisted Hochstetter, for example, in the geological survey of Auckland. In New South Wales, William Romaine Govett, who did a good deal of surveying in the Blue Mountains region during the 1830's, made water-colour drawings of the natives and scenery of the area, which he used to illustrate a series of articles entitled 'Sketches in New South Wales' published in the *Saturday Magazine* in 1835.[29] Robert Russell (1808–1900) was appointed to the Sydney Survey Office in 1832 and took lessons from Conrad Martens in 1835. He made the earliest extant drawings of the Melbourne district when he made the first survey of the Port Phillip area during the same year.[30] Robert Hoddle (1794–1881),[30] the first Surveyor-General of Victoria, likewise made drawings of early Melbourne. William Charles Piguenit (1836–1914) entered the Tasmanian Survey Department in 1849. When he resigned in 1872 to devote himself entirely to landscape-painting he built up a considerable reputation as a painter specializing in huge canvases depicting outstanding features of Australian scenery such as Lake St. Clair (Tasmania) and Mount Kosciusko. His search for the local 'tremendities of nature' may be compared with the work of the American artist, F. E. Church. Charles Conder, who later became well known as a painter in Paris and London, painted his earliest works while employed in a survey camp in New South Wales.

In New South Wales, Sir Thomas Mitchell's own example did much to promote an interest in landscape-painting among surveyors. During service in the Peninsular War he had been engaged upon surveying, mapping, and topographical intelligence work. In 1827, shortly before he embarked for Australia, he published a small and eminently practical textbook on surveying, *Outlines of a System of Surveying, for Geographical and Military Purposes,* 'based on sixteen years experience, and originated among the mountains of Spain and Portugal during the war'. One section is of particular interest in estimating the possible influence of surveying techniques on the production of topographical and panoramic landscapes during the second quarter of the century. This is the section that deals with the construction of field sketches according to the principles of surveying. Mitchell's book contains an illustration of a panorama produced in this manner (Plate 180). By such means Mitchell overcame problems associated with surveying a difficult terrain. Shortly after arriving in New South Wales, for instance, his instructions required him to survey a particularly broken region among the headwaters of the Wollondilly that had defied his predecessors' attempts to survey it. Mitchell left an account of his procedure:

> The channel of the Wollondilly ... after it is joined by the Uningalla near Arthursleigh ... sinks immediately into a deep ravine ... the country west of it being exceedingly wild. The scene it presented, when I stood on the pic of Jellore in 1828, and then commenced a general survey of this Colony, was of the most discouraging description. ... Universal wood, impassable ravines—a total absence

of artificial objects, and the consequent necessity for clearing summit stations for the theodolites, were great impediments; but I made the most of each station when it had been cleared, by taking an exact panoramic view with the theodolite of the nameless features it commanded.[31]

Mitchell's methods were, without doubt, copied by other surveyors in the Colony. Panoramas made by Lt. R. Dale of the 63rd Regiment of the Swan River and King George's Sound[32] in Western Australia, in their clear delineation of hill contours and landmarks recall Mitchell's work. In Dale's panorama of King George's Sound a surveyor (probably intended to represent Dale himself), with native assistants, is drawn in the foreground.

Although explorers like Sturt and Mitchell were quite capable of providing drawings to illustrate the accounts of their explorations, in a number of cases artists were included among exploring parties in order to provide some visual record of the proceedings. G.W. Evans, himself an explorer, surveyor, and topographical draughtsman,[33] made drawings for John Oxley's exploration of the Western rivers. Some of these were aquatinted by Robert Havell & Son to illustrate Oxley's *Journal of Two Expeditions into the Interior of New South Wales* (1820). John Gilbert, an artist and naturalist who came out to Australia with John Gould, attached himself to Ludwig Leichhardt's expedition in 1844 from the Darling Downs to Port Essington, but was killed on the journey by the natives. A similar disaster would almost certainly have overtaken Thomas Henry Huxley, who made some fine drawings of tropical vegetation on the Queensland coast during the short period he was with Kennedy at Rockingham Bay, had his commander, Owen Stanley, agreed to his desire to accompany Kennedy on his fatal trip to Cape York in 1848. Samuel Thomas Gill (1818–80), who later did more than any other artist to depict life on the Australian gold diggings, accompanied Horrocks on his exploring expedition which reached Lake Dutton, South Australia,

180. (*Landscape Sketching by Survey*), Major T. L. Mitchell, *Outlines of a System of Surveying* (1827), pl. 1, f.p. 52

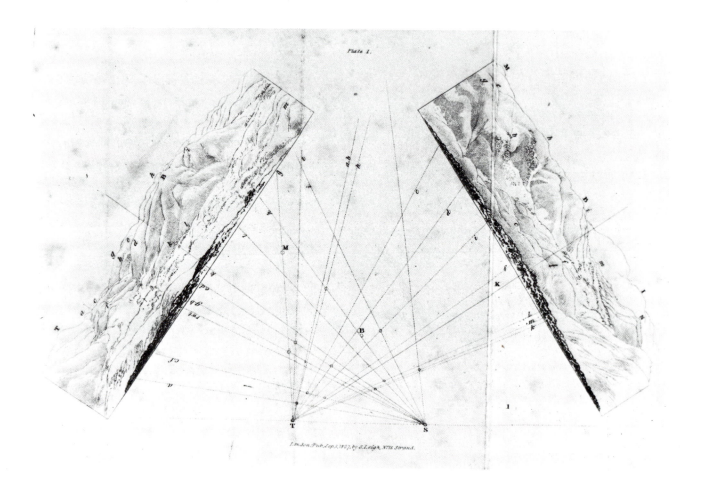

Plate 1.

London Pub. Sep.3.1827, by J. Leigh, N°.76 Strand.

before its leader was fatally injured in a gun explosion. George French Angas[34] accompanied Sir George Grey, Governor of South Australia, in some of his expeditions into the interior of the colony.

The publication of John Gould's *Birds of Europe* in 1837 established him as one of the world's outstanding ornithologists. Having completed the work he decided to embark upon publishing the birds of Australia because the field was still little known, and, as he wrote in his *Introduction to the Birds of Australia* (1848), 'of no ordinary degree of interest, from the circumstances of its being one of the finest possessions of the British Crown, and from its natural productions being as remarkable for the anomalous nature of their forms, as for their beauty, and the singularity of their habits'.[35] After publishing ten coloured plates, from material available in England, Gould became dissatisfied with his results, and decided to visit Australia to gather material himself. Accordingly, armed with letters of introduction from the Home Secretary, the Colonial Office, the Admiralty, and the Royal Geographical Society, he left England for Australia with his wife (who acted as his illustrator), his son and nephew, the collector John Gilbert, and two servants.

Gould arrived in Tasmania in 1838 where he received much help from the Franklins: indeed all the governors of the Australian colonies were of assistance to him. Furthermore, he had the good fortune to arrive in the country at a time when the marine surveying of the tropical waters of Australia and New Guinea was at its height and when Ross was engaged upon his Antarctic voyage. Gould himself travelled extensively in Tasmania, the islands of Bass Strait, South Australia, and New South Wales where he penetrated 400 miles from the coast in search of new species. He sent his assistant Gilbert to explore the western and northern portions of the country. It is not surprising, therefore, having regard for his own activities and the varied assistance at his disposal that Gould was able to add 300 new species of birds to the 300-odd already known.

Gould returned to England in 1840 and began to publish his folio *Birds of Australia*. It appeared in thirty-six quarterly parts, the first part being published on 1 December 1840, and the last on 1 December 1848.[36] Gould later published a supplement which appeared in five parts over an interval of eighteen years. Many finished drawings were made by Gould's wife, Elizabeth, until her death a year after her return from Australia. After Elizabeth's death, finished drawings were made by H. C. Richter, W. Hart, J. Wolf, and Edward Lear.

Gould's decision to study Australian birds in their own habitat is itself a token of the growing realization that naturalists should study their material as much as possible in the field. With this realization is to be associated the increasing naturalism of bird illustration. The finest of the bird books occur somewhat later than the finest of the flower books, and are mainly concerned with the illustration of exotic birds.[37] In its increasing attention to naturalism ornithological illustration followed botanical illustration. In many of his plates (though by no means all) Gould represents birds in their natural habitat. In describing the Chestnut Faced Owl of Tasmania he records how 'it sallies forth from the hollows of large gum trees', and the accompanying illustrations provides a fine description of its habitat (Plate 181).

Elizabeth Gould appreciated the value of naturalistic settings. On one occasion she wrote to her mother: 'I find amusement and employment in drawing some of the plants of the colony, which will help to render the work on the Birds of Australia more interesting.'[38]

Gould, of course, had much in common with his American counterpart, J. J. Audubon (1781–1851), who went even farther than Gould in depicting birds in

283

181. *The Chestnut Faced Owl of Tasmania (Strix Castanops)*, Gould, in John Gould, *Birds of Australia* (1848), vol. 1

natural landscape settings (Plate 182). Invaluable as the contributions of both men were to the science of the day, their lavish publications are of equal value in estimating the nature of its taste and sensibility. 'C'est le plus magnifique monument que l'Art ait encore élevé à la Nature', wrote Cuvier of Audubon's great work.[39] Indeed, just how far the world of taste had been brought towards accepting the empirical methods of the Royal Society may be estimated by John Ruskin's own high regard for the work both of Gould and Audubon. In his third lecture in *The Eagle's Nest* on 'The Relation of Wise Art to Wise Science' Ruskin stressed the general cultural value of the study of ornithology. A few days previously he had visited Gould, and he told his audience how the old man had shown him a bullfinch's nest made from the withered stalks of clematis blossom. The bird, Ruskin said, had produced 'an intricate Gothic boss of extreme grace and quaintness'.[40] The implication clearly was, as Ruskin never ceased to repeat in his works, that only by means of the closest study of nature was it possible to arrive at the truths and the laws of art.

When Charles Darwin arrived in Sydney on the *Beagle* in January 1836 he wrote a letter to his sister in which he expressed the highest admiration for the progress evident on all sides: 'This is really a wonderful Colony; ancient Rome, in her imperial grandeur, would not have been ashamed of such an offspring. When my Grandfather

182. *Arctic Birds*, engraving after J. J. Audubon by Robert Havell, in *Birds of America* (1830–9), iv, pl. 402, no. 81

wrote the lines of "Hope's visit to Sydney Cove" on Mr. Wedgwood's medallion he prophesied most truly.'[41] In so admiring the city's rapid progress Charles Darwin was only voicing a comment made by virtually every European traveller who visited Sydney during the 1830's, but for him there was the added interest of checking in some detail the accuracy of his grandfather's prophecy. Erasmus had written of 'broad streets' and 'stately walls'.[42] Charles reported that the streets were 'regular, broad and clean'..[43] Erasmus had prophesied 'solid roads'. Charles reported that the roads were excellent and made on the Macadam principle. Erasmus had prophesied 'embellished villas crowning the landscape'. Charles reported 'beautiful villas and nice cottages' along the beach. Erasmus had said that 'northern treasures' would 'dance on every tide'. Charles saw a fine house built from the profits made from steam vessels.

The rapid civil progress of Sydney and Hobart during the 1830's gave rise to publications which continued the tradition of colonial urban topography inaugurated locally by John Eyre and George Evans. In 1833 Charles Atkinson, an architect who made a practice of augmenting his income by sketching the homes of more—respectable colonists, published his lithographic *Views Through Hobart Town*—the artist making some concession to contemporary taste by figuring himself upon the frontispiece standing before a gothic ruin. In 1836 J. G. Austin, who had arrived in Australia in 1800 and was an engraver to the Bank of New South Wales, published *A Series of Lithographic Drawings of Sydney and its Environs*. Twenty-four plates were originally planned to be issued in six parts, each containing four drawings. Only twelve views, however, all of Sydney, were published. Two years later Maclehose's *Picture of Sydney* appeared containing 'forty-three engravings of the public buildings and picturesque land and water views in and near Sydney'. A second edition appeared in 1839. In 1842 John Skinner Prout began publishing his *Sydney Illustrated* in parts, each part containing two plates. Fourteen plates were issued, the last two being panoramas of Sydney. When Prout visited Tasmania in 1844 he began publishing another series of plates entitled *Tasmania Illustrated* in a similar manner. Four years later Joseph Fowles (active 1845–78) began publishing his *Sydney in 1848*, which was originally issued in twenty fortnightly parts, each part containing two copper-plate engravings and an accompanying text.

 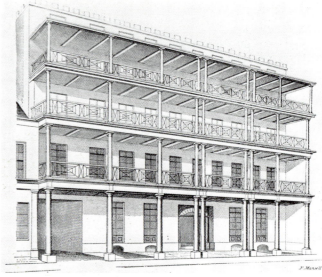

183. *Interior of the Royal Victoria Theatre, Sydney*, engraved after Fowles by F. Mansell, in Joseph Fowles, *Sydney in 1848*, f.p. 32

184. *The Royal Hotel, Sydney*, engraved after Fowles by F. Mansell, in Joseph Fowles, *Sydney in 1848*, f.p. 50

Fowles's object was to 'correct erroneous and discreditable notions current in England' concerning the city of Sydney.

We shall endeavour to represent Sydney as it really is—to exhibit its spacious Gas-lit Streets, crowded by an active and thriving population—its Public Edifices, and its sumptuous shops, which boldly claim a comparison with those of London itself: and to shew that the Colonists have not been inattentive to matters of higher import, we shall display to our Readers the beautiful and commodius Buildings raised by piety and industry for the use of Religion.[44] [Plates 183, 184]

Two years later Conrad Martens published his *Sketches in the Environs of Sydney*, a series of twenty lithographs issued in five parts.

All these publishing ventures, so similar in their intentions, usually combined items of a purely topographical interest, such as public buildings, with items of picturesque interest, and were inspired by similar material being published in Britain by such artists as Turner and the Daniells. In Australia, during the economic depression of the 1840's, artists like J. S. Prout, Fowles, and Martens, found that, despite such difficulties as procuring satisfactory lithographic paper, their ventures into graphic illustration helped to tide them over difficult times.

The appearance of these publications is one of the earliest manifestations of local support for the arts and of the emergence, at a humble level, of taste as a factor in colonial culture. In the preface to his *Picture of Sydney*, Maclehose had proudly asserted that in the colony 'the taste, the pursuits, the comforts, and even elegancies of English society are valued and enjoyed to a far more substantial extent than in many of the large towns of Britain itself'.[45] Pretentious as the claim was, Maclehose was at least accurate in announcing that the cultivation of taste had become a factor in fashionable colonial society; taste, that is in the sense of certain standards of value held by select groups in the community distinguished from the commonalty by virtue either of their official status, their education, or their wealth.

During the period with which we are concerned the pursuit both of art and of science had much in common, as we have seen, in the Pacific. It is not surprising therefore to find that it is among the educated classes who cultivated scientific interests in the Australian colonies, such as the Franklins in Tasmania and the Macleays in New South Wales, that the earliest patrons of the arts are also to be found. The Franklins, for instance, materially assisted the Tasmanian portrait-painter, Thomas Bock; and, apart from the Macleays, Conrad Marten's earliest

286

27. John Glover, *Glover's House and Garden, Mills Plains, Tasmania*, canvas, 30 × 45⅛ in. (*c.* 1834). Art Galley of South Australia

28. John Glover, *Australian Landscape with Cattle*, canvas, 30 × 45 in. (*c.* 1835). Nan Kivell Collection 803, National Library of Australia, Canberra

29. Charles Heaphy, *Mount Egmont from the Southward*, watercolour, 15¼ × 24¼ in. (1839). The Alexander Turnbull Library, Wellington

30. John Skinner Prout, *Valley of Ferns, Hobart*, watercolour (*c.* 1844). Art Gallery of New South Wales, Sydney

patrons in New South Wales included such people as Captain P. P. King, Sir John Jamison, and Governor FitzRoy, brother of Martens's commander on the *Beagle*.

This is not to say that even among such circles whose interests were centred upon science the function of the colonial artist was identified with scientific recording and topographical accuracy. With the rise of a colonial patronage the basic situation of the European artist in the Pacific began to change. So soon as the visual arts became significant as a mode of taste in the colonies it became possible for artists to distinguish, both in their own work and in their writings, between the functions of documentary and topographical art on the one hand, and those aspects of art which sought to express more complex forms of experience, on the other. Whereas it had been the basic function of the artist working in the Pacific since the days of Cook to provide Europeans with true accounts of life and nature in the Pacific, it now became increasingly the professed function of the colonial artist to elevate colonial taste.

The article, already referred to, which appeared in the *Sydney Gazette* on 28 July 1829 will serve to clarify the distinction. The correspondent had noted the great interest shown by the Sydney public when Augustus Earle exhibited his own collection of paintings, and on 30 July asked that 'a miniature gallery ... be got up for a period of the season, by the spontaneous contributions of opulent proprietors, possessed of pictures or engravings of value, which they may be disposed to place for a time in some public depository for general and public inspection. It would be an interesting ... enjoyment to the man of taste, as well as to him possessed of its elements, but devoid of its details'. The same correspondent, however, was also keen to see a permanent exhibition of colonial scenery opened up in London:

> We wish the Government of the Mother Country would do what Mr. Earle is doing on his own account, encourage artists of merit to take connected and detached views of Colonial scenery, and particularly towns and villages, that the British public might be able to form some definite conception of the local circumstances connected with them, when they become subjects of discussion. A Gallery in London with a varied collection of such views, from East, West and South, would constitute a pleasing sought of instruction, and fill up a vacuum in our public institutions much to be deplored and severely felt.[46]

Thus, whereas a local art gallery in Sydney is justified upon the grounds that it will cater for and promote taste in the community, a gallery of colonial paintings in London is justified as a means of conveying new and accurate information.

With the rise of local patrons a period of close analysis and description of the local scene begins to be supplanted gradually by a period of interpretation. In the earlier phase, exotic scenery had been drawn for Europeans resident in Europe, after 1835 an increasing number of landscapes are painted by artists in Australia for people, mainly of British stock settled, most of them, permanently in the colonies.

Drawing and painting as a tasteful occupation is accompanied by the appearance in the colonies of the amateur artist. The *Sydney Gazette* correspondent already referred to, informs us that Governor Darling's family, 'without the least parade, did much to foster and fan the flame of pure taste'. Mrs Darling herself drew 'with great beauty and effect', and was 'deeply skilled in the minutiae of architectural embellishment'. Colonel Dumaresq sketched 'with great beauty in black lead and Indian ink', while Captain Dumaresq contented himself with being 'well versed in the drawing of working models'.[47]

The cultivation of amateur painting was somewhat more widespread in fashionable circles in Tasmania during the 1830's and 1840's than it was in Sydney.

There had been an amateur group in Hobart from the time of the arrival of the Glovers. During the 1840s the group included: G. W. T. B. Boyes, the Colonial Auditor. Bishop F. R. Nixon (1803–79) and Mrs. Nixon; Lieut. F. G. Simpkinson, Lady Franklin's nephew; George Frankland, Surveyor-General of Tasmania (1828–38), and his successor James Erskine Calder; Samuel Prout Hill, journalist, lecturer, and poet, Louisa Ann Meredith,[48] and Thomas E. Chapman.

An outstanding and yet, in many ways, a representative member of this group was George Thomas William Blamey Boyes (1787–1853) who had served like Sir Thomas Mitchell in the Peninsular War and was like him an enthusiast for the romantic and the picturesque. A keen amateur painter, the friend and confidant of every Governor of Tasmania from Arthur to Eardley-Wilmot, and an enthusiastic collector of paintings, Boyes cultivated the arts not as a means towards a better understanding of an unfamiliar part of the world but as a manifestation of taste, culture, and sensibility. His well-written diary together with its family record, its long descriptions of picturesque walks, recipes for water-colour painting, and personal reading lists, also contains a great deal of intelligent satirical comment on contemporary Hobart society. He saw himself, not altogether without reason, as a protagonist of European culture amid colonial barbarism. 'The people of this colony', he wrote on one occasion, 'resemble the Americans in their presumption, arrogance, ignorance, and conceit.'[49] Captain Ross, on his way to the Antarctic, had noted, like many other visitors, during his stay in Hobart, the striking contrast between the educated colonial residents and their Australian-born children And Boyes wrote, 'These Colonial chaps, "Gumsuckers", as they are not inappropriately called—are my aversion—without education or manners, having no ideas beyond a partial and faint glimmer of something supplied by another.'[50] For Boyes the solution to the prevailing barbarism lay in the arts. On another occasion, in a more conciliatory vein, he wrote in his diary, concerning the problem of educating the Tasmanian youth:

> The Arts. We must attract their [young people's] notice and teach them to respect the arts by shewing that wealth and honour attend upon eminence in the practice of them and qualified the professors to be the companions of Princes who were even proud of the association and eager to rank themselves amongst the number of patrons.[51]

The establishment of Mechanics' Institutes in Hobart (1826) and Sydney (1833) provided rallying-points for those like Boyes desirous of raising standards of public taste.[52] When John Skinner Prout arrived in Sydney in 1840 he gave a successful series of lectures on landscape painting, and another series in Hobart in 1843. Prout's appearance in Tasmania stimulated amateur painting, in a fashion neatly described by Mrs. Meredith: '... a landscape sketching and water-colour fever raged with extraordinary vehemence. . . . The art that Mr. Prout taught and practised so well at once became the fashion.'[53] From this enthusiasm came the first exhibition of paintings organized in Tasmania, which was opened in the Legislative Council in January 1845. It consisted partly of loan works and partly of the work of local artists. The second exhibition was held in a gallery erected by Robin Vaughan Hood[54] in May 1846.

During the 1840's exhibitions were held in other colonies. An art exhibition was organized in Adelaide by the artist S. T. Gill in February 1847. In the same year a Society for the Promotion of Arts was established in Sydney, its first exhibition being held in the Australian Library, a second in 1849. In January 1848 the Launceston Mechanics' Institute held an exhibition in the Cornwall Assembly Rooms:

Though there was a most creditable collection of pictures and other works of art, the financial result was a deficit of 5s 9d. Disappointed, the Board was not disheartened, feeling assured that public taste would be awakened and stimulated by the Exhibition, and that the objects of the Institute would be to that extent promoted.[55]

Paralleling this new concern for the visual arts was a growing interest in horticulture and landscape gardening. Australia's early botanic gardens had been established to hold Australian plants awaiting shipment to England and to acclimatize plants introduced from abroad for general cultivation in Australia. They were the direct result of Sir Joseph Banks's interest in New South Wales.[56] By the 1830's the introduction of European plants and extensive clearing for settlement had wrought a considerable modification upon the Australian scene in areas close to the towns. The change was most noticeable in Tasmania in the vicinity of Hobart. In 1831 John Glover, as we have seen, had painted his Hobart town house in order to show his countrymen how well their own cottage plants could thrive at the other end of the earth (Colour Plate 27). And Mrs. Meredith upon arrival in Hobart noted that:

> ... the little gardens before and between many houses in the middle of the town, with their great bushes of geraniums in bloom, were all full of sweet English spring flowers, looking happy and healthy, like the stout rosy children that everywhere reminded me of HOME.[57]

And even farther afield the scenery reminded her of England:

> The scenery around Newtown is the most beautiful I have seen on this side of the world—very much resembling that of the Cumberland Lakes: the broad and winding estuary of the Derwent flows between lofty and picturesque hills and mountains.... But the most English, and therefore the most beautiful things I saw here, were the hawthorn hedges.... It seemed like being on the right side of the earth again.[58]

The modifications wrought upon the Tasmanian landscape noted by Mrs. Meredith and many of her contemporaries represent the successful application of English agricultural and horticultural methods to the Tasmanian soil and climate. But by the 1830's gardening was not only a useful practical pursuit, it had become an expression of colonial taste. Although Daniel Bunce (1813–72) in his *Manual of Practical Gardening adapted to the Climate of Van Diemen's Land* provides essential information on the kitchen and fruit garden, it is to be noted that in his preface he champions the cause of gardening as a fashionable pursuit: 'If we follow the steps set us in the Mother Country, we shall not fail in an especial degree to cultivate a taste for gardening among the rising generation. From the lowest to the highest at this time in England, it is the favorite and fashionable pursuit.'[59]

In New South Wales, horticulture as a fashionable pursuit was greatly advanced by William Macarthur and Alexander Macleay, both of whom owned extensive gardens. 'It is to these two gentlemen', wrote Thomas Shepherd, 'that the settlers in this colony as well as myself are principally indebted for the numerous sorts and varieties of fruit' introduced into the Colony.

Shepherd had arrived in Sydney from New Zealand in February 1826. He had learnt the principles of horticulture from his father, head gardener to Lord Lindesay, upon whose estate he had studied landscape gardening. Shortly after his arrival Shepherd was granted some land by Governor Darling near the city of Sydney on the understanding that he would establish a public nursery and fruit garden upon it. This he did successfully. In 1835 the Sydney Mechanics' School of Arts invited him to give a series of four lectures on horticulture. The lectures were, like Bunce's *Manual*, primarily concerned with the practical problems of horticulture and aroused wide interest. At the conclusion of the series, Shepherd promised to deliver a series of lectures on landscape gardening during the following winter. But he died on 31 August 1835 having only delivered the first of the series. The full series of lectures, however, which he had prepared in advance were published in 1836. They were dedicated to Alexander Macleay, one of Shepherd's close friends, 'by whom was imported for his nursery, and eventually for the use of the Colonists at large, every rare and costly Botanical production ... from all quarters of the world'.[60]

In his opening lecture Shepherd complained that, apart from some romantically situated country residences recently embellished, the art of landscape gardening had been totally neglected in New South Wales. By developing landscape gardening in Australia it would be possible to interest 'gentlemen of taste and fortune who resided in other countries' to migrate and to purchase improved estates at considerably advanced prices. This would in time create a commerce in the purchase and sale of estates.

Shepherd was perhaps the first to advocate the retention, for aesthetic reasons, of indigenous trees upon large estates. He directed the attention of landowners to 'a better mode of laying out their grounds, than has generally prevailed' asserting that they should 'spare their indigenous trees to embellish and give a park-like appearance to their Domains'.[61] The very nature of the country lent itself admirably to such improvements:

> ... in place of cutting down our splendid forests right forward without distinction, we have only to thin out, and tastefully arrange and dispose them, to produce the most pleasing effects. The country could by this means, at a very small cost, and with less labour than is required by the indiscriminate destruction of our native trees, present an exterior to the eye of the stranger and the resident in the Colony, such as no other country in the world I believe could furnish. Besides the pastoral nature of this country would favour such embellishments, as not an acre of ground would be lost—sheep might feed on our lawns and parks, adding the pleasure of seeing living objects enjoy the benefits of improved scenery.[62]

Furthermore the improvements could be made at considerably less expense than similar improvements in England:

> Extensive parks may ... be made in the first style of magnificence here, at a comparatively trifling expense, when contrasted with the large sums of money which have been expended on similar objects in Britain. New South Wales is a pastoral, more than an agricultural country, and therefore, it is much more adapted for park scenery than Britain, as no loss can possibly be sustained by the establishment of extensive parks.[63]

Indigenous trees should not be indiscriminately cut out of estates but thinned 'to form intricacies' and grouped in 'every wild irregular manner'. The sombre and monotonous appearance of the eucalypt could be effaced by plantations of trees differing in habit and growth. Shepherd proceeded to give details as to the best and most economical methods of clearing land. A well-proportioned building should be the principal object in the landscape, and the view of its façades should be entirely unhindered. (Plate 185)

185. L. Haghe, *Penshanger (Panshanger), the seat of Joseph Archer, Esq., County of Cornwall, Van Diemen's Land,* coloured lithograph $8\frac{3}{8} \times 12\frac{1}{2}$ in. Nan Kivell Collection 468, National Library of Australia

The interest in gardening led to the formation of horticultural societies. The Australian Floral and Horticultural Society came into existence in Sydney in 1836, the year Shepherd's *Lectures on Landscape Gardening* was published. Three years later a Horticultural Society was established in Hobart. During the 1840's similar societies were established in Victoria and South Australia.

The growing popularity of botany, horticulture, and landscape gardening, together with the enjoyment of picturesque scenery and the practice of landscape-painting in water-colours among amateurs, are so many allied aspects of the emergence of taste in colonial society. The interplay of such interests as these in the expression of taste is to be found not only in the writings and enthusiasms of people like G. W. T. B. Boyes and Mrs. Louisa Anne Meredith but in the lectures delivered at the Sydney, and the Hobart, Mechanics' Institutes.

The series of lectures delivered at the Hobart Mechanics' Institute for the first part of the session of 1849 was largely devoted to a consideration of the role of the arts, science, and taste in civilized society. They provide an insight into the aesthetic interests of educated members of Tasmanian society at the time. The lectures included 'The Perception of the Beautiful as an Element in Civilization' by the Rev. John Lillie, 'The Principles of Taste', by Samuel Prout Hill, 'The *School of Athens* as it Assimilates with the Mechanics' Institution' by Benjamin Duterreau, 'Expression as Applied to the Fine Arts' by Dr. Bedford, and 'The Philosophy of Botany' by J. E. Bicheno. In these lectures the arts, the sciences, and taste are considered as civilizing processes which improve mankind, and the Mechanics' Institutions are agencies whereby such improvements may be effected.[64] The lecture of the Colonial Secretary, J. E. Bicheno, may be taken as an example. Bicheno informed his audience that 'the civilization of nations is betokened by their love of gardens' for gardening 'is but another form of Nature improved by art'.[65] Gardens were the material evidence of man's improvement and his love of nature. The awareness of nature's beauty constituted taste, and taste was a manifestation of man's civilized progress. 'The man who has acquired an eye and a taste for the beautiful has so far raised himself as an individual of his species—he has made a step upwards, and placed himself at a higher point in the scale of being.'[66] But men can also exercise their taste by the enjoyment of natural beauties quite untouched by the hand of man:

Who can look upon that magnificent mountain [alluding to Mount Wellington], which towers above our city, without feeling a pleasing gratitude for the gift of being rendered capable of perceiving the intellectual and glorious delights of the sublime and beautiful? To view it with its varying cloak of mist or shroud of snow, and when clear and distinct in feature beneath the bright blue sky,—or to gaze on the vale of Derwent with its mirror-like winding stream ... always raises in my mind the most exciting feelings of delight.[67]

Bicheno's delight in the changing appearances of Mount Wellington, like Shepherd's desire to preserve wherever possible 'our splendid forests', is indicative of a changing attitude to Australian nature. Whereas in Phillip's time human progress was symbolized by the imposition of law and order upon the untamed wilderness, in Bicheno's time human progress comes to be spoken of as a capacity to enjoy the unspoiled beauties of Australia in their sublime aspects. Certainly we have here no more than the transition from an Augustan to a Romantic attitude towards nature—in an Australian context. But the importance lies elsewhere; it lies in the fact that educated colonists were now beginning to apply traditional aesthetic categories to Australian nature whereas in earlier decades, apart from an occasional painter like Thomas Watling or a *litterateur* like Barron Field, such an approach was exceptional. During these earlier decades the Australian scene had tended to arouse curiosity because of its novelty, or melancholy because of its monotony. But during the 1830's and 1840's an increasing number of settlers began to derive considerable aesthetic satisfaction from their surroundings. It is not surprising that Tasmania, with its mountainous scenery (which recalled for so many the Lake District of England), and its soil and climate so suitable for the cultivation of the fruit, flowers, and hedgerows of England, was the first area in which a circle of British colonists accommodated themselves aesthetically to their new surroundings. Curiously enough one of the writers who assisted in this process was Humboldt who, as we have seen, encouraged many Europeans to take an aesthetic interest in landscapes which had previously appealed only as exotic novelties. 'If there is one man I would set up as an ideal', declared Bicheno in his lecture, 'Humboldt would be the man.... He possessed the power of combining general principles with the capacity of minute analysis.'[68] And that, after all, was precisely what the colonial *cognoscenti* of Hobart Town were attempting to do in the 1830's and 1840's—apply general aesthetic principles to a landscape being scrutinized at the same time by botanists, zoologists, geologists, and meteorologists.

Humboldt's influence in assisting colonials to accommodate themselves aesthetically to the Australian landscape is also revealed in James Martin's essay on the 'Sublime in Nature' which he published at the age of eighteen in his *Australian Sketch Book*, a series of essays modelled on the style of Washington Irving. It appeared in 1838, eleven years before Bicheno delivered his lecture. Martin was concerned with the question whether all men are capable of apprehending the sublime:

> All men's feelings are not susceptible of those exquisitely fine impressions which actuate and thrill the truly sensitive individual.... But I feel convinced there is a height of grandeur an extent of sublimity which must enrapture anyone, how indifferent soever may be his feelings, in wonder and astonishment.... There are sights which it is impossible for human eyes to behold and remain unmoved. An untutored Indian could scarcely pass the snowy tops of Chimborazo or Cotopaxi, in the Andes, or stand on the summit of the White Cliff, in the Himalaya Mountains, without feeling an indescribable something within his breast.[69]

Martin, like Wentworth, was Australian born. He does not refer to European examples to illustrate the sublime in nature, but to his acquaintance, direct or indirect, with the writings of Humboldt. His *Australian Sketch Book*, one of the first books of essays published in Australia, bears witness to a new reflective attitude to Australian nature.

This reflective attitude was promoted by the growing popularity of picturesque travel. During the early 1840's a number of artists undertook picturesque excursions in New South Wales, Tasmania, and South Australia. Apart from Conrad Martens, the most important artist of the time, the three most notable were Louisa Anne Meredith, John Skinner Prout, and George French Angas.

Before considering their work and travels it is to be noted that picturesque travel in Australia differed from picturesque travel in Europe in two cardinal respects. First, Australia possessed neither ancient monuments nor places hallowed by historical associations. In consequence the picturesque traveller in Australia was precluded from drawing upon one of the great sources of romantic sentiment. And, because the material evidence of the past did not trench everywhere upon immediate experience, picturesque travellers concerned themselves to a greater extent with the visual rather than the associational elements of the picturesque sensibility. Secondly, it is more difficult to distinguish the interests of the scientific traveller from the interests of the picturesque traveller in Australia. The distinction is often more one of degree than kind. A professional scientist, like Thomas Henry Huxley, often proves to be a keen amateur artist; a professional artist, like George French Angas, often proves to be a keen amateur scientist.

Scientific and picturesque interests were allied aspects of the taste of Louisa Ann Meredith (1812–95). A prolific writer, her earliest books bear witness to the continued popularity of botany as a fashionable interest and tasteful diversion. The widespread popular interest in botany had created a new literary genre, the sentimental flower book. It originated in France in the works of the botanical illustrations of Charles Malo and Pancrace Bessa (1772–1835). The translation of Charlotte de Latour's *Le Langage des fleurs* (1833) illustrated by Bessa gave rise to many English imitations. Among the best known are those written and illustrated by Louisa Ann Twamley before her marriage to Charles Meredith.[70] Her first publication, *Poems* (1835), reveals both her sentimental interest in flowers and her love of picturesque travel. The plates illustrating the book, etched by the author herself, included views of Tintern Abbey and Kenilworth Castle together with pictures of flowers. The poems referred both to the picturesque scenes and the flowers. She dedicated her second book, *Romance of Nature or the Flower Seasons Illustrated* (1836), to Wordsworth, and wrote in the preface, 'I love Flowers as forming one of the sweetest links in the God-written Poetry of Nature'. The book proved popular and ran through three editions in as many years. There followed *Flora's Gems* (c. 1839) and *Our Wild Flowers* (1839), a children's book. In the same year she published a book of picturesque travel *An Autumn Ramble on the Wye*, with twenty engravings from drawings by Copley Fielding, David Cox, and other artists. It is a youthful exercise in romantic sentiment containing long descriptions of her visits to Chepstow and Raglan castles, Tintern Abbey, and similar places of historic interest. For her, far more than for such eighteenth-century travellers in search of the picturesque as William Gilpin, the historical associations of the places she visited were of great significance. She is clearly speaking of herself when she writes:

> To persons of refined taste and retentive memory, few enjoyments are greater or more permanent than the sight of grand and beautiful scenery. While present, it creates a feeling of rapturous delight, almost of inspiration. The hills seem to heave with a deeply murmured eloquence, and we understand their tales of times gone by;

the rivers roll along their volumed and rapid waters, and we hear in the mighty music, the voices of 'men of olden days,' who dwelt, fought, or died within its sound. We gaze on the summer heaven, and the eyes of the young and beautiful, whom Poets sung, and Princes loved, seem to look on us, and we live in a Fairyland of thought and fancy.[71]

It is clear from such a passage that for Mrs. Meredith the very conception of beautiful scenery is inextricably interwoven with an enjoyment of the historical past. It is of interest, therefore, to examine her reactions to Australian scenery with its lack of historical associations. In the year her *Autumn Ramble* was published she married her cousin, an Australian squatter, and migrated to New South Wales. There she maintained her practice of keeping a journal from which she published the first of the many books dealing with her Australian experiences, *Notes and Sketches of New South Wales during a Residence in that Colony from 1839 to 1844*. Compared with her *Autumn Ramble*, with its romantic digressions and fulsome descriptions of feudal architecture, the book is written in a more practical vein with an eye to the interests of prospective migrants: 'I believed that a few simple sketches from nature, however devoid of scientific lore, would be a welcome addition to the present small fund of information on common every-day topics relating to these antipodean climes; and of such belief, this little work is the result.'[72] Nevertheless, her approach was still essentially that of the picturesque traveller, and it is of particular interest to compare her romantic interpretation of a view in the Wye Valley with a view in the Blue Mountains. Whereas for earlier picturesque travellers, like Barron Field, it was the visual novelty of the Blue Mountains which made them unpicturesque, for Mrs. Meredith it is the lack of historical associations. In her *Autumn Ramble* she had described in some detail the view of the Wye Valley from Windcliff:

It seems as if the genius of the Wye and its fair banks, had here set up his giant-throne, whence he might look abroad over his vassal-hills, and hold communion with the mountain kings of Cambria.... In many parts of Wales I have gained views more extensive, and of more wild grandeur—the grandeur of solitude and desolation:—but I doubt if there be one of more rich and varied beauty than this, 'all bonny England through'. The two fine rivers, seen for some distance inland, and also their junction, and final mingling with the ocean:—the pervading character of luxuriant richness given by the abundant woods around:—the mountains, hills, and crags, from the distant Welsh alps, to the fantastic rocks in the foreground of the picture:—and not less the cultivated and cheerful appearance of green pastures and waving cornfields in the valleys below; all combine to render their prospect surpassingly beautiful.[73]

A year later Mrs. Meredith was making her way over the Blue Mountains, not without considerable discomfort, in a bullock dray; and viewing with considerable distaste a landscape ravaged by bushfires and two years of severe drought.

We continued our journey through a wild and barren country, utterly destitute of herbage; the inhospitable Blue Mountains were before, behind, and on either side of us, rising in grand and dreary monotony of form and colour. Forests of tall gum trees covered them from base to peak, but instead of a beauty in the landscape, these were a deformity.... The steepest ravines had not the semblance of water in their dry dreary depths, and but for the fearful quagmires and deep holes in the road (which made the utmost care in driving requisite to avoid an upset over the precipice), one would not have thought that rain or dew ever visited this desert region.[74]

Despite all this the peculiar formation of the mountains at times stimulated Mrs. Meredith's romantic fancy:

> Our road now lay over hilly ground again, sometimes skirted by live trees and a slight semblance of herbage, and often approaching in wild sterile grandeur the scenery we had before traversed. A singular range of perpendicular cliffs form a striking feature in the landscape at a place called 'Hassan's Walls'. These walls or cliffs rise, I should think, to a height of about 300 feet perpendicularly above the road, and their summits, broken and fissured in various fantastic forms, exactly resemble a ruined castle crowning the brow of the sheer precipice, with here and there a stunted tree or graceful shrub growing from crevices in the dark rock. Had I been travelling in an old country I should at once have decided that these were truly the ruins of some mighty mountain-fortress of former days; loop-holes, arches, battlements, and buttresses were, as it seemed, so clearly remaining, and extending far along the airy heights of these genii-haunted crags, for such I fancied them. . . . I thought of the mysterious castle of St. John, with its wizard transformations, and of how much romance would attach to these fantastic crags in a romantic or legendary country; but the existence of poetry or imagination in New South Wales is what none who know and have felt the leaden influence of its ledger and day-book kind of atmosphere would believe it guilty of suffering.[75]

Mrs. Meredith was only one of a number of travellers who, influenced by the contemporary interest in Gothic architecture, allowed her fancy to turn rocks into castles and battlements. Even Sir Thomas Mitchell, well trained both as a surveyor and geologist, mistook (or claimed he mistook) a rocky outcrop for a castle keep. Nor was the ledger and day-book atmosphere of New South Wales so far removed from current medieval sentiment as Mrs. Meredith imagined. While she was writing her book, neo-gothic turrets were rising above the eucalypts along the foreshores of Sydney harbour, and new town mansions were being erected for merchants and pastoralists grown wealthy on Pacific trade or an annually increasing wool clip. As early as 1821 Francis Howard Greenway had completed a commodious new Government stables for Lachlan Macquarie in a castellated style which contained many of the features his master, John Nash, had incorporated into *Luscombe* (1800) (Colour Plate 31). In 1837, the new Government House was begun in the Gothic manner of Edward Blore. Thenceforth the neo-gothic became one of the most popular styles for large town houses. As might have been expected, Sir Thomas Mitchell built his own house *Carthona* in the neo-gothic style (*c.* 1845).[76]

Gothic revival arthitecture was one of the forms in which romantic taste expressed itself in the colonies (Plate 186). But the picturesque traveller with nothing of historical interest to engage his attention was drawn increasingly, like the travellers before him, towards a study of the natural productions of Australia and the manners and occupations of the colonists. In Australia Mrs. Meredith became increasingly absorbed in a study of the flora and fauna of Australia, particularly after she settled in Tasmania in 1840. Her interests, for all that, are never quite those of the professional botanist or zoologist. Things are described in a subjective context of personal or aesthetic relationships, as when she mentions, to take an example, the grass tree (*Xanthorrhoea arborea*): 'Groups of this very singular plant often give a picturesque and somewhat Oriental aspect to an otherwise uninteresting landscape.'[77]

186. J. Skinner Prout, *The Cathedral Church of St. Mary, Sydney, New South Wales*, lithograph, 15 × 10¼ in. (1842). Mitchell Library, State Library of New South Wales

The second picturesque traveller of note to visit Australia was John Skinner Prout (1806–76), a nephew of Samuel Prout (1783–1851), whose renderings of medieval architecture John Ruskin so much admired. John Skinner Prout was largely self-trained as an artist. Before coming to Australia he had travelled about a good deal in the west of England making topographical views of ancient monuments, and had published *The Antiquities of Chester* and *Castles and Abbeys of Monmouthshire* (1838). In the production of the latter work he had occasion, like Mrs. Meredith, to visit the Wye Valley. He appears to have been living in rather straitened circumstances in 1840, and decided to migrate with his family to New South Wales.

Although Prout was a humble practitioner of topography in England, in the Colonies he became a prophet of taste in the visual arts. Both in Sydney and Hobart, as has been shown, he set out to develop an interest in painting as an art form. In consequence, he is the first itinerant painter in the colonies whose work ceases to be dominated by the requirements of topographical accuracy. Many of his landscapes, painted with breadth and freedom, seek only to capture an effect of light and colour. It is true, as indicated earlier, that the precarious life of the travelling artist and the economic difficulties of the 1840's made it necessary for him to publish lithographic views in order to carry on. The great majority of Prout's paintings, however, are more concerned with picturesque effects than with topographical accuracy. His drawings consist of a few lines swiftly stated to indicate the basic structure of a scene. Upon these he applied colour washes directly, indicating rocks, foliage, and other details with broadly hatched brushwork, and body-colour for the lights. Like such contempo-

187. J. Skinner Prout, *Grass Trees, Richmond Road, Van Diemen's Land*, watercolour, 10 × 7 in. (1844). Nan Kivell Collection 571, National Library of Australia, Canberra

raries as Copley Fielding he delighted in rural subjects, effects of mist and mountain, free renderings of sea and shore. It is significant that as a champion of taste in the Colonies he accepted Australian scenery as normal material to be interpreted by the artist—though the interest in exotic curiosities lingers.

There is evidence that Prout's free manner of sketching was at first received with disfavour. Boyes described a drawing Prout had made for him as a 'poor washy thing not worth a frame'.[78] On another occasion after examining two paintings Prout had made for Francis Simpkinson he criticized them as 'flimsy gaudy things'.[79] Boyes, for all that, copied Prout's paintings[80] and carefully noted the range of colours he used.[81] Indeed Prout's manner affected the work of Hobart's amateur circle of landscape-painters quite profoundly. Francis Simpkinson's style is modelled closely on Prout's, and the work of Bishop F. R. Nixon, Mrs. Nixon and that of Boyes himself reveals the influence of Prout's teaching. In New South Wales although Conrad Martens was critical of Prout's work, possibly due to professional jealousy, it seems likely that Prout's work helped Martens towards the cultivation of a broader and freer style.

Prout remained in Australia for eight years, making many excursions in search of picturesque material in New South Wales (1840–4) and Tasmania (1844–8), including a trip to the Port Phillip District in 1846. A detailed itinerary could be gained from his numerous signed and dated paintings. He has left a detailed account of one of these journeys. In an account written for an English weekly periodical years later[82] Skinner Prout tells how he visited every point of interest in the environs of Hobart during the two years following his arrival there, but these were merely half-holiday excursions which did not fully satisfy his artistic longings. 'I pined to be out and away upon a real sketching tour', he wrote, 'to turn my back upon civilization and town life . . . for the companionship of the woods, the mountains and the fields.'[83] Lake St. Clair in the centre of the island had been discovered only five years before by George Frankland (1797–1838), the Surveyor-General who had made sketches of it. Prout saw these sketches. 'They so impressed me, revealing as they did glimpses of scenery full of natural grandeur, of unchecked wildness, and savage majesty, that from the moment my eye fell on them I determined the direction of my tour in search of the picturesque.' Prout's account of his excursion is a combination of picturesque description and colonial adventure, and his sketches included not only such things as lake scenes, so normal to the picturesque repertoire, but also drawings of exotics such as fern valleys (Colour Plate 30) and grass-trees, which, as Mrs. Meredith had said, gave an oriental air to the scene (Plate 187).

In Australia, then, Prout had been a strong champion of the taste for the picturesque and of the right of the artist freely to interpret rather than merely to imitate the scene before him. On his return to England, however, Prout realized that he could put his drawings to a profitable and useful purpose by using them to convey information to interested persons in Britain, especially prospective migrants. Accordingly he used them as the basis for a series of dioramic views of Australia. These were exhibited in the theatre of the Western Literary and Scientific Institution, Leicester Square, in 1850. The scenes chosen were of a nature likely to be of interest to anyone contemplating migration and included: *A Bivouac of Emigrants in the Blue Mountains*, *A Clearing in a Forest with an Emigrant's Residence*, and pictures purporting to portray the habits both of the aborigines and the bushrangers. A printed catalogue was available for those viewing the diorama. It expressed the hope that the views would 'enable the spectator to realise many of those scenes which are most strikingly characteristic of this distant and interesting country'.[84] It also assured him that the views were all made on the spot, so that their fidelity could be relied upon. A broadside announced that the exhibition was accompanied by a lecture on the Australian colonies and by appropriate music.

The third picturesque painter of the period, George French Angas (1822–86), produced work which was even more closely associated with the promotion of migration than Prout's work. Like Prout and Mrs. Meredith, Angas had journeyed in search of the picturesque and published his material before he embarked for Australia. The son of George Fife Angas (1789–1879) he was born at Newcastle-upon Tyne and studied under Waterhouse Hawkins, a natural-history painter. At the age of nineteen he made a trip to the Mediterranean, keeping a journal and making sketches of the towns, the characteristic costumes, and the ancient ruins of Malta and Sicily. On his return he lithographed his sketches and published them with his journal in *A Ramble in Malta and Sicily in the Autumn of 1841*, which was dedicated to Queen Adelaide, who had recently visited Malta.

George Fife Angas was closely concerned with the promotion of the South Australian Company, and it was this intimate connexion with the fortunes of the new colony in South Australia which doubtless caused his son to try his fortunes there painting the yet little-known life and scenery of the region. During 1843 he travelled extensively in the colony, at times accompanying Governor Grey on his journeys into the interior and outlying settlements.

Angas described himself as 'a disinterested observer, who went to the Antipodes actuated by an ardent admiration of the grandeur and loveliness of Nature in her wildest aspect'.[85] The programme which he thus set himself combined pictorial

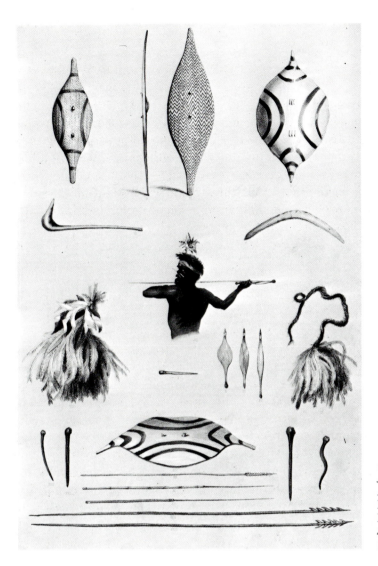

188. George French Angas,
*Native Weapons and
Implements,* (from tribes at
Mount Barker and
Encounter Bay) from his
South Australia Illustrated
(1847), pl. vi

topography with a search for picturesque material. But despite Angas's undoubted interest in the picturesque, both the colonies he visited and the English patronage he sought required him to devote himself to topography to a greater extent than Mrs. Meredith or John Skinner Prout. The colonies of South Australia and those in New Zealand (which he visited later) were much younger than those of New South Wales and Tasmania and possessed no local patronage capable of sustaining an artist economically. Furthermore, they were less well known in England and this placed an emphasis upon the provision of faithful visual records.

Angas announced the details of his artistic programme in South Australia in the preface to his *South Australia Illustrated* (1847). The new colony afforded a unique spectacle of civilized and savage life in conjunction. Angas set out, therefore, to record this spectacle before the advance of civilization swept the primitive life of the tribesman away for ever (Plate 188). He took the same pessimistic view of the future of native races taken by George Catlin, the American artist, who had set himself a programme similar to Angas's a few years before. In the pursuit of his object Angas visited all parts of the colony in order to make himself conversant with the material culture and social organization of the aborigines of South Australia, as yet little known to the world.

Angas proceeded to New Zealand from South Australia returning to England in 1846, via the Cape. He lost no time in arranging for an exhibition of his work in the

Egyptian Hall, Piccadilly. The catalogue explained that it was the 'result of a residence of nearly three years, and a journey of 40,000 miles, in Countries with which the People of England are still but only very imperfectly acquainted'. Visitors were assured that the artist's purpose had been 'to represent the Natives and Scenery of New Zealand and South Australia, with unexaggerated truth and fidelity'.[86]

The exhibition was noticed by the *Art Journal* which gave its approval to the faithful topography employed in providing a visual record of peoples so little known to Europeans. It made no suggestion that the aesthetic value of the drawings should be distinguished from their ethnographical value:

> The subjects amount in number to two hundred and seventy—all elaborated with the utmost care, and landscape sketches of a highly interesting character. In this collection we read a history of the inhabitants—nothing appertaining to them is forgotten—for, besides very numerous drawings representing individuals of all ages, every object—personal, sacred and domestic—is shown; thus at once affording a key to their habits, customs and institutions.[87]

The primary interest of the exhibition was clearly popular and ethnographical. There were, for instance, not only 200 portraits of Maoris, but also paintings of their 'carved buildings, colossal images, canoes, temples, houses, tombs, pahs, fortifications, dances, games, manners, customs, and entire domestic economy, autographs, tattooing, etc.'[88] To increase the interest of the exhibition a young New Zealand chief in native costume was in constant attendance at the exhibition, which was advertised as being under the special patronage of the Queen and Prince Albert. During the same year the exhibition was shown at the Assembly Rooms, Liverpool. George Fife Angas appears to have used the paintings executed by his son when lecturing in the provinces upon the advantages of migration to the new colonies in South Australia and New Zealand.

189. George French Angas, *Waungerri Lake and the Marble Range. Beyond Point Lincoln*, from his *South Australia Illustrated* (1847), pl. xx

In 1847, George French Angas began publishing his *South Australia Illustrated*. At the time John Gould's *Birds of Australia*, published in quarterly parts since 1840, still had one year to run before completion. That Angas had Gould's publication in mind when he projected the publication of his own large views is revealed by a note in a prospectus published in 1847: 'The work will be published in Imperial folio Parts, the size of Mr. Gould's *Birds*.'[89] The publication was to consist of ten parts, each containing five plates, appearing at two-monthly intervals at the price of a guinea to subscribers.

While there is no need to doubt that George French Angas was indeed actuated to travel because of a love of nature 'in her wildest aspect' and may be classified as a picturesque painter, it is quite clear that the purposes which his paintings came to serve were considerably wider than those normally served by picturesque paintings. In addition they became ethnographical documents of considerable value. The landscapes were used to illustrate the nature of the country awaiting settlement in the new colonies and so to promote migration, as the letterpress of so many of his illustrations indicate. That which describes *Waungerri Lake* (Plate 189) is typical; 'In a few years, no doubt, all this district will be thickly settled and cultivated; the margin of Waungerri Lake presents an enticing spot for a settler's homestead; and should I ever again visit this locality, the sights and sounds of civilisation and busy industry, will no doubt have taken the place of the kangaroo feeding silently.'

Angas, trained under a natural-history painter himself, included many drawings, in his exhibitions and books, of value to the natural historian and ethnologist. Indeed Angas became a proficient amateur natural scientist himself, a member of the Linnean and Zoological societies, and secretary of the Australian Museum, Sydney, from 1853 to 1860. He amassed a fine collection of shells and contributed several articles on conchology to the *Proceedings of the Zoological Society*.[90] During the period under discussion little real distinction can be drawn between the intentions of a scientific illustrator, like Gould, who dedicated himself to the production of fine bird books, and a picturesque artist like Angas, who sought to advance science by means of the information contained in his paintings.

The varying influences of science and taste upon the pursuit of art in the Pacific during the second quarter of the nineteenth century is particularly well exemplified by the work of Conrad Martens (1801–78). He was the son of J. C. H. Martens, a German who came to England as Austrian consul and later settled there as a merchant. Conrad was born at Crutched Friars, near the Tower, and had two brothers who also became artists.[91] After the death of his father in 1816 he studied landscape-painting under Copley Fielding (1789–1855). Later, while residing with his mother at Exeter, he made many sketching excursions along the Devon coast and neighbouring valleys in search of picturesque material.

Either late in 1832 or early in 1833 Captain Blackwood of the *Hyacinth* offered to take Martens on a three-year cruise to India, which he accepted.[92] While the *Hyacinth* was at Rio de Janiero, Martens heard that Captain FitzRoy of the *Beagle* desired to engage an artist; Augustus Earle, who had joined the expedition as its painter, being about to leave because of ill-health. Martens, therefore, left the *Hyacinth* and made for Montevideo where he joined the *Beagle*. His arrival was noted by the ship's naturalist, Charles Darwin, in a letter to his sister: 'poor Earle has never been well since leaving England, and now his health is so entirely broken up that he leaves us;—a Mr. Martens, a pupil of C. Fielding and excellent landscape painter, has joined us, and like all birds of that class, full up to the mouth with enthusiasm'.[93]

Although Copley Fielding was probably the most fashionable teacher of watercolour painting in London his methods were not ideal for training a painter destined to become a landscape topographer to a marine survey expedition. It is possible to gain some idea what Martens learnt from Fielding by turning to the remarks of John Ruskin, who became Fielding's pupil a few years after Martens. In *Praeterita* Ruskin recorded what he had learnt from Fielding:

> ... Copley Fielding taught me to wash colour smoothly in successive tints, to shade cobalt through pink madder into yellow ochre for skies, to use a broken scraggy touch for the tops of mountains, to represent calm lakes by broad strips of shade with lines of light between them ... to produce dark clouds and rain with twelve or twenty successive washes, and to crumble burnt umber with a dry brush for foliage and foreground.[94]

Conrad Martens's Devonshire water-colour paintings reveal that he also learnt such things from Fielding. Broad free washes, frequently raw and bright in colour, are used to capture an occasional effect of light and shadow playing over an old cottage in a turn of road, or upon a copse by a meadow.

Broad washes and a free picturesque treatment in the manner of Fielding (or Skinner Prout) was not the best method to adopt when recording little-known landscapes and shore lines on a marine survey dedicated to scientific accuracy. Martens found himself, like Hodges and Westall before him, thrown among a party of scientists and naval men who were skilled observers and some of them proficient draughtsmen. It is not surprising, therefore, that the work Martens executed during his period on the *Beagle* is more detailed, empirical, and topographical than the picturesque sketches he painted directly under Fielding's influence in Devonshire. Marten's drawing of *Valparaiso from the Anchorage* (Mitchell Library, Sydney), for example, is economical in line yet sharp, precise, and detailed in its visual account of the ships in the harbour, the buildings and the topography of the harbour itself.

Martens also became more fully aware of the geological structure underlying a landscape during the voyage. Even the poor engravings by T. Landseer after his work, which were published in FitzRoy's account of the voyage, clearly reveal this.

190. *Basalt Glen-River Santa Cruz*, engraving after Conrad Martens by T. Landseer, in Fitzroy, *Narrative of the Voyages of the Adventure and Beagle*, London (1839), ii, f.p. 348

31. Conrad Martens, *Government House and Stables* (detail), canvas, 18¼ × 25½ in. (1841). Dixson Galleries, Sydney. By permission of the Trustees of the State Library of New Sòuth Wales

32. Sir Oswald Brierly, *First Arrival of White Men amongst the Islands of the Louisiade Archipelago* (detail), watercolour and gouache on vellum, 24 × 42¼ in. (*c.* 1860). National Library of Australia, Canberra

191. Conrad Martens, *Rio Santa Cruz*, wash, $7\frac{1}{4} \times 10\frac{1}{4}$ in. (1834). Dixson Library, Sydney. By permission of the State Library of New South Wales

During an expedition up the Santa Cruz river, Patagonia, Martens worked in particularly close co-operation with the *Beagle*'s scientists. His illustration of Basalt Glen, Santa Cruz (Plate 190), may be taken as an example. Both FitzRoy and Darwin wrote detailed descriptions of the place. FitzRoy wrote:

> The glen ... is a wild looking ravine, bounded by black lava cliffs. A stream of excellent water winds through it amongst the long grass, and a kind of jungle at the bottom. Lions or rather pumas shelter in it, as the recently torn remains of guanacoes showed us. Condors inhabit the basaltic cliffs. Near the river some imperfect columns of basalt give to a remarkable rocky height, the semblance of an old castle. Altogether it is a scene of wild loneliness fit to be the breeding place of lions.[95]

In his drawing Martens sought to capture not only an accurate visual account but also something of the mood of the place. The high, dark, basaltic terraces are clearly indicated, with the river winding below. A puma is seen leaping after a guanaco. The engraving, though not altogether devoid of a certain romantic feeling, incorporates facts of value both to the geologist and zoologist. On another occasion Martens painted a lonely creek running beside a high ridge of mountains where only condors are to be seen preying upon the remains of a guanaco (Plate 191). Although this water-colour with its broad and simply stated washes appears at first sight only to be a study in melancholy landscape it does contain information of value to the zoologist. For Darwin it would have been of special interest, since it concerned the habitat and ecological relationship of two animals which he had occasion to mention years later in the *Descent of Man*.[96]

307

It is not at all unlikely that Darwin's unsurpassed analytical observation affected Martens's practice as a painter. During the voyage they appear to have become close friends. When it was necessary for Martens to leave the *Beagle* at Valparaiso in October 1834 Darwin wrote to his sister with obvious regret: 'It is necessary also to leave our little painter Martens, to wander about the world.'[97] When Darwin arrived in Sydney in 1836 Martens had already established himself as an artist there and Darwin bought two of his water-colours from sketches made on the *Beagle*,[98] one being of the Santa Cruz river. When he sent a message to Martens by a friend about to leave for Australia twenty-eight years later, Darwin told him that the two paintings were still hanging in his study.[99]

Drawings of plants collected in South America also appear in Marten's *Beagle* sketch-books, and his association with Darwin doubtless caused him to take great interest in the characteristic qualities of plants. He delineated the luxurious undergrowth of tropical jungle with much greater detail than he painted the homely countryside of Devon. And in these cases it is likely that Humboldt rather than Fielding was his guide. Darwin was a great enthusiast for Humboldt and took copies of his works with him to read on the *Beagle*. It was Humboldt who opened Darwin's eyes to the beauties of tropical scenery.[100] And since Humboldt had a good deal to say of great interest to any artist working in South America it is likely that Martens read Humboldt too. Humboldt's descriptions of South American vegetation, his discussions of the effects of light and haze in tropical and subtropical landscapes, and his suggestions to travelling landscape-painters would have been of great interest to him.

· There was one aspect of his art training, however, that must have stood Martens in good stead during the voyage. Copley Fielding, according to Ruskin, 'produced some of the most perfect and faultless passages of mist and rain-cloud which art has ever seen'.[101] It was Fielding, doubtless, who first interested Martens in the portrayal of weather effects. But Fielding, as Ruskin rightly points out, was preoccupied with the study of the rain-cloud. He did not concern himself with the shape, structure, and classification of clouds: 'So surely as Copley Fielding attempts the slightest hint at cloud form, beyond the edgeless rag, which is tossed and twisted in the drift of rain, does he become liny, hard, and expressionless.'[102] It was not from Fielding but from the Captain of the *Beagle*, Robert FitzRoy,[103] that Martens must have learnt to observe and classify clouds and to study their formations and dispersal with the interest of a meteorologist. For FitzRoy, from the moment he joined the *Beagle* in 1828, paid the greatest attention to meteorological phenomena. It was his greatest personal interest. His account of the voyage reveals his great interest in atmospheric effects. More important still he published as an appendix to the volume a classification of cloud forms based on the systems developed by Luke Howard and Thomas Ignatius Forster[104] and illustrated the principal cloud types with engravings made from his own drawings. FitzRoy was himself a proficient draughtsman both in figure and landscape work, some of his drawings being used to illustrate his account of the voyage. It is likely, therefore, that FitzRoy communicated his knowledge and interest in cloud formation to Martens in whose sketch-books cloud studies are not infrequent. Martens also jotted down from time to time notes concerning the formation of clouds. After leaving the *Beagle* at Valparaiso Martens shipped on board the *Peruvian* bound for Tahiti. A few days after leaving port he included the following note in his sketch-book:

> In evening skies, a short time before sunset you will frequently observe two kinds
> of clouds a lower and an upper strata the lower cumuli or cumulo-strati; of a rich

192. Conrad Martens, *Moonlight*, watercolour, $5\frac{1}{4} \times 5$ in. (date not known). Dixson Library, Sydney. By permission of the State Library of New South Wales

warm colour such as yellow orange and purple while the upper cloud is cirrus, and exceedingly high and minute in form, will be really without colour, or of a subdued white—but immediately after the sun has set, the contrary will be the case, normally, the lower cloud—of a cold grey like dark smoke, and the cirri high above still receiving the sun's rays—and of a bright warm yellow or orange-note, this kind of sky gives a good evening effect.[105]

In this note we find Martens applying the vocabulary and the vision of the meteorologist to his examination of the sky, and then proceeding to appreciate the pictorial possibilities of his observations. On another occasion he includes notes on a squall observed at sea:

A dark sky. warm grey. coming down flat and unbroken to the horizon light and broken in the upper part. the sun high up above the centre of the picture—the sea not very rough but sufficient to show a squall, and worked out only by lights upon a ground of exactly the same tone and colour as lower parts of sky-lights—the reflection of the sun strongest at the horizon with bright lights thinly scattered as they approach the foreground—and a very few touches of true dark to assist the appearance of the water—a schooner close reefed.[106]

The pictorial effects of sunsets delighted Martens as they did so many of the artists of his day. Not infrequently he will make a sketch and add accompanying notes, as when he writes on the voyage to Tahiti: 'Sunset—perfect calm—azure grey down into orange—with indistinct forms of clouds at lower part of a red colour—great mass of clouds very dark and at some places edged with red.'[107]

Conrad Martens remained a keen student of atmospheric effects throughout his life, as may be seen from such studies as *Moonlight* (Plate 192), but his notebooks are the best source for his meteorological interests. In a lecture upon landscape-painting given many years after leaving the *Beagle* he claimed that the ability 'to judge the true color of familiar objects seen through the intervention of atmosphere' was 'a faculty of all others the most to be desired by a landscape painter'.[108] We may take it that Martens's own great ability to judge atmospheric colour truly, admirably expressed in such fine water-colours as *Sydney from Vaucluse* (Plate 193), owed much to his years on the *Beagle*.

Arriving in Tahiti from Valparaiso, Martens remained sketching on the island for several weeks. Then on 4 March 1835 he left in the *Black Warrior* of Salem, which put in to the Bay of Islands for five days and then came on to Sydney, where Martens disembarked on 17 April 1835.

It is most probable that Martens on leaving Valparaiso was intending to complete a tour of the world hoping to return to England with a portfolio of sketches to be used for the publication of an illustrated travel book, or for work upon larger finished paintings. Immediately after disembarking at Sydney he began to sketch in the environs of the city and farther afield. In May he was at Emu Plains making sketches along the Nepean. In June he was sketching along the foreshores of Sydney harbour and Botany Bay. In July he visited the Illawarra, attracted there, doubtless, by reports of the beauty of its sub-tropical scenery. In August he was sketching in the Blue Mountains. In September, north of Sydney at Broken Bay. Meanwhile, Martens had found lodgings in Cumberland Street, in a fashionable quarter of Sydney known as the Rocks, and had begun to take pupils. One of his first was Robert Russell, the surveyor.[109]

193. Conrad Martens, *Sydney from Vaucluse*, water-colour, $17\frac{1}{2} \times 26$ in. (1864). Dixson Library, Sydney. By permission of the Trustees of the State Library of New South Wales

In order to move about freely, Martens acquired a pony[110] and began to make longer excursions into the country in search of picturesque scenery. He also began to make drawings and paintings of the residences of prominent settlers. Or he would paint the view as seen from the residence. By such means Martens was able to maintain a somewhat precarious livelihood based entirely upon local patronage. In this he was a pioneer. For Glover had settled as a pastoralist and his colonial

paintings, as we have seen, were primarily intended for the English market. Augustus Earle, though he obtained local commissions, was essentially a bird of passage. But Martens married two years after arriving in the Colony, and by dint of consistent and methodical work succeeded in maintaining a wife and two children entirely from the proceeds of his paintings, teaching, and the sale of his lithographs, until he was appointed Assistant Parliamentary Librarian in New South Wales in 1863.

Martens arrived in Sydney at a time when the Colony was prospering from the rapid expansion of the pastoral industry. Within a short time of his arrival he had gained the patronage of a small circle drawn from the socially *élite* of the Colony. From the account books which Martens kept most methodically from the time of his arrival in Sydney to the day of his death in 1878 we may obtain exact information as to the people who purchased his paintings together with the prices they paid for them.[111] Numbered among his early patrons were a number of persons who had helped to promote scientific organization in Australia: Sir John and Lady Franklin, Alexander and William MacLeay, Sir Thomas Mitchell, Sir John Jamison, Colonel Breton, and Captain P. P. King. The Governors of New South Wales, Sir Richard Bourke, and later Sir Charles FitzRoy, also assisted him.

Colonial patronage was fitful and unreliable, however. Martens, therefore, partly in search of new scenery to paint and partly to gain some help from squatters settled in outlying areas (by painting their homesteads), began to travel farther afield. In 1841 he was travelling north of Newcastle in areas opened up by the Australian Agricultural Company. Ten years later he took ship to Brisbane and from there made an extensive tour through the Darling Downs and the New England Tableland, painting scenery and homesteads for squatters who had established themselves in these regions during the previous decade.[112]

The economic depression of the 1840's reduced Martens and his family to straitened circumstances for a number of years. To meet the difficulty he began to experiment with lithography. His first plate *Sydney from the North Shore* (1842) sold steadily for a number of years. Eight years later he was able to write to his brother Henry: 'my coloured print continues to sell well. I have in the long run made a very good thing of it. I sell none but coloured. They sell at a guinea.... I do not think, however, that it would be possible to raise anything like fifty pounds at this time for a similar publication.'[113] Martens was having an extremely difficult time and was apparently receiving some help from his family in England. This is suggested in a letter which deserves to be quoted at length for the picture it gives of art and life in Sydney immediately before the discovery of gold:

> Indeed I have never known so great a depression in business of all kinds than there is at present. The people are leaving the country by hundreds for California by every ship that goes; and to charter a vessel for that place is now, I believe, one of the best specs going. When this mania will end or how it will end I cannot even guess. It is true the ups and downs have always succeeded each other in pretty quick succession, but as the artist is perhaps the last to feel the depression so he is also the last to benefit by the improvement of the times. The money will be most acceptable when it comes. I am altogether at a loss to account for such great stagnation of business....
>
> I cannot help looking out somewhat anxiously for the arrival of the cash you mention: indeed I should have been fairly aground some time since had it not been for a haul of about £60 which I made by the Art Union Exhibition which was, I think, about to take place when I last wrote. It was as good an exhibition of colonial

talent as I could have expected, but in all other respects a decided failure that is to say, firstly, the proprietors of good pictures would not lend them, visitors were not so numerous as I might have expected, and subscribers to the Art Union did not number more than, I think, 62. There was not a single picture sold during the exhibition, but fortunately for me, the prize holders were almost unanimous in selections from my works, so that where I could not meet them with a picture of exactly a corresponding figure to the amount of their ticket the balance was paid. . . . Since that time however I have sold but one drawing; nor have I at present any pupils; in short something else must be thought of to keep the pot boiling till better times come round.[114]

Martens decided to get out more lithographs to tide him over the bad times, and accordingly in 1850–1 produced his *Sketches in the Environs of Sydney*, mentioned above.

The drawings and paintings Martens produced in the years immediately following his arrival in Sydney are still very much in the topographical tradition. But as the years passed he became much more interested in endowing his paintings with romantic grandeur. The question of interpreting a landscape took on greater importance, and the need to elevate his themes above the level of topography was always present in his mind. For Martens was no longer producing landscapes that would convey information to Europeans, he was painting to satisfy the requirements of colonial taste—and doing what he could to improve it.

Martens, however, even in the most romantic landscapes he painted in New South Wales, never returned completely to the broad and fluent picturesque facility of his Devonshire paintings. If we compare his *Hey Tor, Dartmoor*,[115] painted directly under Fielding's influence, with the *Five Islands, South Coast, New South Wales* (Plate 194) we

194. Conrad Martens, *The Five Islands, South Coast, N.S.W.*, watercolour. Mount Gilead, New South Wales

are immediately aware of the greater degree of visual analysis which Martens has sought to incorporate into his interpretation of the latter scene. The delicate transitions of colour suffusing sea and sky may be contrasted with the simple recipe employed in the Devonshire painting. For Martens here paints marine horizons with years of observation and close association with an outstanding meteorologist behind him. Similarly vegetation, though generalized, is rendered to conform to the requirements of botany. Martens has included not only the eucalypt and the cabbage-tree palm, together with the hanging vines so characteristic then of the Illawarra, he has also incorporated two typical plants, the waratah and the grass-tree, as foreground embellishments. And by painting the flat sandstone platforms which overlook the coast in this region, he has given some account of the geology of the district. Here, in short, Martens has sought to elevate exotic topography to the full stature of an artistic interpretation. The painting conforms very well to the type of landscape Humboldt had in mind when he dealt with the subject in his *Cosmos*. In this connexion some comments on a discussion Martens had with Marshall Claxton[116] are especially revealing:

> ... we have occasionally great arguments about the necessity of preserving the character and true delineation of the trees, plants, etc. in the landscapes of this country, a point which I have ever considered of great consequence so long as it does not amount to absolute servility.[117]

The qualification was important. When Martens delivered a lecture on landscape-painting in Sydney in 1856 he placed great emphasis upon the value of studying works of art. Only through the medium of art could we learn to see nature truly. Therefore all those who aspired to art in a distant colony like New South Wales laboured under many disadvantages. Martens admitted the value of a drawing made on the spot, having no further aim than accurate topography, and cited David Roberts's *Sketches in the Holy Land* as good examples to examine. But his own preference was for what he called 'true sketching', and he drew the attention of his audience to Turner's *Liber Studiorum*:

> ... a book *to be studied* with the *greatest advantage*. Here will be found *breadth, grandeur*, and a total absence of all petty details ... 55 degs of the circle, is the most that should be included from the left to right of the subject.... Taking now ... a smaller angle, say 40 degs for the extent of the picture; grandeur and magnitude will be the result; without in the least departing from the truth ... and I may here take the opportunity to add that this was one of the first practical lessons which I myself learnt by carefully comparing the drawings of Turner with the scenes which he represented.[118]

Martens attached great importance to breadth in painting. Breadth was an extension of light and shade over and above that necessary for stating their actual form. By means of breadth, light and dark masses were formed in a painting. These masses, Martens pointed out, could be made to take on agreeable shapes without reference to the subject: 'so that the picture when seen at such a distance that the subject is not intelligible, shall yet have an agreeable effect upon the eye'.[119] If the principles of breadth was properly understood it was possible to go 'very far beyond the mere imitator'.

Marten's lecture was intended to be of practical use to an amateur group of landscape-painters and was full of practical suggestions. These may be taken as a guide to his own practice. In choosing a subject, he said, a principal object should be selected and the highest lights and deepest darks made to assist each other by being brought to bear upon this object. The strongest darks should be reserved for the foreground. And these darks should be detached from the side of the picture since by contact with the frame they lose their visual force. However, when surrounded by middle tints (wherever the highlights do not make contact with them) they will then yield their utmost force and effect. When preparing to sketch a scene it was wise to place oneself in such a position as to obscure much of the middle distance in order that a considerable portion of the foreground might be brought into the immediate contact with the extreme distance.

The methods which Martens advocated were derived from his own studio practice, as an examination of his paintings will show. But his practice itself was developed not only from his training under Fielding, his experiences on the *Beagle*, and his study of the works of Turner; he also derived many ideas from his readings of Reynolds's *Discourses*, John Burnet's *Practical Treatise on Painting* (1827), and the paintings of such men as Danby, Stanfield, Cattermole, and Cox. In his work we may trace one endeavour to solve the aesthetic problem set by the explorations of the preceding century: the reconciliation of a scientific and an aesthetic vision in the painting of unfamiliar landscapes.

During the 1830's and 1840's artists working in Australia, as we have seen, sought to accommodate an analytical and descriptive method of recording exotics with the traditional practice of landscape art, namely the presentation of a scene as an ordered unity. In a somewhat similar fashion, visiting scientists continued to be fascinated by the country's novelties and to fashion hypotheses that sought to explain or to subsume the apparent exceptionalism of the country's natural productions. Charles Darwin himself recorded how important the voyage of the *Beagle* was in determining the subsequent course of his life and thought. It was the parallel which he observed between the prehistoric life of South America revealed in its fossil record, and the nature of the country's living plants and animals, which first suggested to him the possibility of an organic evolution of life upon the earth. His later work in the Galapagos and his long research into the formation of coral islands, which involved an exhaustive reading of Pacific voyage literature, helped to confirm his speculations. The way in which the natural productions of Australia helped further to promote his questioning of the accepted explanation of the natural order is revealed in a note which he wrote in his *Journal* when making a trip from Sydney to Bathurst across the Blue Mountains:

> I had been lying on a sunny bank, and was reflecting on the strange character of the animals of this country as compared with the rest of the world. An unbeliever in everything beyond his own reason might exclaim, 'Two distinct Creators must have been at work; their object, however, has been the same, and certainly the end in each case is complete.' [120]

A similar view that Australia presented a coherent, complete, and yet quite distinct order of nature from the rest of the world was expressed by Strzelecki when he visited the country three years later. He found it a matter for surprise that European fruits and animals should thrive so well in a climate which had produced so different a natural order. In New South Wales, Strzelecki wrote, 'nature unfolds annals of wonders; not indeed, that they can be so called, as furnishing new lights upon the origin of things, but as yielding additional evidence that the structure to which they relate is analogous to that of the rest of the globe'. [121]

Strzelecki did not appreciate that an adequate explanation of Australia's 'analogous' forms might throw new light upon the origin of things. Not so Joseph Dalton

Hooker who arrived in Australia shortly after Strzelecki. Hooker appears to have grasped early the full significance of making a complete study of the apparent exceptionalism of the Australian flora, a study which caused him to make a radical alteration in his own views upon the origin of species. In the General Remarks which he wrote prefacing his essay *On the Flora of Australia*, Hooker expressed in some detail the reasons which led him to undertake his detailed study, the most important since Brown's *Prodromus Florae Novae Hollandiae*:

> The Flora of Australia has been justly regarded as the most remarkable that is known, owing to the number of peculiar forms of vegetation which that continent presents. So numerous indeed are the peculiarities of this Flora, that it has been considered as differing fundamentally, or in almost all its attributes, from those of other lands; and speculations have been entertained that its origin is either referable to another period of the world's history from that in which the existing plants of other continents have been produced, or to a separate creative effort from that which contemporaneously peopled the rest of the globe with its existing vegetation; whilst others again have supposed that the climate or some other attribute of Australia has exerted an influence on its vegetation, differing both in kind and degree from that of other climates. One of my objects, in undertaking a general survey of the Australian Flora, has been to test the value of the facts which have given rise to these speculations, and to determine the extent and comparative value of a different and larger class of facts which are opposed to them, and which might also give some clue to the origin of the Flora, and thus account for its peculiarities.[122]

At the conclusion of his work Hooker had indeed revealed the inadequacy of the extravagant hypotheses advanced by earlier thinkers like Erasmus Darwin and François Péron. But in the course of his work he became convinced that his earlier conviction that species were immutable was false. Working always in close contact with his friend Darwin, Hooker first admitted the truth of the descent and modification of species in his *Flora of Tasmania*. It appeared in December 1859, a few weeks after the appearance of the *Origin of Species*.

The influence of the Pacific upon Darwin's other great friend Thomas Henry Huxley was not such that it led him directly to evolutionary theory. But it did, by bringing him into direct contact with the most primitive forms of marine life, lead him directly towards fundamental discoveries in comparative morphology. On the *Rattlesnake* he became a general biologist, by being brought directly in touch with a great variety of the physical world and with primitive man.[123] Confronted with a chaotic array of nondescript marine material, Huxley hit upon the notion of classifying according to an archetypal principle, according, that is, to a fundamental structural plan revealed by a study of many individuals, rather than according to superficial resemblances in appearance or mode of life. At first an abstract concept invented to solve a problem, in the light of evolutionary principles it became clear that the archetypal common plan was a badge of common descent. Furthermore, the study of zoological individuality became an important one for Huxley in the study of such colonial structures as Portuguese men of war. He came to the conclusion that biological individuality was a process; that individuality was not to be expressed in static but in dynamic terms. Moreover, his study of primitive man laid the basis for his outstanding work in physical anthropology. Clearly, Huxley's years on the *Rattlesnake* prepared him well for the years when he was to become the most militant champion of Darwinism in England.

11. *The Ignoble and the Romantic Savage, 1820–50*

DURING the first half of the nineteenth century one aspect of faithfully recording life and nature in the Pacific continued to present difficulties; the portrayal of man himself. The incursion of evangelical Christianity into the Pacific mission field, as we have seen, did much to present the unredeemed savage as an object of pity or dislike. One of the results of this attitude was a considerable modification of the pictorial image of the savage which had been created by the artists of the eighteenth century. Something of the change was already apparent in Smirke's *Cession of Matavai Bay* (Plate 99), discussed above.

Few missionaries were artists or even draughtsmen of any distinction. They were not interested in drawing landscapes, natives, or objects of natural history for the sake of science or art. There were some exceptions. Illustrations of mission establishments were made to preserve an account of developments achieved and to inform the Societies at home. For a similar reason views of churches erected and of natives converted to Christianity were sent back to England (Plate 196). But the graphic repertoire of the scientific voyages—plants, animals, landscapes, native peoples, and natural wonders—was mostly ignored.[1] This is not surprising. To most of the early missionaries the nakedness of the savage, his clothing, rites, dances and, above all, his 'idols' were not only repulsive but, to a greater or lesser degree, diabolical.

Missionary societies, however, found it desirable to publish illustrations of native life in the Pacific in order to bring their work before the public. The *Cession of Matavai Bay* was, as we have seen, produced with that end in mind. The usual practice, however, was to search the atlases of Pacific voyages for suitable pictorial material. Consequently engravings from the published voyages of Cook, La Pérouse, d'Urville, and others, which illustrated Pacific religious beliefs and ritual practices were reproduced extensively. Webber's *Human Sacrifice at Tahiti* (Plate 196) became one of the best-known illustrations of the century.

Missionary publications were for the most part cheaply produced. The translation of the elegant engravings of Woollett and Sherwin into small and cheap woodcuts or lithographs did much to nullify most of the dignity and nobility with which they, and others, had invested the savage. But there were other factors, such as the selection of subject-matter which invariably presented the unredeemed native in a light unfavourable to them in the eyes of Europeans.

In April 1818 the Missionary Society began to publish *Missionary Sketches*, a small periodical pamphlet which reported on work in the mission field for the information of members and contributors. It provided illustrations in the form of woodcuts. Aspects of native life were selected that tended to promote work in the field: illustration of native rites, 'idols', natives accepting Christianity, natives casting their 'idols' to the flames, and so on. The issue for October 1837 published Webber's *Human Sacrifice at Tahiti* as a woodcut (Plate 198). As a result both of the cheaper form of publication and of the evangelical aversion for any ennobling of savage life the woodcut differs

195. Jacques Arago, *Savage of New Holland coming from Battle*, in his *Narrative of a Voyage round the World* (1823), pl. 22

317

considerably from its original. Webber did not in his own work seek to ennoble savages in the manner of Cipriani, Reynolds, Sherwin, and Zoffany. Neither did he attempt to suggest that they were a degraded form of humanity. But in the woodcut Tahitians appear as a squat, very swarthy, and barbaric people, while the skulls surrounding the place of sacrifice have been picked out for special emphasis.

Such editing of voyage illustrations was not confined to the purposes of missionary propaganda. Evangelism in a greater or lesser degree permeated all phases of British life and thought during the first half of the century and the graphic portrayal of Pacific islanders in general took on an evangelical purpose and direction. New popular editions of Cook's Voyages published after 1820 were frequently edited with the thought of the missionary enterprise much in mind. Material such as that which had offended so many when reading Hawkesworth was discreetly omitted. To accounts of the religious beliefs and funerary customs of Polynesia were added reflections upon the abject spiritual state of the natives and the moral duties of Christians. Illustrations in such editions followed the practice of the missionary publications— the native appearing as a squat, swarthy, highly emotional type of being completely lacking in any personal dignity. There is some evidence that the image of an ignoble savage which so evolved became, like the noble savage before him, a pictorial stereotype. Just as all noble savages were alike in drawing their virtue from the simple life of nature, so all ignoble savages were alike in the spiritual darkness of their paganism. This visual stereotype of an ignoble savage at times confounded the physical characteristics and adornments of quite different peoples. In the edition of Cook's Voyages edited by Wright (1843), for instance, Webber's *Human Sacrifice* (Plate 199) again appears. On this occasion the Tahitian chieftain who speaks with Cook has been endowed with the adornments and gestures of a Bodhisattva.

A particularly interesting example of the ignoble savage as a pictorial convention occurs in George Baxter's print of the death of John Williams at Eromanga. Williams had played a remarkable role in the growth of South Sea mission activity after his arrival in Tahiti in 1817. He became famous both in the South Seas and in Britain. After he was murdered by natives at Eromanga in 1839 he became a kind of protestant martyr, and the example of his life provided a spur to mission work for many years. Baxter's print, *The Massacre of the Lamented Missionary, the Rev. John Williams*, with its accompanying letterpress, was one of the ways adopted to make his life's work better known to the British public, and the theme looks back directly to

196. *A Dying Christian Chief*, lithograph, in *Missionary Scenes*, ii (Mayence, 1852). Nan Kivell Collection 786, National Library of Australia

197. *A Human Sacrifice, in a Morai, in Otaheite*, engraving after John Webber by Woollett, in Cook and King, *Voyage to the Pacific Ocean* (1784), pl. 25

198. *The Offering of a Human Sacrifice in Tahiti*, woodcut after John Webber, in *Missionary Sketches* (1837)

199. *The Ceremony of a Human Sacrifice in Tahiti*, engraving by J. F. Read, in Cook's *Voyages* (pub. W. Wright, 1843)

200. *The Massacre of the Lamented Missionary, the Rev. John Williams*, Baxter oil print (1843)

201. *Massacre of the Rev. John Williams*, watercolour, 10¾ × 18 in., (1843). Nan Kivell Collection 150, National Library of Australia, Canberra

Webber's print of the death of Cook. A comparison of the print (Plate 200) and an original water-colour design, made in its preparation by an unidentified artist employed by Baxter (Plate 201), is illuminating. Pictorial elements of the noble savage type survive in the latter. There is, for instance, a tall well-built savage who stands on a rock holding a club aloft with an heroic gesture. The natives running into the water to murder Williams are fine physical specimens with hair flowing wildly. Williams, in turning to resist the onslaught, has fallen into shallow water to adopt something like a Lamentation-type pose. The print, however, differs radically from the painting. The reason for many of the alterations is made clear by remarks in Baxter's handwriting on the painting. These remarks clearly sought to make the illustration more amenable to evangelical taste. The natives were to be made darker in complexion; Williams was to be made 'more heavenly'. In the print these directions have been fulfilled and the appearance of the natives has been transformed. They are now much more squat in proportion, and their arched eyebrows, staring eyes, bared teeth or open mouths endow them with an air of savage ferocity. The heroic savage with a club in the right foreground has been replaced by a ferocious archer. Williams is shown with an arm and eyes raised in silent prayer and supplication to God, while in the distance his companions are being speared and clubbed to death. Such a print was admirably designed to suggest the saintliness of Williams and the spiritual depravity of his murderers.[2]

202. *The Death of Cook*, engraving from Cook's *Voyages* (ed. John Barrow, 1874), f.p. 176

203. Henry Anelay, *The Rev. John Williams on board ship with Native Implements, in the islands*, watercolour, $6\frac{3}{4} \times 13\frac{1}{2}$ (date not known). Nan Kivell Collection 187, National Library of Australia, Canberra

The image of the ignoble savage is present not only in missionary literature. It spread widely in contemporary illustrated books and journals of all kinds. The ferocious savage who stabs Cook in the back, used to illustrate a popular account of Cook's voyages (Plate 202), is typical of the brutish creature so widely used to illustrate boys' adventure books during the second half of the century. It is worth noting that the book was edited by Sir John Barrow who, as we have seen, described the Australian Aborigine as 'an animal of prey . . . more ferocious than the lynx, the leopard or the hyena'.

The missionary enterprise in the Pacific was also responsible for promoting an active dislike in Europe for the figural arts of Pacific peoples. For the missionaries the question was inextricably bound up with idol worship. Figured carvings, whether in two or three dimensions, were usually denounced as 'the creation of a corrupt imagination' and evidence of the degraded condition of the heathen. Biblical authority existed for denouncing images which resembled things in the heavens above, the earth beneath, and the waters under the earth. But in a century which treasured realism in the visual arts more than any other, idols which failed to resemble things with any accuracy were held up for special scorn and ridicule. 'What sort of deities must they be, of which images, so ridiculously fantastic, so monstrously uncouth, so frightfully distorted, as many heathen idols are, are yet considered by their worshippers as the appropriate and worthy representatives?'[3]

Henry Anelay painted Williams on board ship pointing with a smug and scornful gesture at a collection of Pacific artefacts in which the image of a Polynesian god is appropriately overturned (Plate 203). In order to impress upon their public the utter beastliness of idols, missionary publications not infrequently resorted to distortions of their own which had nothing to do with the distortions of the heathen. In a series of

204. *A New Zealand Idol*, woodcut vignette from W. H. G. Kingston, *Voyages of Captain Cooke*. London, Religious Tract Society (1871)

322

205. *New Zealand War Canoes*, lithograph, in *Missionary Scenes* ii, xiii (Mayence, 1852). Nan Kivell Collection 786, National Library of Australia

206. *The Tahitian War Fleet*, engraved illustration to *The Voyages of Captain Cook* (pub. W. Wright), 1843.

207. William Hodges, *Review of the War Galleys of Tahiti*, oil on panel, $9\frac{1}{2} \times 18\frac{1}{2}$ in. (1774). National Maritime Museum, London

208. Augustus Earle, *Herald
or Peacemaker*, in his *Sketches
of the Native Inhabitants of
New Zealand* (1838)

missionary sketches, for example, published in 1852, the figure-head of a Maori canoe is picked out for special emphasis (Plate 205). This version of the rather formalized carving of the Maori was naturalistic enough to render it repulsive to contemporary Europeans. In a similar fashion a small vignette in W. H. G. Kingston's edition of Cook (1871) written for a juvenile audience, represents a *New Zealand Idol* as pot-bellied and pigeon-toed (Plate 204). Or again, in Wright's edition of Cook, the size and proportion of the figure-heads upon Tahitian canoes are greatly exaggerated (Plate 206) in a cut, derived from Hodges's *Review of the War Galleys of Tahiti* (Plate 207). Pacific peoples converted to Christianity however could be depicted in a highly sympathetic manner. Compare the Christ-like visage of Augustus Earle's *Peacemaker* (Plate 208) with the satanic countenance of Jacques Arago's *Savage of New Holland coming from Battle* (Plate 195).

A nascent enjoyment of the arts of Oceania, as we have seen, manifested itself during the late eighteenth century in the formation of ethnological cabinets of Pacific art by such virtuosi as Sir Ashton Lever and George Keate. But such frivolities did not appeal to the high-minded evangelism of the century that followed. 'A view of these Otaheitian gods will fill every spectator with amazement at the weakness and folly of human nature.' (Plate 209)[4] The figured sculpture and carving of the Pacific was not

324

to be enjoyed again by Europeans until the last decades of the century when the hold of evangelical values upon matters of taste was relaxing.

The ignoble savage continued to exist as a conventional figure in British poetry. When the subject of 'Australasia' was set for the Vice-Chancellor's Prize Poem at Cambridge for 1823 some mention of the missionary enterprise in the Pacific was evidently expected. Mackworth Praed, who won the competition, managed to combine the rather contradictory interpretations of Pacific peoples created by the early voyagers on the one hand and the missionaries on the other. Much of the poem is devoted to assembling a traditional picture of a southern Arcadia, but it also deals at length with the dark hatreds, viciousness, and cannibalism of savages. In the beautiful lands of the Pacific, Praed could see 'nothing dark except the soul of man'. Every prospect pleased but only man was vile. That was the accepted evangelical view which Bishop Heber had already written into his famous missionary hymn, 'From Greenland's Icy Mountains'. William Charles Wentworth, the Australian who was placed second to Praed, attributed his lack of success to the fact that he had not even mentioned the missionary enterprise. In a self-critical preface to his own poem he observed:

> The author feels that his poem would have been much more perfect, if some allusion had been made in it to the religious improvement which has been effected in Australasia, and particularly to the great missionary efforts which are now in progress in the Polynesian Archipelago ... its omission too was less excusable, as it may be considered a species of *ascriptio glebae* to the ancient and religious manor from which the subject sprung.[5]

Similary Thomas Hervey, whose poem *Australia* (1825) has been discussed above in another connexion, is based upon the threefold scheme of arcadian landscape, ignoble savage, and the call for missionary enterprise.

Two years later James Montgomery wrote his *Pelican Island*, a poem inspired by a passage from Flinders's *Voyage*. The poem bears some striking similarities to Hervey's. Like Hervey, Montgomery was fascinated by the growth of coral[6] and by the idyllic descriptions of Pacific islands written by early navigators. And as a well-known evangelical poet he naturally stressed in his poem the degraded spiritual condition of

209. *Destruction of the Idols of Otaheite; pulling down a Pagan Altar, and building a Christian Church*, woodcut, in *Missionary Sketches* (July 1819)

the people of the South Seas and the importance of missionary activity. In the later cantos of his poem Montgomery drew a detailed picture of the ignoble savage in his natural paradise. Cook, noting that daily toil did not appear to be a condition of existence for the Society Islanders, suggested that they might have been exempt from the primeval curse. Montgomery had no doubt at all that the islanders had fallen from grace like the rest of mankind; but the natural fertility of Tahiti constituted something of a problem for him:

> The curse was here; and yet the soil untill'd
> Pour'd forth spontaneous and abundant harvests.

Such a denial of the divine law could only occur for men who had given themselves over entirely to the Devil, and indeed they appeared to have taken on his image:

> Large was their stature, and their frames athletic;
> Their skins were dark, their locks like eagles' feathers;
> Their features terrible;—when roused to wrath,
> All evil passions lighten'd through their eyes,
> Convulsed their bosoms like possessing fiends,
> And loosed what sets on fire the course of nature,
> —The tongue of malice, set on fire of hell,
> Which then, in cataracts of horrid sounds,
> Raged through their gnashing teeth and foaming lips
> Making the ear to tingle, and the soul
> Sicken, with spasms of strange revolting horror,
> As if the blood changed colour in the veins.
> Their visages at rest were winter clouds,
> Fix'd gloom, whence sun nor shower could be foretold:
> But, in high revelry, when full of prey,
> Cannibal prey, tremendous was the laughter.

Evangelical opinion did not, however, entirely eradicate the belief in the noble savage. The romantic savages which appear in the poetry, art, and fiction of the nineteenth century draw both upon the enthusiastic description of the early voyagers and upon the less favourable accounts of the missionaries; the romantic savage was, in a sense, child both of noble and of ignoble savage. And as the noble savage had been an epitome of the virtues of the natural man of the Enlightenment so the romantic savage became an epitome of the virtues treasured by the romantics. A great love of personal freedom, a devotion to race and 'nation', a temperament which reacted violently and immediately to experience, courage, great emotional depth, and a childlike warmth and generosity of feeling characterized his personality. He was of course, like the noble savage, essentially a European fiction; but it was a fiction that lay closer to the truth than its predecessor, for it was grounded upon a longer and better acquaintanceship with primitive peoples. Faulty as knowledge still was, the conception of the romantic savage was a genuine effort on the part of the European imagination to make contact with the personal life of primitive peoples. In the eighteenth century, as we have seen, Oberea and Omai became convenient stock figures of literary satire to burlesque European fashions and vices. But writers made no serious attempt to bridge the gulf that lay between the real people and the convention which they embodied. The Tahitian princess of Byron's *Island* and Queequeg of Melville's *Moby Dick* are also literary conventions, but they are conventions within which it was possible for poet and novelist to go much farther in their endeavour to understand the native and the native point of view.

326

The *Bounty* mutiny did much to sustain in the minds of Europeans a romantic view of Pacific Island life. For the mutiny provided a clear case of men born and reared in a civilized society deliberately choosing to live permanently among native people. There had been earlier cases but none that drew such public interest. That interest was due not only to the exciting story of the mutiny itself but also to the fact that the mutineers chose to accomplish in real life an ideal that lay close to the romantic view of life—the desire to live in intimate and continuous contact with nature. The mutiny was a sharper criticism of civilization than any of the clever remarks voiced by literary noble savages. Coleridge, at one stage, was tempted to write a poem about the mutiny, but the project came to nothing. Mary Russell Mitford's *Christina, The Maid of the South Seas* (1811) was directly inspired by accounts of the mutiny. In it the transposition of sentiment normally associated with tales of Gaels, Goths, and Vikings was easily made. The ballad form adopted follows Scott closely and the names of the heroes of the ballad—Hubert and Fitzallen—have the desired medieval ring. We are informed in the poem how Fletcher Christian turned away in disgust from 'the Druid rite' he saw enacted before a Tahitian *marae*, and Fitzallen recounts the tale of the mutiny in the manner of a romantic bard,

> Oft soaring on the wings of thought,
> The bard the patriot's flames has caught
> With force resistless, pour'd along
> The rousing eloquence of song.

The poem draws heavily upon motifs already well established in the imaginative use of Pacific material. Hubert and Henry (the purely British and the half-caste), rivals for the hand of Christine (daughter of Fletcher Christian by a native woman), at one point in the story enter a 'wondrous cave' upon the island of Pitcairn. The description of the cave was based upon a visit which the poetess made to the Cave of Fingal in Staffa. Echoes of the *Et in Arcadia Ego* theme are preserved in Christine's moonlight visit to the tomb of her mother in a beautiful tropical glade. And the Pacific island here appears once again as a terrestrial paradise. But the poem is by no means a piece of unqualified primitivism. Despite the romantic bent of her thought Miss Mitford was not uninfluenced by evangelical sentiment and ideas of progress. The ideal expressed in the poem is not purely primitive but a judicious blending of civilized and savage. In presenting Pitcairn as an island whose natural riches and beauty have been augmented by the fruits and flowers of Europe, and by presenting Henry and Christine, children of the mutineers, as ideal people combining the virtues of the British and the Polynesian races she attempted to make the best of both worlds.

Byron's poem *The Island* or *Christian and his Comrades* (1823), also based upon the *Bounty* mutiny, though a far finer poem, has much in common with *Christina, The Maid of the South Seas*. Again we meet the courageous British sailor who longs for the golden islands of the Pacific, the love-idyll between sailor and native girl, and the grotto, which, on this occasion enables the lovers to escape their enemies:

> Wide it was and high,
> And show'd a self-born Gothic canopy;
> The arch uprear'd by nature's architect,
> The architrave some earthquake might erect;
> The buttress from some mountain's bosom hurl'd,
> When the Poles crash'd, and water was the world;
> Or harden'd from some earth-absorbing fire,
> While yet the globe reek's from its funeral pyre;

210. *Reine des Carolines vue à Tinian*, lithograph by Langumé after Arago, in his *Promenade autour du monde, Atlas* (1822), pl. 15

The fretted pinnacle, the aisle, the nave,
Were there, all scoop'd by Darkness from her cave.
There, with a little tinge of phantasy,
Fantastic faces mop'd and mow'd on high,
And then a mitre or a shrine would fix
The eye upon its seeming crucifix.
Thus Nature play'd with the stalactites,
And built herself a chapel of the seas. (Canto iv, ll. 144–60)

Byron's Pacific grotto was like a Gothic cathedral, and the songs of Polynesia for him as for Douglas were analoguous to the sagas and ballads of northern Europe:

Such was this rude rhyme—rhyme is of the rude—
But such inspired the Norseman's solitude,
Who came and conquer'd; such, wherever rise
Lands which no foes destroy or civilise,
Exist: and what can our accomplish'd art
Of verse do more than teach the awaken's heart? (Canto ii, ll. 97–102)

And Byron proceeded to describe the Polynesians themselves as 'the naked knights of savage chivalry'. To give his poem a greater sense of reality, however, he freely introduced native words and free translations of two native songs which he had drawn from Mariner's *Account of the Tonga Islands* (1817). The most notable features of the poem are the romantic descriptions of the Pacific, and of Neuha, the native girl; descriptions that serve to remind that it was the initial impressions of the early navigators in the Pacific which made the most fundamental and lasting impression upon the European imagination. Not that Byron's conception of the South Seas is a simple statement of arcadian bliss and natural virtue. As in all sustained imaginative conceptions taking the Polynesian islands for their subject the theme of mutability makes its appearance:

> We'll cull the flowers that grow above the dead,
> For these most bloom where rests the warrior's head;
> And we will sit in twilight's face, and see
> The sweet moon glancing through the tooa tree,
> The lofty accents of whose sighing bough
> Shall sadly please us as we lean below. (Canto ii, ll. 7–12)

The romantic interpretation of Pacific people was not confined to poetry, it also made an appearance in the graphic work of scientific expeditions during the first half of the nineteenth century, particularly in the Atlases to the voyages of Freycinet (1817–20) and d'Urville (1826–9). The work of Jacques Arago, Freycinet's artist, both in his illustrations and in his writings, is highly coloured by romantic attitudes. He delighted in the portrayal of scenes of native prowess and violence. His *Savage of New Holland coming from Battle* (Plate 195) has the wild look, glistening eyes, and tousled hair favoured by the illustrators of evangelical publications, but unlike them Arago presents his savages as fine physical specimens and gives them an air of wild dignity, placing them at times in a lowlying landscape to increase the impression of size and power. This was a trick of composition also used by Augustus Earle, another painter of romantic savages. By such means it was possible to combine a realistic drawing with an heroic presentation. Arago's *View Taken in the Interior of New Holland*[7] afforded him the chance of combining his interest in native combat with that geological curiosity, the natural arch, so favoured by romantic taste.

Arago wrote a series of letters to a friend describing the voyage. They were translated into English in 1823 the year Byron wrote the *Island*. And the sultry, erotic beauty of Arago's *Reine des Carolines* (Plate 210) with her melting expression, upturned eyes, and long flowing hair forms a suitable visual equivalent to the voluptuous heroine of Byron's tale. Arago's portraits of male natives are usually much fiercer characterizations. But fierce as they were the portraits were still intended to convey something of the manliness and freedom of the hard primitive life. 'Let us therefore, leave these good people to their early habits and inclinations', he wrote to his friend concerning the Hawaiian islanders, 'why teach them desires and wants? If repose, comfort, tranquillity and pleasure constitute happiness, they are happy; what do they want more?'[8] It was only, however, in the peoples of Polynesia that Arago found romantic exemplars of the hard primitive life. The New Hollanders and Fuegians were by contrast little better than beasts.

Augustus Earle who visited New Zealand in 1827 held a similar opinion concerning the contrast between the natives of New Holland and New Zealand. 'The natives of the former', he wrote, 'seem of the lowest grade—the last link in the great chain of existence which unites man with the monkey.... While the natives of the latter are "cast in beauty's perfect mould": the children are so fine each might serve as a model for a statue of "the Infant Hercules": nothing can exceed the graceful and athletic forms of the men, or the rounded limbs of their young women. These possess eyes beautiful and eloquent, and a profusion of long, silky, curling hair. . . .'[9]

Earle's paintings of Maori women took the form of the dark and soulful romantic type of feminine beauty favoured by the fashion of the time. Earle admired much in the Maori life and culture but he did not see them as self-sufficient primitives best left to their own devices. They were for him a people emerging from barbarism and ready to take the first steps towards civilization. Their chiefs, orators, war canoes, and fighting men reminded him of the heroic age. He drew a war party assembled by the shore (Plate 211). 'To me', he wrote, 'it almost seemed to realize some of the passages of Homer, where he describes the wanderer Ulysses and his gallant band of warriors.'[10] Surely, thought Earle, such people, like the Greeks in Homer's time, stand upon the threshold of a glorious future:

> Surely every one who is interested in tracing our own form of government, from the present time up to its first rude outline, will perceive the similarity of causes and events, and will anticipate the glorious prospect of beholding a clever, brave, and, I may add, noble race of men, like the New Zealanders, rescued from barbarism.[11]

In the year that Earle visited the Bay of Islands d'Urville was on the New Zealand coast in the *Astrolabe*. He had sailed from Port Jackson in December 1826. The striking contrast between Australian aborigine and New Zealand Maori was equally apparent to him, and his artist de Sainson in his drawings revealed the sharpest distinction between the extremely primitive culture and poor physique of the aborigines and the sturdy manliness of the Maoris. Indeed the portraits of *Rangui* and *Natai* (Plates, 212, 213) are among the outstanding characterizations of the romantic savage produced by the artists of the times. De Sainson has depicted the Maori as an intelligent barbarian whose destiny lies in the future. This after all was the crucial distinction between the noble and the romantic savage: the former was self-sufficient and most happy in his natural state, the later was a representative of the childhood of

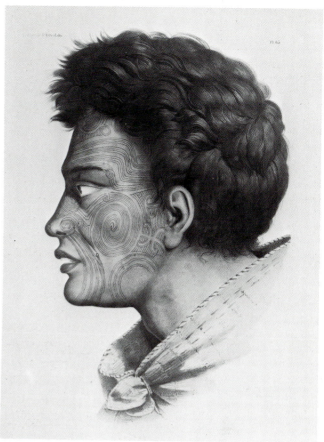

man, interesting because he possessed the unrealized accomplishments of the child. The noble savage expressed the classical desire for a state of natural perfection, the romantic savage expressed the ideal of life as a voyage, a continuous movement towards an ever-receding goal. When this romantic ideal was applied to the fields of history and sociology it tended to produce a theory of social undulation—man's genius being progressively expressed in societies which, like organisms, are born, flourish, and decay. The idea, as we have seen, had been frequently put into service by travellers and writers reflecting upon the future of the Pacific. But it was d'Urville, among Pacific voyagers, who gave the idea its most adequate expression. He knew the Aegean well from his marine survey work there in 1820. It was on this station that he first recognized the value of the recently discovered *Venus de Milo* (Plate 214) and induced the French Government to purchase it for the Louvre. [12] While at work in Tokomaru Bay, New Zealand, seven years later he suddenly became aware of a remarkable similarity between the Maori *pa* and the Greek *polis*. It produced a flood of reflection, by no means lacking in historical insight, in which the romantic savages of New Zealand were pictured as the likely ancestors of a great future civilization:

214. *Venus de Milo* (*c.* 200 or later). Paris, Louvre.

The coast, which from Houa-Houa Bay had been lofty and mountainous, drops after Toko-Malou [Tokomaru] Bay and slopes gently down to the sea. The surrounding country offers to the gaze of the navigator smiling woods, lovely valleys, and two or three *pas* of some considerable size. One of them, especially, situated about a league from the sea, a white patch in the middle of a space cleared of trees, with its regular lines of huts forming an amphitheatre, reminded me somewhat of the little towns in the Greek Archipelago. This spontaneous comparison of the cradle of the highest European civilization with these wild shores in our antipodes, induced in my mind a flood of reflections on the destinies of peoples

331

and the unforeseen causes which can suddenly bring them out of obscurity to play, each in turn, a brilliant role on the stage of the world. I thought of the Gauls, bandits looked upon with such scorn by the organized Greeks; of the Britons, savage creatures whom Rome did not deign to conquer in the most brilliant periods of her empire: twenty centuries have sufficed to raise them to the first rank among the nations. The first have just made Europe tremble at the sound of their arms, and to-day the latter dominate the whole world by the influence of their wealth and the overwhelming power of their ships. Still more recently, the Russians, who less than two centuries ago had scarcely been heard of, have emerged as if by a miracle from the obscurity in which they were plunged; and have they not already become a formidable power? And what of the North Americans, freed from the yoke of Albion, proud and happy men who came into existence as a nation scarcely a half century ago? If only they preserve their simple way of life, their wisdom and their industry, will they not before many years have run, be able to challenge the English rule of the seas?

If, as everything leads one to think, Australia is destined to become the seat of a great empire, it is inconceivable that New Zealand should not follow her impetus, and her children, civilized and intermingled with the posterity of England, will themselves become a powerful and formidable people. Everything seems to point to their playing an important part at sea. Like Great Britain, New Zealand, while surrounded on every side by ocean waters, and provided with excellent harbours, also possesses forests which could supply the finest timbers for masts and shipbuilding generally, plants yielding fibres suitable for the manufacture of the best rope and cordage and a soil that would lend itself to cultivation of all the products of temperate regions. It cannot, therefore, be questioned that its inhabitants will make very rapid progress towards a civilized life, as soon as Europeans or Australians are willing to assume responsibility for the task, or perhaps from the moment that from among themselves there emerges a genius of extraordinary powers, capable of becoming a lawgiver to his fellows and of uniting them in one national body.

Then these shores, at present without human habitation, except for a few isolated *pas*, will be alive with flourishing cities; these bays of unbroken silence, crossed occasionally by frail canoes, will be highways for ships of every type. And a few centuries hence, were it not that henceforth printing will record by its indestructible means the deeds and discoveries of modern times, future members of the Academy of New Zealand would not fail to question or at least to argue laboriously about the narratives of the earliest explorers, when they found them speaking of the wilderness lands, and the savages of their country, and most of all, the total absence of any animals that are useful to man on this great globe.[13]

Dumont d'Urville's idea of a new civilization in the south proved to be a most attractive one to colonial nationalists during the second half of the century, especially in Australia. But it provided European thinkers with yet another reminder of the transience of human institutions; as when, in the full flight of prophecy, Macaulay imagined the melancholy day upon which 'some traveller from New Zealand shall, in the midst of a vast solitude, take his stand on a broken arch of London Bridge to sketch the ruins of St. Paul's'.[14] *Et in Arcadia Ego.*

332

12. *The Triumph of Science, 1820–50*

THE published accounts of the voyages to the Pacific organized by the French, Russians, British, and Americans between 1819 and 1850 testify to the culmination of that alliance between art and science which has been one of the main concerns of this investigation. They provided a great wealth of evidence, which it will not be necessary to deal with here in detail, as to the way the sciences of visible nature, geology, botany, zoology, anthropology, meteorology, and the like, imposed their interests upon the graphic arts.

The impact of geology is particularly noticeable. The drawings of artists like the Viscount de la Touanne, artist on Bougainville's voyage (1824–6), of Paul Mikhailov, artist on Bellingshausen's voyage (1819–21), of de Sainson, artist on Dumont d'Urville's first voyage (1826–9), and of Frederick William Beechy on his own voyage (1825–8), reveal a great interest in the delineation of geological features in landscape (Plate 215). The Geological Society had been formed in England in 1807, and geology was a fashionable enthusiasm throughout Europe. The young Ruskin's passionate interest in rocks is typical of the 1820's and 1830's, and reveals how narrow the gap between science and taste was at this time, and how quickly the interests of science could be transformed into the enthusiasms of art.

In these later voyages, too, travelling artists learned to assist the sciences of enthnology and anthropology by bringing a more objective approach to the delineation of native peoples. The published accounts of Dumont d'Urville and Wilkes provided a comprehensive account of the native peoples visited; and the atlases to these voyages (as if in reply to Herder's plea for an accurate gallery of the world's peoples) made a special feature of anthropological and ethnological illustration. Native physiognomy was indicated by carefully drawn profile and full-face portraits. Even the so-called picturesque views which depicted natives in their natural environment aimed, for the most part, at highly realistic presentations. It is true, of course, that even in these years the artist could not escape entirely the prevailing stereotypes of the time. Even de Sainson's careful representations veer occasionally towards the ignoble and comic savage when he depicts Australian aborigines, as they err on the side of the romantic when he depicts the Maori. But his drawings do mark a considerable advance upon the work of his predecessors. Published illustrations of native peoples in their natural settings no longer distorted and vitiated in any marked degree drawings made on the spot. When Cipriani and Bartolozzi altered Buchan's original sketches of Fuegian natives the scientific world of the time condemned Hawkesworth's *Voyages*, as we have seen, in no uncertain terms. But when Le Breton, an artist upon Dumont d'Urville's second voyage (1837–40), published his drawing of a similar subject (Plate 216) over seventy years later, the gulf between science and taste had been closed. During the intervening years the 'picturesque' had taken unto itself so much of the documentary discipline of science that the artist was able to publish a painting with an appeal both for the scientist and the man of taste. For

333

215. *Landing in Bounty Bay*, engraving after F.W. Beechey by Edward Finden, in Beechey, *Narrative of a Voyage to the Pacific* (1831)

216. *Groupes de Patagons* (Hâvre Peckett), lithograph after L. le Breton, in Dumont d'Urville, *Voyage au Pole Sud, Atlas Pittoresque* (1846), pl.13

despite the painting's obvious affiliation with French romantic painting and its artfully contrived composition, it did succeed in presenting a faithful account of Fuegian life.

The publication of Dumont d'Urville's second voyage marks, in fact, the end of a chapter in the history of the depiction of native peoples. A separate volume was devoted to *Anthropologie et Physiologie Humaine*, and illustrated by an album of fifty colour plates. The greatest care was taken to see that these plates should meet the requirements of science, not only drawing but also modelling, photography, and cephalometic instruments being brought into service to render the illustrations accurate:

> Toutes les figures ont été dessinées d'après nature ou d'après des reliefs moulés sur nature, et en même temps d'après des images daguerriennes faites rigoureusement à demigrandeur naturelle. Les bustes sont vus en perspective de trois quarts. Les crânes et les cerveaux sont vus de face et de profil. Enfin tous les objets ont été photographiés dans une direction verticale, à la même hauteur et à la même distance et éclairés sur le même angle; leur grandeur a été déterminée par les procédés de la trigonométrie sphérique, afin que leurs images fussent aussi exactes que possible et pussent servir aux études d'ethnologie, d'esthetique, de physiologie, de physiognomie et de phrénologie....[1]

When illustrated under these rigorous scientific safeguards the Maoris Taha-Tahala and Heroua (Plates 217, 218) whose fine heads had reminded d'Urville of the busts of Socrates and Brutus, appeared in a light no more favourable than that of the Tasmanian aborigines Worraddey and Trouggarnanna (Plates 219, 220) who, for d'Urville, were somewhat worse off than the beasts. The noble and the ignoble, the comic and the romantic savage, withered under the dry light of science. But under that same dry light all sense of compassion for peoples less powerful than Europeans gradually withered also. The young Trouggarnanna of Sullivan's Cove was destined to become the last full-blood member of her people to die.

The objectivity with which natives came to be depicted is paralleled by the near-photographic accuracy of the landscapes published in the *Atlas Pittoresque* to Dumont d'Urville's second voyage. In such paintings as *Site dans l'Isle Managa-Reva* (Plate 221) by Ernest Auguste Goupil, artist on the *Zélée*, no other interest than the faithful depiction of light and shade and the characteristic forms of vegetation appears. No attempt at composition is apparent and it seems most probable that on this occasion the artist used a camera lucida, an instrument invented by Dr. Wollaston in 1807 for projecting a distant image upon paper as an aid to accurate draughtsmanship. Goupil's drawings are not so much typical landscapes as transcripts of nature. The artists Drayton and Agate, who accompanied the United States Exploring Expedition (1838–42) under the command of Charles Wilkes, made considerable use of the camera lucida in the preparation of their work.[2] Like d'Urville's artists they set out to convey graphically in highly finished drawings, which were lavishly illustrated in the published account of the voyage, a great deal of geological and botanical information in their landscapes as in their scientific illustrations. Indeed Wilkes employed Drayton, as Hamilton had employed Fabris many years before, to assist him in the study of volcanic action.[3] Concerning his examination of the crater of Mauna Loa he wrote:

> As I proposed remaining here a few days on my return, I determined to await until then for the exploration of the volcano. Some of the observations then made

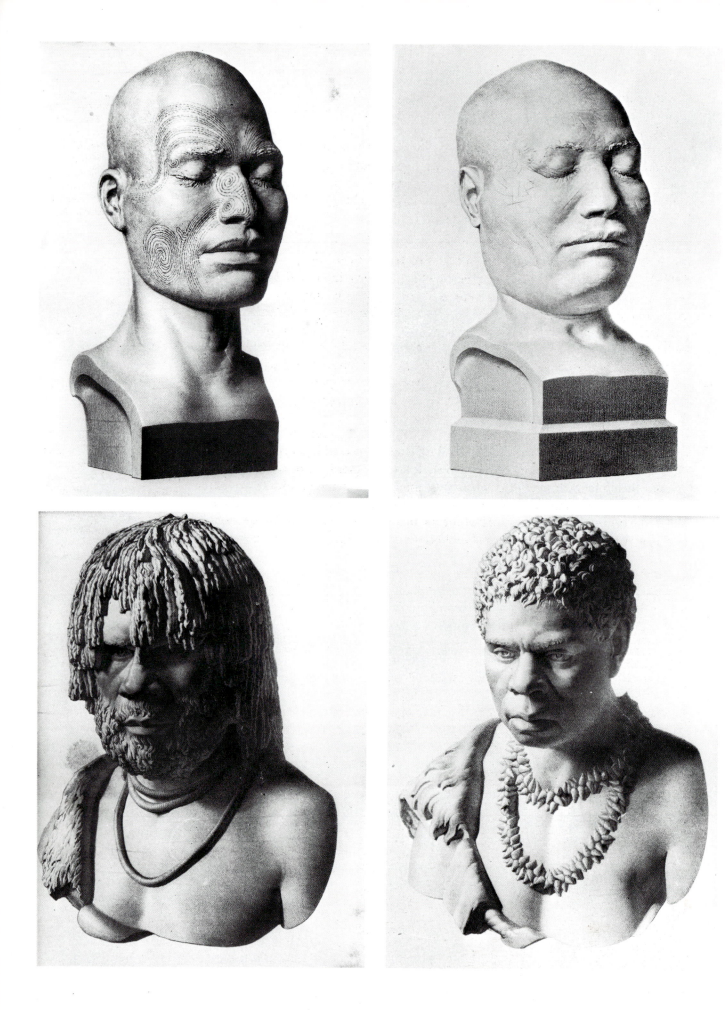

will be noticed at present, that the nature of the lavas may be more fully understood. This day was employed in becoming acquainted with its paths, and in making sketches. One made by Mr. Drayton, with the camera lucida, is very characteristic, and was taken from one of the best positions for viewing this wonderful place.... These sketches I conceived would enable me to ascertain if any, and what, alterations should take place between our two visits, for I could not but imagine it must be continually undergoing change. For this purpose we multiplied our camera lucida drawings....[4]

When Wilkes and Dumont d'Urville sailed on their voyages artists were still an essential part of any scientific expedition. But before their voyages were officially published the French painter Daguerre, who had long interested himself in the production of naturalistic effects, invented photography. The invention brought the close alliance between art and science which had characterized the exploring expeditions of the preceding seventy years to a close. Science adopted photographic methods for making its graphic records; art became increasingly a vehicle of personal expression. Yet even before the appearance of photography scientific draughtsmanship was revealing a tendency to move away from a preoccupation with the graphic delineation of surfaces towards an analytical interpretation of the structure of things. The desire to express the geological facts about a given landscape was an example of this tendency, for it involved to some extent a neglect of the vegetative surface of the earth and an emphasis in drawing upon fault lines and stratifications. In botanical illustrations the Bauers popularized the practice of incorporating drawings of dissections in their plant illustrations. But it was upon the drawing of minute and often transparent marine animals, such as plankton, that scientific illustrators in the first half of the century lavished so much of their skill and patience. Just as Huxley sought to classify such animals by the use of archetypes so scientific draughtsmen sought to

221. *Site dans L'Île Manga-Reva*, lithograph after E. A. Goupil, in Dumont d' Urville, *Voyage au Pole Sud, Atlas Pittoresque* (1846), pl. 41

217 (facing page top left). *Taha-Tahala, Natif de Otago, Ile Tavaï, Pounamou. Nlle Zélande (Polynésie)*, lithograph by Léveillé after busts modelled from nature, photography by Bisson, under the direction of Dr. Doumoutier, in Dumont d' Urville, *Voyage au Pole Sud, Anthropologie (Atlas)* (1842–7), pl. 13

218. (facing page top right). *Heroua, Native de Otago. Ile Tavaï, Pounamou. Nlle Zélande (Polynésie)*, lithograph by Léveillé after busts modelled from nature, photograph by Bisson, under the direction of Dr. Doumoutier, in Dumont d' Urville, *Voyage au Pole Sud, Anthropologie (Atlas)* (1842–7), pl. 13 (bis)

219. (facing page bottom left). *Worraddey, Chef de L'ile Bruny, Canal d'Entrecasteaux Wan Dieménie (Mélanésie)*, lithograph by Léveillé after busts modelled from nature, photography by Bisson, under the direction of Dr. Doumoutier, in Dumont d' Urville, *Voyage au Pole Sud, Anthropologie (Atlas)* (1842–7), pl. 13 (bis)

220. (facing page bottom right). *Trouggarnanna, Native de Sullivan Cove. Wan Dieménie (Mélanesie)*, lithograph by Léveillé after busts from nature, photography by Bisson, under the direction of Dr. Doumoutier, in Dumont d' Urville, *Voyage au Pole Sud, Anthropologie (Atlas)* (1842–7), pl. 13

GEORGII EDVARDI
ORNITHOLOGIA NOVA

222. Frontispiece to George Edwards, *History of Birds* (1743–64)

reveal their true nature in plans and dissections. Scientific photography, as it perfected its techniques, was to follow a similar path. But the programme which Banks and his circle of friends set themselves in the late 1760's was concerned with the faithful representation of appearances. There was something heroic about the undertaking, for it implied the assembling of a systematic, empirical, and faithful graphic account of all the principal kinds of rocks, plants, animals, and peoples in the world.

The same ambitious programme had been graphically illustrated at the outset by George Edwards, in the frontispiece which he used for his *History of Birds* (1743–64). In it we see Minerva and Juno, with the assistance of Time encouraging the artist to depict the real, not the imaginary creatures, that inhabit the earth and sky (Plate 222).

And surprisingly enough, a century later, the programme was virtually complete. The great bulk of the work involved in the descriptive phases of the biological sciences (and to a lesser extent geology) had been assembled. In the process, the descriptive discipline of science had transmitted to the visual arts an analytical naturalism which did much to determine the nature of landscape painting during the nineteenth century. Apart from the basic work of Banks it was Humboldt who had played the dominant role in this alliance between art and science. It is most revealing therefore to find how enthusiastically Humboldt received the invention of photography; in it he saw the possibility of actually realizing the ambitious programme which he had outlined for artists in his *Cosmos*. Photography, like a great tropical mountain, would record something of all the climatic regions of the world. In a letter to his friend Fox Talbot, the English pioneer of photography, Humboldt exclaimed in delighted enthusiasm, 'Daguerre is my Chimborasso!' [5]

In 1759 Dr. Johnson, through the mouth of one of his characters in *Rasselas*, claimed that it was not the business of a poet 'to number the streaks of the tulip, or describe the different shades in the verdure of the forest'. And some years later Reynolds made it quite clear that such interests were still less the business of the landscape-painter who sought perfection in the highest branches of his art. One hundred years after Dr. Johnson had summed up the neo-classical position in his memorable statement, Ruskin, with an authority equal to that both of Reynolds and Johnson, expressed the opposite view, in a statement equally memorable. 'If you can paint one leaf', he wrote, 'you can paint the world.' [6] The remark was timely; for in the century which elapsed between the two remarks, navigators and explorers had provided European artists with a world to paint. And so pervasive was the influence of science upon illustration and landscape-painting during the period that it might be said with some truth that already by 1859 the painters of leaves had painted the world. So far had the artist, in the course of a century's collaboration in the business of recording the appearance of man and nature, subjected his own vision of reality to the service of science.

Abbreviations

Banks Corr., D.T.C.	Transcripts of Sir Joseph Banks's correspondence in the British Museum (Natural History) known as the Dawson Turner copies.
Brit. Mus.	British Museum.
Brit. Mus. (Nat. Hist.)	British Museum (Natural History).
N.L.A., Canberra	National Library of Australia, Canberra.
D.G., Sydney	The Dixson Galleries, Sydney.
D.L., Sydney	The Dixson Library, Sydney.
Gent. Mag.	*Gentleman's Magazine.*
H.R.A.	*Historical Records of Australia.*
H.R.N.S.W.	*Historical Records of New South Wales.*
J.H.I.	*Journal of the History of Ideas.*
J.R.A.H.S.	*Journal of the Royal Australian Historical Society.*
J.P.S.	*Journal of the Polynesian Society.*
Met. Mus. Bull.	*Bulletin of the Metropolitan Museum.*
M.G., Sydney	Mitchell Galleries, Sydney.
M.L., Sydney	Mitchell Library, Sydney.
M.P.	*Modern Philology.*
Nat. Mar. Mus., Greenwich	National Maritime Museum, Greenwich.
N.K., Canberra	Nan Kivell Collection, National Library of Australia, Canberra.
P.Q.	*Philological Quarterly.*
Phil. Trans.	*The Philosophical Transactions*, Royal Society.
Walpole Soc.	The Walpole Society.

Notes

Notes to the Preface to the Second Edition

1. e.g. Alan Moorehead, *The Fatal Impact. An Account of the Invasion of the South Pacific*, London, 1966.
2. See Hugh Honour, *The European Vision of America*, Cleveland Museum of Art, 1976, and Hugh Honour, *The New Golden Land. Images of America from the Discoveries to the Present Time*, London, 1975.
3. *The Structure of Scientific Revolutions*, University of Chicago Press, 2nd ed., 1970. p.x.
4. Ibid.

Notes to the Preface to the First Edition

1. *Place, Taste and Tradition*, a study of Australian art since 1788.
2. Trans. S. Godman. London, 1950.
3. *Journal of the Warburg and Courtauld Institutes*, xiii (1950), 13–47.
4. *Journal* cit. ii (1938), 116–27.

Notes to Chapter One

1. And the famous journey of Pallas into Siberia (1768–74), entered upon like the *Endeavour*'s voyage to observe the 1769 transit of Venus, did not foreshadow the opening up of northern Asia to Europeans in the way that Cook's entry into the Pacific foreshadowed its speedy penetration by scientists, missionaries, and merchants.
2. G. White, *The Natural History and Antiquities of Selborne* (ed. R. Bowdler Sharpe), i. 178.
3. Better known as Linnaeus.
4. J. D. Hooker, *On the Flora of Australia*, p. cxiv.
5. J. E. Smith, *Tracts relating to Natural History*, p. 11; see also F. A. Stafleu, *Linnaeus and the Linneans*, 1971.
6. J. E. Smith, *A Specimen of the Botany of New Holland*, p. 9.
7. See Lovejoy and Boas, *Primitivism and Related Ideas in Antiquity*, p. 10 *et passim*.
8. A. F. Frézier, *Relation de Voyage de la mer du sud aux côtes du Chily et du Pérou fait pendant les années 1712–1713 et 1714*, Paris, 1716.
9. Anson, G. *A Voyage Round the World* (comp. by R. Walter), London, 1748, Int.
10. J. Forster, *Observations*, p. ii.

Notes to Chapter Two

1. Bacon, *Essays* (Everyman), p. 54.
2. Hakluyt, ii. 98.
3. *Phil. Trans.* i (1665/6), 140–2. Quoted by Frantz, *The English Traveller and the Movement of Ideas 1660–1732*, p. 22.
4. Ibid.
5. See Trollope, *A History of Christ's Hospital*, p. 188; and Pearce, *Annals of Christ's Hospital*, pp. 159 ff.
6. The Educational writings of John Locke (ed. J. L. Axtell), London, 1968, p. 265.
7. Quoted in Martin Hardie, *Water-colour Painting in Britain*, III, p. 251.
8. *Phil. Trans.* lviii (1768), 1–12. Sir William Hamilton (1730–1803); diplomatist, vulcanologist, and archaeologist; envoy extraordinary and plenipotentiary at the court of Naples, 1764–1800.
9. i.e. a vent opened up by the eruption.
10. *Phil. Trans.* lviii (1768), 3.
11. *Phil. Trans.* lviii, p. 12.
12. *Campi Phlegraei, Observations on the Volcanos of the Two Sicilies*, p. 5.
13. See on the English virtuosi: W. E. Houghton, 'The English Virtuosi in the 17th Century', *J.H.I.* iii (1942), 51–73, 190–219 and cf. Gilbert White: 'Poor Mr. Banks! his Undertakings are virtu in excess!' *History of Selborne*, i. 89.
14. *Archaeologia*, i (3rd ed. 1784), p. i.
15. M. Whinney and O. Millar, *English Art, 1625–1714*, pp. 265–9.
16. E. Smith, *Life of Banks*, pp. 12–13.
17. See Blunt, *The Art of botanical Illustration*, pp. 143–55.
18. i.e. Newfoundland plants not Icelandic, as stated in H. C. Cameron, *Sir Joseph Banks*, p. 78.
19. Pennant to Banks, 29 Apr. 1767, *Banks Corr.* D.T.C., vol. 1, f. 4.
20. Ibid., 11 May 1767, vol. 1, f. 7.
21. Parkinson exhibited a painting of flowers on silk at the Free Society of Arts Exhibition, 1765, and two more flower pieces and a drawing in red chalk in 1766.
22. *Phil. Trans.* lviii (1768), 91–99.
23. *The Literary Life of Thomas Pennant*, p. 3.
24. Thomas Falconer (1738–92), classical scholar and antiquary.
25. T. Falconer to Banks, 15 Feb. 1768, *Banks Corr.*, D.T.C., vol. 1, f. 18.
26. See C. Mitchell, 'Zoffany's *Death of Cook*', *Burl. Mag.* lxxxiv (1944), 56–62.
27. See Sir Henry T. Wood, *A History of the Royal Society of Arts*, pp. 14–15 and D. G. C. Allan, *William Shipley*, 1968.
28. Cust, pp. 113 ff.
29. Farington, *Diary* (ed. Greig), i. 27.
30. See A. P. Oppé, *The Drawings of Paul and Thomas Sandby . . . at Windsor Castle*, p. 17.
31. Possibly in 1773. The late Paul Oppé referred to a note on the back of a drawing, which he saw in a sale in

1928 and copied down. It stated that Banks, Lightfoot, the Hon. Mr. Lloyd, and Paul Sandby stayed in the cottage at Llanberis (depicted) for six days in July 1776. Banks, however, is not known to have made any tour of Wales in 1776; but he did make one in the summer of 1773 when Lightfoot was of the party. It is likely that this was the occasion the party stayed at Llanberis, for they climbed Snowdon towards the end of the tour; and Banks was back in London in Aug. 1773. Paul Oppé, *in litt.* 5 Aug. 1955; J. C. Beaglehole, *in litt.* 30 Mar. 1957.

32. E. Waterhouse, *Painting in Britain 1530 to 1790*, p. 229.

33. Banks, MS. Journal of a Tour in Holland, 18 Feb 1773.

34. *MS. cit.*, 11 Mar. 1773.

35. J. Bulmer to Banks, 10 Nov. 1792, *Banks Corr.*, Kew.

36. John Holland to Banks, 29 Mar. 1801, *Banks Corr.*, Kew.

37. For Banks and Stubbs see B. Taylor, *Animal Painting in England*, p. 36 and his, *Stubbs*, p. 35. Considering that Stubbs was probably working from a stuffed or blown-up specimen he provided a credible likeness of a kangaroo and also the first credible resemblance in a painting to the open savannah quality of the Australian landscape, and the character of the eucalypt. This landscape was probably derived from a lost drawing, or drawings, by Sydney Parkinson. See also A. Lysaght, 'Captain Cook's Kangaroo', *New Scientist*, XXII (1957), 17–23.

38. W. T. Whitley, *Artists and their Friends in England 1700–1799*, i. 296.

39. Falconer to Banks, 16 Jan. 1773, *Banks Corr.*, D.T.C., vol. 1, f. 43.

40. E. Smith, p. 16.

41. *Journals of Captain James Cook* (ed. Beaglehole), 1. cclxxxii–cclxxxiv. See also the *Hints* offered to the consideration of Captain Cooke, Mr. Bankes, Doctor Solander, and other Gentlemen who go upon the Expedition on Board the *Endeavour*, by the Earl of Morton (1702–68), President of the Royal Society (1764–8), pp. 514–19.

42. Kitson, *Captain James Cook*, p. 63.

43. See R. A. Skelton, in *Mariner's Mirror*, xl (1954), 92–119.

44. Banks, *Journal of the Right Hon. Sir Joseph Banks ... in H.M.S. Endeavour* (ed. Hooker), p. 79.

45. See Solander, MS. Notebooks, *Endeavour* voyage, Brit. Mus. (Nat. Hist.).

46. W. T. Stearn, 'A Royal Society appointment with Venus', *Roy. Soc. Notes and Records*, vol. 24, no. 1. June 1969, pp. 64–90.

47. Solander MS., p. 563. It is now called *Eucalyptus terminalis*.

48. For Frederick Polydore Nodder (*fl.* 1777–1800), Botanic Painter to Queen Charlotte, see Blunt, p. 151.

49. The importance of the botanical collections made on Cook's three voyages has been examined in great detail in Elmer Drew Merrill's *The Botany of Cook's Voyages*, 1954.

50. Captain Samuel Wallis: the discoverer of Tahiti, who circumnavigated the globe in the *Dolphin*, 1766–8.

51. *Journals* (ed. cit.), i. 168.

52. Certain views and coastal profiles (B.L. Add MSS 15507–8 and 23920–1) previously unidentified or ascribed to Parkinson were identified as the work of Spöring by Alwyne Wheeler and Averil Lysaght. *in litt* A. Lysaght, 24 Jan. 1955; R. A. Skelton, 2 May 1955.

53. See also illustrations by Parkinson in Cook's *Journals*, i (ed. cit.).

54. Banks, *Journal* (ed. Hooker), p. 192

55. On the taste for grottoes among English *cognoscenti* see E. W. Manwaring, *Italian Landscape in Eighteenth Century England*. Cook, who was not a grand tourist, was much more matter-of-fact in his description: '... at the entrance into the Bay are two high rocks, the one is high and round like a corn sack but the other is long with holes thro' it like the arches of a bridge', *Journals*, i. 185.

56. Banks, *Journal* (ed. cit.), p. 198.

57. For the connexion between grottoes, geology, and romantic taste see Robert Aubin, 'Grottoes, Geology, and the Gothic Revival', *S.P.* xxxi (1934), 408–16.

58. See also A. Lysaght, 'Banks's Artists and his Endeavour Collections', *British Museum Yearbook*, 3 (1979), 29–30.

59. Paris, 1795.

60. p. 157.

61. *La Peyrouse, ein Schauspiel in zwei Aufzügen*, Leipzig, 1797.

62. *La Pérouse, a drama in two acts ... as performed at the Theatre Royal, Drury Lane*, London, 1799.

63. Pennant, *Tour in Scotland* (1774 ed.), pp. 262–3.

64. 'Letter from M. E. Raspe ... containing a short account of Some Basaltic Hills in Hassia (Hessia)', *Phil. Trans.* lxi (1771), 580–3.

65. Cf. O. Pächt, 'The human figure was the last of nature's creations from which the medieval ban on analytical observation was lifted', 'Early Italian Nature Studies', *Journal of the Warburg and Courtauld Institutes*, xiii (1950), 13–47. This splendid article provides many illuminating anticipations in early Italian art of processes studied in this book.

66. Abel Janszoon Tasman's *Journal*, ed. J. E. Heeres, p. 15.

67. The evidence is summarized in Hawkesworth, i, pp. ix–xvi, and in P. P. King, *Narrative of the Surveying Voyages of the Adventure and Beagle*, i. 28.

68. Hawkesworth, i. 28; and for a full account see H. Wallis, 'The Patagonian Giants' in *Byron's Journal of his Circumnavigation* (ed. Gallagher), pp. 185–199.'

69. Banks, *Journal* (ed. cit.), p. 59.

70. See Smith, *Art as Information*, pp. 8–9 *et al*.

71. Hawkesworth, i, p. xvi.

72. Monboddo, *Origin and Progress of Language*, i. 267–8 n.

73. For a description of this collection see Crone and Skelton, pp. 129–30.

74. Walter Veit has objected to the use of the word 'falsified' in this context claiming that both Buchan, Cipriani and Bartolozzi could only 'see' according to the ruling perceptions and visual conventions of their time. But if this was so, how would it be possible for anyone to provide an account of how any new thing observed is drawn and seen to be new? Both the artists on voyage and the engravers who interpreted them were influenced by the ruling conventions of their time (how strongly is in each case an empirical question) but their perception was never entirely determined by those conventions. This book assumes throughout that objective reality can be observed through the supporting and distorting veils of ideology and culture. See W. Veit, 'Intellectual Tradition and Pacific Discoveries' in *Captain James Cook: Image and Impact*, (ed. W. Veit), II, 110 ff.

75. Cook, *Journals*, i. 45.

76. For a detailed documentation of hard primitivism in antiquity see Lovejoy and Boas, *Primitivism and Related Ideas in Antiquity*.

77. Hawkesworth, ii. 59.

78. See p. 169.

79. *The Adventures of Telemachus*, London, 1769.

80. His sister, Sarah Sophia, in her MS Catalogue (in

the British Library) of her brother's library lists two
copies of Fénelon's book, one held at Soho Square, the
other at Revesby Abbey.

81. Fénelon, *Les Aventures de Télémaque* (3rd ed.), Paris,
    1729, i. 315.
82. Ibid., 318–19.
83. Banks, *Journal*, pp. 55–56.
84. The figure of the boy at the right is one of the many
    amorini used by Cipriani in his decorations. Cf. the
    amorini at the extreme right in *Drawing for a mytholo-
    gical Frieze*, Cipriani, P.D. 168, 3436–78, Print Room,
    Victoria and Albert Museum, London.
85. *Gentleman's Mag.* lv (1785), 52.
86. See M. Holmes, *Captain James Cook, A Bibliographical
    Excursion*, pp. 25–26, 52–55; Cook, *Journals*, i. ccliv.
87. For an interesting and well-documented, but not
    wholly convincing, presentation of the view that
    Hawkesworth did not see the Fuegians as noble
    savages and was not favourably disposed towards
    primitivism, see W. H. Pearson, 'Hawkesworth's
    Alterations', *Journal of Pacific History*, vii (1972),
    45–72.
88. See H. N. Fairchild, *The Noble Savage*, p. 108.
89. Banks, *Journal*, p. 90
90. Ibid., p. 79.
91. Bougainville (trans. Forster), *A Voyage round the
    World*, p. 249.
92. Ibid., p. 219.
93. Ibid., pp. 244–5.
94. Ibid., p. 252.
95. Ibid., pp. 228–9.
96. Bougainville, op. cit., 222–3; see also the remarks of
    P. Commerson, physician and naturalist of the
    Boudeuse, Corney, *Quest and Occupation*, ii. 461–6.
97. Banks, *On the Manners*, ff. 1c, 1d.
98. Banks, *Journal* (ed. cit.), 74.
99. (1806 ed.), pp. 213–14. A primitivistic view which
    persisted. Cf. for example Karl Marx's much-quoted
    statement, 'The Greeks were normal children. The
    charm their art has for us does not conflict with the
    primitive character of the social order from which it
    had sprung.' *Contribution to the Critique of Political
    Economy*.
100. See G. Chinard, *L'Amérique et le rêve exotique*, vi–vii *et
    passim* and T. Kendrick, *British Antiquity*, pp. 123–4.
101. Solander note-book, Marsden MS 12023. Library
    of the School of Oriental and African Studies, Uni-
    versity of London.
102. Cook, *Journals*, i. 121.
103. Hawkesworth, ii. 186.
104. Ibid., 101.
105. Ibid., 102.
106. *Tupapa'u*: 'a corpse, a ghost or apparition, the sup-
    posed spirit of the dead', Williamson, i. 203.
107. Banks, *Journal* (ed. cit.), p. 112
108. Hawkesworth, ii. 253.
109. Alan Frost has drawn attention to the fact that it
    was the most popular title in the Bristol Library from
    1773 to 1784, being borrowed 115 times between 1773
    and 1775, and 201 times over the whole period. See his
    'Captain James Cook and the Early Romantic Imagi-
    nation', p. 94, and 'New Geographical Perspectives
    and the emergence of the Romantic Imagination',
    typescript of paper presented to the Cook Conference,
    Simon Fraser University, April 1978, pp. 4–5. The
    information is from P. Kaufmann, *Borrowings from the
    Bristol Library*, Charlottesville, 1960.
110. *An epistle from Mr. Banks, Voyager, Monster-Hunter,
    and Amoroso, to Oberea, Queen of Otaheite*, London (1774).
111. Cf. James Gillray's cartoon of Banks 'The Great
    South Sea Caterpillar transformed into a Bath Butter-
    fly', National Portrait Gallery. See H. C. Cameron, *Sir

Joseph Banks, Pl. 8, facing p. 268.
112. John Scott-Waring (1747–1819): agent of Warren
    Hastings; member of the House of Commons and
    pamphleteer.
113. *Otaheite: A Poem*, 1774; on satire arising from the
    Endeavour voyage, see also C. Roderick, 'Sir Joseph
    Banks, Queen Oberea and the Satirists', in *Captain
    James Cook: Image and Impact* (ed. W. Veit), I, 1972,
    pp. 67–89.
114. C. Mitchell, 'Benjamin West's "Death of Wolfe"
    and the Popular History Piece', *Journal of the Warburg
    and Courtauld Institutes*, vii (1944), 28.
115. For Jenyns and King and a detailed discussion of
    the chain of being see A. O. Lovejoy, *The Great Chain of
    Being*, pp. 203 f., 212–23 *passim*.
116. *Natural History of Selborne*, ii. 114.
117. For antipodal inversion see Cumont, *After Life in
    Roman Paganism*, pp. 79–80; Kimble, *Geography in the
    Middle Ages*, pp. 35–37; G. A. Wood, 'Ancient and
    Medieval Conceptions of Terra Australis', *J.R.A.H.S.*
    iii (1916), 455–65; R. Wittkower, 'Marvels of the East,
    a Study in the History of Monsters', *Journal of the
    Warburg and Courtauld Institutes*, v (1942), 159–97.

NOTES TO CHAPTER THREE

1. Banks to Hooker, 19 June 1813, *Hooker Correspondence*,
   Kew., quoted by Cameron, p. 87.
2. Cf. the remarks of Baron Cuvier (1769–1832): 'This
   voyage deserves to be noted as forming an epoch in the
   history of science. Natural history having thus con-
   tracted an alliance with astronomy and navigation,
   now began to extend its researches over a wider
   sphere.... governments have learned how nearly related to each other are all the sciences, and how much
   their value is increased by combining their labours.'
   Quoted by Tomlinson, p. 66.
3. Quoted by Cameron, pp. 319–20.
4. An account of the disagreement will be found in
   Cameron, pp. 46–56, and Cook, *Journals*, ii,xxvi–xxxii.
5. Banks to Sandwich, 30 May 1772, quoted by
   Cameron, p. 286.
6. (John Marra), *Journal of the Resolution's Voyage*, 1775,
   p. iv.
7. *Phil. Trans.* i (1665/6), 142.
8. Falconer to Banks, 16 Apr. 1768, *Banks Corr.*, D.T.C.
9. Add. MS. 9345. Ascribed on the flyleaf to Buchan.
   But the style is Parkinson's and Buchan could not have
   made the New Zealand drawings. See also R. A.
   Skelton, 'The Graphic Records', *The Journals of
   Captain James Cook* (ed. Beaglehole), i. cclxix.
10. For the state of water-colour painting in the 1760's
    see: Redgrave, *Des. Cat. of Water-Colour Paintings in the
    South Kensington Museum*, p. 10; H. Lemaitre, *Le Paysage
    Anglais a l'Aquarelle 1760–1851*, Paris, 1955, pp. 34–50
    passim.
11. Advertised (as published) in *Gentleman's Mag.*, Apr.
    1772.
12. Or Johann George Adam Forster.
13. On his return he became Professor of Natural
    History at Cassel and Wilna, and, later, librarian to
    the Elector of Mayence; he died in Paris in 1794 while
    acting as a Deputy from Mayence to the National
    Assembly.
14. *Phil. Trans.* lx (1770), 100–36, 137–78.
15. For a more detailed account of the life of Wales, his
    mastership of the Mathematical School of Christ's
    Hospital (1775–98) and his likely influence upon
    Coleridge, see my 'Coleridge's *Ancient Mariner* and
    Cook's Second Voyage', *Journal of the Warburg and

16. J. R. Forster, *Observations*, pp. 55–56.
17. e.g. Brit. Mus. Add. MS. 15743.4.5.6.
18. P.R.O., Adm. 55/107. Rep. in Cook's *Journals, Charts and Views*, pl. xxix.
19. See H. T. Wood, p. 183.
20. 'There is a fairly reasonable chance that Hodges and Wright knew each other, or at the very least knew about each other.... In Wright's account book is this entry: Two grottoes by the sea side in the gulf of Salerno ... Mr. Hodges ... 105 0 0 (£s)', Charles E. Buckley, *in litt.*, 22 Mar. 1955.
21. For his connexion with Joseph Whitehurst, a member of the Lunar Society, see below, p. 104 and B. Nicholson, *Joseph Wright of Derby*, London, 1968, p. 83 *et seq.*
22. Waterhouse, p. 178. A statement which does him less than justice.
23. W. G. Constable, *Richard Wilson*, p. 139.
24. Cook to Stephens, 18 Nov. 1772, *H.R.N.S.W.* i. 370. Hodges exhibited *A View in the Island of Madeira* (169) in the Academy of 1777. A painting, traditionally attributed to Wilson, entitled *Funchal, Madeira*, formerly in the possession of Sir Edmund Bacon, was attributed to Hodges by W. G. Constable, p. 139. See also A. P. Oppé, Wilson, Hodges, and the View of Woburn Abbey', *Burl. Mag.* xcvi (1954), 86
25. Cook, *Voyage towards the South Pole*, i. 19.
26. Cook to Stephens, 18 Nov. 1772, *H.R.N.S.W.* i. 370.
27. Herbert Furst was the first to note the unusual qualities of the painting: 'A great surprise in these galleries (i.e. The National Maritime Museum, Greenwich) is the work of William Hodges. He is here represented by several paintings of astonishing vigour and originality, despite the recognisable affinity with Wilson, notably the serene *Tahiti Revisited* and the dramatic *Cape of Good Hope*. They seem to belong more to the late nineteenth than to the eighteenth century'. *Apollo*, xxv (1937), 326.
28. See Wales, *Remarks on Mr. Forster's Account of Captain Cook's last Voyage round the World*, 1778.
29. Wales, MS. Journal, 14 Mar. 1774.
30. Wales, *Remarks*, p. 29 *et passim*.
31. Wales, MS. Journal, 21 June 1774.
32. Sparrman, *A Voyage round the World with Captain James Cook*, p. 26. Parkinson had also been called a 'gentleman adventurer'. See Cook, *Journals*, i. 448 n.
33. G. Forster, i. 30.
34. See also G. Callender, ' "Cape Town" by William Hodges', *Burl. Mag.* lxxix (1941), 93–94.
35. Cook to Stephens, 18 Nov. 1772, *H.R.N.S.W.* i. 370. It was exhibited in the 1774 exhibition of the Society of Artists, a year before the return of the expedition, together with six other pictures Hodges had painted at St. Jago and Madeira.
36. Cook, *Voyage towards the South Pole*, i, p. xxxiii.
37. Contained in 'Original sketches ... collected by Admiral Isaac Smith', Mitchell Library, Sydney PXD 11.
38. G. Forster, i. 117.
39. Cf. Wilson's *Torre della Grotte*, which Hodges engraved, see B. Ford, *Drawings of Richard Wilson*, pl. 43.
40. J. R. Forster, *Observations*, p. 72; Wales, MS. Journal, 29 Jan. 1774. See also Livingstone Lowes, *Road to Xanadu*, pp. 143 f. for the ice-blink in voyage literature.
41. Sparrman, p. 34.
42. G. Forster, i. 349.
43. He was elected A.R.A. in 1787; R.A. in 1790.
44. Cf. 'In his paintings of South Sea and Indian subjects Hodges tends to a crisper handling, with sharply accented lights; and tends to treat the planes of his design somewhat like stage scenery', W, G. Constable, p. 139.

45. Cf. *A Toupapow with a corpse*, Cook, *Voyage towards the South Pole*, pl. xliv.
46. J. R. Forster, *Observations*, pp. 106–7.
47. Cf. '... in the development of naturalism ... the lower genres, intrinsically more naturalistic and which make up by far the greater proportion of the art of their period, are slowly, step by step, rising to higher rank'. F. Antal, 'Reflections on Classicism and Romanticism,' *Burl. Mag.* lxxviii (1941), 19.
48. G. Forster, i. 124.
49. Reynolds, *Discourses* (ed. Fry), p. 124.
50. G. Forster, i. 190–2.
51. Ibid., i. 194.
52. Hawkesworth, ii. 395.
53. Farington, *Diary*, vi. 266–7.
54. Reynolds, *Discourses*, p. 385.
55. See my article in *Journal of the Warburg and Courtauld Institutes*, xix (1956), 117–54.
56. A waterfall at Dusky Sound induced Wales to quote 17 lines verbatim from Thomson's *Seasons*, and to describe it as 'one of Natures most romantic scenes', MS. Journal, 29 Apr. 1773.
57. See *Voyage of Gonzalez*, Hakluyt Soc. Ser. II. xiii. 15.
58. Cook, *Voyage towards the South Pole*, i. 294–6.
59. G. Forster, i. 589.
60. Ibid., 593–4.
61. In the Royal Academy Cat. for 1785, Hodges records that (S.) Gilpin drew the animals in two of his Indian scenes.
62. G. Forster, i. 427–8.
63. Wales, *Remarks*, p. 29.
64. Cf. E. Wind, '... one of the sources of modern history painting lies in the painting of *mirabilia*', 'The Revolution in History Painting', *Journal of the Warburg and Courtauld Institutes*, ii (1938), 121.
65. The *London Packet or Lloyd's New Evening Post*, 25 Apr. 1777. Contemporary comments of this kind together with such paintings as *Province of Oparee* and *Monuments of Easter Island* greatly weaken the force of Philip Conisbee's claim that 'It was the subsequent generations of painters, from Constable and Corot to Cezanne, who would take this tradition (i.e. plein air sketching) as a starting point, and would bring a fusion of the landscape 'sketch' and the 'finished' work, where, as far as possible and increasingly so, the pure sensation of the first response to nature could be carried over into a grander scale'. See 'Pre-Romantic Plein-Air Painting!', *Art History* (December 1979), 426; and my 'William Hodges and English *plein-air* painting, *Art History* (June 1983), 143–52.
66. Edwards, *Anecdotes*, pp. 241–5.
67. *The Works of the Late Edward Dayes*, p. 332.
68. Cf. the list cited by Sir William Foster, 'British Artists in India', *Walpole Soc.* xix (1930–1), 88; on Hodges in India see M. Archer and R. Light bown, *India Observed*, Victoria and Albert Museum, 1982, and I. C. Stuebe (1973 and 1979).
69. Hodges, *Travels*, p. 2.
70. Ibid., p. 35.
71. See also T. S. R. Boase, 'Illustrations of Shakespeare's Plays in the 17th and 18th centuries', *Journal of the Warburg and Courtauld Institutes*, x (1947), 101.
72. Waterhouse, p. 208.
73. Cook, *Journal*, 2 Jan. 1773.
74. G. Forster, i. 320.
75. Hodges, p. 155.
76. Reynolds, *Discourses*, p. 21.
77. Hodges, pp. 155–6.
78. Quoted by Edwards in his article on Hodges, *Anecdotes*, pp. 241–51.
79. *Gent. Mag.* lxvii (1797), 255.
80. For a more detailed account of Hodges's last days see

Stuebe, *op cit*, 72–8, and Farington's *Diary*, the basic source.

81. Hodges, p. 153. For Hodges see also Farington, *Diary*, iv. 8–11 *et passim*; *Gent. Mag.* lxvii (1797), 255, 552; Cats. of the R.A. and Society of Artists; W. Hayley, *Life of Rommey*, pp. 258–61; *Bengal Past and Present*, xxx, July–Dec. 1925; Foster, 'British Artists in India', *Walpole Society*, xix (1930–1), 1–88; W. G. Constable, *Richard Wilson*, p. 139, and Stuebe *op cit*.

82. On Omai see Tinker, *Painter and Poet*, pp. 56–58, and *Nature's Simple Plan*, pp. 75–89; Fairchild, *The Noble Savage*, pp. 71–74, 483–4; Clark, *Omai, First Polynesian Ambassador to England*, and McCormick, *Omai*, (1977). Bougainville had returned earlier with a Tahitian, Aotourou. He did not, however, achieve the success in Paris of Omai in London.

83. In England Omai dressed in the conventional dress of the time: reddish-brown coat, white waistcoat, breeches, and sword. See Tinker, *Nature's Simple Plan*, p. 76.

84. Quoted in Cook, *Journals* (ed. Beaglehole), II, 949–50.

85. Hawkesworth's comments on the Tahitian language (*Voyages*, ii. 228–30) and Scott's references to it, may best be understood in the light of the great interest being taken at the time in the origin of primitive language and the beginnings of poetry. See Lois Whitney, 'Primitivistic Theories of Epic Origin', *M.P.* xxi (1924), 337–78.

86. A name given (*c.* 1770) to exquisites who affected Italianate manners extravagantly. Banks was lampooned as a macaroni, see E. Smith, p. 176.

87. Diderot, *Supplément au voyage de Bougainville*, ed. G. Chinard, pp. 119–20, 123–4.

88. G. Forster, i. 303.

89. Ibid., 368.

90. Published 1779.

91. Quoted by Lovejoy, *The Great Chain of Being*, p. 290.

92. See below, p. 87.

93. Du Bos, *Reflexions critiques sur la poesie et sur la peinture*, 1719 (esp. pt. 2, secs. 14–20). The book went through several editions, and the discussion of the relation between the artistic excellence and the climate of nations was much in the air, as the contrary arguments of Reynolds and James Barry plainly testify. See Barry, *Works*, ii. 177.

94. *L'Esprit des lois*, 1748.

95. *Geschichte der Kunst des Alterthums*, 1764.

96. It was based on the information contained in his Journal, recently published for the first time. *The Resolution Journal of Johann Reinhold Forster 1772–1775* (ed. M. E. Hoare), London, 1981.

97. In this he was doubtless following Bougainville who had launched a sarcastic attack upon armchair philosophers in the introduction to his *Voyage autour du monde* (pp. 16–17), which Forster himself had translated into English. See also H. Jacquier, 'Le Mirage et l'exotisme tahitiens dans la littérature', *Bulletin de la Société des études océaniennes*, vii (Dec. 1944), 16–17.

98. J. Forster, *Observations*, p. ii.

99. See also O. H. K. Spate, *The Compass of Geography*, p. i.

100. *Outlines of a Philosophy of History*, p. x.

101. *Bemerkungen auf seiner Reise um die Welt*, Berlin, 1783.

102. Herder, *op. cit.*, p. 2.

103. G. Chinard in his edition of Diderot's *Supplément au voyage de Bougainville* incorrectly sees in Taitbout a precursor of modern sociology on the basis of such borrowings (pp. 79–83).

104. Hodges, *Travels*, p. iv.

105. *Discourses*, p. 367.

106. Hodges, *Travels*, pp. 126–7.

107. Hodges, *Select Views in India*, 1786.

108. Hodges, *Travels*, p. 66.

109. Ibid., p. 64.

110. Ibid., p. 65.

111. Ibid., p. 66.

112. Ibid., pp. 67–68.

113. Ibid., p. 68.

114. Ibid., p. 64.

115. Ibid., pp. 75–76.

116. See G. Chinard in the introduction to his edition of Diderot's *Supplément au voyage de Bougainville*, p. 91 *et passim*.

117. See R. L. Meeks, *Social Science and the Ignoble Savage*, Cambridge, 1976.

118. Monboddo, i. 226.

119. Ibid., 227–8. And cf. Banks's remarks in a letter to his sister, a week after the *Adventure* returned with news of the massacre of some of Furneaux's men in New Zealand, 'ten of the Adventure's people have been rosted and eaten by our friends in New Zealand'. Banks to his sister, Sarah, 21 July 1774, *Banks Corr.*, vol. 16. M.L., Sydney.

120. Monboddo, i. 239.

121. Ibid., p. 242.

122. Ibid., p. 251.

123. Ibid., p. 252.

124. Ibid., p. 252.

125. Bowman, p. 52.

126. Ibid., p. 64.

127. Ibid., pp. 65–66.

128. Ibid., p. 62.

129. Monboddo, i. 221.

130. Ellis, *op. cit.*, pp. v–vi.

131. For Sir Ashton Lever's Museum see below, p. 127.

132. Baron Ignatius von Born (1742–91): mineralogist and metallurgist with wide general scientific interests. In 1766 arranged the Imperial Museum for Maria Theresa at Vienna, where he was a Councillor of State.

133. See below, pp. 213–214.

134. Martyn, *Universal Conchologist* (2nd ed. 1789), p. 36.

135. Farington (ed. Greig). iv. 10.

136. Forming Pt. I of *The Botanic Garden*.

Notes to Chapter Four

1. Cook, *Voyage to the Pacific Ocean*, i, p. xxxiv.

2. Ibid. 5. Cook had approached the Navy Board to obtain a boy about to leave the mathematical school at Christ's Hospital to embark with him (ibid.). The preparation of charts and views was a part of the curriculum of the school. (See above, p. 9.)

3. For an account of Webber see the entry under John Webber by D. Cole in *the Dictionary of Canadian Biography*.

4. Cook, *Voyage to the Pacific Ocean*, i. 5.

5. Cf. H. V. S. and M. S. Ogden, p. 60 *et passim*.

6. Cf. M. H. Grant, 'The hand of Webber is not difficult to detect for he imitated none and had no imitators, unless it be Joseph Farington ... who evidently admired him to the extent of adopting largely his assiduous but tedious brushing of foliage.' *Old English Landscape Painters*, p. 137.

7. Redgrave gives Webber as one of the first watercolour painters to work in the 'stained' or 'tinted' manner in England. *Water-colour Paintings in the South Kensington Museum*, p. 12.

8. Reynolds, *Discourses*, pp. 304–7.

9. For Thornton see Blunt, pp. 203–8. It is to be noted that Thornton described his plates on a title-page of vol. iii as 'Picturesque Botanical Plates of the Choicest Flowers of Europe, Asia, Africa and America'.

10. *Outlines of a Philosophy of the History of Man*, p. 289.
11. In 1808 Boydell's published a folio volume of Webber's *Views in the South Seas*. On the importance of Cook's artists in the field of costume design see Jöppien, R. 'The Artistic Bequest of Captain Cook's Voyages—Popular Imagery in European Costume Books of the Late Eighteenth and Early Nineteenth Centuries' in *Captain James Cook and his Times* (ed. R. Fisher and H. Johnston), Vancouver, 1979, pp. 187–210.
12. Quoted by Jöppien, p. 202.
13. Cf. F. Antal, in *Fuseli Studies*, 1956, p. 28 ff., *et al.*
14. Herder, *Outlines*, p. 290n
15. P. Oppé, *John and Alexander Cozens*, p. 95.
16. Hussey, *The Picturesque*, p. 120.
17. Quoted by E. A. Benians in *The Cambridge History of the British Empire*, ii. 3.
18. Philip James de Loutherbourg (1740–1812); an Alsatian painter who became a member of the French Academy, 1767; arrived in London, 1777, and became Garrick's stage and scene designer; an important innovator in theatrical design; opened the *Eidophusikon*, a panoramic peep-show in 1781.
19. For the importance of the play in the history of the English theatre see William Huse's excellent article, 'A Noble Savage on the Stage', *M.P.* xxxiii (1936), 303–16, to which this section is indebted.
20. *London Chronicle*, 20–22 Dec. 1725.
21. *Memoirs of the Life of John Phillip Kemble*, 1825, i. 311–12. Quoted by Huse.
22. Whitley, *Artists and their Friends in England, 1700–1799*, ii. 354. On the genesis and decor of the play see also R. Jöppien, 'Philippe Jacques de Loutherbourg's Pantomime "Omai, or a Trip round the World" and the Artists of Captain Cook's Voyages' in *Captain Cook and the South Pacific*, British Museum Yearbook 3, London 1979; and E. H. McCormick, *Omai*, 313–20.
23. M. Arnould, *La Mort du Capitaine Cook*, p. 3.
24. The heroizing of Cook is considered more fully in my 'Cook's Posthumous Reputation' in *Captain James Cook and his Times* (ed. R. Fisher and H. Johnston), Vancouver, 1979. pp. 159–85.
25. I am here particularly indebted to the following articles: E. Wind, 'The Revolution in History Painting'. *Journal of the Warburg and Courtauld Institutes*, ii (1938), 116–27; C. Mitchell, 'Zoffany's *Death of Captain Cook*', *Burl. Mag.* lxxxiv (1944), 56–62; C. Mitchell, 'Benjamin West's *Death of Wolfe* and the Popular History Piece', *Journal of the Warburg and Courtauld Institutes*, vii (1944), 20–33.
26. See Mitchell, 'Zoffany's *Death of Captain Cook*, *Burl. Mag.* lxxxiv (1944), 60–61.
27. For the iconography of the death of Cook see *Bibliography of Captain James Cook*, (ed. Beddie), 1970, p. 380 ff.
28. Boswell, *Life of Johnson* (ed. by G. B. Hill and L. F. Powell), iv. 331. Unfortunately, Johnson did not record his reaction to the lines in which the poetess clothed Flora in *tapa* cloth and provided Fauna with a pet kangaroo.
29. Quoted from Sparrman, pp. 186–7.
30. Ibid., p. 187.
31. *Banks Corr.*, D.T.C., i, f. 45.
32. See C. Mitchell, 'Zoffany's *Death of Cook*', p. 56.
33. Parkinson, p. 90.
34. Ibid., pp. 129–30.
35. Ibid., p. 96.
36. Ibid., p. 129.
37. Ibid., p. 79.
38. Ibid., p. 119.
39. Cook, *Journals*, i. 131.
40. Ibid., 283.
41. Parkinson, p. 98.
42. G. Forster, i. 227.
43. Ibid., 226.
44. Ibid., 438.
45. Cook, *Voyage towards the South Pole*, i. 219.
46. Cook, *Voyage to the Pacific Ocean*, i. 159–60.
47. Ibid, 294.
48. Cook, *Voyage towards the South Pole*, i. 293.
49. G. Forster, i. 567.
50. Ibid., 228.
51. Ibid., 580.
52. Ibid., 227.
53. Ibid.
54. Ibid., 291–2.
55. Ibid., 456.
56. Cook, *Voyage to the Pacific Ocean*, i. 397.
57. *With Captain James Cook in the Antarctic and Pacific The private journal of James Burney* ... (ed. B. Hooper), pp. 56–7.
58. *Ibid.*, p. 84.
59. James King (1750–84): second lieut. on the *Resolution* on the third voyage; later commanded the *Discovery*.
60. See J. D. Freeman, 'Polynesian Collection of Trinity College, Dublin; and the National Museum of Ireland', *J.P.S.* lviii (1949), 1–18.
61. *Companion to the Museum (Late Sir Ashton Lever's)*, 1790.
62. The items from the Pacific listed and described in the *Companion* cover 21 pages.
63. Hawkesworth, iii. 463.
64. *Companion*, p. 7.
65. Ibid., p. 11.
66. Since this was written, Dr. Adrienne Kaeppler has greatly enlarged our knowledge of the destination and present provenance of many Pacific artifacts collected on Cook's voyages. See her 'Artificial Curiosities.' An Exposition of Native Manufactures Collected on the three Pacific Voyages of Captain James Cook, R.N.', Honolulu, 1978 and bibl.
67. For the impact of the Near East upon contemporary English literature see W. C. Brown, 'The Popularity of English Travel Books about the Near East 1775–1825', *P.Q.* xv (1936), 70–80; and 'English Travel Books and Minor Poetry about the Near East', 1775–1825, *P.Q.* xvi (1937), 249–71.
68. Winckelmann (trans. Lodge), i. 134.
69. Cook, *Voyage to the Pacific Ocean*, i, p. lxviii. Over ten years before Lord Monboddo had expressed a somewhat similar view: 'The communication and intercourse that has been betwixt the several parts of the old world on this side of the globe, and likewise betwixt the old and the new world discovered by Columbus, during these last three hundred years, has made so great a change in the manners and way of living of men in those countries, that it is not there we are now to look for people living in the natural state, but in another part of the world, as yet very imperfectly discovered, and with which we have had hitherto very little intercourse, I mean the countries of the South Sea, and such parts of the Atlantic Ocean as have not been frequented by European ships', *Origin and Progress of Language*, i. 250.
70. Cook, *Voyage to the Pacific Ocean*, i, pp. lxviii–lxix.
71. Ibid., p. lxix.
72. Memoirs of Thomas Jones, *Walpole Soc.* xxxii (1951), 37.
73. Cook, *Voyage to the Pacific Ocean*, i, p. lxx.
74. Cf. 'The women at sunset always bared their bodies down to the waist.' Banks, *Journal* (ed. Hooker), p. 132
75. Tahiti was at times an image of the East as well as an image of the South Seas. Thus our contemporary re-

viewer of *Omai* writes: 'This pantomime is founded on an Eastern tale' and speaks of 'a Morai, or repository for the bodies of the Eastern Kings in Otaheite'. The *London Chronicle*, 20–22 Dec. 1785, p. 595.

76. Parkinson, p. 23.
77. Sparrman, p. 49.
78. J. R. Forster, *Observations*, p. 465.
79. G. Forster, i. 456.
80. Quoted by Fairchild, p. 456.
81. See Fairchild who also discusses the romantic identification of early British poetry and the songs of the American Indians, p. 455 *et passim*.
82. Watling, *Letters*, pp. 29–30; see below, pp. 135–9. Cf. also Lord Kames's comment: 'It is remarkable that these people (i.e. the Tahitians) roast their meat with hot stones, as the Caledonians did in the days of Ossian', *Sketches of the History of Man*, i. 34; and Dr. Johnson's, 'If we know little of the ancient Highlanders, let us not fill the vacuity with Ossian. If we have not searched the Magellanick regions, let us forbear to people them with Patagons', *Journey to the Western Islands of Scotland* (1775), p. 108.
83. G. Forster, i. 567.
84. Péron, *Voyage*, p. 63.
85. See E. Wind, 'The Revolution of History Painting', *Journal of the Warburg and Courtauld Institutes*, ii (1938), 117–19.
86. On Cook's voyages and the romantic imagination see also the articles by Alan Frost (1972) cited above.

NOTES TO CHAPTER FIVE

1. Keate, *Account of the Pelew Islands*, p. vii.
2. Ibid., p. viii.
3. Keate, p. xiii.
4. Ibid., pp. 261–3.
5. Devis later travelled in Bengal and upon returning to England became well known as a history-painter; one of his best-known paintings being a death of Nelson.
6. Keate, pp. 102–5 *et passim*.
7. Two views by Devis relating to this voyage, formerly attributed to Webber, are held in the Rex Nan Kivell Collection, National Library of Australia, Canberra, NK 52Q and 52R.
8. Voltaire, *Complete Romances* (New York, 1927), p. 214.
9. Keate, pp. 250–1.
10. Voltaire, op. cit., p. 210.
11. Keate, p. 349.
12. In *To a Young Lady with a Poem on the French Revolution* (1794).
13. T. Martyn, *The Universal Conchologist*, p. 16; for Martyn see below, pp.
14. Scott, *La Pérouse*, pp. 41–42.
15. Cook, *Voyage to the Pacific Ocean*, i, p. xxxiv.
16. Ferguson, *Essay on the History of Civil Society*, pp. 3–4.
17. Monboddo, *Origin and Progress of Language*, i. iv.
18. *Outlines of a Philosophy of the History of Man*, i. 289–91.
19. *La Pérouse*, i. 37–38.
20. Ibid.
21. Ibid., 42.
22. Ibid. 327.
23. Ibid. ii. 130–1.
24. It appeared before Milet Mureau's edition of La Pérouse's voyage.
25. *Découvertes dans la mer du Sud*, p. 7.
26. Ibid., p. 25.
27. Ibid., p. 52.
28. Ibid., pp. 67–68.
29. i.e. Sandwich.
30. *A Letter from Omai*, pp. 1–2.

31. Ibid., p. 4.
32. Ibid., p. 13.
33. Ibid., p. 23.
34. IBid., p. 24.
35. 'The Apostolic Commission', *Sermons preached in London . . .*, 1795, p. 12.
36. Letter from Rev. T. Haweis, *Evangelical Magazine*, July 1795, p. 263.
37. Minutes. Meeting of Directors, London Missionary Society, 23 July 1798.
38. Gunner on the first voyage of the *Duff*, and later its commander.
39. Minutes. Meeting of Directors, London Missionary Society, 23 July 1798.
40. Ibid., 11 July 1799.
41. J. Sterling, *Essays and Tales*, i, p. xx.
42. And of comparative value, therefore, for the study of the beginnings of art in Australia. See the following chapter.
43. Edwards, *Voyage of H.M.S. Pandora*, pp. 108–9.
44. See H. N. Fairchild, pp. 140 ff.
45. Labillardière, *Atlas*, pl. 25a.
46. Labillardière, *Voyage* (London, 1800), p. v.
47. Ibid., pp. v–vi.
48. Ibid., *Voyage*, pp. vi–vii.
49. Marchand, *Voyage*, London, 1801, i..337n–8n.
50. Ibid., 338.
51. Ibid., 352–4.
52. Ibid., 258.
53. Coleridge, of course, acknowledged the value of Bowles's poetry in the development of his own poetry.
54. Chateaubriand, *Génie du Christianisme*, p. 434.
55. Ibid., pp. 434–5.

NOTES TO CHAPTER SIX

1. Cf. 'Concluding that it would be a desirable Object to bring home for his Majesty's Botanic Garden at Kew some of the many beautiful and useful Plants with which the Country in the neighbourhood of Jackson's Bay is known to abound, I beg leave to suggest to you, sir, that if the tafferell of the ship *Guardian* be fitted for the reception of pots in the same manner as we have done in the case of the *Bounty*, and one Line along the sides of the Great Cabin, she will be able, without inconvenience to the officers, to bring home a great number.' Banks to Nepean, 27 April 1789, *H.R.N.S.W.*, vol. i, pt. 2, 229–30.
2. See letters to Banks (various refs.) *H.R.N.S.W.*, vols. i–vii; and *Banks Corr.*, M.L.
3. Phillip to Banks, 3 Dec. 1791, *Banks. Corr.*, M.L., Sydney.
4. Note, however, F(rancis) F(owkes), to whom G. Mackaness attributes *Sketch and Description of the Settlement at Sydney Cove, Port Jackson, April 1788*. See Mackaness, *Phillip*, f. p. 128.
5. An A.B. on *Sirius* until 30 Sept. 1787 when he became a midshipman; lieut., 17 June 1797. See O. Salvin, *Proc. Zool. Soc.* (1877), pp. 95–96; G. P. Whitley, *Aust. Mus. Mag.* vi (1938), 291–304.
6. It is quite possible that this artist was Henry Brewer (1745–96), who was an old friend of Governor Phillip, and acted as a clerk for him on several of his ships. Edward Spain in his MS. journal in the Mitchell Library writes: 'Now Mr. Brewer was just such a man as the Governor wanted what excellent plans, drafts and views of places he could draw, which I can send home to my patrons Harry was accordingly appointed and sailed with his old Captain to new South Wales, where he was appointed Provost marshall and there he

died peace to his shade if honesty merits heaven, Harry is there.' See also Mackaness, *Phillip*, f. p. 356. See also R. and T. Rienits, (1963), pp. 30 ff. *et al.*

7. Work attributed to Raper (including signed drawings) is to be found in collections in the Brit. Mus. (Nat. Hist.), the Mitchell Library, Sydney, and the Alexander Turnbull Library, Wellington. An excellent account of the known facts about Raper and comments on his work are to be found in Rienits (1963).

8. Raper Drawings, ff. 17. 21 and 'Watling' Drawings, no. 86. 31. Brit. Mus. (Nat. Hist.).

9. Item *D 311.

10. Item 205.

11. Reproduced in Mackaness, *Phillip*, f. p. 108.

12. Ibid., f. p. 240.

13. Bradley, *Journal*, f. p. 38.

14. Ibid., f. p. 90.

15. On Bradley see Rienits (1963), 21–6.

16. *Memoirs of James Hardy Vaux*, 1819, i. 205.

17. *Voyage of Governor Phillip to Botany Bay*, p. i.

18. John Abbott (1751–c. 1842), see F. C. Sawyer, 'Notes on some original drawings of birds used by Dr. John Latham', *J. Soc. Bibl. Nat. Hist.* ii (1949), 173–80.

19. Aylmer Burke Lambert (1761–1842): botanist and collector, Vice-President of the Linnean Society, 1796–1842.

20. John White (c. 1750–1832), chief surgeon to the first fleet.

21. Better known as Carolus Linnaeus.

22. See Blunt, pp. 190–2, *et passim.*

23. *Voyage of Governor Phillip to Botany Bay*, pp. 294–5.

24. Sibthorp to Banks, 10 June 1793, *Banks Corr.*, vol. 18, M.L., Sydney.

25. Smith, *Specimen*, p. 20.

26. Ibid., p. 52.

27. Francis Bauer, *Exotic Plants*, Preface.

28. i.e. *Nelumbo nucifera*, the 'East Indian Lotus'. The species is found from southern Asia to the northern part of Australia.

29. Duchess of Portland to Banks, *Banks Corr.*, vol. 16, M.L., Sydney. See plate 64 for Thornton's illustration of the plant.

30. Smith, *Specimen*, pp. 45–46.

31. George Shaw, *Musei Leveriani Explicatio*, London, 1796, pp. 38–9.

32. The history of the idea has been traced in detail by A. O. Lovejoy, *The Great Chain of Being*.

33. 'Reflections on the Study of Nature', trans. J. E. Smith, *Tracts Relating to Natural History*, p. 11.

34. J. E. Smith, *Specimen*, p. 2. Cf. also Southwell, D., *Journal*, *H.R.N.S.W.* ii. 667.

35. Smith, *Specimen*, p. 9.

36. Hunter, p. 68.

37. E. Darwin, *Zoonomia* (Philadelphia, 1818), i. 392–3.

38. Dampier, *New Voyage* (ed. Masefield), i. 453.

39. Cook, *Journals* (ed. Beaglehole), i. 399.

40. Banks, *Journal*, (ed. Hooker), pp. 315–16.

41. Ibid., p. 265.

42. Kames, *Sketches of the History of Man*, p. 23.

43. See Lovejoy, p. 197 *et passim.*

44. Monboddo, i. 420.

45. Shaw, p. 2.

46. And often a strong erotic appeal.

47. Item 220.

48. Tench, *Complete Account*, p. 10.

49. Ibid., p. 17.

50. Ibid., p. 22.

51. Ibid., pp. 23–24.

52. Ibid., p. 200.

53. Ibid., p. 129.

54. Ibid., p. 187.

55. See Lovejoy, *Essays in the History of Ideas*, pp. 69–77.

56. See L. Whitney, *Primitivism and the Idea of Progress*.

57. Diderot, *Supplément au voyage de Bougainville*, pp. 91–96 *passim.*

58. *Voyage of Governor Phillip to Botany Bay*, pp. 122–3.

59. In his 'Neuholland und die brittische Kolonie in Botany-Bay,' *Historischer Kalender vom Jahre 1786*, Göttingen. See L. Bodi, 'Georg Forster: the Pacific Expert of 18th Century Germany', *Historical Studies Aust. and N.Z.*, ix (1959), 345 *et seq.*

60. See also *Economy of Vegetation*, ii. 317–18.

61. See F. Rathbone, *Josiah Wedgwood on the Clay of Sydney Cove*, Birmingham, n.d.

62. Tuckey, pp. 189–90.

63. Hawkesworth, iii. 622.

64. Parkinson, p. 134.

65. Hunter, p. 77.

66. S. M. Onslow, *Some Early Records of the Macarthurs*, p. 48.

67. Cf. 'Brown . . . reduced the new irregular landscaping to a system of his own in which the main elements were clumps, belts and lakes distributed in an otherwise close-shaven terrain' J. Summerson, *Architecture in Britain, 1530–1830*, p. 291. Doubtless Australia's natural parklands reminded some travellers of estates improved by Brown.

68. A. Bowes, MS. journal, M.L., Sydney; *H.R.N.S.W.* ii. 392.

69. *H.R.N.S.W.* ii. 666.

70. Thomas Watling (1762–?): limner of Dumfries; sentenced to 14 years' transportation, 1789, for forging guinea notes upon the Bank of Scotland; arrived Sydney on the *Royal Admiral*, Oct. 1792; granted conditional pardon, Sept. 1796; appears to have practised as a miniature-painter in Calcutta (1801–3) after leaving Sydney; tried and acquitted of forging five-pound banknotes of the Bank of Scotland, at Edinburgh Jan. 1806. See Gladstone, pp. 70–133.

71. Watling, *Letters from an Exile at Botany Bay to his Aunt in Dumfries*, pp. 7–8.

72. Ibid., 15.

73. Pennant *Outlines of the Globe*, iv. 104.

74. i.e. the plain on which Sydney is situated.

75. Watling, pp. 1–2.

76. Ibid., pp. 8–9.

77. Gilpin, *Observations . . . made in 1772, on Several Parts of England, part. the Mountains and Lakes of Cumberland and Westmoreland* (1786), pp. 59–60.

78. Watling, p. 9.

79. Gilpin, *Observations . . . on . . . Cumberland and Westmoreland* (1786), p. 83.

80. Gilpin, *On the Principles on which the Author's Sketches are Composed* (1804), pp. 35–36.

81. Gilpin, *On the Principles on which the Author's Sketches are Composed* (1804), pp. 35–36.

82. Now only faintly discernible because of the fugitive quality of the paint employed.

83. Gilpin, *Observations made in 1772, etc.*, p. 106.

84. Watling, p. 26.

85. Ibid., p. 12.

86. Watling, p. 11.

87. Collins, i. 563.

88. A detailed discussion of early opinion and comment upon the Australian aborigines will be found in D. J. Mulvaney, 'The Australian Aborigines 1606–1929: Opinion and Fieldwork', *Historical Studies Aust. and N.Z.*, viii (1958), 131–51, 297–314.

Notes to Chapter Seven

1. E. Scott, p. 176.

2. To continue Cook's survey of the north-west coast of

America, 1791–5.

3. Flinders, *Voyage to Terra Australis*, i. 11.
4. In his, *On the Flora of Australia*, p.cxiv.
5. See Blunt, pp. 200–1.
6. See Sitwell and Blunt, pp. 10–11, passim.
7. Flinders, i. 221.
8. In a letter to the Royal Colonial Institute, 9 Nov. 1889; Library of the Royal Commonwealth Society, London.
9. Flinders, i. 96.
10. Westall to Banks, 31 Jan. 1804. *Banks Corr.*, vol. 4. M.L., Sydney. Westall may have been misled concerning the route to be followed when offered the position of landscape-painter, for on 28 Mar. 1801 Thomas Daniell informed Joseph Farington that his nephew William was to embark with Flinders, 'to explore and make out the boundaries of New Holland, abt which there are some doubts, that is whether a *Mediterranean Sea* does not pass between those parts which have been supposed to be one island. They are also to visit some Islands situated further out than Otaheite.' Farington, *Diary*, i. 304.
11. Westall to Banks, 31 Jan 1804
12. *Art Journal*, xii (1805), 104.
13. Sir William Foster, 'British Artists in India', *Walpole Soc.* xix (1931), 77.
14. Farington, v. 182. Banks most likely had in mind Labillardière's *Relation du voyage à la recherche de La Pérouse* (Paris, 1800; London, 1802), and Péron's *Voyage de découvertes aux terres Australes* (Paris, 1807).
15. T. M. Perry and D. H. Simpson, *Drawings by William Westall*, p. 62.
16. *Art Journal*, xii (1850), 105.
17. On Westall see also T. M. Perry, and D. H. Simpson, *Drawings by William Westall*, London, 1962; and R. J. Westall, 'William Westall in Australia', *Art and Australia*, vol. 20, no. 2 (1982), 252–6.
18. Péron, *A Voyage of Discovery to the Southern Hemisphere* (London, 1809), p. 85.
19. Quoted from the *American Journal of Sciences and Arts* (Sept. 1849), p. 206.
20. Ibid., p. 207.
21. This is not to suggest that typical landscape appeared for the first time at the end of the eighteenth century. H. V. S. and M. S. Ogden in their *English Taste in Landscape in the Seventeenth Century* have shown how one form of typical landscape arose from the mergence of the topographical and the ideal traditions in landscape towards the end of the seventeenth century. 'The particular scene is lost in the type of scenery, and an image that is a generalized symbol for a region or a kind of terrain is presented' (p. 163). But it was during the nineteenth century that the typical landscape achieved its most complete expression, for only then did Europeans become fully aware of the varied scenery of the earth's surface.
22. Plomley (1983), 162.
23. See J. M. Degérando, *The Observation of Savage Peoples*, trans. F. C. T. Moore, London, 1969. In an otherwise illuminating introduction to this important work, Dr. Moore unfortunately does not place Degérando's work in the context of the publications arising from Cook's voyages, particularly J. R. Forster's *Observations*. By 1799 most of these publications were readily available in French translations.
24. For Lesueur in America see R. W. G. Vail, 'American Sketchbooks of Charles Alexandre Lesueur, 1816–1837', *Proc. Am. Ant. Soc.*, April 1938.
25. See T. Sutton, *The Daniells, Artists and Travellers*.
26. For a comprehensive list of such books see J. R. Abbey, *Travel in Aquatint and Lithography*, Curwan Press, London, 1956–7.
27. Payne Knight, *Analytical Enquiry* (1806), p. 149.

28. *Northanger Abbey*, p. 111.
29. Hazlitt, *Works* (ed. Howe), viii. 317.
30. *Table Talk and Omniana of Samuel Taylor Coleridge* (1917), p. 443.
31. Payne Knight, *Analytical Enquiry*, p. 80.
32. Ibid., p. 169.
33. *The Works of the Late Edward Dayes*, pp. 285–6.
34. Humboldt, *Cosmos* (trans. Sabine), London, 1848, ii. 5.
35. Humboldt, *Aspects of Nature* (trans. Sabine), ii. 13–14.
36. Ibid., ii. 18.
37. Price, *Essays on the Picturesque*, 1810, i. ch. 8.
38. Cf. the remarks of Barron Field, p. 240–1 below.
39. Humboldt, *Aspects*, ii. 29.
40. Humboldt, *Aspects*, ii. 31.
41. *John Constable's Clouds*, pp. 23–34.
42. See T. S. R. Boase, 'The Decoration of the New Palace of Westminster, 1841–1863', *Journal of the Warburg and Courtald Institutes*, xvii (1954), 319–58.
43. *Pictorial Maps for the Illustration of the Land, the Sea, and the Heavens, on the Walls of Large Buildings, and Georamas. A Letter addressed to C. L. Eastlake, Esq., R.A. Sec. to the Commission of Fine Arts*. London, 1849, p. 6.
44. *Works*, v. 428.
45. Ibid. xxxix. 271.
46. Ibid. i. 67 ff.
47. Ibid. vii. 175–7.
48. For Humboldt's influence on American landscape-painting see A. T. E. Gardner, 'Scientific Sources of the Full-length Landscape: 1850', *Met. Mus. Bul.* iv (1945), 59–65.
49. Choris, *Voyage pittoresque*, p. iii.
50. Adalbert von Chamisso (1781–1838): naturalist on Kotzebue's first voyage; botanist and poet; author of *Peter Schlemihl*, the man who lost his shadow.
51. *Vues et paysages*, p. 3.
52. Ibid., pp. 2–3.
53. Humboldt, *Aspects*, ii. 21.
54. Ibid., 21–22.

NOTES TO CHAPTER EIGHT

1. Thomas Martyn, *The Universal Conchologist* (2nd ed. 1789), p. 6.
2. Ibid., p. 36.
3. See P. Mander Jones, 'John William Lewin a Memoir', *Biblionews*, vi (1953), 36 ff.; and A. McEvey's introduction to his critical edition of the 1838 edition of Lewin's *Birds of New South Wales*, Melbourne, 1978.
4. *H.R.A.* ii. 127.
5. Drury Papers, Entomological Library, Brit. Mus. (Nat. Hist.).
6. *Trans. Linnean Soc.* i. 46.
7. Drury Papers, *loc. cit.*, Invoice of Goods deliv'd on board the *Buffalo* for Mr. J. W. Lewin ... 22 Mar. 1798.
8. C. H. Smith, 'Memoir of Dru Drury', *Naturalist's Library*, quoted by P. Mander Jones, p. 38.
9. *Trans. Linnean Soc.* i. 45.
10. *Drury Papers*, 7 Mar. 1803.
11. Cf. Ferdinand Bauer's difficulties in 1813, above, p. 141.
12. See Blunt, p. 208.
13. Banks to Caley, 25 Aug. 1808, *Banks Corr.* vol. 8, M.L., Sydney.
14. Entry for 29 Nov. 1784, Enrolment of Indentures, Mar. 1781–Aug. 1806. Birmingham Reg. Coventry City Archives.
15. Entry in Freedom Roll, 7 Aug. 1792, Coventry City Archives.

16. *Coventry Mercury*, 21 Feb. 1799; N.S.W. Col. Sec., Indents, 1801; General Muster, 1811.
17. The Public Library, Coventry, possesses a copy of the second, and the British Museum a copy of the third edition. I have not seen a copy of the first.
18. The letter written 'by a Manchester man' is dated 4 June 1811.
19. NSW Col. Sec: Register of Conditional Pardons 1791–1825, p. 21; quoted by R. and T. Rienits, (1963), p. 237.
20. *Sydney Gazette*.
21. On rare occasions these are replaced by officials or a group of hunters.
22. They were engraved as aquatints by Clark, possibly John Heaviside Clark. See Rienits (1963), 197.
23. Péron, pp. 271 ff.
24. e.g. Blake's *Family of New South Wales* (93) recurs in Joseph Lycett's *Distant View of Sydney*, and the *View of Sydney* by Paul Mikhailov. See *The Voyage of Captain Bellingshausen to the Antarctic Seas*, i. 160–1.
25. S. Smith, *Works*, p. 26.
26. In the Mitchell Library, Sydney.
27. e.g. the five drawings of aborigines in the Nan Kivell Collection. Item 215 N. K. Canberra. See also James Finucan's *Tippahee (Te Pahi) a Chief of New Zealand* (1808). M.L., Sydney for an early comic Maori.
28. 19 Jan. 1811. Quoted by P. Mander Jones.
29. Michael Massey Robinson (1747–1826): London attorney convicted of attempted extortion; transported for life; clerk to various judge advocates and magistrates; recited birthday odes regularly at Government House, Sydney, on the birthdays of George III and Queen Charlotte.
30. Macquarie to Bathurst, 8 Oct. 1814, *H.R.A.* Ser. 1. v 368.
31. Péron, *Voyage de découvertes aux Terres Australes*, i. 381.
32. Péron, *Voyage of Discovery*, p. 286.
33. Ibid., p. 109.
34. Ibid., pp. 291 ff.
35. Ibid., p. 306.
36. O'Hara, p. 54.
37. S. Smith, *Works*, ii. 254.
38. Barron Field (1786–1846): son of the apothecary of Christ's Hospital, where Leigh Hunt was his elder contemporary. Read law at the Inner Temple; dramatic critic to *The Times*; contributed to Hunt's *Examiner*, and accompanied Hunt to prison, 1813; app. Supreme Court Judge of New South Wales, 1817; recalled 1824; Chief Justice, Gibraltar, 1829–35; between 1841 and 1846 edited five texts of Heywood for the Shakespeare Society. Died, Torquay, 1846.
39. See also above, p.
40. *Sydney Gazette*, 10 June 1815; Mackaness, *Fourteen Journeys*, i. 71–82.
41. See *Sydney Gazette*, 10 June 1815; Mackaness, *Fourteen Journeys*, i. 75.
42. Ibid.
43. See P. R. Stephenson, *The Foundations of Culture in Australia*, Sydney, 1936. pp. 36–52.
44. Wentworth, *Statistical Description*, pp. 14–15.
45. Flinders, *Voyage*, ii. 586–7.
46. Oxley, p. 113.

Notes to Chapter Nine

1. See T. M. Perry, 'The Spread of Rural Settlement in New South Wales, 1788–1826', *Historical Studies: Aust. and N.Z.* vi (1955), 377–95.
2. W. Dixson, *J.R.A.H.S.* v (1919), 243.
3. Oxley, *Journals*, see plates facing pp. 275, 300.
4. Wallis, p. 1.
5. Ibid.
6. Ibid., p. 40.
7. See, e.g., drawings of corroborees by H. Darcy (N.K. 212), W. R. Govett (*Saturday Mag.*, 1836–7), lithographs by Captain Hext (N.K. 421) and W. H. Fernyhough (1836), and paintings by John Glover (*c.* 1835).
8. *Sydney Gazette*, 21 June 1822; 13 Sept. 1822.
9. Lycett, *Views*, the Advertisement.
10. Ibid., p. 15.
11. His method may be examined clearly in the landscape on the title-page of his *Views* (132).
12. Since the first edition, the second set of drawings on which the engravings are based has re-appeared. Auctioned at Sothebys, 9 July 1962 (lot 237) they are now divided among several collections.
13. Field, *On Reading the Controversy between Lord Byron and Mr. Bowles*, a poem included in the second edition of *First Fruits* (1823).
14. Field, *Geographical Memoirs*, pp. 421–2.
15. Ibid., p. 423.
16. Charles Darwin, who made the trip across the Blue Mountains thirteen years later, was inspired to write in a similar vein, and he too seems to have Humboldt at the back of his mind: 'The inhabitants of this hemisphere and of the intertropical regions, thus lose perhaps one of the most glorious, though to our eyes common, spectacles in the world, the first bursting into foliage of the leafless tree. They may, however, say that we pay dearly for this, by having the land covered with mere naked skeletons for so many months. This is too true; but our senses thus acquire a keen relish for the exquisite green of the spring, which the eyes of those living within the tropics, sated during the long year with the gorgeous productions of those glowing climates, can never experience.' Darwin, *Voyage of the Beagle*, iii, 518.
17. Field, *Geographical Memoirs*, pp. 429–30.
18. Field, *Geographical Memoirs*, pp. 430–1.
19. Ibid., p. 443.
20. Ibid., p. 445.
21. Mackaness, *Fourteen Journeys*, ii. 30.
22. Ibid., 91 from *The Australian*, 24 Mar. 1827.
23. Cunningham, i. 126.
24. Ibid., 132.
25. See Mackaness, *Fourteen Journeys*, i. 18.
26. Cunningham, i. 126.
27. The native group in this illustration is clearly based on Blake's *Family of N.S.W.* (93).
28. Mackaness, *Fourteen Journeys*, i. 85.
29. Field, *Geographical Memoirs*, p. 429.
30. Mackaness, *Fourteen Journeys*, ii. 20.
31. See Pliny Earle, *Ralph Earle and his Descendents*, 1888.
32. Dunlap, ii. 322.
33. Ibid.
34. Earle, *Narrative of a Nine Months' Residence*, pp. iv–v.
35. Dunlap, ii. 324.
36. *Cat. of Paintings ... etc.... Ex. at the Pennsylvania Academy of Fine Arts*, July 1818.
37. Earle, *Narrative of a Nine Months' Residence*, p. vi.
38. Graves, *The Royal Academy*.
39. Ibid.
40. See Earle, *Narrative of a Nine Months' Residence*, pp. 287–371.
41. Ibid., p. 291.
42. Ibid., pp. 287–371.
43. *Sydney Gazette*, 28 July 1829.
44. Nan Kivell Collection, Canberra.
45. *Sydney Gazette*, 31 Oct. 1825.
46. Ibid., 28 July 1829.
47. Ibid., 30 July 1829.

48. Ibid., 289.
49. *Sydney Gazette*, 28 July 1829.
50. Ibid.
51. Harris, *Settlers and Convicts*, pp. 29 ff.
52. Philip Astley (1742–1814), a celebrated equestrian performer and theatrical manager of London.
53. Field, *Geographical Memoirs*, p. 464.
54. Cunningham, i. 115–16.
55. On the noble frontiersman see R. Ward, *The Australian Legend*, pp. 228–36.
56. See Badt, *John Constable's Clouds*, 36, 41 ff.
57. Nan Kivell Collection, 12. 25.
58. Robert Burford (1791–1861): maintained panoramas in the Strand and later in Leicester Square.
59. *Sydney Gazette*, 9 May 1829; 28 July 1829.
60. On Earle see also J. Hackforth Jones, *Augustus Earle Travel Artist*, Canberra, 1980.
61. See Basil Long, 'John Glover', *Walker's Quarterly*, xv (Apr. 1924), for the most complete account of Glover's English career.
62. But a MS. statement by a former pupil of Glover's in the possession of Dr. W. L. Crowther, Hobart, reads: 'He would probably have made a large fortune but for the conduct and extravagance of his eldest son which involved him in such difficulties he was obliged to go to Australia.'
63. B. Fitzpatrick, *British Imperialism and Australia*, pp. 278–9.
64. Backhouse, p. 147.
65. Button, *Flotsam and Jetsam*, p. 120.
66. John Glover junior to his sister Mary, 20 Feb. 1831, *Glover MSS.*, M.L., Sydney.
67. Ibid., 15 Sept. 1833.
68. Boyes, *Diary*, 31 Oct. 1831.
69. John Glover junior to his sister Mary, 15 Sept. 1833, *Glover MSS.*, M.L., Sydney.
70. Ibid.
71. Moore, i. 32.
72. Glover junior to John Lord, 16 Oct. 1831, *Glover MSS.*, M.L., Sydney.
73. *A catalogue of Sixty Eight Pictures descriptive of the Scenery and Customs of the Inhabitants of Van Diemen's Land, together with Views in England, Italy, etc., painted by John Glover ... now exhibiting at 106 Bond St., London.*
74. B. Long, art. cit., p. 4.
75. B. Long, art. cit., p. 18.
76. Effectively prevented by the return of Napoleon according to Long. But Henry Button claims the medal was struck and presented to Glover. After his death Glover's son presented the medal to the Queen Victoria Museum, where it remained until stolen from its case on 20 Jan. 1904 (Button, pp. 119–20).
77. John Glover junior to his sister Mary, 8 Sept. 1833, *Glover MSS.*, M.L., Sydney.
78. Button, p. 121.
79. *Old Newtown*, in the Tasmanian Museum and Art Gallery, is another painting which might be ascribed to John Glover junior.
80. Glover junior to his sister Mary, 12 July 1839, *Glover MSS.*, M.L., Sydney.
81. Glover junior to his sister Mary, 20 Feb. 1831, *Glover MSS.*, M.L., Sydney.
82. Ibid., 22 Sept. 1833.
83. Ibid., 20 Feb. 1831.
84. Glover junior to John Lord, Hobart Town, 16 Oct. 1831.
85. George Augustus Robinson (c. 1788–1866): Protector of Aborigines in Tasmania and later in Port Phillip. Induced Tasmanian aborigines to lay down their arms and settle on Flinders Island, 1835.
86. On Glover see also J. A. McPhee, *John Glover—The Prints and associated material*, Queen Victoria Museum

and Art Gallery, Launceston, 1976; and *The Art of John Glover*. Melbourne, 1980.
87. Australian reactions to the continuing aboriginal presence are discussed more fully in my *The Spectre of Truganini: The Boyer Lectures, 1980*, Sydney (1981): see also J. J. Healy, *Literature and the Aborigine in Australia 1770–1975*, St. Lucia, Queensland, 1978; and A. T. Yarwood and M. J. Knowling, *Race Relations in Australia*, 1982.
88. Dawson, p. 103.
89. Holman, iv. 473.
90. *Encyclopaedia Britannica*, 6th ed., iv. 218.
91. Roberts, pp. 112–13.
92. Cf. 'Australia is the land of contrarieties ... her zoology can only be studied and unravelled on the spot, and that only by a profound philosopher.' Field, *Geographical Memoirs*, p. viii.
93. See *Encyclopaedia Britannica* (7th ed., 1842) which incorporated the *Supplement* (pub. 1815–24), iv. 218.

Notes to Chapter Ten

1. W. J. Hooker, *Botanical Miscellany*, i. 48–78.
2. Ibid., 76.
3. Ibid., 71–72.
4. For George Gray, see A. Musgrave, *Bibliography of Australian Entomology, 1775–1930*, pp. 128–9.
5. For a more detailed account of the Tasmanian Natural History Society see K. Fitzpatrick, pp. 194–200.
6. F. Darwin, *Charles Darwin*, p. 27.
7. L. Huxley, i. 154.
8. Ibid., 57.
9. Ibid., 61.
10. Ibid., 62.
11. Ibid., 63.
12. Ibid., 61.
13. For Fitch see Blunt, pp. 223–8 *et passim*.
14. L. Huxley, i. 62.
15. Ibid., 173.
16. Concerning Leader's landscapes Sir Kenneth Clark has written: '... there is no unity of any kind. Nature has not been perceived as a whole but described piece by piece. Leader still thinks of the world as made up of a number of "things" which have to be treated separately. This was a perfectly reputable way of composing a landscape in an age which expressed itself through symbols. ... It was not a possible procedure in a landscape which was supposed to render the truth of a visual impression' (Clark, *Landscape into Art*, p. 90). It has been argued throughout this book that many landscape-painters of Leader's day did not seek so much to render 'the truth of a visual impression' but truthful concepts about the world of appearances that were grounded in such sciences as botany and geology. For this reason they saw the world 'as made up of a number of "things"'.
17. See also J. Huxley, plates 2, 7.
18. The Royal Society of Tasmania has a folio of his drawings. One is reproduced in K. Fitzpatrick, facing p. 76.
19. Vaucluse House, Sydney.
20. R. Joppien, 'Sir Oswald Walters Brierly's *First Arrival of White Men amongst the Islands of the Louisade Archipelago*: A Nineteenth-Century Painting of New Guinea and Related Sketches', in *Australia Art and Architecture* (ed. A. Bradley and T. Smith), Melbourne, 1980.
21. Mitchell, *Three Expeditions*, ii. pl. 42.
22. Ibid., pl. 47.

23. Sturt, *Southern Australia*, i. xiv.

24. Sturt, *Central Australia*, i. 73.

25. Sturt, *Southern Australia*, i. lvii.

26. Mitchell, *Tropical Australia*, p. v.

27. See J. H. L. Cumpston, *Thomas Mitchell*, Surveyor-General and Explorer.

28. For Charles Heaphy see E. H. McCormick, pp. 33–35 *et passim*.

29. The originals are now in the Nan Kivell Collection, Canberra.

30. A collection of his drawings are in the State Library of Victoria.

31. Mitchell, *Eastern Australia*, 11. 318–19.

32. Engraved by Havell & Son, 1834.

33. See above, p. 164.

34. See below, pp. 230–2.

35. Gould, *Introduction*, p. 1.

36. See Ferguson, iv. 190.

37. Cf. S. Sitwell: '. . . it is safe to say that it would never have occurred to the Victorian ornithologists to have paintings made of the various kinds of game cocks, any more than one could expect the botanists who collected wild plants in China in the beginning years of the century to show an interest in the auriculas or tulips of the handloom weavers of Lancashire and Cheshire'. *Find Bird Books, 1700–1900*, 1954.

38. A. H. Chisholm, *The Story of Elizabeth Gould*, p. 49; see also A. McEvey, *John Gould's Contribution to British Art*, Sydney, 1973.

39. *Encyclopaedia Britannica* (9th ed.), article on Audubon, iii, 70–71.

40. Ruskin, xxii. 157.

41. *Charles Darwin and the Voyage of the Beage* (ed. Barlow), p. 132.

42. *The Voyage of Governor Phillip to Botany Bay*, p. v.

43. *Narrative of the Voyages of the Adventure and Beagle*, iii. 516.

44. Joseph Fowles, *Sydney in 1848*, 'To the Public' on fly-leaf.

45. Maclehose, p. vi.

46. *Sydney Gazette*, 30 July 1829.

47. Ibid.

48. See below, pp.

49. Hudspeth, p. 112.

50. Hudspeth, p. 111.

51. Boyes, MS. Diary, 14 Aug. 1834.

52. For the Mechanics Institute movement in Australia see my *Place, Taste and Tradition*, Sydney, 1945, and G. Nadel, *Australia's Colonial Culture*, Melbourne, 1957.

53. Quoted by W. Moore, i. 153.

54. Robin Vaughan Hood: arrived in Hobart, 1833; framer, lithographer, and dealer in fine art; sent Tasmanian woods to the Great Exhibition, 1851; upon retirement devoted himself to the geological exploration of Tasmania.

55. *Jubilee of the Launceston Mechanics' Institute*, p. 9.

56. See J. H. Maiden, 'The History of the Sydney Botanic Gardens', J.R.A.H.S., xiv (1928), 1–42.

57. Meredith, *My Home in Tasmania*, i. 22.

58. Ibid., 25–26.

59. Bunce, iii.

60. Shepherd, p. v.

61. Ibid., p. vii.

62. Ibid., p. 2.

63. Ibid., p. 4.

64. I have discussed these lectures in more detail in *Place, Taste, and Tradition*, pp. 90–94.

65. *Lectures delivered at the Mechanics' Institute, Hobart Town . . . 1849*, p. 10.

66. Ibid., p. 6.

67. Ibid., p. 9.

68. Ibid., p. 10.

69. Martin, p. 9.

70. See Blunt, pp. 219–20.

71. Meredith, *Autumn Ramble*, p. 10.

72. Meredith, *Notes and Sketches*, p. vii.

73. Meredith, *Autumn Ramble*, p. 43.

74. Meredith, *Notes and Sketches*, p. 70.

75. Ibid., pp. 79–80.

76. His country house *Parkhall* was designed by Edward Blore, who designed Scott's *Abbotsford*. Cumpston, p. 168; see also J. Kerr and J. Broadbent, *Gothic Taste in the Colony of New South Wales*, Sydney, 1980.

77. Meredith, *Notes and Sketches*, p. 81.

78. Boyes, MS. Diary, 14 Oct. 1845.

79. Ibid., 15 Aug. 1847.

80. Ibid., 22 Mar. 1845.

81. Ibid., 11 June 1845.

82. 'The Sketcher in Tasmania', *Once a Week* (1 Mar. 1862), pp. 275–80; (8 Mar. 1862), pp. 304–8.

83. Ibid., p. 275.

84. Prout, *Dioramic Views of Australia*.

85. Angas, *Savage Life and Scenes*, p. vii.

86. Angas, *Catalogue of Paintings . . . illustrative of the Natives and Scenery of New Zealand*, see Ferguson, iv (4217).

87. *Art Journal*, viii (1846), 140.

88. Angas, *Handbill of New Zealand and Australian Exhibition*, see Ferguson, iv (4218).

89. See Ferguson, p. iv (4457).

90. See e.g. *Proc. Zoo. Soc.* (1877).

91. Henry Martens (known as 'Battle' Martens) and J. W. Martens.

92. See *Aust. Town and Country Journ.*, 31 Aug. 1878. The fact is questioned by Lindsay (*Life of Conrad Martens*, p. 3) who states that Martens arrived at Montevideo in Aug. 1832, at a time when Captain Blackwood had still to be appointed to the command of the *Hyacinth*. However, a drawing in the Mitchell Library by Martens is inscribed by him 'Star Cross, 11 August 1832'. Martens, therefore, was still in England in Aug. 1832, and on the evidence of Darwin's letter (quoted below) joined the *Beagle* in Nov. 1833.

93. Darwin to Caroline Darwin, 13 Nov. 1833, quoted in N. Barlow, *Charles Darwin and the Voyage of the Beagle*, p. 95.

94. Ruskin, xxxv. 215.

95. *Voyage of the Beagle*, ii. 348.

96. C. Darwin, *Descent*, pp. 472, 500 *et passim*.

97. Barlow, p. 108.

98. Ibid., pp. 133–4.

99. See Martens to Darwin, 20 Jan. 1862, *Martens Corr.*, D.L., Sydney Pub. Lib., New South Wales.

100. F. Darwin, *Charles Darwin*, p. 55.

101. Ruskin, iii. 398.

102. Ibid., p. 399 n.

103. Robert FitzRoy (1805–65): entered navy 1819; served on the *Thetis* in the Mediterranean; and on the American station under Otway; app. commander of the *Beagle*, Nov. 1828; Governor of New Zealand, 1843–5; app. Director, Meteorological Department, Board of Trade, 1854; published *Weather Book*, 1863.

104. For the influence of Howard and Forster upon John Constable see Badt, *John Constable's Clouds*.

105. Martens, 1 Sept. 1834, *Sketchbook No. 4*, D.L., Sydney.

106. Ibid., 24 Dec. 1834.

107. Ibid.

108. Martens, MS. Lecture, M.L., Sydney, f. 6n.

109. Martens, MS. Account of Pictures Painted at Sydney, D.L., Sydney.

110. Letter to Henry Martens, 13 Sept. 1850, *Martens Corr.*, D.L., Sydney.

111. Martens, MS. Account of Pictures, D.L., Sydney.

112. See J. G. Steele, *Conrad Martens in Queensland*,

Brisbane, 1978.

113. Quoted by Lindsay, pp. 8–9.

114. Letter to Henry Martens, 19 Nov. 1849.

115. Lindsay, Pl. II.

116. An English painter of history and biblical subjects who visited Sydney in the 1850's.

117. Conrad to Henry Martens, 18 Mar. 1851. *Martens Corr.*, D.L., Sydney.

118. MS. Lecture, M.L., Sydney, ff. 12, 29, 31–32.

119. MS. Lecture, M.L., Sydney, f 16.

120. *Voyage of the Beagle*, iii. 526. A questioning of the biblical account of creation to which in its original manuscript form was added: 'A Geologist perhaps would suggest that the periods of Creation have been distinct and remote the one from the other; that the Creator rested in his labour'. Barlow, p. 383. The image of the Creator resting had already occurred to Barron Field in connexion with Australia's faunal curiosities, see p.　Charles Darwin's Diary of the Voyage of H.M.S. *Beagle*, Ed. from the MS. by Nora Barlow. Cambridge, 1933, p. 383.

121. Strzelecki, p. 51.

122. J. D. Hooker, *On the Flora of Australia*, p. xxvii.

123. See *T. Huxley' Diary on the Voyage of H.M.S. Rattlesnake* (ed. J. Huxley), to which the comments that follow are indebted.

NOTES TO CHAPTER ELEVEN

1. Note, however, the excellent *written* accounts of William Ellis, *Journal of a Tour Around Hawaii* (1825), and *Polynesian Researches* (1829).

2. On Williams see also G. Daws, *A Dream of Islands*, 1980.

3. 'The Contemplation of Heathen Idolatry an Excitement to Missionary Zeal', an account of a sermon by Rev. M. Wardlow, *Missionary Sketches No. III*, Oct., 1818.

4. Rev. M. Wardlow, op. cit.

5. W. C. Wentworth, *Australia, A Poem*, 1823.

6. See John Williams, *Narrative of Missionary Enterprises in the South Seas* (1837), p. viii, for a criticism of geophysical notions based on a belief in the rapid growth of coral.

7. Arago, pl. 24. The original drawing is in the Mitchell Library.

8. Ibid., p. 120.

9. Earle, *Narrative of a Nine Months' Residence*, p. 258.

10. Ibid., p. 65.

11. Ibid., p. 239.

12. See *Voyage au Pole Sud*, x. 93–4.

13. O. Wright, *New Zealand 1826–1827, from the French by Dumont D'Urville*, pp. 126 ff.

14. T. B. Macaulay, 'Von Ranke', *Critical and Historical Essays*, iii. 101.

NOTES TO CHAPTER TWELVE

1. D'Urville, *Voyage au Pole Sud, Anthropologie* (ill. folio), 1842–7, Avertissement.

2. Wilkes, iv. 134; v. 122.

3. Ibid., iv. 134, 272 *et passim* and see above p.

4. Ibid. iv. 134.

5. Moholy, p. 38.

6. Ruskin, *Works*, vii. 52.

Bibliography and Graphic Sources

THE subject of this book shades into so many related fields that no bibliography could possibly be complete. The following selection lists the sources, contemporary and modern, found useful in its preparation.

For Cook's voyages the Hakluyt Society's *Journals of Captain James Cook*, edited by J. C. Beaglehole is indispensable. A list of manuscript, printed, and graphic sources for each voyage is included in each of the first three volumes. Other valuable bibliographical sources for the study of Cook are the *Bibliography of Captain James Cook* (Sydney, 1970) and Sir Maurice Holmes's *Captain James Cook, R.N., F.R.S., A Bibliographical Excursion* (London, 1952).

For Pacific exploration in general the bibliographies in *The Exploration of the Pacific* by J. C. Beaglehole, 2nd edition, 1947; the *Catalogue de l'histoire de l'Océanie* by George A. Barringer, Bibliothèque Nationale, Paris, 1912, and *The Cambridge History of the British Empire*, vol. 7, part 1, chapter xii, are the most useful. For the Pacific in general see C. R. H. Taylor, *A Pacific Bibliography* (Wellington, N.Z., 1951); and I. Leeson, *A Bibliography of Bibliographies of the South Pacific*, 1954.

The outstanding bibliography for the study of the beginnings of Australian history, art, and ideas is J. A. Ferguson's *Bibliography of Australia, 1784–1900*, 7 vols. (Sydney, 1941–55). W. Moore's *Story of Australian Art* (Sydney, 1934), was a pioneering account still of considerable value as a reference book.

A great deal of the graphic material discussed is contained in public collections in the British Museum; British Museum (Natural History); National Maritime Museum; The Admiralty; The Mitchell and Dixson Collections, State Library of New South Wales; The National Library of Australia, Canberra; the Tasmanian Museum and Art Gallery, and the various state galleries of Australia.

COLLECTIONS OF DRAWINGS AND PAINTINGS

The following list includes the more important public collections in which original work by artists mentioned in the text will be found. It is a guide to the graphic sources and is not intended to be a detailed inventory, e.g. the European work of Hodges, Webber, and Westall is not included as it is outside the field discussed. The listing of a collection under an artist's name indicates that it includes some of his work, though it is not necessarily his work entirely.

Angas, George French. Water colours in the National Gallery of South Australia, Adelaide.

Banks, Sarah Sophia. *A Ms Catalogue of the Library and collection of prints belonging to Sir Joseph Banks*. British Library, 460.d.13.

Bauer, Ferdinand. 202 w/c drawings of plants and 49 of animals coll. on Flinders's voyage. Botanical Library, Brit. Mus. (Nat. Hist.).

—— Botanical drawings (of Australian plants). Botanical Dept. Naturhistoriches Museum, Vienna.

Boyes, G. W. T. w/c drawings. Roy. Soc., Tasmania, Hobart.

Browne, R. 9 w/c drawings of Australian aborigines. N.K. 149, Canberra.

Browne, R. (copyist of). 5 drawings of Australian aborigines. N.K. 215, Canberra.

Browne, T. R. w/c drawings illustrating a MS. prepared by Thomas Skottowe. M.L., Sydney.
—— w/c drawings of Australian aborigines. M.L., Sydney.
Brierly, Sir Oswald. w/c and gouache paintings in the Art Gallery of New South Wales, and the N.L.A., Canberra.
Buchan, Alexander. Drawings of animals coll. on Cook's 1st voyage. Zoological library Brit. Mus. (Nat. Hist.)
—— Coastal views, &c. (Cook's 1st voyage). Brit. Mus. Add. MSS. 15507, 15508.
—— Views and ethnological drawings (Cook's 1st voyage). Brit. Mus. 23920.
Chapman, J. E. 7 w/c drawings (c. 1847) of Tasmanian views. Roy. Soc. Tas., Hobart.
Earle, Augustus. 161 w/c paintings, formerly in the poss. of Herbert Warrington Smyth. N.K. 12, Canberra.
—— 2 oil-paintings. N.K. 9, 14, Canberra.
Ehret, George Dionysius. w/c drawings of plants collected in Newfoundland by Sir Joseph Banks. Botanical library, Brit. Mus. (Nat. Hist.).
Ellis, William. 16 w/c drawings (Cook's 3rd voyage). N.K. 53, Canberra.
—— 115 w/c drawings (Cook's 3rd voyage). Botanical library, Brit. Mus. (Nat. Hist.).
Evans, George William. w/c views of Hobart, &c. D.G., Sydney.
Eyre, John. w/c views of Sydney. D.G., Sydney.
Forster, J. G. A. 261 foll. of w/c and pencil drawings made during Cook's 2nd voyage. 2 vols. Botanical library, Brit. Mus. (Nat. Hist.).
Glover, John. Sketch-books. N.K. 644, Canberra; National Gallery of Victoria.
—— Field sketches made during an Italian tour. Queen Vict. Mus., Launceston, Tasmania.
—— Oil-paintings: M.G., Sydney; Tasmanian Mus. and Art Gall., Hobart; Queen Victoria Mus., Launceston; National Gallery of Victoria; Art Gallery of South Australia; N.K. Collection, Canberra.
Govett, William Romaine. 12 w/c drawings (c. 1836). N.K. 775, Canberra.
Hodges, William. Wash drawings made on Cook's 2nd voyage. Brit. Mus. Add. MS. 15743.
—— Oil-paintings from drawings made on Cook's 2nd voyage in poss. of the Admiralty on loan to the Nat. Mar. Mus., Greenwich.
—— Wash drawings (one signed) in the coll. of drawings, charts, &c., made by Admiral Isaac Smith. M.L. D. 11.
—— Drawings of Pacific Islanders. Pub. Archives of Canada, Ottawa.
—— Red crayon drawings and pen drawings of Pacific Islanders. N.L.A., Canberra.
Hunter, John. Signed drawing of a man of Lord Howe's group. N.K. 220, Canberra.
King, Phillip Gidley. Wash drawing of Australian aborigines commonly ascribed to King. Banks Corr. A 20–23. M.L., Sydney.
Leseur, Charles Alexandre. w/c drawings of animals made on Baudin's expedition. Bibliothèque centrale, Museum Nationale d'Histoire Naturelle, Paris.
—— Landscape views and drawings of Aborigines. Museum Naturelle, Havre.
Lewin, John William. w/c views of Emu Plains, Blue Mts., and the Bathurst district, painted for Major H. C. Antill. M.L., Sydney, SV1B/Blue M.
—— w/c drawings of plants of New South Wales, formerly in the poss. of the family of P. G. King M.L., Sydney. C 304.
—— 6 Natural history drawings. N.K. 139, Canberra.
—— w/c views, M.G., and D.G., Sydney (see also P. Mander Jones, *Bib. of Lewin*, 12–17. M.L., Sydney).

Lycett, Joseph. w/c views formerly in the poss. of the Earl of Derby. D.L., Sydney.
Martens, Conrad. Drawings and sketch-books. M.L., Sydney. C. 284, C. 292–300, C. 387–91; and D.L., Sydney.
—— Drawings and paintings in the Mitchell and Dixson Galleries, Sydney; the Art Galleries of New South Wales, Queensland, Victoria and South Australia; the Royal Society of Tasmania; N.K., Canberra; and C.N.L., Canberra.
Miller, John Fredrick. Finished drawings after Parkinson coll. during Cook's 1st voyage. 18 fol. vols. Brit. Mus. (Nat. Hist.).
—— Finished wash drawings of ethnological subjects. Brit. Mus. Add. MS. 15508.
Mitchell, Sir Thomas. Sketch-book. M.L., Sydney.
Nixon, Anna Maria. Drawings. Roy. Soc. Tas., Hobart.
Nixon, Francis Russell. Sketch-book. M.L., Sydney.
Parkinson, Sydney. w/c drawings and sketches of plants coll. on Cook's 1st voyage. About 260 finished drawings signed and 16 unsigned, together with about 676 unsigned sketches, contained in 18 fol. vols. bound with finished drawings by F. P. Nodder, and others. Botanical library, Brit. Mus. (Nat. Hist.).
—— 83 signed drawings, and others unsigned, of animals collected on Cook's 1st voyage. Zoological library, Brit. Mus. (Nat. Hist.).
—— Coastal views, sketches of birds, native craft, &c., taken on board the *Endeavour*. Brit. Mus. Add. MSS. 9345; 15507.
—— Views, ethnological drawings, &c., made on Cook's 1st voyage. Brit. Mus. Add. MSS. 23920, 23921.
'Port Jackson Painter'. Drawings of natives, animals, and plants from the neighbourhood of Port Jackson. Banks MS. 34 (Dryander, *Cat. Bibl. Banks* 1, 253), Botanical library, Brit. Mus. (Nat. Hist.).
—— 512 w/c and gouache drawings of views, natives, animals, and plants in the neighbourhood of Port Jackson, by various hands, commonly known as the 'Watling' drawings. Zoological library Brit. Mus. (Nat. Hist.).
—— 6 w/c and gouache paintings. N.K. 144, Canberra.
Prout, John Skinner. 26 w/c drawings. N.K. 306–11, 567–75, Canberra.
—— 9 views in Australia, 1847–52. D 327. M.L., Sydney.
—— 47 drawings and w/c paintings. Roy. Soc. Tas., Hobart.
—— w/c paintings in the National Galleries of New South Wales and South Australia.
Raper, George. Views taken on the voyage to Botany Bay, at Port Jackson, &c. (1788–92). Formerly in the poss. of Lady Alice Godman. General Library. Brit. Mus. (Nat. Hist.).
—— w/c drawings of Australian flowers, fishes, and insects. 2 fol. vols. D 17–18. M.L., Sydney.
—— w/c drawings of plants and animals. Alexander Turnbull Library, Wellington, N.Z.
Roberts, Henry. Charts with views. Brit. Mus. Add. MS. 15500.
—— Drawings, charts, &c., coll. by Admiral Isaac Smith. D 11. M.L., Sydney.
Simpkinson, F. C. 5 fol. books of w/c sketches. Roy. Soc. Tas., Hobart.
Spöring, Herman Diedrich. Drawings of animals coll. on Cook's 1st voyage. Zoological library, Brit. Mus. (Nat. Hist.).
—— Coastal views (Cook's 1st voyage). Brit. Mus. Add. MS. 15507.
—— Unsigned drawings of views and ethnological subjects. Brit. Mus. Add. MSS. 23920, 23921.
Stanley, Charles Owen. Drawings made on the voyage of

the *Britomart*, 1837–43, presented by his widow. Roy. Soc. Tas., Hobart.
—— Drawings in the N.L.A., Canberra.
Sturt, Charles. w/c drawings made on an expedition into central Australia (1844–5) in a coll. of 13 w/c drawings; a gift of Her Majesty the Queen Mother, on the occasion of her Australian Tour, 1958. N.L.A, Canberra.
Wallis, Samuel. 8 coastal views of islands in the Pacific. N.K. 31, Canberra.
Watling, Thomas. w/c and gouache drawings of views, natives, plants, and animals in the neighbourhood of Port Jackson, by various hands, commonly known as the 'Watling' drawings; 4 signed views, 10 signed and 3 unsigned ethnological drawings, and about 150 natural-history drawings. Zoological library, Brit. Mus. (Nat. Hist.).
Webber, John. Drawings and w/c paintings made on Cook's 3rd voyage. Brit. Mus. Add. MSS. 15513, 15514, 17277.
—— Drawings, Brit. Mus. Print Room.
—— 4 oil-paintings in the poss. of the Admiralty; one on loan to the Nat. Mar. Mus., Greenwich.
—— 46 w/c paintings (Cook's 3rd voyage). D.L., Sydney.
Westall, William. Coastal views and profiles taken on Flinders's voyage. 4 vols. N.L.A., Canberra.
—— 10 oil-paintings (from drawings made on Flinder's voyage) in the poss. of the Admiralty; one lent to the Nat. Mar. Mus., Greenwich.
William, John. 30 large w/c drawings used on lecture tours to raise mission funds. N.K. 1224, Canberra.

MSS SOURCES

Angas, G. F. MSS. M.L., Sydney. A. 272; A. 732. A a. 11.
Banks, Sir Joseph. *Correspondence.* M.L., Sydney. A. 77-A. 85.
—— Dawson Turner Transcripts of Correspondence. 21 fol. vols. Brit. Mus. (Nat. Hist.), London.
—— Journal of a Tour in Holland in 1773. D.L., Sydney.
—— Thoughts on the Manners of Otaheite (1773), written in Holland for the Amusement of the Prince of Orange. N.L.A., Canberra.
—— 720 drafts and letters. Library, Royal Botanic Gardens, Kew.
—— Transcript of a letter from J.R. Foster (with Captain Cook) to Sir Joseph Banks. Original in the York Gate Library, Royal Geographical Soc., Adelaide.
—— A manuscript catalogue of the library and collection of prints belonging to Sir Joseph Banks. In the handwriting of his sister, Sophia Sarah Banks. [1800–1815?]. British Library.
—— [A Manuscript Inventory of the Library of Sir Joseph Banks, as received by the British Museum]. 2 vol. [1827]. British Library.
—— Natural History Drawings by various Artists, namely d'Auvergne, Cleveley, Colnett, Engleheart, Gilpin, Greenwood, Metz, Miller, Paillou, Perrin, Rymsdyk, Sowerby *et al*, in the Collection of Joseph Banks. folio. vol. 199* B 4, Print Room, British Museum.
Bowes, A. Journal of a Voyage to New South Wales in the *Lady Penrhyn*, 1786–9. M.L., Sydney, Safe p.h. 9.
Boyes, G. T. W. B. Diary. Roy. Soc. Tas., Hobart.
Bradley, W. Journal 1786–1792. M.L., Sydney. Safe p.h. 8.

Cook, J. Journal of H.M.S. *Endeavour.* 1768–71. N.L.A., Canberra.
—— 'Journal of the Proceedings of His Majesty's Bark the Endeavour in a Voyage Round the World Performed In the Years 1768, 69, 70, & 71', MS. *Ships' Logs Supplementary*, Series II, Adm. 55/40, P.R.O.
—— 'Log Book', MS. *Ships' Logs Supplementary* Series II, Adm. 55/104 (MP1 94), P.R.O.
—— *The Journal of H.M.S. Endeavour.* Facsimile edition. Genesis, Guildford, 1977.
Drury, D. Dru Drury Papers. Entomological library, Brit. Mus. (Nat. Hist.).
Evans, G. W. Calder Papers. Correspondence. M.L., Sydney. A. 594. f. 699.
Farington, Joseph. Diary, Notebooks and Papers, 1788–1821. Typescript copy in Department of Prints and Drawings, British Museum, of original MS in Royal Library, Windsor.
Gilbert, J. Log of H.M.S. *Resolution.* P.R.O. Adm. 55/107.
Glover, John. The Letters of John Glover (son of the landscape-painter) to his sister Mary and to his brother-in-law John Lord. M.L., Sydney.
(London) Missionary Society. Directors' Meetings, Minutes 1798–9. Livingstone House, London.
Martens, C. Copies of Draft Letters. D.L., Sydney.
—— Account of Pictures Painted at Sydney, New South Wales. D.L., Sydney
—— Sketch-books. M.L., and D.L., Sydney.
Martens, C. Lecture upon Landscape Painting delivered at the Australian Library, 21 July 1856. M.L., Sydney. C. 338.
Parkinson, Sydney to Fothergill, John. 16 October 1770. Religious Society of Friends Library, Euston Road, London.
Roberts, H. Log with views, kept on Cook's 3rd voyage. D.L., Sydney.
Skottowe, T. Select Specimens from Nature of the Birds, Animals, etc., etc. of New South Wales. Newcastle, New South Wales, 1813, the drawings by T. R. Browne. M.L., Sydney. A. 555.
Solander, D. C. Notebooks on Natural History kept on the *Endeavour*'s Voyage. Botanical library, Brit. Mus. (Nat. Hist.).
—— Notebook. Marsden MS 12023. Library, School of Oriental and African Studies, London.
Spain, Edward. Reminiscences, 1774–1802. M.L., Sydney. C. 266.
Tobin, G. Journal on H.M. *Providence.* M.L., Sydney.
Wales, W. Journal on the *Resolution* 1772–1774. M.L., Sydney. Safe p.h. 18, no. 4.

CONTEMPORARY WORKS

Angas, G. F. *A Ramble in Malta and Sicily in the Autumn of 1841.* London, 1842.
—— *A Catalogue of Paintings, by George French Angas, illustrative of the Natives and scenery of New Zealand and South Australia; also Sketches in Brazil, Cape Verde Islands, New South Wales, etc., etc.* London (1846).
—— *Savage Life and Scenes in Australia and New Zealand; being an artist's impressions of countries and people at the Antipodes.* London, 1847. 2 vols.
—— *South Australia Illustrated.* London, 1847.
—— *Description of the Barossa Range and its neighbourhood, in South Australia, By 'Agricola'. Illustrated with maps and coloured plates, from original drawings made on the spot, By George French Angas.* London, 1849.
Anson, G. *A Voyage round the World.* (Comp. by R. Wal-

ter). London, 1748.

Arago, J. *Narrative of a Voyage round the World*, London, 1823.

Arnould, M. *La Mort du Captaine Cook, à son troisième voyage au nouveau monde*. Pantomime en Quatre Actes. Paris, 1788.

Aspin, J. *Cosmorama; a View of the Costumes and Peculiarities of all Nations*. London (1826–7).

Atkinson, C. *Views through Hobart Town*. (Hobart, 1833.)

Atkinson, J. *An Account of the State of Agriculture and Grazing in New South Wales*. London, 1826.

Audubon, J. J. *The Birds of America*. London, 1827–38. 4 vols.

Austen, J. *Northanger Abbey* (ed. R.W. Chapman). 3rd ed. London, 1933.

Austin, J. G. *A Series of Lithographic Drawings of Sydney and its Environs*. Sydney, 1836.

Backhouse, J. *A Narrative of a Visit to the Australian Colonies*. London, 1843.

Balfour, J. O. *A Sketch of New South Wales*. London, 1845.

Banks, Sir Joseph. *Journal of the Right Hon. Sir Joseph Banks During Captain Cook's First Voyage* (ed. Sir Joseph D. Hooker). London, 1896.

—— *The Endeavour Journal of Joseph Banks 1768–1771*. J. C. Beaglehole (ed.). 2 vols. Public Library of New South Wales in association with Angus and Robertson, Sydney, 1962.

—— (Anon.). *An Epistle from Mr. Banks, Voyager, Monster-hunter, and Amoroso, to Oberea, Queen of Otaheite*. London (1774).

Bannister, S. *Pictorial Maps for the illustration of the land, the sea, and the heavens, on the walls of large buildings, and georamas. A letter addressed to C. L. Eastlake, Esq., R.A. Secretary to the Commission of Fine Arts*. London, 1849.

Baston, Abbé G. A. R. *Narrations D'Omai*, Paris, 1790. 4 vols.

Baudin, Nicolas. *The Journal of Post Captain Nicolas Baudin* (trans. C. Cornell), Adelaide, 1974.

Bauer, Francis. *Delineations of Exotick Plants Cultivated in the Royal Garden at Kew....* London, 1796.

Bays, P. *A Narrative of the Wreck of the Minerva Whaler of Port Jackson, New South Wales*. London, 1831.

Beechey, F. W. *Narrative of a voyage to the Pacific and Beering's Strait*. London, 1831. 2 vols.

Bellingshausen, T. von. *The Voyage of Captain Bellingshausen to the Antarctic Seas, 1819–1821*, trans. from the Russian (ed. F. Debenham). London, 1945. 2 vols.

Bennett, G. *Wanderings in New South Wales, Batavia, Pedir Coast, Singapore, and China*. London, 1834. 2 vols.

Bérenger, J. P. *Collection de tous les voyages faits autour du monde par les différentes nations de l'Europe*. Paris, 1788–9. 9 vols.

Bewick, T. *A General History of Quadrupeds*. London, 1790.

Boaden, J. *Memoirs of the Life of John Phillip Kemble*. London, 1825. 2 vols.

Boswell, J. *Life of Johnson* (ed. by G. Birkbeck Hill and L. F. Powell). Oxford, 1934.

Bougainville, L. Antoine de, *Voyage Round the World* (trans. by J. R. Forster). London, 1772.

Bowles, W. L. *The Spirit of Discovery; or the Conquest of Ocean*. London, 1804.

Bowman, H. (pseud.). *The Travels of Hildebrand Bowman*. London, 1778.

Breton, W.H. *Excursions in New South Wales, Western Australia, and Van Diemen's Land*. London, 1833.

Brockett, W. E. *Narrative of a Voyage from Sydney to Torres' Straits*. Sydney, 1836.

Brown, R. *Prodromus Florae Novae Hollandiae*. London, 1810.

Bunce, D. *Hortus Tasmaniensis, or A guide to the flora of Van Diemen's Land*. (Hobart, 1850.)

—— *The Australian Manual of Horticulture*. Launceston, 1850.

—— *Manual of Practical Gardening, adapted to the Climate of Van Diemen's Land*. Hobart, 1838.

Burford, R. *Description of a view of the Town of Sydney, New South Wales; the Harbour of Port Jackson, and surrounding country; now exhibiting in the Panorama, Leicester Square*. London, 1829.

—— *Description of a View of Hobart Town, Van Diemen's Land, and the Surrounding Country, now exhibiting at the Panorama, Strand*. London, 1831.

Burney, J. *A Chronological History of the Discoveries in the South Sea or Pacific Ocean*. London, 1803–17. 5 vols.

Burney, James. *With Captain James Cook in the Antarctic and Pacific. The private journal of James Burney Second Lieutenant of the Adventure on Cook's Second Voyage 1772–3* (ed. B. Hooper). Canberra, 1975.

Byron, John. *Byron's Journal of his Circumnavigation* (ed. R.E. Gallagher). Cambridge, 1964.

Callendar, J. *Terra Australis Cognita*. London (1766–8). 3 vols.

Catlin, G. *North American Indians ... written during Eight Years' Travel amongst the Wildest Tribes in North America, 1832–1839*. Edinburgh, 1926. 2 vols.

Chateaubriand, F. A. R., Viscount de, *Le Génie du Christianisme*. Paris, 1865.

Choris, L. *Voyage pittoresque autour du monde*. Paris, 1822.

—— *Vues et paysages des régions équinoxiales*. Paris, 1826.

Churchill, J., and A. Churchill. *Collection of Voyages and Travels*. London, 1752 8 vols.

Clark, J. H. *Field Sports, etc., of the Native Inhabitants of New South Wales; with ten plates by the Author*. London, 1813.

Collins, D. *Account of the English Colony in New South Wales*. London, 1798–1802. 2 vols.

Cook, J. *The Journals of Captain James Cook on his voyages of discovery ... J. C. Beaglehole and others (ed.).* Pub. for the Hakluyt Society. Cambridge, 3 vols, 1955–68. (= Cook, *Jounals*).

—— *Captain Cook's Journal during his First Voyage Round the World* (ed. W. J. L. Wharton). London, 1893.

—— *A Voyage towards the South Pole, and Round the World*. London, 1777. 2 vols.

—— *Captain Cook's Voyages round the World*, London, W. Wright, 1834. 2 vols.

—— and J. King. *A Voyage to the Pacific Ocean*. London, 1784. 3 vols.

Corney, B. G. *The Quest and Occupation of Tahiti ... 1772–76*. London, 1913–19. 3 vols.

Cotton, J. *The Correspondence of John Cotton* (ed. G. Mackaness). Sydney, 1953. 3 vols.

(Courtenay, J.) *An Epistle (Moral and Philosophical) from an Officer At Otaheite*. London, 1774.

—— *A Poetical Epistle (Moral and Philosophical) from an Officer At Otaheite*. London, 1775.

Cox, D. *A Treatise on Landscape Painting*. London, 1845 ed.

Crozet, Lt. *Crozet's Voyage to Tasmania, New Zealand, the Ladrone Islands, and the Phillippines* (trans. H. L. Roth). London, 1891.

Cunningham, P. *Two Years in New South Wales*. London, 1827. 2 vols.

Dale, R. *Descriptive Account of the Panormic View, etc. of King George's Sound, and the adjacent country*. London, 1834.

Dalrymple, Alexander. *Essay on the Most Commodius Methods of Marine Surveying*. London, 1771.

—— *General Introduction to a Collection of Plans of Ports, etc. in the Indian Navigation*. [London, 1774–]

Dampier, W. *A New Voyage Round the World* (ed. N. M. Penzer). London, 1927.

—— *Voyages* (ed. J. Masefield). London, 1906. 2 vols.

Darwin, C. *Narrative of the ... Voyages of H.M.S. 'Adventure' and 'Beagle'. Vol. III*. London, 1839.

—— *The Structure and Distribution of Coral Reefs*. London, 1842.

357

—— *Geological observations on the Volcanic islands, visited during the voyage of H.M.S. Beagle.* London, 1844.

—— *The Origin of Species.* London, 1859.

—— *The Descent of Man.* London, 1871.

Darwin, E. *Poetical Works.* London, 1806. 3 vols.

—— *Zoonomia.* Philadelphia, 1818. 2 vols.

Darwin, F. *Charles Darwin.* London, 1908.

Dawson, R. *The Present State of Australia.* London, 1831.

Dayes, E. *The Works of the Late Edward Dayes* (ed. E. W. Brayley). London, 1805.

Degérando, M. J. *Considérations sur diverses méthodes d'observation des peuples sauvages.* Paris, 1801.

—— *The observation of savage peoples* (trans. and introductory essay by F. C. T. Moore). London, 1969.

Diderot, D. *Supplément au voyage de Bougainville* (ed. G. Chinard). Paris, 1935.

Donovan, E. *The Naturalist's Repository, or Miscellany of Exotic Natural History.* London, 1834.

Drury, D. *Illustrations of Exotic Entomology.* London, 1837. 3 vols.

Du Bos, J.B. *Réflexions critiques sur la poësie et sur la peinture,* 3 vols. (6th ed.). Paris, 1755.

Dumont d'Urville, J. S. C. *Voyage de la Corvette L'Astrolabe.* Paris, 1830–5. 5 vols. Atlas 2 vols.

—— *Voyage Pittoresque autour du monde.* Paris, 1834. 2 vols.

—— *Voyage au Pole Sud.* Paris, 1841–55. 23 vols., with atlases to 7 vols.

—— *New Zealand 1826–1827, from the French by Dumont D'Urville* (trans. O. Wright). Wellington, 1950.

Eastlake, C. L. *Contributions to the Literature of the Fine Arts.* London, 1848.

(Eden, W.) *The History of New Holland,* London, 1787.

Edwards, E. *Anecdotes of Painters.* London, 1808.

Edward, Capt. E., and G. Hamilton. *Voyages of H.M.S. Pandora* (int. Basil Thompson). London, 1915.

Edy, J. W. *Boydell's Picturesque Scenery of Norway . . . From Original Drawings made on the Spot, and engraved by John William Edy, with Remarks and Observations made in a Tour through that Country, and revised and corrected by William Tooke.* London, 1820. 2 vols.

Ellis, W. *Journal of a Tour around Hawaii.* Boston, 1825.

—— *Polynesian Researches.* London, 1829. 2 vols.

—— *The History of the London Missionary Society.* London, 1844.

Farington, J. *The Farington Diary* (ed. J. Greig). London, 1922–8. 8 vols.

—— *The Diary of Joseph Farington.* 14 vols. to date. (ed. by Kenneth Garlick and Angus Macintyre, and Kathryn Cave for The Paul Mellon Centre: Studies in British Art.) New Haven and London, 1978–.

Fénelon, F. *The Adventures of Telemachus* (trans. J. Hawkesworth). London, 1769.

Ferguson, A. *An Essay on the History of Civil Society.* Edinburgh, 1767.

Fernyhough, W. H. *Twelve profile portraits of the Aborigines of New South Wales.* J. G. Austin, Sydney (1836).

Field, B. *First Fruits of Australian Poetry.* Sydney, 1819. 2nd edition, 1823.

—— *Geographical Memoirs on New South Wales.* London, 1825.

(Fitzgerald, G.) *The Injured Islanders; or, the influence of art upon the Happiness of Nature.* London, 1779.

Fitzgerald, W. *An Ode to the Memory of the late Captain James Cook.* London, 1780.

FitzRoy, R. *Narrative of the . . . Voyages of H.M.S. 'Adventure' and 'Beagle',* Vol. II. London, 1839.

Fleming, J. *The Philosophy of Zoology.* Edinburgh, 1822. 2 vols.

Flinders, M. *A Voyage to Terra Australis, 1801–1803.* London, 1814.

Forster, G. *A Voyage Round the World.* London, 1777.

Forster, J. R. *Observations made during a Voyage Round the World.* London, 1778.

Forster, Johann Reinhold. *The Resolution Journal of Johann Reinhold Forster 1772–1775* (ed. by Michael E. Hoare). London, 1981.

Fowles, J. *Sydney in 1848: illustrated by copper-plate engravings of its principal streets, public buildings, Churches, Chapels, etc., from Drawings by Joseph Fowles.* Sydney, 1848.

Gilpin, W. *Observations . . . made in 1772, on Several Parts of England, particularly the Mountains, and Lakes of Cumberland and Westmorland.* London, 1786.

—— *On the Principles on which the Author's Sketches are composed.* London, 1804.

—— *Observations . . . on Several Parts of Great Britain particularly the Highlands of Scotland.* London, 1808.

—— *Three Essays.* London, 1808.

Glover, J. *A Catalogue of Sixty eight pictures, descriptive of the scenery and customs of the inhabitants of Van Diemen's Land, together with views in England, Italy, etc. painted by John Glover.* London, 1835.

Goodridge, C. M. *Narrative of a Voyage to the South Seas . . . and eight years' residence in Van Diemen's Land.* London, 1832.

Gould, J. *A Synopsis of the Birds of Australia.* (London, 1836.)

—— *An Introduction to the Birds of Australia.* London, 1848.

—— *The Birds of Australia.* London, 1841–8. 7 vols.

Gray, G. R. *The Entomology of Australia.* London, 1833.

Hakluyt, R. *The Principal Navigations, Voyages, Traffiques and Discoveries of the English Nation* (ed. J. Masefield). London, 1927.

Hale, H. *United States Exploring Expedition . . . under the command of Charles Wilkes. Ethnography and Philology.* Philadelphia, 1846.

Hamilton, Sir William. *Campi Phlegraei Observations on the Volcanos of the Two Sicilies.* Naples, 1776.

(Harris, A.) *Settlers and Convicts.* London, 1847.

Hawkesworth, J. *An Account of the Voyages undertaken by the Order of His Present Majesty for making Discoveries in the South Hemisphere.* London, 1773. 3 vols.

Haydon, G. H. *Five Years' Experience in Australia Felix.* London, 1846.

Haygarth, H. W. *Recollections of Bush Life in Australia.* London, 1848.

Henderson, J. *Observations on the Colonies of New South Wales.* Calcutta, 1832.

Herder, J. G. *Outlines of a Philosophy of the History of Man* (trans. T. Churchill). London, 1803. 2 vols.

Hervey, T. K. *Australia, with other Poems.* London, 1824.

Hext, Capt. *Views in Australia and Tasmania.* Liverpool (c. 1833).

Hodges, W. *Travels in India.* London, 1793.

Holman, J. *A Voyage round the World, including Travels in Africa, Asia, Australasia, America.* London, 1834. 4 vols.

Hood, J. *Australia and the East.* London, 1843.

Hooker, Sir Joseph D. *The Botany of the Antarctic Voyage of H.M. Discovery Ships Erebus and Terror in the years 1839–1843.* London, 1844.

—— *On the Flora of Australia, its Origin, Affinities and Distribution. Being an Introductory Essay to the Flora of Tasmania.* London, 1859.

Hooker, Sir William J. *Botanical Miscellany.* London, 1831–3. 3 vols.

Hovell, W. H., and H. Hume. *Journal of Discovery to Port Phillip, New South Wales* (ed. W. Bland). Sydney, 1831.

Hudspeth, W. H. *An Introduction to the Diaries of the Rev. Robert Knopwood, A. M. and G. T. W. B. Boyes.* Hobart, 1954.

Hügel, C. A. Anselme, Baron de. *Enumeratio Plantarum.* Vienna, 1837.

Hugues, Pierre François called d'Hancarville. *Collection of Etruscan, Greek, and Roman Antiquities, from the Cabinet of the Hon. W. Hamilton, etc.* 4 vols. Naples, 1766–7.

Humboldt, Alexander von. *Aspects of Nature* (trans. Mrs. Sabine). London, 1849. 2 vols.

—— *Cosmos* (trans. Mrs. Sabine). London, 1846–58. 4 vols.

Hunter, J. *An Historical Journal of the Transactions at Port Jackson and Norfolk Island*. London, 1793.

Huxley, L. *Life and Letters of Sir Joseph Dalton Hooker*. London, 1918. 2 vols.

—— *Life and Letters of Thomas Henry Huxley*. London, 1900. 2 vols.

Huxley, T. H. *T. H. Huxley's Diary on the Voyage of H.M.S. Rattlesnake* (ed. J. Huxley). London, 1935.

Johnson, Dr. Samuel. *Journey to the Western Islands of Scotland*. London, 1775.

Jones, T. 'Memoirs of Thomas Jones', *Walpole Soc.* xxxii (1951), 37.

Jukes, J. B. *Narrative of the surveying Voyage of H.M.S. Fly*. London, 1847.

Kames, Henry Home, Lord. *Sketches of the History of Man*. Edinburgh, 1813. 3 vols.

Keate, G. *An Account of the Pelew Islands*. London, 1788.

—— *The Monument in Arcadia*. London, 1773.

King, P. P. *Narrative of the Surveying Voyages of His Majesty's Ships 'Adventure' and 'Beagle'*. Vol. I. London, 1839.

Knight, R. Payne. *The Landscape, a didactic Poem*. London, 1794.

—— *The Progress of Civil Society*. London, 1796.

—— *An Analytical Enquiry into the Principles of Taste*. London, 1806.

—— *Alfred, a Romance in Rhyme*. London, 1823.

Kotzebue, A. F. Ferdinand von. *La Pérouse, a drama in two acts, From the German of Augustus von Kotzebue; by Benjamin Thomson ... as performed at the Theatre Royal, Drury Lane*. London, 1799.

Kotzebue, Otto von. *A new Voyage Round the World* (trans. from the Russian). London, 1830.

—— *A Voyage of Discovery into the South Sea and Beering's Straits* (trans. from the Russian). London, 1821. 3 vols.

Krusenstern, A. Johann von. *Voyage round the World on the Nadeshda and Neva* (trans. from the Russian). London, 1813. 2 vols.

Labillardière, Jacque Julien de. *An Account of a Voyage in search of La Pérouse* (trans. from the French). London, 1800.

Lang, J.D. *An Historical and Statistical Account of New South Wales*. London, 1834. 2 vols.

La Pérouse, J. François Galaup, Comte de. *Voyage of La Pérouse around the World* (ed. M. L. A. Milet-Mureau; and trans. from the French). London, 1798. 4 vols.

—— (Anon.) *Découvertes dans la Mer du Sud. Nouvelles de M. de la Peyrouse*. Paris (1795).

Launceston Mechanics' Institute, *Jubilee of the Launceston Mechanics' Institute*. Launceston, 1892.

Ledyard, J. *Memoirs of the Life and Travels of John Ledyard, from his journals and correspondence* (ed. Jared Sparks). London, 1828.

Leigh, W. H. *Reconnoitering Voyages and Travels, with Adventures in the new colonies of South Australia*. London, 1839.

Lesson, R. P. *Voyage autour du Monde ... sur la Corvette La Coquille*. Paris, 1839. 2 vols.

Leverian Museum. *A Companion to the Leverian Museum*. London, 1790.

Lewin, J. W. *Prodromus Entomology. Natural History of Lepidopterous insects of New South Wales*. London, 1805.

—— *Birds of New Holland*. London, 1808.

—— *Birds of New South Wales*. Sydney, 1813.

—— *A Natural History of the Birds of New South Wales*. London, 1822.

—— *A Natural History of the Birds of New South Wales, London, 1838* (ed. A. McEvey). Melbourne, 1978.

Lhotsky, J. *A Journey from Sydney to the Australian Alps*. Sydney, 1835.

—— *Illustrations of the Present State and Future Prospects of the Colony of New South Wales*. Sydney 1835.

Lindley, J. *A Sketch of the Vegetation of the Swan River Colony, with nine coloured plates*. London, 1840.

Little, G. (ed.) *Barron Field's Memoirs of Wordsworth'* Sydney, 1975.

Locke, John. *Thoughts Concerning Education*. London, 1693. Quoted in *The Educational Writings of John Locke* (ed. by James L. Axtell). London and New York, 1968.

Lycett, J. *Views in Australia*. London, 1824.

(Macarthur, J.) *New South Wales; its Present State and Future Prospects*. London, 1837.

Mackaness, G. (ed.). *Fourteen Journeys over the Blue Mountains*. Sydney, 1950–1. 3 pts.

Mackenzie, D. *The Emigrant's Guide; or Ten Years' Practical Experience in Australia*. London, 1845.

Maclehouse, J. *Maclehose's Picture of Sydney; and Strangers' Guide in New South Wales, for 1839. Embellished with forty four engravings of the public buildings and picturesque land and water views in and near Sydney*. Sydney, 1839.

Malthus, T. *Essay on the Principles of Population*, 2nd edition. London, 1803.

Mann, D. D. *The Present Picture of New South Wales*. London, 1811.

Marchand, E. *Voyage Round the World ...* (trans. from the French). London, 1801.

Mariner, W. *An Account of the Natives of the Tonga Islands*. London, 1817. 2 vols.

(Marra, J.) *Journal of the Resolution's Voyage ...* London, 1775.

Martens, C. *Sketches in the Environs of Sydney*. Sydney, 1850.

Martin, J. *The Australian Sketch Book*. Sydney, 1838.

Martyn, T. *The Universal Conchologist*. London, 1784.

Martyn, W. F. *A New Dictionary of Natural History; or, Compleat Universal Display of animated nature with accurate representations of the most curious and beautiful animals*. London, 1785.

Mechanics' Institute, Hobart Town. *Lectures Delivered at the Mechanics' Institute, Hobart Town, during the first part of the session of 1849*. Hobart Town, 1849.

Melville, H. S. *The Adventures of a Griffin*. London, 1867.

—— *Sketches in Australia and the Adjacent Islands selected from a number taken during the surveying voyages of H.M.S. Fly and Bramble*. London, 1849.

Meredith, L. A. (*see* Twamley, L.A.).

Mitchell, Sir Thomas L. *Outlines of a System of Surveying for Geographical and Military Purposes*. London, 1827.

—— *Three Expeditions into the Interior of Eastern Australia*. London, 1838–9. 2 vols.

—— *Journal of an Expedition into the Interior of Tropical Australia*. London, 1848.

Mitford, M. R. *Christina, the Maid of the South Seas*. London, 1811.

Monboddo, James Burnett, Lord. *Of the Origin and Progress of Language* (2nd ed.). Edinburgh, 1774–92. 6 vols.

Montgomery, J. *The Pelican Island and other Poems*. London, 1827.

More, H. *Slavery, a Poem*. London, 1788.

Mortimer, G. *Observations and Remarks made during a Voyage ... in the Brig Mercury*. London, 1791.

(O'Hara, J.) *History of New South Wales*. London, 1817.

O'Keefe, J. *A Short Account of the New Pantomime called Omai, or, A Trip Round the World*. London, 1785.

Omai (Anon.). *A Letter from Omai to the Right Honourable the Earl of xxxxxxxx. Translated from the Ulaietean tongue....* London (1780).

Omiah (Anon.). *An Historic Epistle, from Omiah, to the Queen of Otaheite; being his Remarks on the English Nation.*

London, 1775.
—— *Omiah's Farewell; inscribed to the Ladies of London.* London, 1776.
Onslow, S. Macarthur. *Some Early Records of the Macarthurs of Camden.* Sydney, 1914.
Otaheite: A Poem. (Anon.). London, 1774.
Oxley, J. *Journals of Two Expeditions to the Interior of New South Wales . . . 1817–18.* London, 1820.
Parkinson, S. *Journal of a Voyage to the South Seas in his Majesty's Ship, The Endeavour.* London, 1773, 1784.
Patmore, C. *The Table Talk and Omniana of Samuel Taylor Coleridge.* Oxford, 1917.
Pearce, E. H. *Annals of Christ's Hospital.* London, 1901.
Pennant, T. *Tour in Scotland* (2nd ed.). London, 1774.
—— *The Literary Life of Thomas Pennant.* London, 1793.
—— *The View of the Malayan Isles, New Holland, and the Spicy Islands.* London, 1800.
Péron, F., et Louis Freycinet. *Voyage de découvertes aux terres Australes.* Paris, 1807–16. 2 vols.
—— *A Voyage of Discovery to the Southern Hemisphere* (trans. from the above). London, 1809.
(Perry, J.) *Mimosa: or, the Sensitive Plant; A Poem.* London, 1779.
Petit-Thouars, Abel du. *Voyage autour du monde sur la fregate la Venus, pendant les années 1836–1839. Atlas Pittoresque,* Paris, 1841. *Atlas de Botanique,* 1846. *Atlas de Zoologie,* 1846.
(Phillip, A.) *The Voyage of Governor Arthur Phillip to Botany Bay.* London, 1789.
Pickering, C. *The Races of Man; and their Geographical Distribution.* London, 1850.
Pindar, Peter (J. Wolcot). *Poetical Works.* London, 1823.
Pinkerton, J. *Modern Geography.* London, 1807. 3 vols.
Portland Museum. *A Catalogue of the Portland Museum.* London, 1786.
Praed, W. M. *A Poem on Australasia which obtained the Chancellor's Medal at the Cambridge Commencement 1823.* Burnley, 1840.
(Preston, W.) *Seventeen Hundred and Seventy-Seven; or, a Picture of the Manners and Character of The Age. In a Poetical Epistle from a Lady of Quality.* London, 1777.
Price, U. *Essays on the Picturesque.* 1810 4 vols.
Prinsep, A. *The Journal of a Voyage from Calcutta to Van Diemen's Land.* London, 1833.
Prout, J. S. *Castles and Abbeys of Monmouthshire.* Bristol and Clifton, 1838.
—— *Journal of a voyage from Plymouth to Sydney.* London, 1844.
—— *Sydney Illustrated.* Sydney, 1844.
—— *Tasmania Illustrated.* Hobart, 1844.
—— *Views of Melbourne and Geelong* (1847).
—— *Prout's Dioramic Views of Australia, illustrative of Convict and Emigrant Life.* London, 1850.
—— 'The Sketcher in Australia', *Once a Week* (1 March 1862), pp. 275–80; (8 March 1862), pp. 304–8.
Prout, S. *Hints on Light and Shadow Compositions.* London, 1838.
Pye, H. J. *Naucratia; or Naval Dominion. London, 1798.*
Reynolds, Sir Joshua. *Discourses* (ed. R. Fry). London, 1905.
Richardson, J. *The Zoology of Captain Beechey's Voyage.* London, 1839.
[Rickman, John]. *Journal of Captain Cook's last voyage to the Pacific Ocean.* London 1781.
Roberts, J. *Two Years at Sea: being the narrative of a Voyage to the Swan River and Van Dieman's Land 1829–31.* London, 1834.
Robinson, M. M. *Birthday Odes* (ed. G. Mackaness). Sydney, 1946.
Rodius, C. *Twelve lithographs of Australian Aborigines.* Sydney, 1834.
Ross, J. C. *A Voyage of Discovery and Research in the Southern and Antarctic Regions.* London, 1847. 2 vols.

Rousseau, J. J. 'A Dissertation on the Origin and Foundation of Inequality among Mankind', *Works* (trans. from the French). London, 1773–4.
Ruskin, J. *Works* (ed. E. T. Cook and A. Wedderburn). London, 1903–12. 39 vols.
Samwell, D. *A Narrative of the Death of Captain James Cook.* London, 1786.
(Schomberg, Sir Alexander.) *An Ode to the Memory of Captain James Cook.* Dublin, 1780.
Schultes, Dr. 'Schultes's Botanical Visit to England', *Botanical Miscellany* (ed. W. J. Hooker), i. 48–78. London, 1830.
(Scott, J.) *An Epistle from Oberea, Queen of Otaheite, to Joseph Banks, Esq.* London, 1774.
—— *A Second Letter from Oberea, Queen of Otaheite, to Joseph Banks, Esq.* London, 1774.
Seward, A. *Elegy on Captain Cook.* London, 1780.
Shaw, G. *Zoology of New Holland.* London, 1794.
—— *Musei Leveriani Explicatio.* London, 1796.
—— and F. P. Nodder. *The Naturalist's Miscellany: or coloured figures of natural object; drawn and described immediately from nature.* London, 1789–1813. 24 vols.
Shepherd, T. *Lectures on the Horticulture of New South Wales. Sydney, 1835.*
—— *Lectures on Landscape Gardening in Australia.* Sydney, 1836.
Shillibeer, J. *A Narrative of the Briton's Voyage to Pitcairn Island.* London, 1817.
Skelton, R. A. *Captain James Cook after Two Hundred Years.* British Museum Publications, London, 1969.
—— (ed.). *Charts and Views drawn by Cook and his Officers and reproduced from the original manuscripts.* Published for the Hakluyt Society. Cambridge University Press, 1955.
Smith, Sir James E. *A Specimen of the Botany of New Holland. London, 1793.*
—— *Tracts Relating to Natural History.* London, 1798.
Smith, Sydney. *Works. London, 1854.*
Snip, Simon (pseud.). *The Philosophical Puppet Show, or Snip's Inauguration to the President's Chair, addressed to Sir J—B—.* London, c. 1783.
Society for the Promotion of the Fine Arts in Australia. *Exhibition of the Society for the Promotion of the Fine Arts in Australia.* Sydney, 1847. (*Second Exhibition,* Sydney, 1849.)
Southwell, D. 'The Southwell Papers', HRNSW, ii. 661–734.
Sparrman, A. *A Voyage to the Cape of Good Hope, towards the Antarctic Polar Circle, and Round the World* (trans. from the Swedish). London, 1785. 2 vols.
Sparrman, A. *A Voyage Round the World with Captain James Cook in H.M.S. Resolution* (int. and notes by O. Rutter). London, 1944.
Sterling, J. *Essays and Tales,* London, 1848. 2 vols.
Sturt, C. *Narrative of an Expedition into Central Australia.* London, 1849. 2 vols.
—— *Two Expeditions into the interior of Southern Australia.* London, 1833. 2 vols.
Strzelecki, Count Paul E. de. *Physical Description of New South Wales and Van Diemen's Land.* London, 1845.
Sweet, R. *Flora Australasica, . . .* London, 1827–8.
Taillemite, E. (ed.). *Bougainville et ses Compagnons auteur du Monde 1766–1769.* 2 vols. Paris, 1977.
Taitbout, M. *Essai sur l'Isle D'Otahite. . . . Paris, 1779.*
Tasman, A. J. *Journal* (ed. J. E. Heeres). Amsterdam, 1898.
Tench, W. *Narrative of the Expedition to Botany Bay.* London, 1789.
—— *A Complete Account of the Settlement at Port Jackson. London, 1793.*
Townsend, J. P. *Rambles and Observations in New South Wales.* London, 1849.
Tuckey, J. *Account of a Voyage to Establish a Colony at Port*

Philip in Bass's Strait. London, 1805.
Turnbull, J. *Voyage Round the World 1800–4*. London, 1805.
Twamley, L. A. *Poems, with original illustrations drawn and etched by the Authoress*. London, 1835.
—— *Romance of Nature; or, the Flower Seasons Illustrated*. London, 1836.
—— *Flora's Gems, or the Treasures of the Parterre*. London, 1837.
—— *An Autumn Ramble by the Wye*. London, 1838.
[Meredith] L. A. (née Twamley). *Notes and Sketches of New South Wales, during a Residence in that Colony from 1839 to 1844*. London, 1844.
—— *My Home in Tasmania during a Residence of Nine Years*. London, 1852. 2 vols.
Tyerman, D., and G. Benne. *Journal of Voyages and Travels* (ed. J. Montgomery). London, 1831. 2 vols.
Vancouver, G. *A Voyage of Discovery to the North Pacific Ocean, and round the World*. London, 1798. 3 vols. and atlas.
(Vason, G.) *An Authentic Narrative of Four Years' Residence at Tongataboo* (ed. S. Piggott). London, 1815.
Vaux, J. H. *Memoirs of James Hardy Vaux*. London, 1819. 2 vols.
Wales, W. *Remarks on Mr. Forster's Account of Captain Cook's last Voyage round the World*. London, 1778.
—— *Astronomical Observations, made in the Voyages Which were Undertaken By Order of His Present Majesty, for making Discoveries in the Southern Hemisphere*. London, 1788.
—— and Bayly, W. *The original Astronomical Observations, made in the course of A Voyage towards the South Pole, and Round the World*. London, 1777.
Wallis, J. *An Historical Account of the Colony of New South Wales*. London, 1821.
Walpole, F. *Four Years in the Pacific*. London, 1850. 2 vols.
Watling, T. *Letters from an Exile at Botany Bay to his Aunt in Dumfries*. Penrith (1794).
Webber, J. *Views in the South Seas*. London, 1808.
Wentworth, W. C. *Australasia: a Poem written for the Chancellor's Medal at the Cambridge Commencement, July, 1823*. London, 1823.
—— *A Statistical, Historical and Political Description of the Colony of New South Wales*. London, 1820.
West, A. *Views in New South Wales*. Sydney, 1812–14.
West, J. *The Fine Arts: A Lecture, delivered at the request of the Committee of the Launceston Mechanics' Institute*. Launceston, 1848.
Westmacott, R. M. *Sketches in Australia*. Exeter, 1848.
White, G. *The Natural History and Antiquities of Selborne* (ed. R. Bowdler Sharpe). London, 1900. 2 vols.
White, J. *Journal of a Voyage to New South Wales*. London, 1790.
Whitehurst, J. *Inquiry into the Original State and Formation of the Earth*. London, 1778.
Wilkes, C. *Narrative of the United States Exploring Expedition*. Philadelphia, 1844–74. 24 vols.
Williams, J. *Narrative of Missionary Enterprises in the South Sea Islands*. London, 1837.
Wilson, J. *A Missionary Voyage to the Southern Pacific Ocean, 1796–98 in the Ship Duff*. London, 1799.
Winckelmann, J. *The History of Ancient Art* (trans. G. H. Lodge). London, 1881. 2 vols.
Woolls, W. *Australia: A Moral and Descriptive Poem*. Sydney, 1833.
—— *Miscellanies in Prose and Verse*. Sydney, 1838.

LATER WORKS

Allen, D. G. C. *William Shipley*. London, 1968.
Anderson, C. R. *Melville in the South Seas*. Columbia, 1939.

Antal, F. 'Reflections on Classicism and Romanticism V', *Burl. Mag.* lxxviii (1941), 14–22.
—— *Fuseli Studies*. London, 1956.
Archer, Mildred. 'British Painters of the Indian Scene: The Sir George Birdwood Memorial Lecture'. *Royal Society of Arts*. Oct. 1967, pp. 863–79.
—— and Lightbown, Ronald, *India Observed, 1760–1860*. Victoria and Albert Museum, London, 1982.
Aubin, R. 'Grottoes, Geology, and the Gothic Revival', *SP*, xxxi (1934), 408–16.
Auckland City Art Gallery. *Captain James Cook: his Artists and Draughtsmen*. Auckland, New Zealand, Oct.–Dec. 1964.
Badt, K. *John Constable's Clouds* (trans. by S. Godman). London, 1950.
Baily, J. T. Herbert. *Francesco Bartolozzi R.A. A Biographical Essay*. London, 1907.
Beaglehole, J. C. *The Exploration of the Pacific* (2nd edition). London, 1947.
Beaglehole, J. C. *The Life of Captain James Cook*. London, 1974.
—— *The Life of Captain James Cook*. London, 1974.
Beddie, M. K. (ed.). *Bibliography of Captain James Cook*. State Library of New South Wales, Sydney [2nd edn.], 1970.
Begg, A. Charles and Begg, Neil C. *James Cook and New Zealand*. Wellington, New Zealand, 1969.
Binyon, Lawrence. *Catalogue of Drawings by British Artists and Artists of Foreign Origin Working in Great Britain, Preserved in the Department of Prints and Drawings in the British Museum*. 4 vols. London, 1898–1907.
Blunt, W. *The Art of Botanical Illustration*. London, 1950.
Blunt, W. and Stearn, W. T. *Captain Cook's Florilegium*: a selection of engravings from the drawings of plants collected by J. Banks and D. Solander, with introduction by W. B. and botanical notes by W. T. S. [30 engravings from original plates in the Brit. Mus (Nat. Hist.).] Drawn by S. Parkinson and others. Lion and Unicorn Press, London, 1968.
Boase, T. S. R. 'Illustrations of Shakespeare's Plays in the 17th and 18th Centuries', *Journal of the Warburg and Courtauld Institutes*, x (1947), 83–108.
—— 'The Decoration of the New Palace of Westminster, 1841–1863', *Journal of the Warburg and Courtauld Institutes*, xvii (1954), 319–58.
Bodi, L. 'Antipodean Inversion and Australian Reality', in *Captain James Cook: Image and Impact* (ed. W. Veit), II, Melbourne, 1979, 76–94.
—— 'Captain Cook in German Imaginative Literature', in *Captain James Cook: Image and Impact* (ed. W. Veit), I, Melbourne, 1972, 117–37.
Bradley, A. and Smith, T. *Australian Art and Architecture Essays presented to Bernard Smith*. Melbourne, 1980.
Brown, W. C. 'The Popularity of English Travel Books about the Near East', *PQ*, xv (1936), 70–80.
—— 'English Travel Books and Minor Poetry about the Near East, 1775–1825', *PQ*, xvi (1937), 249–71.
Callender, Geoffrey. '"Cape Town" by William Hodges R.A.', *Burl. Mag.* lxxix (1941), 93–94.
Cameron, H. C. *Sir Joseph Banks K.B., P.R.S., The Autocrat of the Philosophers*. London, 1952.
Campbell, I. C. 'Savages Noble and Ignoble: The Preconceptions of Early European Voyages in Polynesia', *Pacific Studies*, Fall 1980, pp. 45–59.
Carrington, H. *Life of Captain Cook*. London, 1939.
Carter, Harold B. *Cook's Oxford Tutor: Sir Joseph Banks and European Expansion in the Pacific Region 1767–1820*. Typescript of paper delivered at the conference 'Captain James Cook and his Times', Simon Fraser University, April 1978.
Chinard, Gilbert. *L'Amérique et le rêve exotique dans la littérature Française au XVIIe et au XVIIIe Siècle*. Paris, 1934.

Chisholm, A. H. *The Story of Elizabeth Gould*, Melbourne, 1944.

Clark, Sir Kenneth. *Landscape into Art*. London, 1949.

Clark, T. B. *Omai, First Polynesian Ambassador to England*. San Francisco, 1941.

Cobbe, Hugh (ed.). *Cook's Voyages and Peoples of the Pacific*. British Museum Publications, London, 1979.

Colenso, W. 'Manibus Parkinsonibus sacrum: a brief memoir of the first artist who visited New Zealand', *New Zealand Institute Transactions* (1897), pp. 108–34.

Constable, W. G. *Richard Wilson*. London, 1953.

Crone, G. R., and R. A. Skelton. 'English Collections of Voyages and Travels, 1625–1846', in *Richard Hakluyt and his Successors* (ed. E. Lynam), pp. 63–140. London, 1946.

Cumont, F. V. M. *After Life in Roman Paganism*. Yale, 1922.

Cumpston, J. H. L. *Thomas Mitchell Surveyor-General and Explorer*. Melbourne, 1954.

Cust, L. *History of the Society of Dilettanti*. London, 1898.

Davidson, J. W. *The Study of Pacific History*. Canberra, 1955.

Daws, G. *A Dream of Islands. Voyages of Self-Discovery in the South Seas*. New York, 1980.

Dawson, W. R. *The Banks Letters*. London, 1958.

Dixson, W. 'Notes on Australian Artists', J.R.A.H.S. v, 225–48, 283–300; vii, 100–4, 158–60, 212–16, 379–80; ix, 46, 161.

Dunlap, W. *A History of the Rise and Progress of the Arts of Design in the United States*. New York, 1834. 2 vols.

Fagan, L. A. *Catalogue Raisonné. The Engraved Works of William Woollett*. London, 1885.

Fairchild, H. N. *The Noble Savage. A Study in Romantic Naturalism*. New York, 1928.

Fisher, R. and Johnston, H. (ed.). *Captain James Cook and His Times*. Vancouver and London, 1979.

Fitzpatrick, B. *British Imperialism and Australia 1783–1833*. London, 1939.

—— *The British Empire in Australia. An Economic History 1834–1939*. Melbourne, 1941.

Fitzpatrick, K. *Sir John Franklin in Tasmania 1837–1843*. Melbourne, 1949.

Ford, B. *Richard Wilson's Drawings*. London, 1951.

Force, R. W. and Force, M. *Art and artifacts of the 18th Century. Objects in the Leverian Museum as painted by Sarah Stone*. Bishop Museum Press, Hawaii, 1968.

Foster, Sir W. 'British Artists in India', *Walpole Soc.* xix (1930–1), I 88.

Frantz, R. W. *The English Traveller and the Movement of Ideas: 1660–1732*. Lincoln (Nebraska), 1934.

Freeman, J. D. 'Polynesian Collection of Trinity College, Dublin; and the National Museum of Ireland', *Journal of the Polynesian Soc.* lviii (1949), 1–18.

Frost, Alane. 'Captain James Cook and the Early Romantic Imagination', in *Captain James Cook: Image and Impact* (ed. E. Veit), I, Melbourne, 1972, 90–106.

—— 'New Geographical Perspectives and the Emergence of the Romantic Imagination', in *Captain James Cook and His Times* (ed. Robin Fisher and Hugh Johnston). Vancouver and London, 1979.

—— 'The Pacific Ocean—The Eighteenth Century's "New World"', in *Captain James Cook: Image and Impact* (ed. W. Veit), II, Melbourne, 1979, 5–49.

Furst, H. 'The National Maritime Museum', *Apollo*, xxv (1937), 322–6.

Gardner, A. T. E. 'Scientific sources of the Full-length Landscape: 1850', *Met. Mus. Bul.* iv (1945), 59–65.

Garfinkle, N. 'Science and Religion in England, 1790–1800: The Critical Response to the Work of Erasmus Darwin', JHI, xvi (1955), 376–88.

Gladstone, H. S. 'Thomas Watling, Limner of Dumfries', *Trans. Dumfriesshire and Galloway Natural History and Antiquarian Society*, 3rd ser., xx (1935–6), 70–133.

Grant, Col. M. H. *Chronological History of the Old English Landscape Painters* (in oil). Vols. i and ii, London (1926); vol. iii, Leigh-on-Sea, 1947.

Graves, A. *The Royal Academy of Arts*. London, 1905–6. 8 vols.

—— *The Society of Artists of Great Britain (1760–91): The Free Society of Artists (1761–1783)*. London, 1907.

Guiart, Jean. *The Arts of the South Pacific* (trans. A. Christie). London, 1963.

Hackforth-Jones, J. *Augustus Earle Travel Artist*. Canberra, 1980.

Haughton, W. E. 'The English Virtuoso in the Seventeenth Century', *J.H.I.*, iii (1942), 51–73, 190–219.

Hazard, P. *European Thought in the Eighteenth Century* (trans. J. Lewis May). London, 1954.

Herrmann, Luke. *British Landscape Painting of the Eighteenth Century*. London, 1973.

Hindwood, K. A. 'John Gould in Australia', *Emu*, xxxviii (1938), 95–118.

HMSO. *Catalogue of Pictures, Presentation Plate, etc. at The Admiralty; on Board H.M. Ships; and in the Naval Establishments at Home and Abroad*. Corrected to 30 April 1911. NS 11041/10.

Hoare, Michael E. *The Tactless Philosopher: Johann Reinhold Forster (1729–98)*. Melbourne, 1976.

—— *The Resolution Journal of Johann Reinhold Forster 1772–1775*. The Hakluyt Society, London, 1980.

Holmes, Sir Maurice. *Captain Cook, R.N., F.R.S. A Bibliographical Excursion*. London, 1952.

Honour, Hugh. *The European Vision of America*. The Cleveland Museum of Art, Cleveland, Ohio, 1975.

Huse, W. 'A Noble Savage on the Stage', *M.P.* xxxiii (1936), 303–16.

Hussey, C. *The Picturesque*. London, 1927.

Huth, H. 'The American and Nature', *Journal of the Warburg and Courtauld Institutes*, xiii (1950), 101–49.

Iredale, Tom. 'Captain Cook's Artists', *The Australian Museum Magazine*, iii, no. 7, July–Sept. 1925, 224–30.

Jacquier, H. 'Le mirage et l'exotisme tahitiens dans la littérature', *Bulletin de la Société des Études Océaniennes*, vii (Dec. 1944), pp. 3–27; (June 1945), pp. 50–76; (Sept. 1945), pp. 91–114.

Jones, P. Mander. 'John William Lewin, a Memoir', *Biblionews*, vi (1953), 36–46.

Joppien, Rüdiger. *Philippe Jacques de Loutherbourg, R.A. 1740–1812*. [Exh. Kenwood, London]. Greater London Council, 1973.

—— 'Three Drawings by William Hodges (1744–1797)', *La Trobe Library Journal*, no. 18, Oct. 1976, 25–33.

—— for Hartnoll & Eyre Ltd. *Drawings from Captain Cook's Voyages: An unrecorded collection of fourteen ethnographical and natural history drawings relating to the second and third voyages*. London, 1976.

—— 'Philippe Jacques de Loutherbourg's Pantomime 'Omai, or a Trip round the World' and the Artists of Captain Cook's Voyages', *British Museum Yearbook 3 Captain Cook and the South Pacific* (ed. T. C. Mitchell). Trustees of the British Museum, London, 1979, pp. 81–136.

—— 'The Dutch Vision of Brazil' in *Johan Maurits van Nassau 1604–1679. A Humanist Prince in Europe and Brazil* (ed. E. van den Boogaart). The Hague, 1979.

—— 'Sir Oswald Walters Brierly's *First Arrival of White Men amongst the Islands of the Louisiade Archipelago*', in *Australian Art and Architecture*. Melbourne, 1980.

Kaeppler, Adrienne L. 'Eighteenth century Tonga', *Man*, vi, no. 2, June 1971, 204–220.

—— 'The Use of Documents in Identifying Ethnographic Specimens from the Voyages of Captain Cook', *Journal of Pacific History*, vii (1972), 195–200.

—— 'A Study of Tongan Panpipes with a Speculative Interpretation', *Ethnos*, 39 (1-4) (1974), 102-128.

—— *"Artificial Curiosities": being an exposition of native manufactures collected on the three Pacific Voyages of Captain James Cook, R.N. ... January 18, 1978–August 31, 1978.* (Bernice P. Bishop Museum Spec. Pub. 65). Honolulu, 1978.

—— 'Cook Voyage Provenance of the "Artificial Curiosities" of Bullock's Museum', *Man* (NS) 9 (1), 68-92.

Kimble, *Geography in the Middle Ages*. London, 1938.

Kippis, A. *The Life of Captain James Cook*. London, 1788.

Kitson, A. *Captain James Cook*. London, 1907.

Lee, S. 'The American Indian in Elizabethan England', *Elizabethan and other Essays*. Oxford 1929.

Lindsay, (Sir) Lionel. *Conrad Martens, the Man and his Art*. Sydney, 1920.

Long, B. 'John Glover', *Walker's Quarterly*, xv, April 1924.

Lonchamp, F.-C. *J.-L. Aberli (1723-1786) ... avec un Catalogue Complet*. Paris and Lausanne, 1927.

Lovejoy, A. O. *The Great Chain of Being*. Cambridge, Mass., 1948.

—— 'The Supposed Primitivism of Rousseau's *Discourse on Inequality*', *M.P.* xxi (1923), 165-86.

—— *Essays in the History of Ideas*, Baltimore, 1948.

—— and G. Boas. *Primitivism and Related Ideas in Antiquity*, Baltimore, 1935.

Lowes, J. Livingstone. *The Road to Xanadu*. London, 1953 ed.

Lysaght, A. M. 'Captain Cook's Kangaroo', New Scientist, xxii (1957), 17-23.

—— *Joseph Banks in Newfoundland and Labrador in 1766*. London, 1971.

—— 'Banks's Artists in the Endeavour', The *Journal of HMS Endeavour 1768-1771*. Facsimile edition. Genesis Publications, London, 1977, pp. 37-47.

—— 'Banks's Artists and his *Endeavour* Collections', *The British Museum Yearbook 3 Captain Cook and the South Pacific*. British Museum Publications, London, 1979, pp. 9-80.

MacCormick, E. H. *Letters and Art in New Zealand*. Wellington, 1940.

—— *Omai: Pacific Envoy*. Auckland and Oxford, 1977.

McEvey, A. *John Gould's Contribution to British Art: A note on its authenticity*. Sydney, 1973.

McPhee, J. A. *John Glover—The Prints and Associated Material*. Queen Victoria Museum and Art Gallery, Launceston, 1976.

—— *John Glover Catalogue of Exhibition*. Queen Victoria Museum and Art Gallery. Launceston, 1977.

—— *The Art of John Glover*. Melbourne, 1980.

Mackaness, G. *The Life of Vice-admiral William Bligh*. Sydney, 1931. 2 vols.

—— *Sir Joseph Banks. His Relations with Australia*. Sydney, 1936.

—— *Admiral Arthur Phillip, founder of New South Wales, 1738-1814*. Sydney, 1937.

Maiden, J. H. *Sir Joseph Banks*. Sydney, 1909.

Manwaring, E. W. *Italian Landscape in Eighteenth-Century England*. New York, 1925.

Marshall, J. B. 'The handwriting of Joseph Banks, his scientific staff and his amanuenses', *Bull. Brit. Mus.* (Nat. Hist.); Bot. ser. vol. 6, no. 1, 28 September 1978, 1-85.

Meek, R. L. *Social Science and the Ignoble Savage*. Cambridge, 1976.

Merrill, Elmer Drew. *The Botany of Cook's Voyages, and its Unexpected Significance in Relation to Anthropology, Biogeography, and History*. Waltham, Mass., 1954.

Mitchell, C. 'Benjamin West's "Death of Wolfe" and the Popular History Piece', *Journal of the Warburg and Courtauld Institutes*, vii (1944), 20-33.

—— 'Zoffany's "Death of Cook"', *Burl. Mag.* lxxxiv (1944), 56-62.

Moholy, L. *A Hundred Years of Photography 1839-1939*. London, 1939.

Moore, W. *The Story of Australian Art*. Sydney, 1934. 2 vols.

Murray-Oliver, Anthony. *Captain Cook's Artists in the Pacific, 1769-1779*. New Zealand, 1969.

Myers, J. L. 'The influence of Anthropology on the course of Political Science', *Rep. Brit. Ass. Adv. Sci.* Winnipeg, 1909, pp. 589-617.

Nadel, G. *Australia's Colonial Culture*. Melbourne, 1957.

Nicholson, Benedict. *Joseph Wright of Derby*. 2 vols. (The Paul Mellon Foundation: Studies in British Art). London and New York, 1968.

Ogden, H. V. S., and M. S. Ogden. *English Taste in Landscape in the Seventeenth Century*. Michigan, 1955.

Oliver, Douglas L. *Ancient Tahitian Society*. 3 vols. Honolulu, 1974.

Oppé, A. P. *The Drawings of Paul and Thomas Sandby in the Collection of His Majesty the King at Windsor Castle*. Oxford, 1947.

—— *Alexander and John Robert Cozens*. London, 1952.

—— 'Wilson, Hodges, and the View of Woburn Abbey', *Burl. Mag.* xcvi (1954), 86.

Ord, G. 'A Memoir of Charles Alexander Lesueur', *American Journal of Science and Arts*, Sept. 1849, pp. 189-216.

Pächt, O. 'Early Italian Nature Studies and the Early Calendar Landscapes', *Journal of the Warburg and Courtauld Institutes*, xiii (1950), 13-47.

Panofsky, E. 'Et in Arcadia Ego', in *Philosophy and History* (eds. Klibansky and Paton). Oxford, 1936.

Parkinson, Sydney to Fothergill, John. 16 October 1770. Religious Society of Friends Library, Euston Road, London.

Pearson, H. *Dr. Darwin*. London, 1930.

Pearson, W. H. 'Hawkesworth's Alterations', *The Journal of Pacific History*, vii (1972), 45-72.

Perret, Louis. 'Herman Diedrich Spöring d.y. Medicinare, natuvetare och forskningsresande', *Nordisk Medicin Historic Arsbok* (1968), 147-57.

Perry, T. 'The Spread of Rural Settlement in New South Wales 1788-1826', *Hist. Stud. Aust. and N.Z.*, vi (1955), 377-95.

Perry, T. M. and Simpson, D. H. (ed). *Drawings by William Westall*. Royal Commonwealth Society, London, 1962.

Pevsner, N. 'Genesis of the Picturesque', *Archit. Rev.* xcvi (1944), 139-46.

—— 'Richard Payne Knight', *Art Bulletin*, xxxi (1949), 293-320.

Pickard, Jane. William Hodges's Paintings of the South Pacific. Unpublished B.A. thesis, Cambridge University, 1973.

Plomley, N. J. B. *The Baudin Expedition and the Tasmanian Aborigines 1802*, Hobart, 1982.

Poignant, R. 'The Improbable Kangaroo', *Geographical Magazine*, April 1962, pp. 671-79.

Rathbone, F. *Josiah Wedgwood on the Clay of Sydney Cove*. Birmingham, n.d.

Redgrave, R. and S. *A Century of Painters of the English School*. London, 1866. 2 vols.

Redgrave, S. *A Descriptive Catalogue of the historical collection of Water-colour Paintings in the South Kensington Museum*. London, 1876

Reynolds, Graham. 'British Artists Abroad. I. Captain Cook's Draughtsmen', *Geographical Magazine*, xix, no. 10, Feb. 1947, 457-466.

Rienits, R. and T. *Early Artists of Australia*. Sydney, 1963.

Robertson, J. G. *Studies in the Genesis of Romantic Theory in the 18th century.* Cambridge, 1923.

Roderick, C. 'Sir Joseph Banks, Queen Oberea and the Satirists', in *Captain James Cook: Image and Impact* (ed. W. Veit). Melbourne, 1972, pp. 67–89.

Sawyer, F. C. 'Notes on some original drawings of Birds used by Dr. John Latham', *J. Soc. Bibl. Nat. Hist.* ii (1949), 173–80.

Scott, Sir Ernest. *La Pérouse.* Sydney, 1912.

—— *The Life of Captain Matthew Flinders, R.N.* Sydney, 1914.

—— *Terre Napoleon: A History of French Explorations . . . in Australia.* London, 1910.

Sitwell, S. *Fine Bird Books 1700–1900.* London, 1954.

—— and Blunt, W. *Great Flower Books 1700–1900. A Bibliographical Record of two Centuries of finely-illustrated Flower Books.* London, 1956.

Skelton, R. A. 'Captain James Cook as a Hydrographer', *Mariner's Mirror*, xl (1954), 92–119.

—— 'The Graphic Records of the Voyage', *The Journals of Captain James Cook* (ed. J. C. Beaglehole). London, 1955. I, pp. cclxv–cclxxi.

—— *Captain James Cook after Two Hundred Years.* British Museum Publications, London, 1969.

Smith, Bernard *Place, Taste and Tradition, a study of Australian Art since 1788.* Sydney, 1945

—— 'European Vision and the South Pacific', *Journal of the Warburg and Courtauld Institutes*, xiii (1950), 66–100.

—— 'Coleridge's *Ancient Mariner* and Cook's Second Voyage', *Journal of the Warburg and Courtauld Institutes*, xix (1956), 117–54.

—— *Art as Information: Reflections on the Art from Captain Cook's Voyages.* (The annual lecture delivered to the Australian Academy of the Humanities, Canberra, 16 May 1978.) Sydney, 1979.

—— 'Cook's Posthumous Reputation', in *Captain James Cook and his Times* (ed. R. Fisher and H. Johnston). Vancouver, 1979, pp. 159–185.

—— *The Spectre of Truganini. 1980 Boyer Lectures.* Australian Broadcasting Commission, Sydney [1981].

Smith, E. *The Life of Sir Joseph Banks.* London, 1911.

Société de Geógraphie. *Centenaire de la mort de Cook.* Paris, 1879.

Stafleu, Frans A. *Linnaeus and the Linneans.* Utrecht, 1971.

Stearn, William T. 'A Royal Society Appointment with Venus in 1769: The Voyage of Cook and Banks in the *Endeavour* in 1768–1771 and its Botanical Results', *Roy. Soc. Notes and Records*, 24, no. 1, June 1969, 64–90.

Steele, J. G. *Conrad Martens in Queensland.* Brisbane, 1978.

Stuebe, Isabel C. 'William Hodges and Warren Hastings: a study in eighteenth-century patronage', *Burl. Mag.*, CXV, Oct. 1973, 657–66.

—— *The Life and Works of William Hodges.* (Garland: Outstanding Dissertations in the Fine Arts.) New York, 1979.

Sutton, D. *The Daniells. Artists and Travellers.* London, 1954.

Taylor, A. Carey. *Le Président de Brosses et l'Australie.* Paris, 1937.

—— *Charles de Brosses, the Man behind Cook.* (Maritime Monographs and Reports No. 2). National Maritime Museum, London, 1971.

Tylor, B. *Animal Painting in England.* London, 1955.

—— *Stubbs.* London, 1971.

Tinker, C. B. *Nature's Simple Plan.* Princeton, 1922.

—— *Painter and Poet.* Cambridge, Mass., 1938.

(Tomlinson, C.) *Sir Joseph Banks and the Royal Society.* London, 1844.

Trollope, W. *A History of Christ's Hospital.* London, 1834.

Turnbull Library, Alexander. 'Oil Paintings by William Hodges, R. A.' (text by A. Murray-Oliver), *Alex. Turn. Lib. Bull.*, xv, June–Sept. 1959, 1–16.

Uggla, A. H. 'Daniel Solander och Linné', *Svenska Linné Sällskapets Arsskrift*, xxxvi (1953).

Vaughan, Thomas and Murray-Oliver, A.A.St.C.M. *Captain Cook, R.N.: The Resolute Mariner.* (Oregon Historical Society). Portland, Oregon, 1974.

Veit, Walter (ed.). *Captain James Cook: Image and Impact.* 2 vols. Melbourne, 1972, 1979.

Wallis, H. 'The Patagonian Giants', in *Byron's Journal of his Circumnavigation* (ed. R. E. Gallagher). Cambridge, 1964, pp. 185–199.

Ward, R. *The Australian Legend.* Melbourne, 1958.

Waterhouse, E. K. *Painting in Britain 1530 to 1790.* London, 1953.

Webster, Mary. *Johan Zoffany 1733–1810.* National Portrait Gallery, London, 1976.

Wedgwood, J. *On the Analysis of a Mineral Substance from New South Wales. Phil. Trans.*, lxxx (1790), 4–19.

Wells, W. 'The Pantheon, Oxford Road', *Leeds Art Calendar*, v (1952), 11–17.

Whitehead, P. P. J. 'Zoological Specimens from Captain Cook's Voyages', *Journal for the Society of Bibliography for Natural History* 5(3), 161–201.

—— *Forty Drawings of Fishes made by the Artists who accompanied James Cook on his three voyages to the Pacific, 1768–71, 1772–75, 1776–80. Brit. Mus. (Nat. Hist.),* London [1969] printed as 1968.

Whitley, G. P. 'Some Early Naturalists and Collectors in Australia', *J.R.A.H.S.* xix (1933), pp. 291–323.

—— 'Naturalists of the First Fleet', *Australian Museum Magazine*, vi (1938), 291–304.

Whitley, W. T. *Artists and their Friends in England, 1700–1799.* London, 1928, 2 vols.

Whitney, L. 'English Primitivistic Theories of Epic Origins', *M.P.* xxi (1924), 337–78.

—— *Primitivism and the Idea of Progress.* Baltimore, 1934.

Willey, B. *The Eighteenth Century Background.* London, 1949.

Williams, G. *Seamen and Philosophers in the South Seas in the Age of Captain Cook. The Eva G. R. Taylor Lecture for 1978. The Mariner's Mirror*, 65, February 1979, 3–22.

Williams, Iola A. 'Thomas Pennant and Moses Griffith', *Country Life*, 2 July 1938.

—— 'Moses Griffith', *Walker's Monthly*, Aug–Sept 1938.

Williamson, J. A. *Cook and the Opening of the Pacific.* London, 1946.

Williamson, R. W. *Religious and Cosmic Beliefs of Central Polynesia.* Cambridge, 1933. 2 vols.

Willson, E. J. *James Lee and the Vineyard Nursery.* [Hammersmith Local History Group] London, 1961.

Wind, E. 'The Revolution of History Painting', *Journal of the Warburg Institute*, ii (1938), 116–27.

Wittkower, Rudolph. 'Marvels of the East, A Study in the History of Monsters', *Journal of the Warburg and Courtauld Institutes*, v (1942), 159–97.

—— *Art and Architecture in Italy 1600–1750.* London, 1958.

Wood, G. A. 'Ancient and Mediaeval Conceptions of Terra Australis', *J.R.A.H.S.* iii (1916), 455–65.

—— *The Discovery of Australia.* London, 1922.

Wood, Sir Henry *A History of the Royal Society of Arts.* London, 1913.

Index

369